Intermediate GNVQ

BUSINESS

Intermediate GNVQ
BUSINESS

SECOND EDITION

Jon Sutherland

and

Diane Canwell

PITMAN
PUBLISHING

PITMAN PUBLISHING
128 Long Acre, London WC2E 9AN
A Division of Pearson Professional Limited

First published in Great Britain 1994
Second edition published 1995

British Library Cataloguing-in-Publication Data
A CIP catalogue record for this book is available from the British Library

ISBN 0–273–61772–9

Typeset by M Rules
Printed in England by Clays Ltd, St Ives plc

10 9 8 7 6 5 4 3 2 1

The Publishers' policy is to use paper manufactured from sustainable forests.

For Joshua and Easter

Contents

Introduction

Welcome to this second edition of *Intermediate GNVQ Business*. There have been a great many changes since preparation of the first edition in September 1994. We have followed a very similar format, but hope you will find this new book even more user-friendly and comprehensive. Unit and Core Skills performance criteria are also listed beside each activity, the Core Skills being represented by C for Communication, AN for Application of Number and IT for Information Technology. A new feature is the Focus studies, which include short case studies relating to that topic. There is now a glossary which covers the main key words, jargon and phrases that will become familiar to you.

We have followed all of the performance criteria, ranges and evidence indicators, Element by Element, across the four Mandatory Units of the learning programme. You will find that each of the Units is capable of being tackled independently in almost any order. At all times we have used the most up-to-date documentation from NCVQ and the awarding bodies in the preparation of the materials included in this book. This has not been a particularly easy task, since there have been a number of changes in the past year.

Throughout the 14 Elements that form the substance of the four Units you will find a common format, which attempts not only to cover all of the performance criteria but also the core skills. Each student activity is labelled with the appropriate performance criteria relating to the task in hand, along with any appropriate core skills that we have identified as being inherent in that activity. There is also, in many cases, an indication of the time which should be allocated to these activities. However, if the activities involve research or the use of information technology, no timing has been indicated. The Element Assignments form the major means of gathering evidence and cover all of the performance criteria in that particular Element. At the end of each Unit there is a 30-question multiple-choice mock test which follows the same format as the real end tests themselves. In addition to this, there is a short answer section before the mock end test, to aid revision.

The major reason behind our choice of format relates to the accessibility of information and immediacy of use to address each of the performance criteria and range statements. Many of the other texts for this subject have opted for a more conventional 'chapter' approach. Personal experience, together with feedback from students and institutions purchasing the first edition, show that our approach is both successful and helpful.

We hope that you will find this book an invaluable tool in the successful completion of this award and that GNVQ Intermediate Business proves to be a sound foundation for your future career plans. Many of the key concepts you will learn throughout this programme will greatly help you if you are interested in continuing your studies into GNVQ Advanced Business.

Jon Sutherland and Diane Canwell
September 1995

Introduction to Intermediate GNVQ in Business – A Student's Guide

So what is Intermediate GNVQ in Business? Let's start by explaining what GNVQ stands for: it means General National Vocational Qualification. In other words, this is a course that has been designed so that you not only gain knowledge of business, but are actually able to use it in the workplace. Depending on the grade you get for this course, it will be worth about the same as four good GCSE passes. There are two other things about the course that are worth remembering. First, you will have some useful skills that could get you a job at the end of the course and, second, you can get on to the GNVQ Advanced Business course.

The Intermediate course asks you to study the following:

- four mandatory units, which everyone will have to do
- two option units – you will have a choice of these if your centre offers a wide variety
- three core skill units, that you will be marked on throughout the course

The four mandatory units cover the business skills and knowledge that will provide you with an understanding of the ways in which businesses work and what it is like to work in one.

The option units cover some of the other features of business and allow you to concentrate on things that interest you. There are some rules about the option that you can choose, but your tutor will be able to tell you about them.

The core skills cover 'use of number' (some maths, statistics and graphs, etc); communication (written, oral and visual); and information technology (the use of computers to present and use information).

New course, new things to remember

There are plenty of new words and phrases that you will have to learn. Don't worry about them too much at the moment, because they will become clear as you get into the course. Here are some of the main ones that you will come across:

- **Unit** – this is a part of the course. There are nine units to complete: four mandatory, two options and three core skills.
- **Elements** – these are parts of the units. There are usually three or four in each of the units. These split up the units in easy-to-understand parts.
- **Performance criteria** – these are probably the most important of all. Each of the Elements is split up into three or more performance criteria. The performance criteria

ask you to prove that you can do something or understand something. The course work that you will be asked to do will be aimed at helping you to provide this evidence.

- **Range statement** – the performance criteria are split up into a number of statements which are all related to one another. The range covers all of the things that make up the wider performance criteria. You will find information on each of the range statements in this book to help you understand what is meant by them. The range statements that are printed in bold on the specification are known as 'range dimensions' and you will cover all of these. The other parts of the range statements are known as 'range categories' and you may not have to cover all of these in the course of your studies.
- **Evidence indicator** – these are descriptions of what you will have to produce as evidence that you understand each of the performance criteria. The activities throughout the book will help you to collect this evidence, but the most important way is to do the assignment at the end of each of the Elements. These assignments give you a series of tasks which exactly match each of the performance criteria. This is the minimum amount of work you will have to do if you want to claim that you have covered all of the performance criteria.
- **End tests** – these are one-hour multi-choice tests that you will be asked to sit during the course. They can be attempted several times if you have trouble with them and your tutor will be able to give you the dates of the tests. Once you have passed these and completed all of the assignments covering all of the performance criteria of a unit, then you have passed that unit. You will only have to sit an end test for each of your mandatory units, although some of the more practical ones may not have an end test. You do not have to do one for the options or the core skills, so you will only have to do three different tests.
- **Portfolios** – this is where you keep the evidence that you have collected to show that you have covered all of the performance criteria. You must make sure that your portfolio is up-to-date and that you have put all of your marked work into it. The ways in which these portfolios are put together will depend upon the way your school or college has decided to organise them.
- **Resubmission** – this is a polite way of saying that there is something wrong with the piece of work that you have handed in. You may have missed out some of the tasks or not answered them sufficiently well. Whatever the reason, you will be asked to do the piece of work again. It may only be one little piece of the work, but you will not have covered all of the performance criteria. You will only be expected to do the parts of the work again that were not good enough in the first place.
- **Grading themes** – there are four grading themes for the course. These are important as your grades for these will decide whether you get a pass, merit or distinction for the whole of the course. The grading themes are:

    1. *Planning* – in which you need to show that you are well organised in getting your work sorted out and that you have made sure that all of the tasks have been covered. You will also need to show that, when you plan how you are going to do a piece of work, you keep an eye on your progress (this is called monitoring).
    2. *Information seeking and handling* – this shows that you can figure out what you will need in order to complete a piece of work and that you have mentioned where you got the information from.
    3. *Evaluation* – you may find this difficult in the beginning and your tutor will be able to give you some more clues about dealing with it. You need to look at your planning and try to say what problems you had in completing the work. The evaluation

is your chance to look back at the way you tackled a piece of work and what you think (after having finished it) of your performance.

4 *Quality of outcomes* – this means that you can get a grade for the way in which the piece of work has been put together (have you covered all of the tasks well?) and your use of language and communication skills.

- **Verification** – there are three different types of people that will have a look at your work. The first is obviously the person who has set you a piece of work and will mark it. The second is another member of the staff at the college or school, who will check the marking of the person who set you the work. This person is known as the Internal Verifier. The third person is the External Verifier, who will not be a member of staff of the college or the school. This person is employed by the awarding body (BTEC, City & Guilds or RSA).

Getting good grades

The grade that you get will be based on just one in three of all of the grades that you get for all of your work. The goods news is that this is the best third of the work! You will only pass or be asked to resubmit work that is not worthy of a merit or a distinction. Above all, you should collect and keep all of the work that you have done. You should also make sure that your tutors have filled in a sheet and signed it to show that you have completed a part of the course every time that you get a piece of work back from one of them.

You will be encouraged to take responsibility for what you do throughout the course. This means that when you have been set a piece of work to do you should get on with it as soon as possible. Letting the work build up just means that you will be putting yourself under pressure later in the course. It will also give you problems with your tutors. Remember that they are only human, too, and would not want to have everything that you should have done weeks ago to mark in the last few days of the course.

We know that this might all sound rather strange to you. Really, there are some things about this course that are similar to the GCSE. The biggest difference is that you will need to keep up to date with the course work, as there will be quite a lot more to do than on a GCSE course. The other major difference is that you will only have to sit three one-hour tests spread out over the whole of the year.

Don't worry too much if this has left you wondering what it's all about. You will begin to understand as you get further and deeper into the course. Remember that this is your course and that the tests are pretty straightforward and used only to check that you have understood the unit itself. If nothing else, keep up to date with the course work.

We really hope that you will enjoy this course. We have tried to make this book as useful as possible and we are sure that you will find nearly everything that you need in it. The options are covered in other books and we have followed the same system of covering all of the units, elements, performance criteria and range. By the time that you start your options, we are sure that you will know as much about the course as we do!

Good luck
Jon Sutherland and Diane Canwell

Portfolio building

Gathering evidence for the Portfolio

Throughout the book we have designed a series of Student Activities and Element Assignments which are both formative and summative in nature. Formative means that students will be learning while they are doing; summative means that the student will be tested after a specific block of information to ensure understanding. In addition, at the commencement of each Element, we have listed the Performance Criteria and Range as specified by GNVQ.

The Student Activities and Element Assignments not only cover the GNVQ Performance Criteria and Range, but also the Core Skills – i.e. students apply technology, are asked to communicate in a variety of ways, and show application of number.

Because these Activities and Assignments cover all the necessary criteria and Core Skills, it is therefore possible to use these to build up the Student Portfolio of Evidence.

What the Portfolio should contain

The Student Portfolio should contain evidence that they have either achieved outcomes or proved competence in the past, or have carried out tasks which test both their knowledge and competence during their GNVQ programme. In effect, this means that the Portfolio can contain both evidence obtained within the institution of study, as well as any external activities.

Examples of evidence which a student could use to claim accreditation for prior learning or experience might be:

- Certificates from qualifications already gained
- A reference from an accredited assessor stating that the student has carried out a certain task competently on a number of occasions
- A log of visitors which a student may have dealt with on a regular basis over a period of time
- Evidence based on the student's part-time work experience

This is not an exclusive list. Other evidence may be negotiated with an External Verifier.

The Portfolio *must* contain evidence of assessment of all the GNVQ elements.

The Range and Evidence Indicators assist in suggesting how this could be carried out.

The Portfolio *must* contain evidence of achievement of the three Core Skills. It is not essential that Additional Core Skills be contained in the Portfolio, as they will not be required to prove competence at Intermediate Level. If, however, these Additional Core Skills have been assessed, then obviously the evidence should be included in the Portfolio.

The Student Activities and Element Assignments in this book are designed to assist in the preparation of the Evidence Portfolio, although naturally additional evidence will also be required or preferred. When students have to prove competence on a number of different occasions, then obviously the centres involved in delivering the Programme will need to provide additional means of assessment.

Core skills

As mentioned in the introduction, in designing the learning, assessment and evidence gathering activities we have borne in mind the Unit specifications demanded within the programme. It is important to think of the core skills as an integral part of the learning programme. Core skills require continuous assessment and testing throughout the programme. In practice, not only will your core skills be assessed on more than one occasion, but you will also find that the particular elements that make up each core skill are similarly tested repeatedly. This process is perfectly acceptable since it gives you the chance to show your ability to reproduce a particular achievement on a number of occasions.

The new core skills are somewhat more complex and detailed than any previous version. While we have repeatedly used the core skills, this has only been detailed to Element level. In order to address the performance criteria for each Element, it would have been necessary to include a complex matrix which cross-checks each of the performance criteria and their related range. Bearing in mind that core skill performance criteria and range are equally as important as the other mandatory performance criteria and range, your tutors will probably map them once they have decided which of the student activities and Element Assignments they intend to use.

Acknowledgements

The authors would like to thank the following individuals and organisations for their help and support in the preparation of this book:

Tracey Birkbeck (British Nuclear Fuels plc)
Julie Conneely (Marks and Spencer plc)
Theresa Gibson (Avon Cosmetics Limited)
Richard Garbutt (Peugeot Talbot Motor Company plc)
Paul Hallett (Department of Trade and Industry)
Her Majesty's Stationery Office
Steve McIvor (British Union for the Abolition of Vivisection)
R C Newstead (Mobil Oil Company Limited)
Amanda Smee (Woolworths; Kingfisher plc)
Edmund Staples (Mercury Communications Limited)
Tracey Suett (The British Petroleum Co plc)
Lowestoft Job Centre
Barclays Bank plc
Lloyds Bank plc
Midland Bank plc
National Westminster Bank plc

We acknowledge the copyright of illustrative materials used as follows:

Avon Cosmetics Limited
The Bank of Education
British Nuclear Fuels plc
British Petroleum Co plc
BUAV
Confederation of British Industry
Department of Trade and Industry
The Equal Opportunities Commission
Federation of Recruitment and Employment Services
Inland Revenue (Her Majesty's Stationery Office)
Kingfisher plc
Marks & Spencer plc
Mercury Communications Limited
Mobil Oil Company Limited
Norfolk and Waveney TEC
Peugeot Talbot Motor Company Limited

Unit 1

BUSINESS ORGANISATIONS AND EMPLOYMENT

Element 1.1

Explain the purposes and types of business organisations

Element 1.2

Examine business location, environment, markets and products

Element 1.3

Present results of investigation into employment

Element 1.1
Explain the purposes and types of business organisations

Performance criteria

A student must:

1 describe **developments** in **industrial sectors**

2 explain the **purposes** of **business organisations**

3 explain the **differences** between **types of business ownership**

4 explain the **operation** of one business organisation

Range

- *Developments*: recent past, present, likely future, growth of the sector, decrease of the sector, typical activities in the sector
- *Industrial sectors*: primary, secondary, tertiary
- *Purposes*: profit, market share, customer service, public service, charitable
- *Business organisations*: private sector, public sector; large, medium, small
- *Differences*: types of liability (limited, unlimited; use of profit (owners, shareholders, government)
- *Types of business ownership*: sole trader, partnership, private limited company (Ltd), public limited company (plc), franchise, co-operative, state-owned
- *Operation*: location, product (goods, services); links with other businesses; purpose, type of ownership

1.1.1 Describe developments in industrial sectors

Developments

As we will see throughout this Element, a variety of different business organisations belong (in one way or another) to a particular industrial sector. While you only really need to remember the three main industrial sectors, we have included in the performance criteria the full listing known as Standard Industrial Classifications. In your investigations into the sectors, you may find that using these classifications as the basis will allow you to find considerably more information that can be used much more easily than using the more simple primary, secondary and tertiary categories.

Recent past

Most of Western Europe is made up of countries with a mixed economy – in other words, there is a portion of the economy in public ownership and the remainder in private ownership. The scale of government intervention is, of course, far higher in the percentage of the economy which is in public ownership. Nationalised industries are owned and operated by an authority which is directly responsible to the government.

In recent years, successive UK Governments have been selling off these state-owned enterprises. This is, perhaps, in response to the fact that countries such as Japan and the USA, who are very active and successful in the world markets, rely very heavily on private industry. Attempting to emulate these two successful countries, many of the UK's nationalised industries have been privatised by selling shares to people and this has consequently reduced the role of the government in the economy.

We can identify that the core of the nationalised industries tended either to be part of the primary sector (concerned with obtaining basic raw materials) or tertiary sector (concerned mainly with distribution of products and services). We can see, therefore, that the government felt that these were key industries, apart from manufacturing, and so were better off in public hands. There was a serious change of opinion at the end of the 1970s which signalled a move away from public ownership to privatisation. This has also produced a valuable source of additional income to fund government expenditure.

PC 1.1.1
C 2.1

Group activity

In pairs, identify a privatised organisation of your choice and try to investigate its fortunes since it was taken into private ownership. Has the move worked for the organisation and for its customers too?

Compare your findings and conclusions with the rest of the group.

Present and likely future

When the UK joined the European Union (or the European Economic Community as it was known then) in 1973, it became part of a political and economic union. There has been considerable debate regarding the membership of the EU and the advantages and disadvantages can best be summed up as follows:

Advantages and disadvantages of EU membership

Advantages

- The EC offers UK industry the prospect of easy access to some 340 million customers.
- The sheer size of the EU offers groups of industries amazing economies of scale.
- By disposing of trade barriers, and subsequently increasing competition, there is an opportunity to reduce costs, increase efficiency and encourage innovation.
- Investment from non-EU countries is positively encouraged and no blocks are placed in the way of this.
- It also offers much greater redistribution of wealth within the EU as the poorer countries are given the opportunity to catch up with their more successful neighbours.
- On an individual level, the EC offers tremendous career opportunities.

Disadvantages

- There have been constant criticisms about the way in which EU funds are spent. The Common Agricultural Policy is cited in particular as a distorted and unfair way of spending EU funds.
- The EU has been much criticised for its bureaucratic nature.
- The EU is regarded with a degree of suspicion by non-EU countries and some have gone as far as to suggest that it is a conspiracy to exclude them from the lucrative European markets.
- Despite the fact that the EU means full European market integration, many member states still put their own national interests before those of the rest of the member states.

PC 1.1.1
C 2.1

Group activity *Time: 20 minutes*

As a group, consider the impact which joining the EU has had on the three main sectors of the economy. (You will find detailed descriptions of the three sectors in the next two sections of this element, or in the Glossary at the end of this book.) Which has suffered the most and which has gained the most as a result of the increased competition and opportunities?

National competitiveness and, consequently, efficiency and productivity, are very much determined by the inflation rate. Considerable progress has been made by member states since the poor performance in the late 1980s. The modest wage increases have helped to signal a sharp rise in productivity. Labour productivity has risen following the laying off of workers in business rationalisation programmes, manufacturing processes having been streamlined and now needing less employees to carry out routine, repetitive tasks. As a result, the real unit labour costs of the total European economy have fallen by 7% over the period 1980–92. At the same time, the Japanese managed to match the decrease in real unit labour costs, while the United States of America only managed a 1.8% drop.

Using a rather complicated formula, it has been calculated that over the 1980–92 period, the following has happened:

- *the EU industries have become 12% more competitive*
- *the USA has become 1.1% more competitive*
- *the Japanese have become 27.8% less competitive*

One of the many reasons for the UK's overseas trading to fall as dramatically as it did in the period was the nature and quality of the products it offered. Basically, manufacturing low-quality products means that they are often the most prone to fluctuations in the fortunes of the overseas markets. It is without doubt that the UK does produce some world-beating products and services, but these also compete in areas that are flooded with the products of other countries. If we take the products offered by the Third World (a term commonly used to describe southern hemisphere countries which are currently underdeveloped), it is impossible for a highly expensive production process in the UK to compete at all. Indeed, there are examples of whole industries being undercut to the degree that they are faced with the prospect of closure. The shipbuilding industry, under pressure from significantly cheaper markets, has all but been closed down as a result.

PC 1.1.1
C 2.1

Group activity *Time: 20 minutes*

In pairs try to discover how competitive each of the three UK industrial sectors is in comparison with the main competitors. Are you able to compare like with like?

Growth of the sector and decrease of the sector

As we will see in later sections of this Unit, there has been a marked decline in the industrial sectors of the economy. This has, in effect, mainly fallen upon the primary and secondary sectors of the economy. With widespread deindustrialisation (which means that the industrial base of the country has suffered very badly and is considerably smaller than it has been in the past) and the closure of many of the traditional forms of primary sector activities (such as coal mining), there has been a shift over to less complex manufacturing and a great switch over to the service (tertiary) sector activities.

PC 1.1.1
C 2.1
C 2.3

Group activity *Time: 20 minutes*

In pairs, and using the Standard Industrial Classifications detailed in the following section of the performance criteria, consider the growth and the decline of the three main sectors in your local region.

What are the trends that you have found in your local area? Do your investigations point to the same conclusions as the other groups? Compare your conclusions.

Typical activities in the sector

There are a number of tables prepared by the government or government agencies. Perhaps one of the more useful and often-used aspects of government statistics is the Standard Industrial Classification. It essentially breaks down the different markets and organisations which make up the economy into ten distinct divisions, as follows:

- *Division 0* – agriculture, forestry and fishing
- *Division 1* – energy and water supply industries
- *Division 2* – extraction of minerals and ores, manufacture of metals, mineral products and chemicals
- *Division 3* – metal goods, engineering and vehicle industries
- *Division 4* – other manufacturing industries
- *Division 5* – construction
- *Division 6* – distribution, hotels and catering, repairs
- *Division 7* – transport and communication
- *Division 8* – banking, finance, insurance, business services and leasing
- *Division 9* – other services

PC 1.1.1
C 2.1

Group activity

In pairs, locate the full listing of the Standard Industrial Classification and identify at least three industries per division.

It is not just the UK government that produces useful statistical information; other government-related organisations and bodies also produce a wide variety of data, including:

- The European Union which publishes such data as the *General Statistical Bulletin*
- The United Nations which produces a *Demographic Yearbook*
- The OECD which publishes *Main Economic Indicators*
- The IMF which releases a *Balance of Payments Yearbook*

There are a number of different agencies or commercial research organisations which produce a variety of statistical information relating to a huge variety of different topics. These agencies and research organisations collect or buy information which they then compile in report form and sell on to other organisations. Typical examples of agencies or commercial research organisations include:

1 **Mintel** – which produces short reports on a single specific consumer market and includes details on the following:

  - *market size*
  - *projected growth*
  - *market share of main competitors*
  - *advertising spending*
  - *market trends*

2 **Euromonitor** – which produces keynote reports which at around 75 pages give a broad outline of the nature and specifics of a particular market.

3 **Retail Audits** – which collects data from supermarkets and other large retail chains with regard to sales figures of particular products. This audit service is very useful for suppliers in assessing how effective their marketing has been and its impact upon other organisations' sales and market share.

As an alternative to these commercial organisations, the various trade associations produce some very useful data. These include:

- *the Market Research Society*
- *the Advertising Association*
- *the Chartered Institute of Marketing*

Individual activity

PC 1.1.1
C 2.1
C 2.2

Using your college library or the local public library, try to find the *Directory of British Associations*. In it you will see details of specific trade associations relating to various industries. Bear this book in mind when you consider the Element assignment, which will shortly follow. You would be wise to contact any trade association that you feel relates to the product which you will have to feature in your presentation.

Industrial sectors – primary, secondary and tertiary

Industry comprises all those organisations which make things or produce raw materials, but also includes banking, insurance and retailing.

PRIMARY (extractive)	SECONDARY (manufacturing, assembly, construction, processing)	TERTIARY (service)	
		Commercial services	**Personal services**
Mining	Shipbuilding	Financial	Medical
Agriculture	Motor vehicle production	Retail	Teaching
Fishing	Road building	Communication	Legal
Forestry	Oil refining	Transportation	Entertainment
Livestock farming		Import/export	Police
		Advertising	

Fig 1.1 Types of production

The government divides up organisations into 111 different types, which go under three categories.

1 Primary

The first is known as primary. These industries are concerned with producing raw materials. They include agriculture, fisheries, forestry and mining.

2 Secondary

The second major group is known as secondary. These industries are concerned with the manufacturing or processing of products. These include car making, food processing, and iron and steel working.

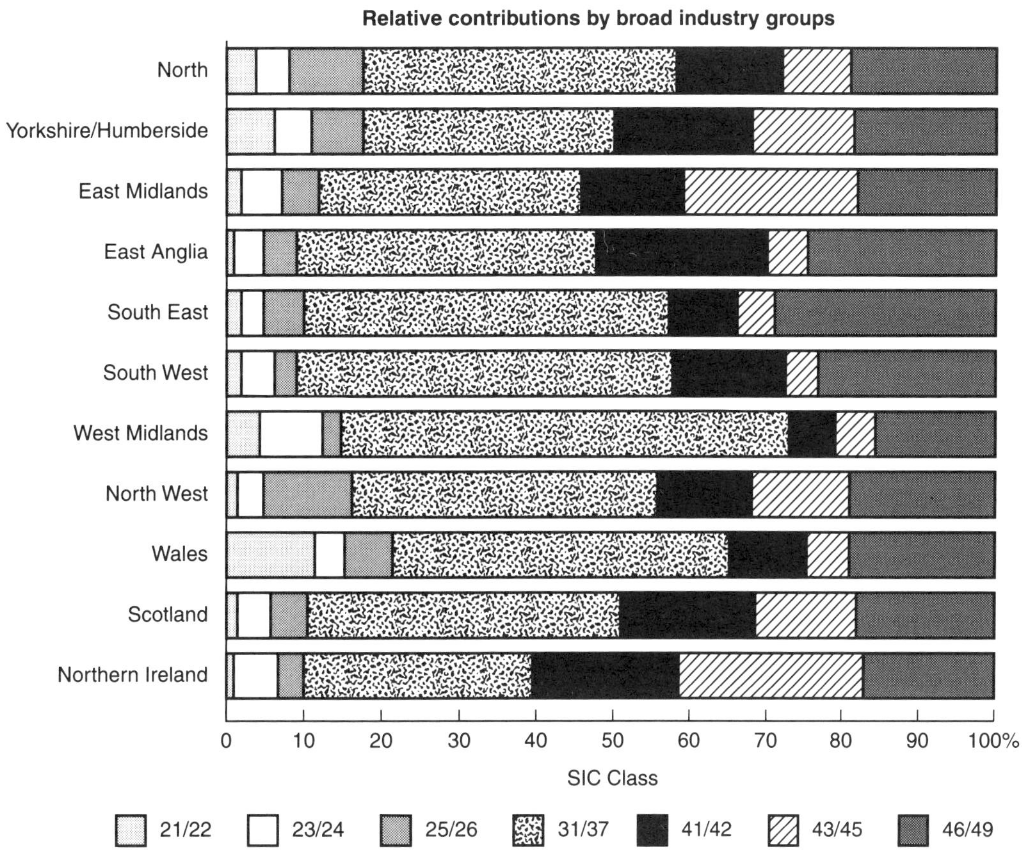

Fig 1.2 Manufacturing employment
(Source: Confederation of British Industry: employment relates generally to 1991)

3 Tertiary

The third group is known as tertiary. This includes service industries, which do not actually produce the goods but sell them. The tertiary group is commonly known as the service sector. In this category are included banking, all of the retailing and distribution businesses, and tourism.

PC 1.1.1
C 2.1

Group activity *Time: 25 minutes*

What is meant by an industrial sector? Why do you think the economy is split up into different sectors? Do you think that there should be more sectors created to cover organisations that do not fit neatly into the existing three? Discuss this as a group.

1.1.2 Explain the purposes of business organisations

Purposes of organisations

The purpose of any organisation is to be successful. Success is measured in many different ways, depending upon the type of organisation concerned. A good starting point for any organisation is to set down guidelines for activity, which serve as a form of standard from which it can measure performance.

There is no ideal organisational structure, as the individual organisation needs to develop gradually over a period of time. It is only when the organisation has clearly set out its goals and objectives that it can identify shortcomings or problems and seek solutions to them.

The business plan

Many businesses begin by setting out their aims, purposes and objectives in a business plan, which is a formal statement of their goals. However, in reality, the day-to-day achievement of these goals may differ from the business plan. Organisations do not exist in isolation. The environment in which they operate is constantly changing and therefore they must be flexible. Any change may require organisational change, when old ways of operating are no longer efficient or advisable in the new circumstances.

PC 1.1.2
C 2.1

Group activity *Time: 45 minutes*

What would you expect to find in a business plan? How would you expect a business plan to be organised? Who would be responsible for putting a business plan together? Who would wish to see the business plan? How closely do businesses adhere to their business plans? Discuss this in pairs.

The mission statement

A mission statement differs from a business plan in that it looks at what the organisation actually stands for. Generally, this is an agreement by both managers and employees. These agreed goals are often more valuable as they have the common consent of all those involved in the organisation. The individuals involved have a shared point of view and perhaps some common ideas of how to achieve it.

PC 1.1.2
C 2.2

Individual activity

The institution in which you are studying this course will have a mission statement. Discover what it is and try to describe in your own words what it actually means.

Once an organisation has established its goals, it must then find methods of achieving them. These are known as the strategies and tactics.

- **Strategies** are the major ways to achieve the objectives and tend to be fairly long term in their approach, e.g. to increase turnover by 50 per cent in 10 years.
- **Tactics**, on the other hand, are more short term and flexible. These are the individual parts of the main strategy, e.g. in order to increase turnover by 50 per cent in 10 years the product range needs to be increased and cheaper suppliers found.

So, strategy answers how the organisation intends to get where it wants to go, and tactics are the means by which it achieves that strategy.

As we have said, businesses exist for many different reasons, and perhaps the most common is profit, but certainly not the only one. Being happy and satisfied is as strong a reason for running an organisation, and this is why many people like to work for themselves. The freedom to make one's own choices is good compensation for not having to work for an organisation that is only interested in profit.

The following are some of the main objectives of organisations.

Profit

Maximising profit

This is the largest possible difference between how much something has cost to produce and how much it can be sold for. In order to achieve this the organisation needs to know as much about the customer and the market as possible. It needs to know where to get its supplies at the cheapest possible rate, the most economical way of getting the product to the customer and the maximum price the customer would be prepared to pay for the product.

Maximising sales

On the face of it, maximising sales would appear to be similar to maximising profit, but this is not the case. It does not necessarily follow that achieving high sales results in achieving high profits. There may only be a small profit to be made from each product. It is only when many thousands of the product are sold that a reasonable profit is made. This particular objective is most common in the retail trade, when even different branches of the same organisation 'compete' with one another to achieve high sales figures. Employees of the branches may be given considerable cash bonuses to encourage them to sell more.

Organisational growth

The larger an organisation is, the more likely it is to attract investors and to be able to produce products on a vast scale. Being big, however, brings its own particular problems. Keeping track of business activity such as sales, stock and profit requires many extra employees. Should a company grow too quickly and overtake its ability to keep track of things, it runs the risk of 'over-trading'. It is therefore very important to be able to monitor all activities when an organisation is growing fast.

Providing a steady income

In some ways, this is the opposite to sales and profit maximisation. An organisation which states that 'providing a steady income' is its principle objective is saying that it would rather attain realistic goals than overstretch itself. This is perhaps a cautious approach to business, but it is one which is often the most workable. Being able to meet sales targets easily, deliver goods on time and maintain high quality standards may mean the difference between survival and failure in an uncertain business world. Many of the organisations which grew very quickly in the 1980s over-extended themselves in pursuit of short-term profits. It can now be seen that companies which 'plodded along' throughout the 1980s are still trading successfully, having provided themselves with a steady income in good times and bad.

Breaking even

This objective can often be used to describe the attitude of a charity or non-profit making organisation (e.g. a local authority or a government department). Any profits that are made are simply ploughed back into the organisation to cover running costs and purchase more products in order to continue the cycle. This can be termed as 'ticking over' and is another objective often adopted by organisations in times of recession.

Providing a return for shareholders and owners

This objective aims to provide a steady and acceptable level of profit to those who own the organisation. In this sense a distinction is made between owners and shareholders. This will be covered in greater detail later.

Shareholders are owners of the business but may only have a small stake in it and look for profits in the form of dividends from the shares they own.

The term 'owners', on the other hand, may refer to either sole traders, partners or major shareholders, who again are looking for income from the organisation related to how much of that organisation they own.

Market share

Being the market leader

A market leader is an organisation that sells more products than any of its rivals, or perhaps all of its rivals combined. There are considerable advantages to being a market leader, since every rival organisation's products are compared to its own products. Once this status has been achieved, profit maximisation may also follow, as each product can be produced cheaper than a rival's because so many more are being produced.

A part-way stage in achieving market leadership is to set an achievable level of market share. In other words, the organisation may not directly seek to be the market leader straight away, but will move towards this in stages by gradually increasing its market share.

Beating the competition

In a sense this objective is similar to being a market leader. However, beating the competition may just relate to achieving higher sales. Measuring this objective in terms of success is difficult, but it can usually be assessed by the level of profit or the organisation's reputation.

Customer service

H/out

Most organisations now appreciate the importance of an efficient and effective customer service programme. In the past, organisations did not always appreciate that this was a crucial aspect of their operations. Customer service is as vital to an organisation which does not have direct contact with its customers as it is to those that deal with customers on a day-to-day basis. When we consider customer service, therefore, we should not simply focus upon the commercial or service sector of the economy. Both public and private sector organisations are under increasing pressure to provide comprehensive customer service programmes.

Some of the main customer service considerations are:

Efficiency and responsiveness

Organisations now value the need to be immediately responsive to customers' requirements. This may be achieved in many ways, such as by answering the telephone quickly, having sufficient products always in stock and being able to repair products at relatively short notice.

Sales service

Throughout the organisation's contact with customers, it is vital that everything possible is done to ensure total customer satisfaction. Well-trained staff and efficient, effective systems are important to the achievement of this goal.

After-sales service

The organisation's responsibility, as far as the customer is concerned, does not cease when the product or service has been sold. It is increasingly important for customer satisfaction that organisations enhance and develop their after-sales service. This may mean having sophisticated systems in place to cope with complaints, queries and returns of damaged or faulty goods.

Individual activity *Time: 3 hours*

PC 1.1.2
C 2.2
C 2.3
AN 2.1
AN 2.3
IT 2.1
IT 2.2
IT 2.3

An organisation monitoring the number of products returned for replacement due to faults would need to keep computerised records of these exchanges or refunds.

How would the organisation estimate the amount of money to be set aside for this purpose?

Using a graph or pie chart produced by means of computer software, prepare an estimate, assuming that 5% of your chosen product will be returned as faulty.

If this were the case in your organisation, what steps would need to be taken to improve this situation? Present your findings in the form of a word-processed report.

Public service

Despite large-scale privatisation, there are still numerous organisations which provide a public service in some form. Primarily, these include:

- *Central government departments*
- *Local authorities*
- *QUANGOs (organisations appointed by the government to provide certain services)*
- *Directly-funded or indirectly-funded organisations (such as hospitals and colleges)*
- *Specialist organisations (such as those set up to advise businesses and direct certain government initiatives)*

In the past many public services were that in name only; they did provide a service, but they were not necessarily accountable or responsive to public needs. Government legislation now requires them to be accessible, responsive and efficient.

Some of the key public service considerations include:

Providing benefits and grants

Organisations such as the DSS (Department of Social Security) or local Councils are responsible for providing a range of benefits and grants, including those to the unemployed or to students. In this respect, the public service aspect of these organisations is obvious, but there are less obvious ways in which some public sector organisations can also provide vital services.

Providing advice and guidance

Councils and central government, through a range of different sub-organisations, provide a vast range of support services to industries and individuals. These services include business advice and guidance through the Department of Trade and Industry, and local support for business via the nearest Chamber of Commerce. Individuals can obtain useful advice from the Citizens Advice Bureaux, which are in nearly all UK towns and cities.

Charitable

Charities have a different perspective on business activity to other organisations. Charities have been described as:

- **Non-profit making** – charities are not necessarily in operation to provide a profit, although a modest profit that could be ploughed back into the operation could be useful. Technically the charity is not owned by anyone, nor are there shareholders who require dividend payments, so the profit motive is not there.
- **Non-loss making** – perhaps this is a slightly better description, but still not quite true. It is obviously advisable for the organisation not to have to dip into its reserves to support its activities. Some organisations, because of the recession, found their income diminishing and had no other choice. Even the Church of England has had to dispose of assets.
- **Profit-making** – this can be said to be true of many charities these days. They do produce a profit from their merchandising and other fund-raising activities, but the money is not distributed to shareholders or owners. In most cases, the funds are used to support new activities, purchase equipment, expand into new countries, or are simply transferred into a reserve fund for contingencies (money set aside for emergencies or unforeseen expenditure).

An organisation with a 'charitable status' is exempt from many of the legal obligations of other organisations. This is not to say that it must not comply with such legal requirements as health and safety, or contracts of employment, but that any profits made are not taxable.

In recent times, in addition to the 'standard' charities like Barnardo's, Oxfam, Help the Aged and Scope, many schools have adopted this form of organisation.

Business organisations

It is probably easier to think of an example of a business organisation than to try to define what a business organisation actually is. Although, as we will see, business organisations can differ enormously, they do have some common features. These are:

- *they often use resources that are in limited supply (such as human resources, money and materials)*
- *they provide something (either a product or a service)*
- *they normally compete with other organisations*

As we will investigate later, each organisation must undertake a wide variety of different tasks or functions to ensure that they operate well within their area of involvement. Some of these functions include:

- *Managing employees* – usually through a personnel (or human resources) department
- *Selling products or services* – providing the customer with the product or service which they require
- *Distributing the product or service* – ensuring that the customer has access to what the organisation provides
- *Purchasing products or services* – ordering stock for either short-term use or long-term needs

- *Marketing a product or service* – researching the customers' needs and then promoting the product or service
- *Keeping financial records* – to monitor the success of the organisation

Also, organisations must ensure that when they need to make a choice they will make the correct decision. This may involve a wide variety of considerations which will have an impact on the decision. It usually involves the use of resources, both of materials and staff, which may be limited, so the organisation as often as possible must ensure that it makes the right decision.

Business organisations do not always have the same purpose. Perhaps the most common, as we will see later, is the profit motive, but not all organisations are driven by this goal.

→ Marks & Spencer – shares plc

Private sector

→ Littlewoods – family owned – Ltd

Generally, the private sector is made up of organisations that are independent of the government. A little later on in this Element we will investigate the specific nature of each of the main private sector organisations, but for now we need to make some simple distinctions between them:

- **Sole traders** are organisations usually owned and run or operated by one person, e.g. the owner of a small shop.
- **Partnerships** are organisations owned by groups of people, e.g. a firm of solicitors.
- **Limited companies** are organisations that are owned by shareholders, who have only limited liability for its debts, e.g. Mercury Communications Ltd.
- **Franchises** are organisations that have been set up by buying the name and expertise of an established organisation, e.g. Fastframe, Kentucky Fried Chicken.
- **Co-operatives** are organisations of groups of people who have joined together to be more efficient and effective, with members producing the goods to be sold (e.g. farm produce) and sharing out the profits.

Public sector

The public sector consists of organisations that are either owned or controlled by the government. The most common forms of public sector organisation are:

- **Government departments or the civil service**, which are responsible for running government activities in a specific area (such as the Department of Trade and Industry which assists businesses).

- **Local government**, such as County, Metropolitan, District or Borough Councils, which provide services, assist business and promote the area.

- **Public corporations or enterprises**, such as the Bank of England, British Steel or British Rail (although, like Railtrack, many parts of this may have been privatised by the time you read this), which provide services in a particular part of the economy. These are also known as nationalised industries.

- **QUANGOS (Quasi-Autonomous Non-Governmental Organisations)** which are funded by the government to provide services. Examples of Quangos include OFTEL (which monitors the communications industry) and the Arts Council (which provides grants to artists, theatres and film makers).

Many organisations were once public enterprises or Quangos, but have been privatised. These include British Telecom, British Gas, British Airways, and the various Electricity Boards and Water Boards.

Group activity *Time: 30 minutes*

Do you think that prisons should be directly controlled by the government or privatised? Discuss this in pairs and decide whether you agree or disagree.

PC 1.1.2
C 2.1

Large organisations

Many organisations have become multinationals or conglomerates, by acquiring or building up their businesses all over the world. For some organisations this is a result of the type of business in which they are involved.

- **Oil companies** discover oil in many parts of the world, refine the crude oil, ship it to storage areas and then distribute it via petrol stations and other means (e.g. BP and Shell).
- **Computer manufacturers** market and sell their products world-wide. Although they may research and manufacture in only one or two countries, they must have support, sales and marketing operations in any country likely to use their products (e.g. IBM and Apple).
- **Retail organisations** have sought to expand into alternative markets throughout the world, particularly important if their major market is in recession or decline (e.g. Marks & Spencer).
- **Franchise organisations** see expansion abroad to be the future and have encouraged people to set up franchises in areas or countries of which the original organisation has little or no knowledge of (e.g. Body Shop).
- **Manufacturing organisations** often need to be able to produce products in the countries in which they compete. This may be to overcome import duties or quotas set by the host country or simply to take advantage of lower wage rates and set-up costs (e.g. General Motors, Nissan and Ford).

Conglomerates

The term 'conglomerate' best describes an organisation that has interests in a variety of different business ventures. An organisation in this position can avoid sudden or gradual downturns in sales and profits for a particular product or in a particular market by spreading its operations and investments over a number of products or services.

International organisations

International organisations can also take advantage of the differences in the value of currencies, as well as the economic growth or recession in different countries. They have enormous buying power and it is thought by many people that they can exert too strong an influence on countries desperate to retain their investment.

International organisations do suffer from some problems that can be encountered as a result of their size. It is often difficult to maintain any sense of international corporate identity. Modern communications technology, such as video-conferencing, E-Mail and faxes have gone some way to solve this problem, as have the use of in-house newsletters and magazines, and corporate logos (symbols).

Just as it is comparatively easy to 'buy into' a market, e.g. by buying a company, if the organisation has the financial strength, so it is also easy to dispose of companies that form part of the organisation if they fail to live up to their promise of profits.

Medium organisations

A wide variety of organisations operate on a national basis in the UK. In all sectors of the economy we can find examples of businesses that have established themselves in most of the major population centres of the UK.

In manufacturing, for example, food processing tends to be based around the areas which produce the required raw materials. Birds Eye / Walls, for example, has positioned itself to exploit the availability of fish and vegetables. The company is careful to choose its locations, since the processing of fresh produce is essential in maintaining its image.

In the service sector of the economy, we will find banks, building societies, travel agents, betting shops and newsagents creating national networks to cover the spread of the population over the UK.

Small organisations

Whether you live in a city, town or in the countryside, there is a network of business organisations to cater for nearly all of your immediate needs and wants. Some may be part of the public sector (such as refuse collection or health care); others will be provided by the private sector (such as supermarkets, newsagents and chemists). Other organisations may not necessarily provide products or services for the local community, but may provide these for the national or international market (such as a mine, a food processing operation, or a government department).

PC 1.1.2
C 2.2
C 2.3
AN 2.1
IT 2.1
IT 2.2
IT 2.3

Individual activity

Time: 2 hours

Undertake a brief 'audit' of your most immediate retail shops. How many of them are independent and local? How many of them are nationally-owned chains? Are there any internationally-owned outlets? Present your findings in the form of a table, by using a computer software package.

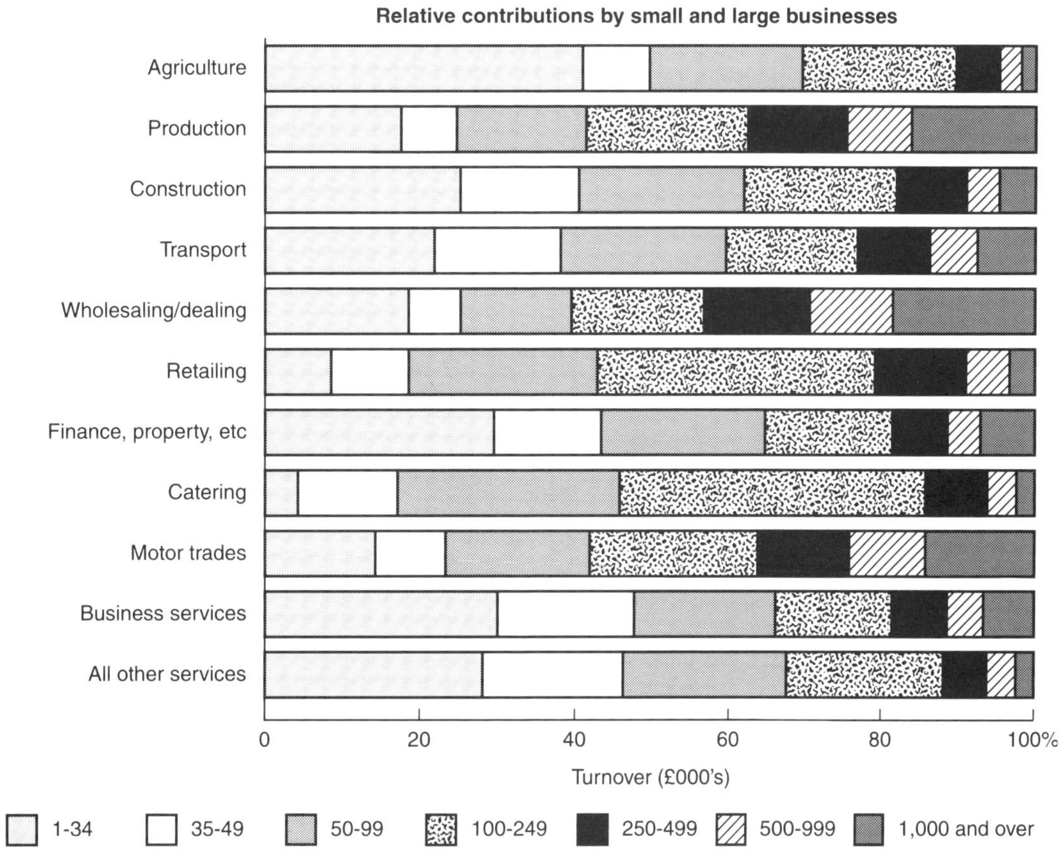

Fig 1.3 Legal units 1993
(Source: Confederation of British Industry)

1.1.3 Explain the differences between types of business ownership

Types of business ownership

There are many ways in which a business can be organised, from a small one-person business to a multinational organisation. You will find that the majority of the business organisations discussed in this section are representative of the private sector, but the public sector is covered in some detail in our consideration of public corporations.

Sole trader

The sole trader is perhaps the most common type of business organisation, although in recent years the numbers of such businesses have been declining.

The sole trader is responsible for all that the operation undertakes. This individual will be responsible for supplying or borrowing all the money required by the business and for actually running the business on a day-to-day basis. Perhaps the most common sorts of sole traders are craftsmen and women – for example, plumbers, decorators, electricians, mobile hairdressers, window cleaners and chiropodists.

Sole trader businesses cover a very wide range of activities, but they all have some features in common, including the way they are started, and that the business can normally be run by one person, although that person has to be very flexible and needs to be willing to work very long hours.

Advantages and disadvantages of setting up as a sole trader

Advantages

- there are no particular legal formalities to complete before commencing to trade
- there are no particular legal requirements governing the layout of their accounts
- the annual accounts do not have to be audited
- decisions can be made quickly, since only one individual is involved
- the owner has the freedom to run the business his/her own way

Disadvantages

- capital is limited to the owner's savings or profits or any other money he/she can borrow
- the owner has sole responsibility for debts – if the owner does fall into financial difficulties it may be necessary to sell his/her own personal possessions to meet the business debts
- responsibility for a range of activities falls upon the shoulders of the one person who runs the business. In other words, the owner is entirely responsible for running the business – dealing with paperwork, customers, filling in tax returns and dealing with day-to-day contact with any employees or sub-contractors
- the success of the business is always dependent on how hard the sole trader wishes to work
- any unforeseen accident or illness could seriously affect the business since all responsibilities rest on the shoulders of that one person

PC 1.1.3
C 2.1

Group activity *Time: 15 mins*

Consult your *Yellow Pages* Directory and try to identify at least 10 local sole traders. What kind of occupations are they in? Compare your findings with those of the rest of your group.

Fig 1.4 Examples of sole traders

Partnership

A partnership may be formed as a way to overcome the problems a sole trader can have in raising capital. A partnership consists of between two and 20 people who set up in business together and share the responsibility for that business. Partnerships of accountants, solicitors and stock exchange members can have more than 20 partners. Each partner is required to contribute some capital and they share out the profits and the losses between all of the partners. The control of the business is the responsibility of all the partners and decisions made by one partner are always binding on the others.

In partnerships, all partners have what is known as unlimited liability. This means that any debts incurred by the partnership have to be met by all the partners.

Individuals may enter into a partnership with one another without any real formal written agreement, but in practice they usually draw up a partnership agreement. Essentially this is a set of rules which will hopefully help avoid disagreements between the partners.

The agreement usually includes the following:

- the amount of capital to be contributed by each partner
- the ratio in which the profits and losses are to be shared. (Usually this is worked out in relation to the amount of capital (money) which each of the partners has put in. So, in other words, the more capital each partner has put in, the more the share of the profits he/she will be entitled to receive.)
- the salaries, if there are any, that are going to be paid to specific partners
- the rules for admitting and expelling partners
- the voting rights of partners – they may have an equal or an unequal share of the decision making
- the rules for ending the partnership

On the question of liability for the debts of the partnership, there is an option which allows a partnership to have limited liability for some of its members – this is known as a limited partnership. In such partnerships, certain partners are known as sleeping partners. They take no part whatsoever in the decision-making process of the business and, should the business fail, they stand to lose no more than their original investment in it. Therefore, they have limited liability. In contrast, the other partners, known as the general partners, still face unlimited liability. In law, there must always be at least one partner with unlimited liability.

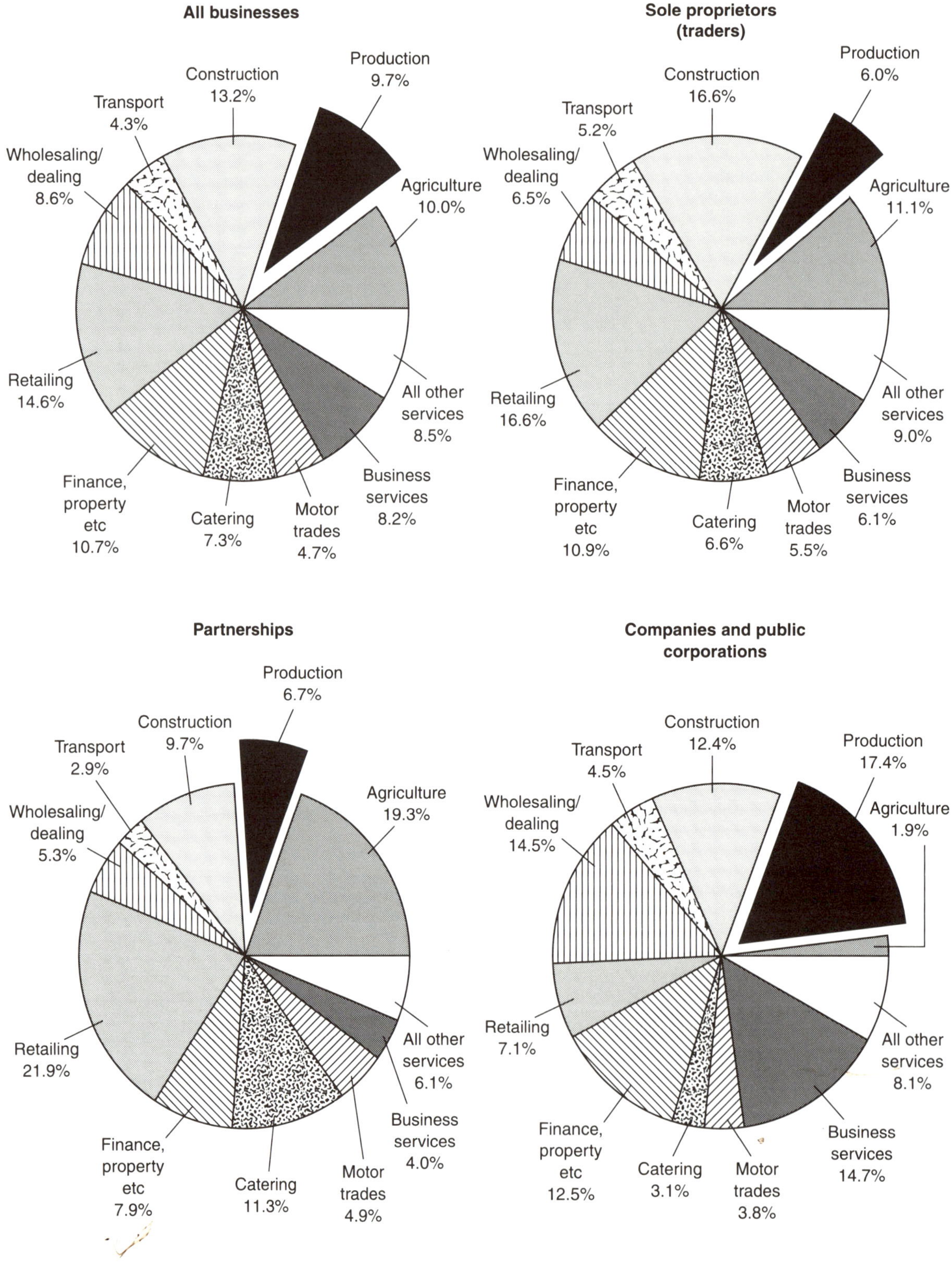

Fig 1.5 Number of legal units 1993
(Source: Confederation of British Industry)

This Partnership Agreement is made this

day of 19

BETWEEN

(hereinafter called

) of the one part and

(hereinafter called

) of the other part

WHEREBY IT IS AGREED as follows—

1. THE parties hereto (hereinafter called "the Partners") shall become and remain Partners in the business of for the term of years from the date hereof if both of them shall so long live

2. THE business shall be carried on under the style or firm of at or at such other place or places as the Partners shall hereafter determine

3. (1) THE capital of the partnership shall consist of the sum of to be brought into the partnership by the Partners in the following proportions namely:—

(A) As to by and

(B) As to by

(2) THE Partners shall be entitled to the capital of the partnership in the same proportions and each Partner shall be entitled to receive interest at the rate of pounds per cent per annum payable half-yearly from the commencement of the partnership on the amount of capital so brought in by h as aforesaid and shall be entitled to receive interest at the same rate payable half-yearly and to commence from the date of the advance on all money which a Partner may hereafter advance to the capital of the partnership

4. (1) THE rent of the business premises and all rates taxes premiums for insurance and other outgoings payable in respect of the same and the wages and remuneration of the persons employed in the business and all other outgoings expenses debts liabilities and losses (including any loss of capital) incurred in the course of the business and all interest payable to either Partner on any capital now brought in or hereafter to be advanced by h shall be paid and discharged out of the gross receipts and out of the capital of the partnership or in case the same shall be insufficient for the purpose by the Partners in the proportions in which they are entitled to share in the net profits of the partnership

(2) ALL interests in land shall be vested in the Partners as joint tenants on trust for sale and they shall hold the rents and profits until sale and the net proceeds in trust for the partnership

5. ALL proper and usual books of account relating to the business shall be kept by the Partners at the partnership premises and all necessary entries made therein and the same shall at all times be open to the inspection of each Partner

6. THE Partners shall be entitled to the net profits of the business (after paying all expenses and outgoings and such interest on capital as aforesaid) in the following proportions:—

(1) As to

(2) As to

7. (1) EACH Partner shall be at liberty to draw out of the profits of the business for h separate use any sum not exceeding the yearly sum of by equal payments of but subject to each Partner repaying to the partnership immediately after the taking of any annual general account any amount so drawn by h in excess of the total amount shown by such account to be due to h for interest on capital brought in or advanced by h and h share of the net profits of the business

(2) THE Bankers of the partnership shall be or such other bankers as the Partners shall from time to time agree

This Partnership Deed is made the

day of 19 **Between**

of the one part and

of the other part:

WHEREAS the parties hereto (hereinafter together called "the partners") have agreed to become partners in the practice or business hereinafter mentioned for the term and subject to the conditions hereinafter appearing:

NOW THIS DEED WITNESSES that in pursuance of the said agreement each of the partners hereby covenants with the other of them as follows:—

1. THE partners shall become and remain partners in the practice or business of for the term of years from the date hereof if both of them shall so long live but subject as hereinafter provided.

2. THE partnership shall be carried on under the style or firm of at or at such other place or places as the partners shall from time to time determine.

3.—(1) THE capital of the partnership shall consist of the sum of £ to be brought in by the partners in the following proportions namely the sum of £ by the said and the sum of £ by the said with such further sums (to be contributed in the like proportions) if any as the partners may agree to subscribe and the partners shall be entitled to the capital of the partnership in the same proportions.

(2) EACH partner shall be entitled to receive interest at the rate of £ per cent. per annum payable half-yearly from the commencement of the partnership or from the date of contribution (as the case may be) on the amount of capital so brought in

1

Fig 1.6 A partnership agreement and partnership deed

(Courtesy of the Solicitor's Law Stationery Society plc)

The most common form of partnership, though, is the ordinary partnership where all partners play an active role in the running of the business. In the event of losses being incurred, each partner has unlimited liability.

It is very important for people setting up a partnership with unlimited liability that all the partners are trustworthy, honest and hard-working. Otherwise, the mistakes of one partner can affect all the others financially.

Partnerships are commonly found in the accounting and legal professions, where specialists in different areas of their profession will join together in a partnership to make the business more attractive to prospective clients.

There are a number of advantages and disadvantages in setting up a partnership.

Advantages and disadvantages of setting up a partnership

Advantages

- as we have said earlier, it is easier for partners than sole traders to raise capital because all of the partners can pool their resources, giving access to more capital than one person could raise
- partners can share their expertise and their workload
- partners can arrange to cover one another at times of illness or holidays, or even during lunch breaks
- a partnership, like a sole trader, does not have to publish its accounts or have them audited
- additional capital can be raised by introducing more partners into the partnership

Disadvantages

- a partner is personally liable for all of the firm's debts
- disagreements can arise between partners about the amount of effort that each of them puts in
- partnerships can only raise limited amounts of capital as compared with businesses like limited companies (which we discuss below)
- decision making can be slow since all partners have to be consulted
- the death or retirement of a member can bring a partnership to an end if such a rule is written into the deed of partnership
- all profits must be shared

PC 1.1.3
C 2.1

Group activity

Investigate at least five local partnership firms in your local area and try to discover the number of partners in each of these businesses. What advantages do they have over sole traders? If you are starting a business, what kind of qualities would you be looking for in your partners? Discuss your findings in small groups.

Private limited company (Ltd) and public limited company (plc)

The limited company is one of the most common forms of business organisation. A limited company is separate in law from its shareholders and directors.

Individuals put capital into the business – they are known as shareholders – and they each therefore own part of the business and will share a percentage of any profits that are earned. They elect a number of directors who will actually run the business on their behalf.

The law requires a meeting of shareholders to be held once a year, and notes, known as minutes, of matters discussed are required to be made. Shareholders normally have no part in the day-to-day running of the business, unless they are also directors or workers who have bought shares.

A number of Companies Acts and other laws have been passed over the years which protect the interests of shareholders, as well as those of creditors who are owed money by limited companies.

It is relatively simple and reasonably cheap to set up a company. In order to set up a limited company, two documents must be drawn up:

1 **Memorandum of Association** This is really the company's rule book. The kind of things that you would find in a Memorandum of Association are:

- *the name of the company*
- *the address of the registered office*
- *the company's activities*
- *the type and amount of capital which has been invested to set up the company*

2 **Articles of Association** This document deals with the inside working of the company. It details the following:

- *the procedures that have to be followed at an Annual General Meeting (known as an AGM)*
- *the duties of the directors of the company*
- *the voting rights of the shareholders*
- *how profits and losses are distributed among shareholders*
- *details of how company officers will be appointed*
- *details of how accounts will be kept and recorded*
- *the rules and procedures for issuing shares and for transferring shares to other people*

Once these two documents have been drawn up, the next step is to send them to Companies House. If everything is in order, the Registrar of Companies will issue a Certificate of Operation, which in effect is like a Birth Certificate for the company.

There are essentially two different types of limited company. Both of them have a minimum of two shareholders.

1 **Private Limited Company** You can always tell that a company is a private limited company when the word *Limited* or *Ltd* is written after the company name. The shares in a private limited company are not freely available to the general public and the transfer of shares is agreed only by the directors. Private limited companies are usually family concerns, or were originally so. This is the form of organisation often chosen when a sole trader wants to expand and wishes to retain control of the company.

2 **Public Limited Company** This tends to be a larger company. It will have 'plc' after the company name. These companies are allowed to raise capital through selling their shares on the Stock Exchange. This gives them greater flexibility in raising capital. They still only need two people to form a Public Limited Company, and there is no stated maximum number of shareholders.

The process of creating a public company is very similar to that of creating a private company. Once a public company has received a Certificate of Operation, it will prepare a prospectus, which is basically an invitation to the public to buy shares. The people forming the company must decide how those shares are to be sold, and how many shares will be allocated to each prospective buyer.

The Registrar of Companies will then issue a Trading Certificate. This means that the business is now up and running.

One feature common to both types of limited company is that they must file a set of audited accounts with the Registrar of Companies. This set of accounts must include:

- *a Directors' Report*

WOOLWORTHS
Building on an unrivalled asset...

We have almost 1,500 stores with sales close to £2bn (excluding VAT) in Britain's high streets through our Woolworths and Superdrug chains. On average nearly 1.8 million customers a day shop with us in these stores, many of them mothers with young children.

Although Woolworths saw a disappointing drop in profits to £51.4m, Superdrug moved ahead strongly and made a record contribution of £38.1m.

WOOLWORTHS
Last year was the first time in seven years that Woolworths failed to increase sales significantly. This was reflected in a loss of share in some of its traditional markets, although the markets grew modestly.

We achieved share increases in entertainment and kidswear but lost ground in toys and stationery. Nevertheless, Woolworths retains leading or significant positions in its chosen markets and continues to attract a broad cross-section of customers. According to independent research, last year more adults visited and bought something from Woolworths than almost any other high street retailer. We recorded more than 330 million customer transactions, with over 50 million alone during the peak Christmas shopping period of December.

The pulling power of Woolworths is highlighted by our share of National Lottery sales. At the time of its launch, with terminals installed in just under half of our stores last November, we achieved 60% of total sales with only 3% of all terminals.

The recovery programme at Woolworths is focusing on re-establishing Woolworths' price proposition and ensuring much improved stock availability throughout the year to reinforce our merchandise ranges and authority. We also plan a more exciting and effective promotional calendar. We will be paying particular attention to our critical second half lines, especially toys and Christmas products. More emphasis on our Chad Valley toy range will be an important feature. Above all a trouble-free Christmas is a priority.

Another exciting initiative last year, was the introduction of newspapers and magazines in 260 stores. An extension to 540 is planned this year. We will also roll-out a bargain books proposition, which performed well over Christmas.

- **EPOS benefits coming through**
- **Woolworths set for recovery**
- **Continued repositioning of Superdrug**

Over the last two years we have invested more than £100m in Woolworths, more than a third of it on the installation of EPOS. All Woolworths stores now have EPOS tills and the benefits will become apparent progressively from now on.

The completion of EPOS installation is an important factor in our longer term strategy to take Woolworths through the rest of the Nineties. During the course of the year we expect to say more about this. However the intention is to build further on Woolworths' powerful brand identity and unrivalled store portfolio.

Throughout the late Eighties and early Nineties we revived Woolworths and consistently grew sales and profits. We did this by a revolutionary programme which focused on merchandise areas where Woolworths had leadership, such as entertainment, gifts and confectionery, kidswear and toys. As a result we increased our authority in those areas and gave customers a better choice.

'Operation Focus,' as we called it, required a radical reduction in the number of Woolworths' product lines and a streamlining of the store portfolio. Its success dramatically reversed Woolworths' fortunes and led to selected new store openings.

What we now propose is further evolution. This will come through differentiating the merchandise offer by store location so that we meet customer needs more precisely.

It is not surprising that with a chain of our size and varied locations, customers use the stores in different ways. For example, there are differences in the offer we need to deliver in our larger stores in city centres which compete against specialists, in our medium sized stores in market towns where Woolworths is often the major retailer, and small suburban stores where we are more of a convenience outlet.

By recognising these differences and adjusting our merchandise ranges to suit them, we can capitalise on the strong brand values that Woolworths still enjoys.

Outlook
The priority this year is to demonstrate recovery at Woolworths through higher sales and profits, while working on the programme for future evolution. With a changed management team in place and the benefits of EPOS coming on stream we are confident about the outlook.

Fig 1.7 Woolworths – a division of Kingfisher plc. This retail operation may be found in most towns and cities in the UK

- *an Auditors' Report*
- *a Balance Sheet*
- *the source and application of funds*
- *an explanation of the accounts*

It is also necessary for public limited companies to file an Annual Return. This gives the details of the Directors, Shareholders and any other information that is actually required by law. All this information is kept on file at Companies House, and is always open to inspection by members of the public for a small fee.

Advantages and disadvantages of setting up a limited company

Advantages

- shareholders have limited liability
- it is easier to raise capital through shares
- it is often easier to raise finance through banks
- it becomes possible to operate on a larger scale since, when additional capital is required, additional shares are offered to the public
- it is possible to employ specialists
- suppliers tend to feel a bit more comfortable in trading with legally-established organisations
- directors are not liable for the debts of the company, provided they follow the rules, and it is easy to pass shares in a company down from one generation to another; in this way control may be kept by the same families
- the company name is protected by law
- there are tax advantages attached to giving shares to employees
- a company pension scheme can give better benefits than those that are available for the self-employed
- the ill-health or death of shareholders does not affect the running of the business

Disadvantages

- the formation and running costs of a limited company can be expensive
- decisions tend to be slow since there are a number of people involved
- employees and shareholders are distanced from one another
- all the affairs of the company are public, through the audited accounts and annual returns that the company makes
- legal restrictions under the various Companies Acts are fairly tight and there are very heavy penalties for companies which break the rules
- large companies are often accused of being impersonal to work for and to deal with
- rates of tax on profits are often higher than those that sole traders and partnerships have to pay

Consolidated Profit and Loss Account

For the year ended 31 March	Note	1994	1993
		£M	£M
Turnover	3		
Continuing operations		**1098**	964
Discontinued operations		**35**	85
		1133	1049
Less net operating costs and expenses	4	**1029**	900
Operating profit	3		
Continuing operations		**103**	128
Discontinued operations		**1**	21
		104	149
Income from associated undertakings		**12**	3
		116	152
Less financial charges	7	**35**	76
Profit on ordinary activities before tax		**81**	76
Tax on profit on ordinary activities	8	**5**	15
Profit on ordinary activities after tax		**76**	61
Profit attributable to minority interests		**1**	2
Profit for the financial year		**75**	59
Dividends	9	**26**	26
Retained profit for the year		49	33

Statement of Total Recognised Gains and Losses

For the year ended 31 March	1994	1993
	£M	£M
Profit for the financial year	**75**	59
Currency translation differences on foreign currency net investments	–	1
Total recognised gains and losses relating to the year	75	60

Fig 1.8 BNFL's consolidated profit and loss account

PC 1.1.3
C 2.1
C 2.2

Group activity

Time: 30 minutes

In pairs, one person taking companies which are plcs and the other taking Ltds, list the main advantages. Take just five minutes to do this, and then together try to agree which has the most advantages. If you agree that plcs are better than Ltds, think about why some companies remain Ltds. If you think that Ltds are better than plcs, why do some companies bother to become plcs?

Franchise

The franchise is a form of organisation which has been imported into the UK and the rest of the world from America, where over a third of all retail businesses are operating on a franchise basis. This is also becoming a very popular form of business organisation in the UK. The main features of franchising are as follows:

- Franchising is hiring out or licensing the use of product lines to other companies. A franchise agreement allows another company to trade under a particular name in a particular area. The firm which sells the franchise is known as the *franchisor*.
- The person who takes out the franchise needs a sum of money for capital and is issued with a certificate from the franchising company. This person is known as the franchisee. The *franchisee* usually has the sole right of operating in a particular area. Examples of franchises can be seen in many of our high streets – Pizza Hut, Prontaprint, Body Shop and Spud U Like.
- Another important feature of the franchise agreement is that the franchisee agrees to buy all of its supplies from the franchisor and the latter makes a profit on these supplies.
- The franchisor also takes a share of the profits made by the franchisee's business, without having to risk any capital or be involved in the day-to-day management of the business.
- The franchisee, on the other hand, benefits from trading under a well-known name and enjoys a local monopoly. In other words, each franchisee is the only business to operate under that name in a particular area.
- The franchise agreement allows people to become their own boss without the normal kinds of risk of setting up a business from scratch.

Fig 1.9 A Fastframe franchise

Individual activity

PC 1.1.3
C 2.2
C 2.3

Franchises have become a very popular way of starting a new business quickly. How many franchises can you find in your local business community? Using research methods, where would you find details concerning franchises? If possible, obtain a brochure and application for the setting up of a franchise. Approximately how much money would you need to buy a franchise operation?

Focus study

Franchises

By the turn of the century McDonald's aims to have 1000 outlets in the UK, which are expected to include some 300 franchised restaurants.

McDonald's joined the franchising business relatively late (1986), and favours granting additional franchises to existing franchise holders. The franchise deal, in the first instance, runs for some 20 years. McDonald's is very careful in choosing its potential franchise holders – it can pick and choose as the enquiry numbers are large. McDonald's looks for outgoing people, with a good financial mind, who are enthusiastic and quite aggressive in business terms. The company also favours individuals setting up franchises in their own town or area.

Training lasts for some nine months. There is a 'Hamburger University' in north London and the total cost of the training is around £40 000.

A typical franchisee would need to find some £125 000 (around 40% of the cost of setting up the restaurant).

If an individual wanted to franchise an existing McDonald's restaurant, then the cost would be between £100 000 and £1m! If a potential franchise is particularly good, but does not have the full 40% investment capital, then with £40 000 a deal could be struck. The balance is paid over a three-year period by putting the restaurant's profits back into the business.

McDonald's franchise operation has been extremely successful; only one franchisee has dropped out so far, although some have also not made it through the training period. Even with the McDonald's name and reputation, there is no guarantee of success. As with all business ventures, it will only be successful if the franchisee works extremely hard.

Co-operative

Co-operatives are an increasingly popular type of business organisation. In the past, co-operatives were found only in agriculture or retailing. More recently there has been a growth in the number of co-operatives in services and in small-scale manufacturing.

In a co-operative all the people who form part of that organisation join together to make decisions, share the work and also share the profits.

Fig 1.10 A Co-op Superstore

The first successful co-operative was a retail co-operative. It was set up at the end of the last century in Rochdale when weavers joined together to start their own shop selling basic grocery items. Their profits were shared, as was the amount of money they spent, and everyone had an equal say in how the shop was run.

The basic idea behind the Rochdale Co-op still stands and Co-ops may be seen in the high streets throughout the country. Nowadays the Co-ops are registered as limited liability companies.

Another major area in which Co-operatives are found is in production, both in manufacturing and food production. In this type of organisation all the members share the responsibility for the success or failure of the business and work together, making decisions together, and taking a share of the profits.

These Co-operatives suffer from a number of problems:

- They often find it difficult to raise capital from banks and other bodies because the Co-operatives are not in business just to make a profit.
- The larger Co-operatives have discovered that they must set up a solid management structure in order that decisions can be made.
- In food production, several farmers will set up what is known as a Marketing Co-operative where each farmer takes responsibility for a particular part of the production of a food product, whether it is packaging, distribution or advertising. The success or failure will depend on the expertise of the members.

Focus study

Co-operatives

The year 1994 saw the 150th anniversary of the founding of the first Co-operative in Rochdale, Lancashire. Twenty-eight working men formed the Rochdale Equitable Pioneers Society with just £28 capital. They opened a shop where they sold good, wholesome food at reasonable prices. Nowadays, the Co-operative movement has never been bigger; the experiment has been copied in over a hundred countries world-wide.

The Co-op is the UK's biggest farmer, with over 45 000 acres of land. They are foremost in the move to stop products being tested on animals and have not done so since 1984. They were the first supermarket chain to ban CFCs, and they have also banned ivory and fur products in their stores, and do not allow fox hunting to take place on their land.

Japan has one of the biggest ranges of Co-op stores, with a replica of the original Toad Lane shop in their training centre; even the Imperial Palace in Tokyo has a Co-op store for employees.

Co-ops have not just restricted their involvement to farming and the sale of products through their supermarket chains. The Co-op Bank was the first in the UK to offer free banking (1973), and supports the film industry and brass bands, as well as making donations to the arts. The Bank financially supports Members of Parliament, Members of the House of Lords, Euro-MPs, and hundreds of Labour councillors. It is active in the insurance industry, in undertaking (170 000 funerals per year) and owns the largest hypermarket in the UK in Stockton-on-Tees (five football pitches in size!).

Internationally, there are 700m Co-op members; one in three Americans are members of Co-ops, and in Moscow there is a road called Rochdale Street in memory of the pioneers.

Commercially, the movement has been a great success, with 99 Tea being the biggest-selling 'own brand' in the world – a staggering 5 million cups of tea are drunk every day!

State-owned

There is a vast range of public sector organisations with an equally vast range of objectives. We are going to look at three main areas:

- *the government itself*
- *the people who operate and work in the public sector*
- *how they relate to the public*

State

It depends on your point of view whether you approve or not, but the fact remains that the government is involved very deeply in the business life of the UK, as indeed also happens in many other countries.

The prosperity of a country, which is measured by the success of the businesses in it, can be either helped or hindered by the kind of policies which its government adopts. The influence of the government is far reaching. Increases in government expenditure, or the creation of government controls over businesses, or even support for businesses in a particular area, can all have a marked effect.

The government has the means to create widescale changes in business activity. Here are some examples:

- If the government increases interest rates, this would reduce the general level of spending in the economy, and at the same time raise the cost of repayment for loans, making it difficult for businesses which have borrowed money to finance projects.
- When the government gives a contract to one firm rather than another, it can make the future of the one business very secure, while destroying the other's possibility of survival.
- If the government reduces the personal taxes that people pay, this may, in fact, prove to be beneficial. The more money a person takes home, the more inclined that person is to work harder. This is known as increasing productivity. In this respect, having additional disposable income is an incentive and employees will realise that their additional productivity payments will not be seriously affected by taxation.
- If the government were to reduce taxes on a particular product, for example lead-free petrol, then this could make it cheaper and so affect the demand for that product. This in turn could lead to changes in how the product is supplied since the supply would need to be increased to match the increased demand.

The government plays a very large role in the economy in general. Here are some examples:

- Some goods and services are actually provided by the government because it is felt that every person is entitled to that product or that service. Good examples of this are health or education.
- Some goods or services from which everyone benefits can only be provided by the government if they are actually going to be provided properly. A good example of this is the police force.
- Taxation aims to try to reduce inequality. This could mean that people who are relatively well off pay a higher tax. This in turn generates money to give to those who are less well off. Some people, however, think that inequality is a good thing because it gives people an incentive to help themselves. Any increases in taxation, of course, will mean that those who are earning higher salaries are taxed more, and in turn they could become less motivated.
- The government needs to make sure that the economic system as a whole is running well. It passes laws to protect consumers or to prevent companies from controlling particular goods or services. It will take measures against polluters or those involved in anti-social behaviour. The government therefore sets rules with which all businesses must comply.

Over time, as the situation changes, the government finds itself required to make amendments to the rules. How are these rules changed? Who loses and who benefits when they change? We will look at these questions later on.

Public enterprises

When we think about government, we tend to think about the Houses of Parliament, Downing Street and Whitehall. Although these are important and they are places where the government can be seen in action, the government has many other parts, including organisations which are controlled by the government in some way. These are known as public enterprises, or public corporations. Here are some examples of these:

- *British Rail*
- *the Bank of England*
- *the Post Office*

Since 1979, however, many public corporations have been returned to private hands. Examples of these are:

- *British Telecom*
- *British Gas*
- *electricity generation*

But why did the government get itself involved in running these organisations in the first place? Here are some of the reasons:

- One of the main reasons was to avoid waste and duplication. In the past many services were offered by different companies. Essentially they were offering the same thing. For example, private railways ran similar services from the same towns, often having lines running parallel to one another.
- Many of these organisations offered services which could not be run profitably. The big debate here is whether a private company would invest in supplying gas or electricity or water to a remote village when even in the long term it would not be able to make a profit.
- The larger the organisation, the more benefits there are in terms of production costs. Organisations which produce lots of goods are able to buy their raw materials in large quantities more cheaply, their labour can be more concentrated and consequently their prices can be lower.
- The government is always concerned about the level of employment. In setting up a public corporation, the government might be taking this into consideration. Good examples of this thinking are Tax Offices and Social Security Offices, where vast headquarters have been set up in relatively remote areas of the country that are suffering high unemployment.
- One of the biggest arguments in favour of public corporations was that the government itself needed to control vital basic goods and services which everybody requires. These are known as the infrastructure. This includes the transport network, water and energy. It was argued that the government had a responsibility to make sure that these were supervised and well maintained.

The process of privatisation which turns public corporations into companies owned by shareholders is proceeding rapidly and is sure to increase during the 1990s.

One of the ways of safeguarding the running of a public corporation is to set up an independent body which keeps an eye on it. This organisation copes with complaints that are made against the enterprise and tackles the enterprise should it wish to put up prices or cut services.

Although these public corporations operate independently, they are controlled to some extent by government. It is the government's responsibility to make decisions about closing down parts of the business or investing large sums of money to improve it. On a day-to-day basis the chairperson of the enterprise and the other managers will make decisions about wages, prices, industrial relations, etc, but the government does still interfere when these decisions affect the public.

We have seen that a limited company needs to make an annual report to its shareholders. So, too, does a public corporation, but it presents its annual report to the government minister who is responsible for taking care of it. This government minister makes a report in Parliament to the Members of Parliament, who will then make criticisms or support the corporation and how it is being run. At the same time a committee made up of Members of Parliament meets on a regular basis to keep an eye on the day-to-day running of the corporation and reports back to Parliament on how it is being operated. This is known as a Select Committee.

In addition to public corporations, there are two other areas where the government gets involved in the business world.

1 The first is when an activity is actually run by a government department. A typical example of this is Customs and Excise. This department deals with the supervision and collection of taxes due on products entering and leaving the country.
2 The second is when the government has a shareholding in a public company.

Local government

Perhaps the most common form of government organisation is one which touches our lives the most, and this is local government. In the UK certain services are run by locally-elected councillors on local councils. These councils usually run local business organisations such as swimming pools, sports centres, bus services, car parks, shopping centres and public conveniences.

Just like public corporations, local council activities have been affected by privatisation. The particular process used by councils for employing businesses to do work for them is that of tendering.

The local council details the service it wishes to offer for tender. Companies which are interested in running the service put sealed bids into the council explaining what it would cost to run the service and what they would be providing. The company that offers the lowest tender is given the job. It is then the council's responsibility to monitor how effective the company is in providing the service. If a company fails to reach certain standards then the contract is taken away from it. Local government pays for these services by receiving a grant direct from central government and by collecting local taxes. These have been variously known as rates, community charge and now council tax (or, for businesses, the uniform business rate).

Local councils also subsidise loss-making activities such as parks which obviously provide benefits to the community.

Perhaps the strangest form of business organisation is that known as the Quango. This stands for 'Quasi Autonomous Non-Governmental Organisation'. These are organisations that have been set up by the government to carry out a specific task. In other words, they have been set up to take responsibility for a certain area of the government's business. A good example of this is the Equal Opportunities Commission.

Individual activity *Time: 15 minutes*

Identify five Quangos other than the Equal Opportunities Commission.

PC 1.1.3

Focus study

Quangos

There is one Quango for every 10 000 people in the UK. Nearly 75 000 people are Quango members and, at a local level, this means that there are twice as many Quango members as elected councillors.

Some 99% of Quangos are not subject to investigation or monitoring by an Ombudsman (a government-appointed official who is responsible for overseeing a particular industry). Only a third are audited by either the National Audit Office or the Audit Commission, and over 90% do not have to invite the public to their meetings or hold an annual general meeting.

It is claimed that Quangos have taken over the responsibility of decision making and public spending that should be the role of elected individuals. A Labour Government would abolish these Quangos and restore the power to local or nationally-elected authorities. At the very least, they would make them subject to supervision by an ombudsman.

Differences between business organisations

We must now turn our attention to the exact nature of the difference between the types of organisation in terms of the following criteria:

- *liability*
- *use of profit*
- *sources of finance*
- *control of the organisation*
- *legal obligations*

In many cases, we have already identified the key aspects when we looked at the different types of business ownership. It is perhaps more valuable to compare the nature of these differences. To this end, we have attempted to put all of the main differences into a single table (*see* Table 1.1).

Type of liability (limited/unlimited)

The term 'liability' applies to liability for debts which may be incurred by a business. (This is different to liabilities in a company balance sheet, for example, which are the sources of finance.)

Limited liability companies or partnerships are those where the owners or shareholders are financially responsible for only the amount that they have invested in the business. Their personal belongings, property and cash are therefore protected from claims by creditors.

In limited liability businesses which fail, the creditors can only claim (and share) cash up to the value of the shareholders' original investment in the organisation. Any potential creditor would know whether the business has limited liability by noting the addition of

Table 1.1 Types of business organisation

	Criteria				
	Liability	*Use of profit*	*Source of finance*	*Control of organisation*	*Legal obligation*
Sole trader	Unlimited	Reinvest: Self	Own assets Loans Grants	Direct	All[4]
Partnership	Unlimited[1]	Reinvest: Partners	Own assets Loans Grants	Direct	All[4]
Private limited company	Limited	Reinvest: Shares	Shares Loans Grants	Directors Managers Owners	All[4]
Public limited company	Limited	Reinvest: Shares	Shares Loans Grants	Directors Managers Owners	All[4]
Franchise	Limited/ Unlimited[2]	Reinvest: Franchisor/ Franchisee	Own assets Franchisor Loans Grants	Managers Franchisor	All[4]
Co-operative	Usually Limited	Reinvest: Members	Members Loans Grants	Members Managers	All[4]
Central Government	n/a	Re-used: Treasury	Treasury	PM Cabinet Ministers Civil Servants	Most[5]
Local Government	n/a	Re-used	Council tax Rates/rent Central government	Councillors Officials	Most[5]
Quangos	n/a	Re-used: Treasury	Central government	Appointees Central government	Nil[6]
Charity	Limited/ Unlimited	Reinvest: Cause in Question	Donations Covenants Grants	Trustees	Most[3]

1 Except in limited partnerships
2 Dependent upon the organisation of the franchise
3 Dependent upon the structure and charitable status
4 Including employment, civil law, trade union, health and safety, etc.
5 Except for some laws depending on nature of authorities
6 Only those imposed by Central Government

'Ltd' (private limited company) or 'plc' (public limited company) after the name of the organisation. This is not often seen as a potential risk to the creditor, but in the early stages of a creditor's relationship with a new organisation it may be that they insist on full or part-payment for goods and services before delivery.

The obvious advantage of limited liability is that potential shareholders know they only risk their actual investment when buying shares in a limited company and do not risk losing their whole lifestyle and wealth.

Use of profit (owners, shareholders, government)

Profit is what is left from revenue (money received) after the costs have been deducted. Therefore:

Revenue – costs = profit

There are, of course, several types of profit, and it is helpful first to understand these in basic terms (although we will look at these in greater detail in Unit 4).

A Profit and Loss Account is the best place to begin. This is simply a statement which records all of the organisation's revenue and costs over a period of time.

- The Profit and Loss Account begins by stating the total revenue (sales total).
- From this is deducted the cost of sales (cost of purchasing the goods and services subsequently sold, and any other directly attributable costs).
- This gives us the gross profit (not the final profit as more costs must be deducted yet).
- From the gross profit we must now deduct the organisation's overheads (indirect and fixed costs such as salaries, rent, lighting and heating).
- This leaves us with the trading or operating profit.
- From this the cost or revenue of 'one-off items' are either added or deducted. This may be revenue from the sale of property, or deductions from the payment of redundancy packages or payments into a pension scheme.
- After this calculation, we are left with the pre-tax profit.
- We now take the tax away from this total (corporation tax in most cases, but in smaller businesses this may be Schedule D: self-employment tax).
- After the tax deduction, we will be left with the total profit after tax. In the cases of limited companies, they must now pay a dividend to their shareholders. A dividend is a share of the profits.
- The total left after payment of the dividend is known as the retained profit. The company keeps this.

So what happens to this retained profit? In most cases, the main use of this cash is reinvestment. This may take a variety of forms:

- *purchase of new materials*
- *payment of long-term liabilities (such as loans)*
- *purchase of premises*
- *acquisition of another organisation*
- *acquisition of another organisation's product or service (for the purpose of owning and producing it in the future)*

PC 2.1.2

Individual activity

Time: 15 minutes

Can you think of any other ways of using the profit? Does this depend upon the type of organisation? Does the size of the organisation help determine where this profit will be spent?

Smaller organisations may use profit to expand their operations. A sole trader, for example, may choose to create a partnership with others and relocate to larger premises. Perhaps the sole trader needs to upgrade or replace machinery or vehicles.

Larger organisations may choose to use their profits to acquire smaller or related organisations. This is known as a merger (when two organisations mutually agree to join together) or a take-over (when one organisation buys another one).

As we have seen from the explanation of the distribution and gradual reduction of profits, the cash needs to go to a number of different individuals, groups and organisations. Tax is the unavoidable consequence of profit. The government insists on clear and honest accounting of the transactions carried out by all organisations, regardless of size or structure.

Any owner or shareholder of an organisation also wants a slice of the profits. After all, the original investments were made to reap the financial benefits of the organisation's activities. As we will see later, the larger organisations which have shareholders have a complex job in deciding the level of their dividend or profit share.

More simple, in one respect, is the distribution of retained profit to partners. This distribution is usually made on the basis of seniority or the level of the original investment in the partnership.

For a sole trader, the distribution could not be easier. If the organisation is wholly-owned and run by a single individual, then he/she will retain all of the profit. Many sole traders will have 'sleeping partners' who do not take an active role in the business. However, they will expect a share in the profits at the appropriate time.

Multinationals or international organisations have complex arrangements in dealing with profits. They are in an excellent position to 'move' profits from one part of the organisation to another to avoid paying tax. In some cases, profit-making parts of the organisation will be deemed to 'owe' another less profitable part of the organisation and thus the profit will have been 'removed' before the stage at which tax is payable. This is not illegal, but a much-used benefit of operating, for example, in a variety of countries. Profits in this case can often be used to bolster or support struggling parts of the organisation. This can, however, cause animosity between the different parts of the organisation as the successful parts feel that they are subsidising the inefficiencies of another part.

1.1.4 Explain the operation of one business organisation

This performance criteria is an integral part of the Element Assignment which follows. It therefore requires you to identify a particular organisation and make some investigations into its nature and its operations. We have provided some very brief guidelines to help you in your search for information, but we can only generalise, since the exact nature of the organisation you chose is unknown to us.

Operation

What is the nature of the business itself? You should look at the sector in which the organisation operates and consider the activities actually undertaken as a matter of routine.

The organisation may be complex and involve itself in a number of different and unrelated areas. In this respect, you should try to identify the core areas of activity and see how the other operations complement (or otherwise) the main areas of activity.

Location

As businesses grow, they may need to consider relocation in order to achieve sustained and permanent growth. Moving closer to the source of raw materials, skilled labour, or better distribution points may be key considerations in this move. More obviously, the move may be brought on by growth itself. Perhaps the organisation simply needs larger premises in order to continue its operations successfully.

An organisation which has a variety of sites needs to adopt a slightly different structure to an organisation in a single site, e.g. one building, in order to accommodate the problems of communication and overall control. Again, the most appropriate business structure may depend upon the nature of the business. In service industries, for example, the organisation would be structured towards providing customer service as a priority. For manufacturing organisations, the main structural considerations would be related to the production process itself, with other departments supporting and servicing the production unit. Organisational structure may, of course, be related to the premises in which the organisation is located. An inappropriate building may preclude the restructuring of the business since the physical location of each part of the organisation remains fixed. This state of affairs is particularly true of organisations which add on new extensions and buildings to their site without really considering the implications of their placement or location. In these cases, the organisation may not have had the time to spend considering the future when immediate demands for expansion and new accommodation were pressing.

You will find a variety of different considerations to look at in relation to location in the next Element of this Unit. The exact location of the organisation may be a result of a number of different and unrelated decisions made many years ago. Indeed, some organisations simply chose to be located close to the homes of their owners, rather than having any real concern about the potential market for their product or service.

Product (goods, services)

What are the key products and services offered by the organisation? Are they the traditional ones that have always been on offer, or has there been a gradual (or for that matter rapid) change from one range of products and services to another? What has influenced the choice of stock or range of services – is it in response to market needs or is it just a case of the owner or directors thinking that they can find a market out there somewhere? You may find some useful ideas in Unit 3 concerning market research and the choice of products and services offered.

Links with other businesses

This really refers to the routine contact that the organisation may have with other businesses. Normally, the main points of contact will be with suppliers and customers. In this respect many of the contacts will be fairly obvious, but you can identify some of the less frequent contacts which may involve the services of specialists (such as solicitors and accountants).

Purpose

We have looked at the main purposes of a typical business in the second Performance Criteria of this Element. We can identify the main ones again:

- *the desire to make a profit*
- *the desire to increase the market share of the organisation*
- *the mission to provide customer service*
- *the requirement to provide public service*
- *the determination to provide charitable assistance*

Note the ways in which we have stated these purposes. The first two are prefixed by the word 'desire', the motive of the owners of the organisation and is not related to any other requirement by an external agency. The word 'mission' infers that the organisation puts the provision of excellent customer service before the desire to make a profit or increase its market share. The word 'requirement' refers to an organisation (usually in the public sector) that is required by law to provide a public service to the population. The final purpose, 'determination', refers to organisations that have a mission to provide charitable assistance to the needy.

Remember that some of these purposes may be interchangeable and complementary, so do not assume that the organisation will only have one purpose; it may have many.

Type of ownership

The type of ownership may be related to the age of the organisation or the desire of the owners to keep the organisation self-manageable. While there may be a natural desire for organisations to grow, this does not necessarily mean that they would wish to change the nature of their business organisation or change their ownership type.

The organisation that you investigate may have considered alternative forms of ownership, but may have rejected them for a variety of reasons. It may be interesting in itself to find out why they have come to certain conclusions. In addition to this, it should be remembered that the move from sole trader to partnership will mean that the original owner has lost some of the control over the organisation to the new partners. Similarly, the move from a partnership or limited company to a plc may mean a loss in the control of the organisation. For some owners, the benefits that come with additional individuals being involved will be outweighed by this loss of independence and control.

Element 1.1 Assignment

PC 1.1.1–4
C 2.1
C 2.2
C 2.3
C 2.4
IT 2.1
IT 2.2
IT 2.3

The purpose of this Element is to help you to collect background information about businesses. This assignment has three main parts aimed at doing this.

Task 1 *PC 1.1.1*

Identify and describe a major development in the primary, secondary and tertiary sectors of industry. You should focus on present growth or decreases in each sector. This short summary should also identify the main activities in each of the sectors.

Task 2 *PC 1.1.2–3*

Identify *seven* examples of different business organisations which have different forms of ownership. For each example of organisational type, give a summary that explains the purposes and differences between it and the other examples of business organisation. You should also make sure that your examples include the following:

- small, medium and large private sector organisations
- at least one public sector organisation

You should present your examples in the form of a chart which can be easily read and cross-referenced.

Task 3 *PC 1.1.4*

Write a short report that focuses on a local or national business organisation. You should explain the following:

- why it is located at the current site(s)
- what product(s) are sold or produced
- what is the purpose of the organisation
- what is the nature of the ownership
- what links it has with other businesses

Notes

In looking at the different types of ownership you should understand that businesses have legal responsibilities in terms of liability and other responsibilities. These include decisions regarding profit distribution.

Your report should be word processed and your charts produced using computer software if this is available to you.

Element 1.2
Examine business location, environment, markets and products

Performance criteria

A student must:

1 explain the **reasons for location** of businesses

2 explain **influences of the business environment** on business organisations

3 describe **markets** for businesses' products based on **demand**

4 identify **products provided** by business organisations

5 explain **activities undertaken by businesses** to improve their market position

6 **propose products** which would meet market demand

Range

- *Reasons for location*: labour supply, natural resources, proximity of other businesses, access to customers, transport services, incentives (local government, national government, European Union)
- *Influences of the business environment*: competition, legal, environmental, public
- *Markets*: domestic markets, international market; value of total market, market share of businesses' products
- *Demand*: needs, wants; wish to buy, ability to buy; created by consumers, created by customers
- *Products*: consumable, durable; goods, services
- *Provided*: to individual customers, to government, to other businesses
- *Activities undertaken by businesses*: marketing research, design, production, marketing communications (advertising, promotion, sponsorship, sales literature), sales, after-sales service
- *Propose products*: new; developed from existing products

1.2.1 Explain the reasons for location of businesses

Reasons for location

Where an organisation chooses to establish its main site of operations can have long-term implications for its success. The costs of establishing the head office or main factory can be very high, so before any decision is made a large number of factors need to be considered. The larger the organisation, the greater the potential pitfalls in setting up in the wrong place. A small business, which may only need relatively small premises, has more flexibility and the exact location is probably less crucial. Whereas almost any area would provide enough work for a small business offering services such as plumbing or electrical installation work, a larger business needs to consider the fact that they may have to cater for regional, national or international customers. Some of the major factors a medium or large organisation would need to consider are as follows.

Labour supply

The availability of labour (workers) and skills is not evenly spread throughout the country. Certain areas, having been the site of now outdated or closed-down industries, have considerable numbers of experienced workers who are available for work. In some cases, they may need additional training for new working practices, but the basic skills are there. If an organisation wishes to move large numbers of its existing workforce to a new location, this can prove to be extremely expensive. It is often the case, therefore, that only key personnel are moved and the bulk of the new workforce is recruited locally.

PC 1.2.1
C 2.1

Group activity

In pairs, research and find a company which has relocated in your area within the last year. Why did it move to your area? What proportion of employees did it bring with it from its previous location?

One of the main factors which prevents large numbers of workers from moving with their organisation to a new location is the cost and availability of housing in the new area. The regional differences in house prices are enormous, as indeed are the differences in the number of houses which are immediately available in a particular area. The process of workers moving from one area to another is known as labour mobility. In times when it is hard to sell homes, or when house prices are very high, labour mobility is low.

PC 1.2.1
C 2.1

Group activity

In pairs, research the housing prices in your local area. What are the average prices for a two-bedroomed and three-bedroomed house? How do these prices compare to the national average? How do house prices in your nearest large city compare with those in the local towns?

Natural resources

Exactly why an organisation may choose to locate in a particular region may be dependent upon the natural resources, such as water or minerals, which are available. As you will remember, there are three main sectors of any economy. The primary sector, since it involves the use of natural resources directly, means that certain industries have traditionally been located in those regions where the natural resources they use have been found. The other two sectors, to varying levels, rely on the natural resources, but not to such a great extent. Let us take a brief look at the natural resources of the UK and the way they influence the location of industry.

Coal

Although the coal industry is in decline, with 31 mines still in operation, all now privatised, we will still find coal fields which have coal mines located in them. Essentially, these are located in the Midlands, the North East of England, south Wales, and southern Scotland. The prosperity of these areas is heavily dependent upon the success of the coal mines and many areas which have suffered the loss of this industry have subsequently declined to such an extent that they have become assisted areas (see later for a description of these).

Minerals

This industry involves the extraction from the earth of various materials, such as chalk, limestone, clay, salt, sand, gravel and shale. The success or failure of these industries may relate to specific industries which use them, such as road building, construction and house building.

Water

The 10 Water Authorities have been privatised. These new companies are responsible for providing a plentiful water supply to their area and for the treatment of sewerage. This means that they are involved in the management of rivers, canals, streams, lakes, reservoirs, wells, springs and underground waterways. Not only do they provide water to homes but also to industry. Depending on the type of industry located within a region, the amount of water required will differ greatly. In agricultural areas, water demands will be related to the rainfall; in other industries, such as the electricity generating sector, vast amounts of water are used daily.

Fig 1.11 Coal mining – a primary sector industry

Gas

The gas industry was privatised in the 1980s and is required to supply gas throughout the UK, either directly or in the form of gas containers. While this industry does offer many jobs offshore in obtaining the gas from under the seabed, it does employ quite large numbers of people at the terminals located on land. Primarily, these terminals will be found in coastal areas.

Oil

The UK is fortunate in the sense that vast oil deposits have been discovered offshore around the coast. Like gas, the oil industry is highly dependent on machinery and so does not employ large numbers of people. It does, however, require additional employees in the processing, refining, storage and transportation of oil. In addition to the offshore deposits, substantial finds have been made on the south coast of England, in southern East Anglia, Wales, the north east of England and southern Scotland.

Forestry

The production of wood has become an increasingly profitable industry in recent years. Indeed, in the past 20 years, production has doubled. Nearly half of all wood production is controlled by the Forestry Commission, which is a government organisation.

Farming

Certain rural areas have traditionally concentrated on particular types of farming. Here is a list of some of these farming regions:

- *South West of Scotland* – sheep and cattle, potatoes and arable (crops)

Fig 1.12 The North Sea has proved to be a vital provider of natural resources such as oil and gas

- *South East of England* – vegetables, potatoes and arable
- *Eastern England* – pigs, poultry, vegetables and arable
- *Midlands* – mainly arable
- *Wales* – sheep and cattle
- *North Midlands* – pigs, poultry and arable
- *Borders* – sheep and cattle, and vegetables
- *Scotland* – sheep and cattle, arable and potatoes
- *Northern Ireland* – sheep and cattle, and potatoes

Fishing

Fishing is vitally important to the UK economy. The fishing fleets operate from many locations in Scotland, the East Coast and the South West coast of England and Northern Ireland. In addition, there is an increasing number of fish farms which are mainly located in the Highlands of Scotland. The UK fishing industry provides nearly two-thirds of all the UK's requirements.

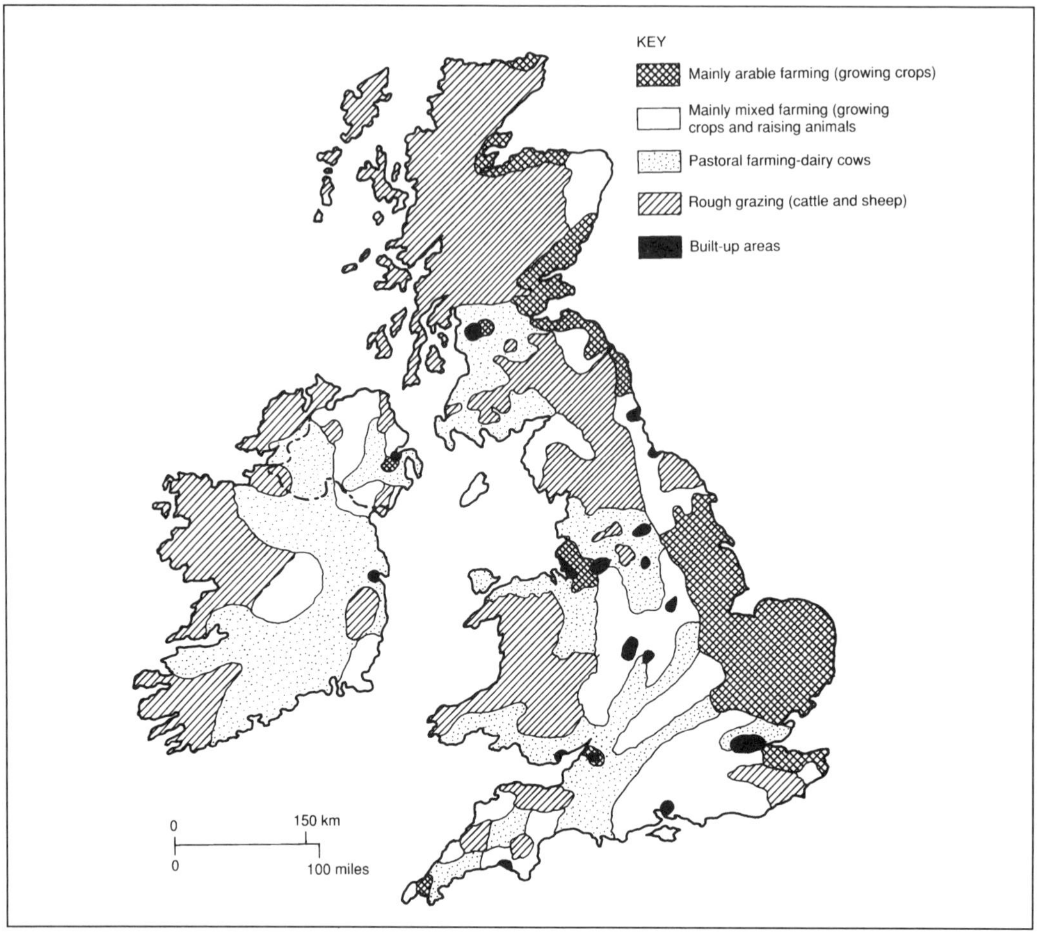

Fig 1.13 Farming types in Britain

Proximity of other businesses

It may be important to the organisation to establish a new factory or offices close to existing premises. Certain businesses rely on regular inter-site communication and exchange of ideas and personnel to function efficiently. Equally, the proximity of similar types of businesses, perhaps competitors, may be an important feature in the decision-making process. This is one of the reasons why London attracts the majority of financial institutions. Other towns or cities may have similar attractions, such as Norwich, which has become relatively important as an insurance centre.

Access to customers

The immediate access to customers should be weighed against the benefits which can be enjoyed by being close to the raw materials or the sources of components and parts. Obviously certain organisations do not have any real choice about where they are located. Those that do have a choice must consider very seriously the comparative benefits of accessibility to customers against the other requirements. Given that it is relatively cheap to transport low-weight and high-volume materials, it may, in fact, be more cost-effective to consider being close to the market in which you will sell your product or services than being close to the source of your raw materials, components or parts.

Transport services

In situations where an organisation needs large amounts of bulky raw materials, it must consider being as close to the source of raw materials as possible. Cities, such as Sheffield, became a natural choice for the manufacturers of steel and other metal works, because of the city's close proximity to the coal fields needed for smelting and the quarries from which the metals were mined. It may be interesting to see, given the level of closure of mines in that area, whether some steel-making industries relocate to coastal areas as they now rely heavily on foreign imports.

Several ports have been the choice of the oil and gas industries for the construction of their rigs, the siting of their terminals and other support services. As the main fields are located close to the coastline, these ports are a natural choice and towns such as Aberdeen and Great Yarmouth have therefore seen periods of relative prosperity. Coastal towns have, of course, always been the ideal place for fishing industries, just as many market towns have flourished close to the main centres of agriculture.

However, in cases when it is more expensive to transport the finished product to the market than it is to transport the raw materials to the factory, organisations have established themselves nearer the market. A good example would be the production of food where an additional factor is the need to get the product to the market in its freshest state.

Fig 1.14 BNFL's purpose-built marine terminal at Barrow-in-Furness

PC 1.2.1
C 2.1

Group activity *Time: 20 minutes*

In pairs, try to agree an ideal location in terms of transportation and distribution for the following organisations:

- **a manufacturer that makes colour televisions**
- **a private hospital**

There are five main services which nearly all industries require, these are:

- *water*
- *gas*
- *electricity*
- *drainage*
- *waste disposal*

We can assume that other essential services, such as telecommunications, are available throughout the country. However, any user of a cellular phone will soon discover that the network only covers around 90% of the UK. To a greater or lesser extent, each of the above five main services are important to the different industries. An industry which produces large amounts of waste would consider waste disposal as the most important. A paper mill uses large amounts of water and would place considerable strain on the local water system if not carefully planned.

PC 1.2.1
C 2.1

Group activity *Time: 20 minutes*

In pairs, using the two types of organisation given in the previous activity, put the five main essential services in ranking order of importance.

Compare your list with that of your partner.

Incentives (local government, national government, European Union)

The UK government is keen for organisations to establish themselves in areas of high unemployment. Some of these areas were previously the sites of now outdated and unwanted types of industry. The government offers a comprehensive package of incentives, often with the help and guidance of local authorities, to attract as many new businesses as possible to the area. Incentives might include financial assistance for relocation, low rents and rates, and subsidised retraining programmes for the local population. There has been considerable argument over which cities, towns and regions should be eligible for government assistance. The type and nature of employment obviously differs from one region to another. There are many reasons for this, and for why economic conditions affect regions in different ways.

Some areas of the country are more successful than others. The more prosperous an area is, the easier it is likely to be to get a job. Obviously, some areas which have large populations and large numbers of organisations sited there will offer better job prospects than more remote, sparsely-populated rural areas. With prosperity comes the ability to provide an extensive transport and communications network, which, in turn, generates more jobs. Some areas with low employment find themselves in a downward spiral from which they cannot escape. If only a few organisations have located in a particular area, there may not be a great deal of investment in transport and communications. This, in turn, means the area is less likely to attract new businesses. Unemployment will stay high and perhaps increase as existing businesses find it impossible to compete with organisations in better-located areas.

The government recognises the unfair advantages related to location. It does not want whole areas to be centres of unemployment. Consequently, it has developed a series of programmes and schemes to encourage 'under-developed' areas to grow. These include the following:

1 **Assisted areas** The Department of Trade and Industry offers a range of grants to companies wishing to set up in a particular area which has been identified as having particular problems. The grant will help them finance the move or set up new premises, assist in the recruitment and training of personnel, and may offer reduced accommodation costs.
2 **Urban programme** This is a similar set of grants to those for assisted area programmes, but relate to city-centre locations
3 **Department of Environment grants** This government department offers specific grants particularly to inner-city development, where previous business activity has reduced to a point where there are many empty premises which could be filled by new businesses. These new businesses are encouraged financially to relocate or set up premises in the run-down areas.
4 **Urban and non-urban development agencies** To help with the allocation of Department of Environment grants, the government has set up these agencies to concentrate on the handing out of funds to increase local employment levels.
5 **Training and Enterprise Councils (TECs)** This is a network of organisations which assist local training needs, offer help to employers in identifying training needs, and encourage closer links with educational establishments and businesses.
6 **Rural Development Commission** To discourage people, particularly the young, from moving away from rural areas to cities, the government has set up this commission. It aims to support rural areas in the following ways:

   - *identifying training needs of businesses in rural locations and help them to get funding from the Training and Enterprise Councils*
   - *encouraging collaboration between organisations within rural locations to exchange ideas and training experiences*
   - *identifying particular dangers in terms of job losses within rural areas, such as the decline of agricultural businesses*
   - *offering a range of additional grants, such as the Training and Enterprise Fund which is available to help promote employment in rural areas*

Since joining the EU, the UK is now eligible for a series of grants aimed at reducing unemployment throughout the whole of the European Union. The main grants available are:

1 **European Regional Development Fund** Which is designed to target areas blighted by high unemployment and offers extensive financial assistance to encourage businesses to locate within the region

2 **European Social Fund** Again, this is aimed at areas of high unemployment, but concentrates on the problems and training of young people within the region

PC 1.1.1
C 2.1

Individual activity *Time: 1 hour*

You are assistant to a managing director who is looking to locate a new site within the UK for a major manufacturing organisation, and hoping to employ at least 500 people. Decide what steps your managing director would need to take to find out whether or not this organisation is eligible for a grant from one of the various funds available. The managing director is prepared to locate these new premises in almost any part of the UK, provided that the communication and transport systems are at least of an acceptable standard.

Having completed your research, write a memorandum to your managing director, outlining the main grants available, the conditions required to be accepted for funding and the addresses to which any applications must be made.

1.2.2 Explain influences of the business environment on business organisations

Influences of the business environment

The business environment can be best defined as the external conditions within which the business operates. Given the fact that the business environment, and consequently businesses, will be subject to constant change, we should identify the main factors which will alter the environment. As you may have already realised, businesses must be able to respond to these changes in order to survive. Some of the influences will constrain business activity; in other words, they will make it more difficult for businesses to operate. On the other hand, other changes or influences may open up opportunities for the business to exploit. The larger the business, the more likely that the organisation will be able to influence the external environment, and we will consider this aspect shortly.

Competition

It is obvious that a business may well be influenced by the activities of its competitors. Broadly speaking, when we use the word 'competitor', we are referring to other organisations operating within the same industry. If an organisation is not sufficiently quick in setting standards and ways of undertaking activities, then it may find that the competitors dictate standards such as reliability, after-sales service and quality.

Legal influences

The UK government and, to an increasing extent, the European Union, pass a great many pieces of legislation which naturally affect the activities of businesses.

The legal environment, in essence, refers to three major areas of legislation:

- *Employment law* – which includes health and safety at work, sex discrimination, and the various Employment Acts.
- *Consumer law* – which includes the Trade Descriptions Act, the Consumer Protection Act and the Sale of Goods Act.
- *Competition law* – which includes the Competition Act and other activities related to the Monopolies and Mergers Commission and the Office of Fair Trading.

Environmental influences

The concept of 'greening' has become a very important feature in relation to business activity. Within this category we will have to consider the disposal of waste, the use of environmentally-friendly products, the use of non-animal tested products and the need of businesses to ensure that the customer does not consider them to be a polluter of the environment.

Fig 1.15 BUAV (British Union for Abolition of Vivisection) campaigns to end animal experiments

Public influences

If the environmental influences can be considered as a government-related pressure on businesses, then we should also look at the activities of various pressure groups which are related to green issues, trade unionism and consumer rights. Indeed, we should not forget that the Confederation of British Industry is also a major pressure group whose objectives are to ensure that the government introduces policies to aid businesses.

1.2.3 Describe markets for businesses' products based on demand

Markets – domestic market, international market, value of total market and market share of businesses' products

The fundamental goal of businesses is profitability, which can only be achieved by gradual growth. This, of course, can be attained by a number of different methods, which include:

- the research and development of new ideas which can become profitable products and services
- the purchase of other organisations that relate in some way to the business of the original organisation
- a merger with another organisation that relates in some way, or is complementary to, the original organisation
- subcontracting or licensing the production of other products from other organisations in order to increase the product range with the minimum of investment and delay

Profits are the key to continued growth, or for that matter any growth in the business. The organisation needs to take a serious look at its resources, which will be used to generate the profits it desires. These resources include:

- *finance*
- *plant and equipment*
- *manpower*
- *organisational ability*
- *recognition of the organisation's marketing possibilities*

A satisfactory marketing mix is dependent upon the recognition of the market's needs, the recognition of the organisation's objectives and the planning of a strategic marketing philosophy which incorporates the various methods of obtaining these objectives. Consideration of the needs of the market must include looking at how to serve all the different segments of the market. Any resulting decision should take account of the need to ensure that the organisation's efforts are co-ordinated in order to reach each of the market segments. The development of the marketing plan should involve a clear definition of the problems, which include:

- *the collection of the facts*
- *the analysis of the data*
- *the selection of the appropriate marketing mix*
- *choosing the appropriate solutions*

The elements that make up the marketing mix are very diverse and may include both external and internal considerations. Among the external factors that may affect the marketing plan are the following:

1. **Socio-economic influences** that can affect the users of the organisation's products

2. **Government regulations**, including restrictions on business, that can also have an impact on the long-term plans of the organisation:

- *seasonal changes*
- *changes in market demand*
- *technological developments*
- *product obsolescence*
- *competition*

Here are some of the internal factors that should be considered as a part of the marketing mix:

- *market research*
- *product quality*
- *pricing*
- *product development*
- *product range*
- *sales force, aids and promotion*
- *after-sales service*
- *advertising*
- *stock levels*
- *credit*
- *public relations*
- *packaging*
- *sampling*

Demand

No matter whether a customer or an organisation, young or old, we all have various wants and needs. The difference between these wants and needs has a great effect upon how we try to get them and what we will do in the process. You could say, 'I want a new car, but what I need is a reliable form of transport. It doesn't have to be a new car.'

Goods and services are produced because people (consumers) want and need them. No matter who they are, everybody has the same basic needs. For example, it does not matter if you are the richest or the poorest person in the world; we all require food, clothing and shelter in order to survive.

Demand is defined as: the quantity of a given good or service that consumers wish to purchase at a particular point in time at a particular price.

Thus a demand curve shows the quantity of a particular good or service that consumers wish to purchase at each conceivable price in a range of prices.

Needs and wants

Having obtained these basic needs, wants are the goods and services that people acquire (or seek to acquire) in order to improve their basic standard of living.

We all make a series of regular purchases every day, e.g. newspapers, canned drinks, chocolates and other food items. The reasoning behind our purchases can be related to our tastes or our opinion or our desire for a particular product. Organisations will seek to influence our decision making when we make a purchase, and we will look at this in more detail later.

We also make special purchases. These are things that we really have to think about before we buy them. Perhaps they are expensive; perhaps they are a luxury. Organisations which make these products, such as cars, televisions, stereo systems and furniture, have to try to predict what the demand will be like for these products and make sure that they have produced enough of them to satisfy demand. These producers of products will have to be ready to react to sudden changes in demand, and be prepared to gear up their production should demand increase in a short space of time. Above all, the product that they make should aim to satisfy the demands of the buyer. If it doesn't, then the buyer will not be satisfied and is unlikely to buy from that organisation or to be a repeat customer.

To be successful, the organisation has to have sufficient products available, at the right price and in the right place. These are the basic business skills required to succeed and survive in a very competitive area of activity. In business jargon, we can use the words production, pricing and distribution.

Wish to buy

Needs and wants therefore represent the demand of consumers for goods and services. However, needing or wanting something is not enough to be able to turn that desire into reality. Effective demand occurs when consumers not only wish to buy a product or service but also have the money to be able to pay for it, thus making their demand effective.

Therefore the demand for a particular product or service is sometimes reliant on the price the consumer is willing to pay, but this is not the whole story. We need to consider something called 'market demand'. This is the amount of a product or service that will be demanded during a particular period of time. Here are some of the factors that will influence that consumption rate:

- **Price** – in most cases the higher the price charged for a particular product or service, the lower the demand for it. As the price falls, there should be a correspondingly higher demand for that product or service. One thing to note here, however, is that, despite the cost, even if it is very low, there is only a comparatively limited demand for a product or service. Eventually, all those who need it will have it.
- **Income** – this refers to the money received by consumers. They may want the product or service but may not have the income to be able to consume it at the rate that they would really like.
- **Availability** – the desirability of a good or service and the income to purchase it effectively, do not necessarily mean that the good or service is available to be purchased.

Ability to buy

One of the main determinants of which products are purchased and the amount that people are able to pay for them is the actual income that people have available to spend.

A basic assumption is that those consumers with higher incomes have more money available to spend than those with lower incomes and that, as income increases, consumers can consume more (as they have more income that they can spend). However, this is not exactly the case. If we split the range of goods and services into two different categories, calling them inferior and superior, then we can begin to see the choices which consumers have. The inferior goods and services are comparatively cheap. The superior goods and services are expensive. When consumers have more income, they can spend it on a greater number of inferior goods and services, which in effect means that they are consuming more. Consumers could switch over to superior goods and services, which are more expensive, so they would use up the additional income, but not actually be consuming more of them. The alternative way of looking at this is to say that those consumers do actually consume more just by buying more superior goods and services.

An example of this occurs when, due to a rise in their income, consumers switch from buying a supermarket's own label product to that of a more upmarket brand name. The consumers are not in effect consuming any more; they are consuming exactly the same amount. However, having switched from an inferior to a superior product, they are paying more for the privilege.

Created by consumers and customers

The ultimate success of any company is related to providing for the needs and wants of the customer. Indeed, to be really successful, an organisation must stay ahead of all its competitors. Having a large market share is one thing, but being a market leader is just as important.

Let us return to the question of customers' needs and wants. Just what is the difference between the two? A need is a requirement for something essential. This, of course, includes the need to eat, drink and keep warm. On the other hand, a want is a specific desire for something you may not necessarily need. If you are hungry, this is a need; but you may want chips.

Organisations spend huge amounts of money trying to assess and manipulate the wants of customers. If it were not for our wants, then there would be no choice in products at all. Marketing experts know this and attempt, by various means, to influence what customers (consumers) want.

The simple fact that one product or another has slightly different features, colours, taste or smell means that our essential need is transformed into want.

The same can be said, to some extent, of the industrial sector of the market. Organisations here will also purchase consumer durables (in their case capital goods such as machines), consumables (such as oil, raw materials and office stationery) and services (perhaps the services of an advertising agency or an accountant). The choice may not be so great as in the consumer market, but there are definite differences between the similar products and services offered by a range of companies.

Essentially, an organisation can be one of the following:

- **Market orientated** – in which case the organisation responds to perceived market need derived from marketing research. The effect of customers' wants in this case would be considerable on the organisation since it would only choose to supply products that it felt the customers intended to purchase. Once the organisation has identified a potential market with a need to be satisfied, it will attempt to supply that market at a level which offers both good market penetration and reasonable profit return.
- **Product orientated** – in which case the organisation has a fixed range of products to offer the market. The organisation has no real choice about what it supplies but it does have a choice about how much it supplies. The level of supply will be affected by the efficiency of the sales force in gaining sales and the willingness of the customer to pay the price which has been set for the product. These organisations are somewhat

vulnerable to others stepping into their market and supplying products at a lower price which may not be cost-effective to the original organisation.

- **Production orientated** – in which case the organisation is very firmly focused to finding markets for a set level of supply. The organisation's production rate is fairly constant and it is restricted to making only minor changes in production output. These organisations need to be either extremely cost-effective and able to supply products at an acceptably low or competitive price, or to have a very good sales force who not only can flood existing markets but can find alternative markets.

1.2.4 Identify products provided by business organisations

Products

Products can take various forms, and we should begin by saying that in many respects you should always consider that the term 'product' is equally applicable to 'service'. Throughout this book, there may be a bias towards the notion that an organisation actually produces something physical as a result of its activities, but this is not necessarily so. Providing and consumption of services and other 'intangibles' forms a huge percentage of all spending and income both in the UK and worldwide.

Consumable products

A consumable product is one that is not durable (lasting). Consumable means that the product can only be used or consumed once. Good examples of consumable products are food, petrol and detergents.

In addition to consumable products, all services would be considered to be consumables. From the organisation's viewpoint, consumable products have the following advantages:

- Consumable products do not share the market saturation problems of durable products. Because of this, demand for consumable products is more constant and they tend to be purchased more regularly, thus enabling the organisation to build up loyalty from their customers.
- Consumable products are more likely than durables to maintain their demand during periods of recession.

Durable products

These are items purchased that should last for a considerable amount of time. They are used, but not immediately used up. Good examples of these are household consumer durables such as washing machines, tumble-driers and dish-washers. They are relatively high-cost items and can be also described as capital goods. In business terms, capital goods are items called 'fixed assets'. You will find out more about fixed assets when you tackle Unit 4 of this programme.

Goods and services

Having identified the two major differences between durable and non-durable products, we should also say that certain products do not have a physical nature at all. They cannot be touched (they are intangible). Whether products handled by the organisation are goods (tangible) or services (intangible), there are costs incurred that determine the price of the product. In this sense, there is no difference in either buying a service or goods. The concept which forms the basis of the pricing decision is known as added value.

Added value

Basically, this means that the organisation which supplies the product adds extra cost to the product as this passes through its hands. An organisation may convert a raw material, through a series of industrial processes, into a finished product. The actual value of the product increases as it reaches the end of its production process. This may appear to be a very different set of circumstances as compared with a service. In the case of services, the organisation is adding value to the service by using expert skills and other specialised knowledge. These skills and knowledge form the basis of the price that is charged for the service itself.

Provided to individual customers, to governments or to other businesses

It should be noted that, regardless of the nature of the customer, each should be equally valued by the organisation. Obviously, this does not always happen, since the larger the customer, the more attention is given to them.

It could be said that an individual person, who will probably form the basis of an organisation's business, is the most potentially difficult and demanding. This is because, although individually customers are not likely to cause a particular problem, collectively they create so many transactions that there are bound to be numerous problems and difficulties. The larger organisations, such as the government or other businesses, while being important in the sense that their transactions with the organisation may be significant, may be equally as difficult in a very different way. Government departments and larger businesses can be significantly more demanding in terms of the service that they require from the organisation. Not only will they demand lower prices, but they will also expect the supplying organisation to recognise the fact that they are contributing greatly to its prosperity.

1.2.5 Explain activities undertaken by businesses to improve their market position

Activities undertaken by businesses

As you will be aware by the time that you finish this learning programme, the activities of an organisation are varied and complex. In this section of the Element, we will be considering only the basic activities of the organisation and we are sure that you will be able to think of a great many more activities that form the routine of businesses that you know.

Marketing research

In order to reduce risk, an organisation needs to know about the intended market for the product that it is going to launch. Market research refers specifically to the research into markets for products, but strictly speaking, marketing research refers to any aspect of the marketing process that requires investigation. In this section we will therefore look at the different types of marketing research, their context and their probable use. Regardless of the type of marketing research to be undertaken, a number of broadly similar questions need to be asked:

- *What is your budget?*
- *What is your timescale?*
- *How accurate does it need to be?*
- *Who exactly do you want to survey?*
- *Where are the people you want to survey?*

Focus study

Marketing research methods

As one well-known advertisement said, 'Eight out of 10 owners who expressed a preference said their cats preferred it'. Many people now believe that if you want accurate information for marketing research, you are better off asking the cat. Marketing research organisations set themselves up as being expert and scientific. However, test results in many polls proved to be either inconclusive or even false. Another good example of this is in relation to television programmes. If you believe market research it will tell you that programmes such as *Spitting Image* and *Blind Date* were in the 'preference to view' category. The fact of the matter was that audience figures for both programmes had dropped considerably. So what is the truth and where can you find it?

Organisations invest huge amounts of money in order to obtain the most accurate and up-to-date market information. So are they just throwing their money away?

The large research organisations obviously disagree. They claim that they find questions and not answers. Research can be the ideal way of discovering the kind of questions that you need to ask about your product or service and not necessarily what people think of it. Critics of market research point to the predictions made of the result of the 1992 General Election. With the exception of one market research organisation, they all predicted a hung Parliament (where no party would have an overall majority). They were wrong. Some cite this as a prime example of the end of quantitative research (asking a quantity of people about a product). On the qualitative research side (choosing people who will give a quality response), group discussions and focus groups have become popular, but the problem with qualitative research is that it only gives information from another individual's perspective. It gives that person's opinion of the proposed product.

The critics of qualitative research claim that you will only get obvious and simplistic results from this form of research. The other major problem which has been unmasked is that large numbers of the participants in these focus groups and discussion groups are in fact fakes. They are paid between £20–£30 for a 90-minute session. This is surely likely to influence their response and might even amount to a fraud on the organisation requesting the research.

Whereas in most countries markets for a product are researched before deciding to produce it, the Japanese, on the other hand, launch a product first and then research it. Admittedly they have had some failures, but largely they are successful. Whether this is testimony to their business sense or the depths of their pockets in terms of advertising spending is another question.

Individual activity

Time: 1.5 hours

PC 1.2.5
C 2.2
AN 2.1
AN 2.2
AN 2.3
IT 2.1
IT 2.2
IT 2.3

Individually, using a software package, create a matrix which cross-references the marketing research methods discussed in the above focus study and the following criteria:

- **accessibility**
- **fitness for purpose**
- **validity**
- **cost**
- **time**
- **reliability**

Head each cross-referencing matrix with one of the following research problems and fill in the matrix as you feel appropriate:

- **washing powder**
- **hand-held remote control for television**
- **decaffeinated tea bags**

Design

Technology, design, research and development are continually introducing new products and services on to the market. In many cases, new products or services simple replace older ones, making them obsolete. Occasionally, a new product or service may enter the market that offers possibilities previously undreamt of. Who would have believed that there could one day be a machine which would replace the need to hand-write additional copies of a book, but it happened when the first printing press was designed. Who would have believed the changes in offices brought about by the photocopier, the telephone and the computer.

These products, whether they are replacing an existing one or not, have to cater for either a need or a want. In the case of replacement, there is an existing need. In the case of a want, this may have to be generated by an expensive advertising campaign which tries to convince the consumers that they really do want the product!

Group activity

Time: 30 minutes

PC 1.2.5
C 2.1
C 2.2

In groups of three, try to make a list of the 10 most-demanded items that a family would require. Then make a list of the 10 most-demanded fashion items.

From your two lists, are there a lot of producers of each item or just a few?

Using your findings and conclusions, say why you think this is so. Compare your findings with those of the rest of your class.

Production

The choice of products available is dependent, therefore, on how businesses and government answer the three questions:

- *What to produce?*
- *How to produce it?*
- *Who should produce it?*

and thus decide upon how resources should be allocated. One of the major influences upon this allocation is to what extent the government and local authorities take it upon themselves to provide goods and services which may not be provided by the private sector.

Marketing communications (advertising, promotion, sponsorship, sales literature)

Whether you have noticed it or not, consumers are consistently bombarded by advertising and marketing strategies. Although as individuals we like to consider that we are largely immune to such devices, the effect of advertising campaigns on the level of demand for goods and services and on consumers' perceptions can be exceedingly influential.

Advertising

Advertising is used by organisations to try to raise the demand for their goods and services. They can do this in several ways. The first is to increase consumer awareness that their products exist and of where they can get them from, because obviously nobody is going to go out and buy a product that they don't know about. By making more consumers aware of their products, organisations hope that more people will buy them and thus increase demand.

Secondly, advertising is used to try to create the perception that a product is better than the competitor's product in one way or another, e.g. better quality, more functions, better after-sales service. The hope is that consumers will switch from buying one brand to another.

Lastly, advertising is used as a means of creating a particular 'image' or brand name for a product.

PC 1.2.5
C 2.1

Group activity

Time: 20 minutes

In groups of two or three, consider the launch of a new product. For example, a chocolate bar, canned drink or a car. How is advertising used to increase the demand for these products?

Sales promotion

Sales promotion, known as 'below-the-line' expenditure, can account for up to half of all marketing spending. Trade sales promotions are very common, such as bulk order discounts, or rebates (cash repayments) based on the amount spent over a year with a supplier. The main aim of the sales promotion is to increase sales. This may sound fairly obvious, but the tactics used can be somewhat more complex than in advertising. Sales promotions, in order to be classified as successful, should generate short-term increases in the sales volume and value. During the period of the sales promotion, customers should also be encouraged to purchase more regularly or in greater quantities per purchase than they would normally do.

Most sales promotions are short term. Certainly in the case of FMCGS (fast moving consumer goods), such as baked beans, confectionery and coffee, the sales promotions may be continuous. Organisations that produce these products will roll one sales promotion straight into the next without a break.

Offering plastic dinosaurs or merchandising from the latest film release can give a brand a temporary edge over the competitors, who are only offering breakfast bowls if you collect ten tokens. In many cases, such as cereals or petrol, the sales promotion replaces the price cut. Price wars do nothing for any of the organisations involved apart from affecting their profit margins and diverting attention away from the quality of the product or service. Having said this, temporary price cuts or special offers can be seen as an alternative method of sales promotion, but not one that is favoured by suppliers. Short-term special offers are fine if the product is a new one that needs to be established in the marketplace, but otherwise they are avoided if possible.

Sales promotions are very much tied in with the concepts of customer loyalty, brand loyalty and the general rewards given to customers who stick with a particular brand name.

PC 1.2.5
C 2.1

Group activity

Time: 15 minutes

Why bother with sales promotions at all? Surely, running a sales promotion only shows that the organisation's advertising and other marketing activities are not working? Discuss this as a group.

Focus study

Focus study – Sales promotion methods

The Institute of Sales Promotion is fighting against the EU's plans to harmonise the rules and regulations that govern the use of sales promotions throughout Europe. They fear that common rules and regulations will remove the possibility of using 'country specific' sales promotion methods that definitely work in a particular country. The laws in the UK are some of the most liberal in the EU. In comparison, Germany has rules and regulations covering nearly every type of sales promotion method.

PC 1.2.5
C 2.1

Group activity

We have identified some of the major variants of sales promotions in this Element, but some of them require investigation and research. In pairs, research the meaning of the above sales promotion techniques and report back your findings and examples to the rest of the group.

Sponsorship

You will find a full description of the nature of sponsorship in Unit 3, which covers all of the main marketing activities. At this point we shall restrict our comments to the more general aspects of sponsorship and how it can be used to enhance the overall activities of the organisation. In return for the prominent display of the organisation's product name, brand names or organisation name, the organisation will sponsor (underwrite or finance) an event. The 1995 Rugby World Cup in South Africa was a sponsorship bonanza, with a variety of different household names sponsoring the matches and the competition in general. Obviously, these high-profile activities which are televised are the sponsor's dream, but more commonly the sponsor will take on an event with a far more local or regional flavour. The sponsorship of football teams, not necessarily in the Premiership or top leagues, is a way for the organisation to get uniquely involved in the leisure activities of the area in which the team is supported.

Sales literature

Sales literature plays a vital role in the ongoing marketing effort of the organisation. It aims to convey to the customer the vital information about the product, service or selling organisation that will help them in making a purchasing decision. To this end, the sales literature needs to be as professional as possible, with a strong company image and some degree of clarity and standardisation. As we have mentioned earlier in this Unit, there is often a communications problem that inhibits the parts of the organisation from understanding what other parts are doing. It is vital that all of the organisation knows the content of the sales literature material and what claims are being made. In some cases, prices and availability are mentioned in the sales literature and the sales department is not informed. They are then faced with the embarrassment of callers quoting from the sales literature and they are not able to respond. The importance of the communication of the content of sales literature can, therefore, not be underestimated.

Sales literature includes the following:

- *brochures*
- *leaflets*
- *information booklets*
- *sales letters*
- *compliments slips*

Group activity

Time: 25 mins

Can you think of some more examples of the use of sales literature and types of material that would contain sales information? Firstly in pairs, and then in groups, consider your ideas.

PC 1.2.5

C 2.1

Brochures and leaflets can be used to send out responses to sales enquiries or for direct mail campaigns. They can also be given out to sales representatives to help to reinforce the sales message. Sales literature is expected to be sent to many potential customers, since it adds credibility to the business.

Brochures and leaflets can be relatively cheap to produce although the style and tone needs to be suitable and consistent. They should not look cheap and nasty, but should be of reasonable quality and follow any conventions that the business has established in terms of logos and slogans, etc.

Brochures should be designed to convey information quickly and clearly, and not be packed with lots of technical details, unless of course, the business is selling technical or specialist equipment. Leaflets are perhaps more flexible, since they are smaller, so cheaper to produce and can be used for a variety of different purposes.

Sales and after-sales service

In Units 2 and 3, we will be looking at the specific roles within the organisation that relate to these two vital activities of most organisations. Obviously, the sales activity of the organisation is of paramount importance since it is through sales that the organisation is able to undertake many of the other activities. Without sales, there can be no profit and without profit there can be no investment. This is a cycle that is the key to all of the business activities of the organisation and proves to be an enduring motive behind much of the activities of businesses around the world. The sales motive is not necessarily the only motive for business activity, as we will see in later Elements of this Unit.

After-sales service is very much an integral part of the sales effort. Without a comprehensive range of after-sales or customer service provision, the organisation cannot hope to be able to manage the needs of the customer or cope with the information and service needs that will arise. Again, this aspect is covered in much greater depth in later Units of this book. If you do wish to investigate them further, you will be given an opportunity in Unit 3 to investigate a particular organisation and assess its provision of after-sales service.

1.2.6 Propose products which would meet market demand

Propose products

New product development is the process through which new product ideas are screened, analysed, developed, tested and finally launched as a new product on the market. This final stage can be described as 'the culmination of a rigorous process of elimination'. Two statements really highlight the need for and risks of new product development by business organisations:

> *'The development and successful marketing of new products is perhaps the most important single factor in long-term growth and profitability for a company.'*
>
> *'This proverb flashes through his head – the many fail, the one succeeds.'*

These two statements really emphasise the need for new product development by companies, and the risk involved in developing a successful new product.

There are several stages involved in new product development:

1. **Generation of ideas** – every new product starts off as an idea. Ideas come from within the organisation itself, e.g. from research and development, marketing department, and executives and workers. Alternatively they come from outside the organisation, from customers, new technology and inventions, and competition.
2. **Screening of ideas** – the main purpose of the first stage in the product development process is to increase the number of good ideas. The main purpose of all the succeeding stages is to reduce the number of ideas, to find those which are the best. The main purpose of screening is therefore to eliminate ideas which are out of line with company objectives or resources, or which carry high-risk cost and little profit opportunity.
3. **Testing the product concept** – once you have a short list of products, concept testing is then carried out. This is where market research can begin to play an important role. The consumer is presented with the idea of the product, using drawings, models, written descriptions, photographs or films, etc., to convey the idea. It is important to look

for an interested reaction to the product. The firm that has a relatively vigorous screening of ideas should be left with a few well-screened products. Then the technical feasibility of the products is examined, looking at such questions as the production costs and the investment needed in research and development.

4 **Development** – this is the product testing stage. Once some prototypes (samples) of the product have been made, the product is tested in controlled conditions (laboratory) to gain consumer reaction to the product, pack, name, etc., so that the firm can compare it with established products. Ratings are also needed so that adjustments can be made, such as too sweet or too dark. This development stage can be very long and it could be a number of years before the organisation puts the products into commercial production.

5 **Test marketing** – up to this stage the reaction of potential customers has not been tested under normal marketing conditions. The idea here is to launch the product in a restricted area in order to make generalisations about the country or market as a whole; it is also a defensive measure, if it is found that the product does not sell, to avoid further losses. There are three main functions of test marketing:

- *to make predictions about the national launch*
- *to find out what went wrong during the test marketing stage*
- *to experiment with different tactics*

6 **Research** – plays a vital role in this stage and it is important that as much data as possible is collected in order to give an indication of how the product will sell nationally. However, it must be emphasised that all products passing this stage are not necessarily successful nationally.

7 **National launch or commercialisation stage** – described as the 'culmination of a rigorous process of elimination' the marketing plan should have been worked out; the salesforce, dealers, etc., should be equipped for the launch; and public relations should be geared for the product's introduction. Management responsibility within the organisation for launching and continued progress of the product should be established. However, even after the launch of the product, the organisation may have failed to anticipate reactions and problems, and here again research can be important in gauging full-scale consumer reaction to the product.

The whole process of new product development is one of continued elimination of ideas at successive stages of new product development. Each stage becomes increasingly costly to an organisation.

The commercialisation stage is the introductory stage of the product life cycle. Lead times from product ideas to the commercialisation stage can often take two to three years or longer.

New products

Continuous innovation is essential for the long-term survival of businesses. Because the purpose is to create a customer need, any business enterprise has two basic requirements – marketing and innovation. A failure by companies to innovate has been termed 'marketing myopia' (shortsightedness). This term was used in relation to the railroads in the 1930s–1960s in the USA, when the argument was voiced that their loss of freight trade was because they were product orientated whereas other commercial carriers were marketing orientated and were providing better transportation services for customers.

Failure to innovate has hit many companies in the past and they have subsequently paid the price. Other, more visionary companies, are increasingly trying to insure themselves against the inevitable obsolescence (outdated and no longer needed) of their existing products. The increasing research and development expenditure by organisations tend to reflect this.

Whether a new technological breakthrough relates directly to the nature or features of the product, or to the production process, substitution of one product by another needs to avoid undermining current products or services. Again, a gradual introduction of the technologically superior product or service is probably the best way of handling the situation.

You only need to look at the prices currently being charged for seemingly outdated computers to appreciate the fact that with each technological breakthrough previous generations of products are rendered obsolete, or, at least, comparatively undesirable.

Group activity

PC 1.2.6
C 2.1
C 2.2
C 2.3
C 2.4

In pairs, in the role of the research and development team of an organisation, create two new products, using the names *Signet* and *Fable*.

Any kind of product is acceptable, but you must choose something which would meet a market need. In addition, you must cover the following aspects:

- **justify why you have chosen these particular products**
- **explain how you believe the names match the products**
- **give physical descriptions of the products**
- **design short questionnaires with the aim of proving that there is a market for your products**
- **produce an outline of a marketing plan for your products**
- **investigate any potential competitors and their market share**
- **assuming that the production of the products will take place in your local area, produce a list of resource considerations (materials required, etc.) related to the products**
- **present any statistical data in the form of pie or bar charts or line graphs.**

Present your findings in the form of a report and be prepared to give a 15-minute presentation to the group, who will take the role of the board of directors. Your report should be word processed and you should make full use of any illustrative material, including any diagrams or models you choose to produce.

Developed from existing products

The release of a product on to the market should never be seen as the end of the marketing research involvement in the operation. It is only through continual monitoring and surveying techniques that an organisation will establish whether the product fully addresses the needs of the customer. Constant attention must be given to the modification of products in order to ensure that they do address customer needs. Innovation or modification in this sense needs to be tempered with a certain degree of caution. An organisation would be ill advised to replace or significantly modify a product before it has had a chance to establish itself on the market. All too often a product will be replaced by a modified version which, in effect, renders the original product obsolete. Subtle and gradual changes are the best ways of ensuring that the product meets the ever-changing demands and requirements of the customer.

Element 1.2 Assignment

PC 1.2.1–6
C 2.1
C 2.2
C 2.3
IT 2.1
IT 2.2
IT 2.3

The key to completing the Element assignment is the understanding of the term 'market share'. In addition to this, you will also have to consider the ways in which an organisation uses its location and marketing activities to manipulate demand despite external influences.

Task 1 *PC 1.2.1*

Create a map of a particular area which identifies the location of a business organisation. On this map you should also include any relevant natural resources, the location of other related businesses and the location in general of the organisation's customers. It would also be useful to include the transportation network. Accompanying this map you should word process a brief explanation of the reason for the location of your chosen business.

Task 2 *PC 1.2.2*

Produce a word processed summary which explains the competitive business environment within which businesses operate. You should include in your summary the following:

- legal influences
- environmental influences
- public influences

Task 3 *PC 1.2.3/1.2.5*

Produce a word processed report on a single identified business organisation. Within your report you should include the following:

- a description of the markets for its goods or services
- the demand for its goods or services
- an explanation of how marketing communications are used by the business to improve its market position

Task 4 *PC 1.2.4/1.2.6*

Produce notes and any relevant sketches to support a proposal for a new or developed product. You should undertake this task with reference to existing products and ensure that your product is not identical to an existing one.

Element 1.3
Present results of investigation into employment

Performance criteria

A student must:

1 describe and give examples of **types of employment**

2 collect, **analyse** and explain **information** about employment in different regions

3 **compare working conditions** for employees in different organisations

4 present results of investigation into employment, or comparison of working conditions

Range

- *Types of employment*: full-time, part-time, permanent, temporary, skilled, unskilled, self-employed
- *Analyse*: in terms of factors contributing to numbers of people employed, growth and decline of manufacturing and service sectors
- *Information*: percentage employed (male, female, by age), percentage employed in manufacturing sectors and service sectors, local, national, EU
- *Compare working conditions*: in terms of travel to work (time, cost), physical conditions, hours of work, pay (wages, extra payments), safety, job security, career opportunities, training opportunities, use of new technology

1.3.1 Describe and give examples of types of employment

Types of employment

Trying to identify the different types of employment in the UK is difficult enough, but when we consider the employment types throughout the EU and beyond, this becomes an almost impossible task. In this Element we will be looking at the trends in employment type and we will be making use of some of the predictions that the Government has made in relation to these differing types of employment. We are sure that you do not need to be told exactly what is a full-time, part-time, permanent or temporary position.

We will now turn our attention to the different types of employment and try to look at the trends in the recent past and the predictions for the future.

Full-time employment

There has been a trend away from full-time employment. It now accounts for around 62% of employment in the UK. This is projected to decrease by a further 0.3m by the year 2001, giving just 57%. This is in the light of the fact that many other forms of employment offer considerably more flexibility to both businesses and individuals.

Part-time employment

Part-time jobs currently account for around 24% of employment. Normally part-time work is no longer than 25 hours per week. It is projected that by the year 2001 the figure will have increased to 28%, which means an increase of 1.3m jobs. Since women are the major part-time work force, this will mean that by the year 2001 they will make up 52% of all part-time workers. This is an increase of over 1.2m. Men will still be the majority of the employed, as considerably more are self-employed.

Permanent and temporary employment

In the temporary category of employment, nearly half of all jobs are in the secretarial field. Very much behind secretarial are the publishing, industrial and technical areas of employment. Just ahead of computing and accounting comes catering. Normally the definition of a temporary full-time post will be that the individual is working on a short fixed-term contract, as discussed later in this Unit. As we will see when we consider the evaluation of types of employment in relation to business needs, the use of the temporary worker has become a steadily more attractive prospect for employers.

Skilled and unskilled

There are a number of current skill supply issues in relation to the needs of the UK. There are three ways of assessing skills:

- **Core skills** – which are very general skills applicable to almost every kind of job. They, of course, include basic literacy and numeracy, the ability to work with others and some understanding of information technology
- **Vocational skills** – these are skills which are needed for a particular occupation but are often less useful outside it. There is still some transferability with these skills. A typical example would be an individual who can operate a specific computer package, who would be likely to be able to use a new one in a different job.
- **Specific job skills** – with these types of skills usefulness is often limited to a fairly narrow range of occupations. It would be perhaps more clear to call these 'specific job skills knowledge'.

As we will see, the availability of jobs in particular regions of the country is often related to the present skills mix within that region. Certain areas will have a predominance of occupational types and consequently will require significantly more individuals skilled in those areas. If we look at the nature of skilled and unskilled work, we will discover that the boundaries between them are becoming increasingly blurred. To this degree it is obvious that even some of the more routine unskilled occupations do require a little more than basic core skills. Increasingly the need to communicate at a number of different levels coupled with the flexibility of multi-skilling is equally as relevant to those involved in more straightforward, less skilled occupations as to those who are involved in complex operations.

Self-employed

Self-employment showed very strong growth throughout the 1980s. However, this growth trend was severely interrupted by the recession. It is widely believed that the growth has now resumed. By the year 2000 it is projected that a further 0.5m more people will be self-employed.

Small businesses themselves also account for a growing proportion of employment. During the 1980s there was a growth from 1.9m to 3.1m. They were, however, the main casualties of the recession and in 1992 only 2.8m had survived. Again, this short-term 'blip' has come to an end and there appear to be underlying trends which suggest that small firms and self-employment have recovered and are growing.

PC 1.3.1
C 2.1
C 2.2
C 2.3
C 2.4

Group activity

In groups of four, find and interview one person from each of the above categories of employment. Between you, you should know several people who fall into these categories. Before the interview, design a list of questions to ask each interviewee. It would be a good idea to let them see the list of questions before the interview takes place, so that they can prepare themselves properly.

When you have undertaken the interviews, compare the answers given in order to determine which employment type offers the following:

- **guaranteed regular income**
- **security**
- **reasonable leisure time**
- **job satisfaction**
- **ability to make your own decisions**

When you have completed this task, compare the results of your investigation with those of at least one other group.

1.3.2 Collect, analyse and explain information about employment in different regions

Analyse in terms of employment

It is widely recognised that there has been a recovery in the labour market. Unemployment itself has been steadily reducing since early 1993. From the summer of 1993 to the summer of 1994 employment actually increased by 230 000. It is expected that the long-term unemployment growth will continue, but at a slower rate. Projections carried out by the Institute of Employment Research suggest the following:

- 1995–97 – employment growth of 0.6% per year
- 1997–2001 – employment growth of 0.9% per year

If these figures are correct, then by 2001 1.6m new jobs will have been created.

Factors contributing to numbers of people employed

The census of employment which measured the work force in employment in June 1994 identified the following figures:

- *male full-time employment – 9.6m*
- *male self-employment – 2.5m*
- *male part-time employment – 1.1m*
- *female full-time employment – 5.7m*
- *female self-employment – 0.8m*
- *female part-time employment – 4.9m*

There are obviously many different reasons why there will be a specific need for a set number of individuals to be employed at any particular time. These may include the following:

1 **Historical reasons** – such as the gradual decline in a particular mode of employment that has become outdated

2 **Geographical reasons** – many of which we will look at later when we consider the nature of regional employment. There may be a particular reason why certain industries congregate around a specific area. This may be related to the fact that certain raw materials are available in that region.

3 **Cultural reasons** – there may have been several migrations of ethnic minorities in a particular region over a number of years, which may have affected the type of employment or the specialisms in that region. Certain ethnic groups are more or less likely to be attracted to different types of employment.

PC 1.3.2
C 2.1

Group activity *Time: 45 minutes*

As a group, try to identify the different ethnic minorities in your region. Remember that you should include any significant group that was not originally associated with the area. In this respect, an ethnic minority could include the English in Northern Ireland, or the Scots in London. In other words, do not restrict your thoughts to West Indians, Asians or Chinese for example.

What are their main areas of occupation? Have they concentrated in any specific types of employment or industry? What has been the impact on the local employment types?

4 **Industrial reasons** – as we intimated in our suggestions regarding the historical and geographical reasons for employment, there are some traditional forms of employment that are common to certain areas. You will recognise that there is a difference between the types of industry that are common on the coast and those of the inland regions.

PC 1.3.2
C 2.1

Group activity *Time: 30 minutes*

Without looking at the regional details which we will cover later in this performance criteria, try to assess the nature of the industrial base (if any) that forms an integral part of the region in which you live. What are the reasons for this type of employment in your region? Is it traditional or historical, or is it as a result of the geographical location of the region?

Discuss your thoughts as a group.

5 **Political reasons** – there has been a series of ongoing initiatives by the government which seek to encourage businesses to relocate in particular areas of the UK. The areas, identified usually for their abnormally high levels of unemployment or loss of traditional industries, are given 'assisted area' or similar status. By being designated as such, they can access both central government funding and EU funding. There are also a number of incentives that businesses can expect if they relocate there. These incentives, given through the local authorities, include rent-free premises, help with finding the right employees and business rate discounts.

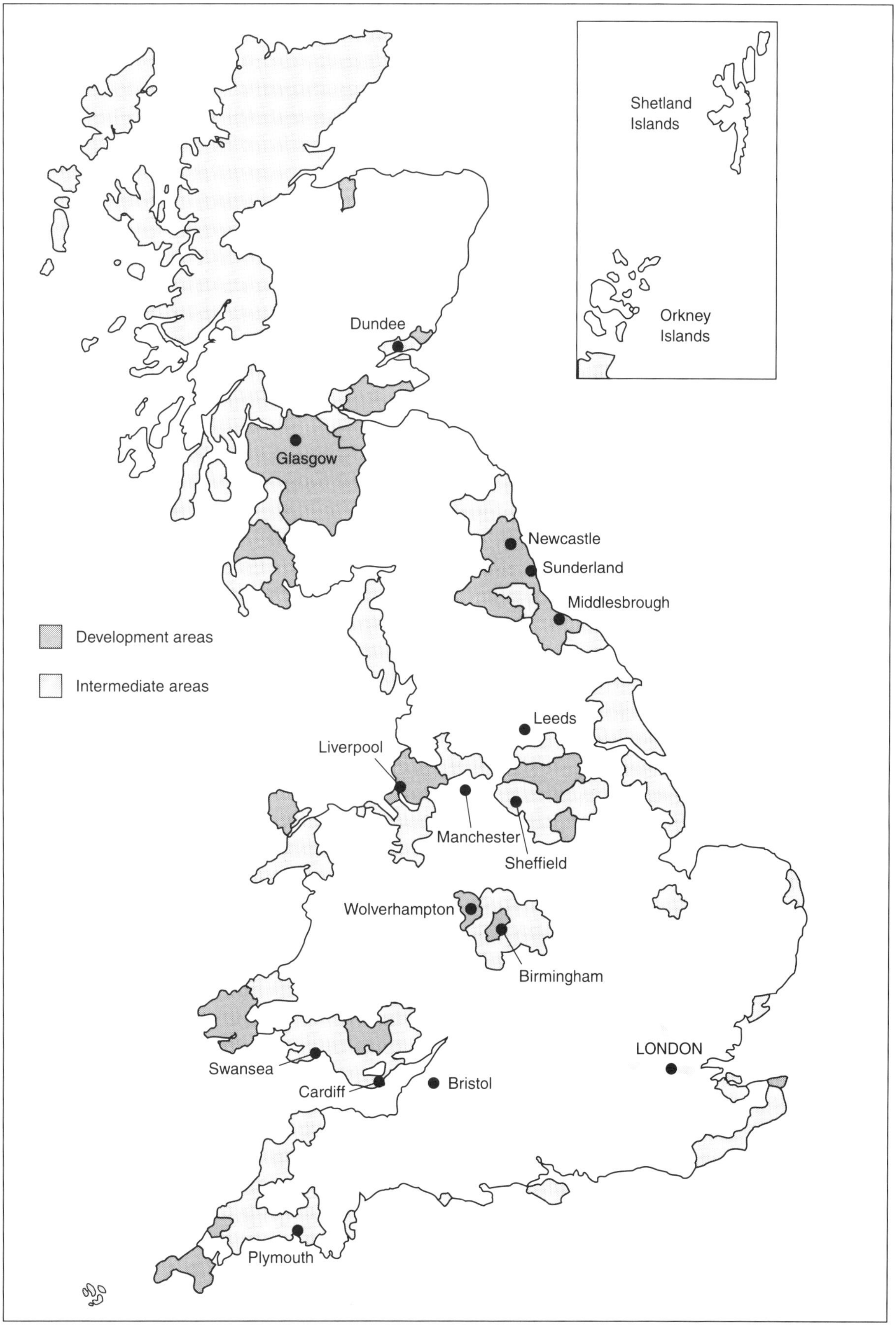

Fig 1.16 Map of assisted areas in England, Scotland and Wales as defined by the Department of Trade and Industry at 1.8.93
(Source: DTI)

6 **Economic reasons** – this very much links in with the prosperity, or otherwise, of the region. If the region is experiencing a fall in the fortunes of key industries in the area, then this will have a 'knock-on' effect on other supporting businesses. If the main employers in the region close down, this will affect all of the businesses that provide services to them, but will also affect the more common forms of business too. With high unemployment, there will be less money to spend and supermarkets, local shops and services will face serious problems too. It is at this point that the government should normally step in and help the region with investments or designation to assisted area status.

Growth and decline of manufacturing sectors and service sectors

There are now around 3m more jobs in service industries and 1.4m fewer in manufacturing. This is compared to the 1981 figures. By 1993 almost 45% of all jobs were in the service industries (this includes both private and public sectors). With another 25% of all jobs in the distribution industries, this left less than 30% in manufacturing, in the primary sector and the construction industry.

It is expected that this trend will continue until 2001, by when it is assumed that around 1.5m extra jobs will have been created in the service industries. At the same time, 0.5m more jobs will be available in distribution and construction. Over the same period 0.5m jobs will be lost from the primary sector and manufacturing combined.

The Institute for Employment Research looked at the trend in overall employment changes between 1993 and 2001 and discovered the following:

- *primary and utility sector* – will lose 12% of the work force
- *manufacturing* – will lose 8% of the work force
- *construction* – will gain 7% of the work force
- *distribution and transport* – will gain 6% of the work force
- *business services and other related services* – will gain 23% of the work force
- *public services* – will gain 8% of the work force

This means that the whole economy will gain around a 6% increase in the work force.

Information

There are some very useful sources of information regarding the regions of the UK and the EU in general. Central government releases a series of data via the Central Statistical Office or the Employment Service. You will find these sets of data in most reference sections of local libraries We have used these sources and have summarised the main trends and information to give you a start in your investigations.

Percentage employed (male, female, by age), percentage employed in manufacturing sectors and service sectors

Technically, part-time workers are those individuals who are working for less than 30 hours per week. There has been considerable growth in this type of employment. Indeed, some 1.4m extra jobs have been created between 1981 and 1993. During the same period the number of full-time employees fell by 2m. As a direct result of this, the overall percentage of employees engaged in part-time work rose from 21% to 28%.

As we have seen, part-time employment is still most commonly done by women. In 1993 women accounted for 80% of part-time workers. In terms of the total number of women working, 42% are in part-time employment. This is compared to just 6% for men. These figures based on 1981 calculations have changed significantly and now they are 46% and 11%.

The Institute for Employment Research expects part-time employee positions to rise by a further 1.3m. Coupled with this is a comparative fall in full-time employment of 0.3m. This will mean that as the number of part-time employees increases it will outstrip the total increase in employees. In other words, by 2001 part-time employment will account for some 32% of all work.

If we refer to some specific sectors we can identify that part-time working is expected to fall slightly. These drops in employment are more than offset by probable increases in the following areas:

- *distribution – up 23%*
- *business and miscellaneous services – up 38%*
- *public services – up 18%*

By referring to the figures which are produced showing the work force in employment, you will see that the majority of individuals, both male and female, are engaged in full-time employment. However, a significant minority, amounting to some 6m, are involved in part-time work of some description. This growing trend, which we addressed earlier in this Element, has had a significant impact on both regional and national employment figures.

Again, as we discussed at the beginning of this Element, there has been considerable change in the balance between the skilled and unskilled employment levels. You will find that as new technology is introduced, there is a decreasing need for skilled employees. Indeed, many of the skills which had been used in the past have been replaced by machinery, automation and robotics.

As we have seen, since the 1960s women's employment has risen while at the same time men's employment has fallen. The predictions of changes throughout the 1993–2001 period infer that, while female employment increases by 1.2m, male employment will fall by 0.2m. The consequence of this means that, while in 1981 women accounted for only 42% of employees, they had gained a 49% share of the labour market by 1993 and are expected for the first time to outstrip their male counterparts in 2001 with a percentage of 52%.

Since women will outnumber men in all other areas except self-employment, this will not mean that they necessarily make up the main share of the employment work force. Predictions do vary, but the current 54% majority of males in employment is expected to fall to at least 52% by the year 2001.

Women's employment is still concentrated in certain sectors of the economy, specifically outnumbering men in the following areas:

- *health*
- *education*
- *other services*
- *textiles*
- *clothing*

In the construction and mining sectors of the economy, women still represent a mere 10% of the work force.

Men in the 35–44 age group still have the highest level of participation in work. By the year 2000 this figure is likely to be 94%. At the same time the number of men over the age of 55 who are working shows a considerable decrease.

Women will play a much greater role in employment than they have ever done in the past. In fact, the participation rates are rising while men's rates are falling. The growth rates of women aged 25–34 will reach 77% by the year 2000. This is in comparison to 61% in 1984 and 72% in 1994. In the next age group of women, 35–44, some 81% are expected to be in work by 2000, compared to just 71% in 1984 and 78% in 1994.

During the period 1983–90 almost two-thirds of all new jobs went to women. From the 1960s there has been a continual rise in women's employment.

Local, national and EU employment

If we consider the projected changes between 1993 and 2001 we will see some interesting trends and possibilities in terms of employment. The categories of occupation as identified by the government are:

- *managers and administrators (M and A)*
- *professionals (Pro)*
- *associate professionals (APro)*
- *clerical and secretarial (Cler)*
- *craft and skilled manual (C and SM)*
- *personal and protective services (P and P)*
- *sales (S)*
- *plant and machinery operators (PMO)*
- *other elementary occupations (OEO)*

In order to examine these, we will look at each of the regions in turn:

- **UK** – the largest employment group in the UK is the M and A category. This accounts for around 4.03m; following closely behind is the C category at 3.95m. It is expected that between 1993 and 2001 M and A will increase by 770 000 while C falls by 120 000.
- **Northern Ireland** – there is a total of 620 000 jobs in Northern Ireland, predominantly skewed towards the C and SM and the P and P categories. In the run up to 2001 it is expected that an extra 30 000 jobs will be created. This is a 5.3% increase and compares rather unfavourably to the projected 6.9% increase across the UK as a whole.
- **Scotland** – of the 2.2m jobs in Scotland, the M and A and the C categories have significantly lower proportions than the UK average. The OEO category is significantly

larger. The expectation of a 4.8% growth (or 110 000 extra jobs) by 2001 is the second lowest rate of growth.

- **Wales** – Wales has some 1.1m jobs. There is a significant bias towards manual jobs; in other words the C and M, PMO and P and P categories are much higher than the UK average. All other categories are significantly smaller in percentage terms. With an expected growth of 7.8% before 2001 this will mean that 90 000 jobs will be created. This is a higher percentage growth than the UK as a whole can expect, with the biggest gains being in the P and P category.
- **North** – there is also a considerable bias towards manual jobs in the 1.2m work force. With the exception of M and A, Pro, APro and C categories, all other occupational groups are significantly higher in percentage terms. Unfortunately, the North is expected to have a 4.8% growth in the run up to 2001. Although this will mean 60 000 extra jobs, this is the second slowest growth in the UK.
- **North West** – with a significant majority of the 2.6m jobs in the PMO category, the North West is looking forward to a rather low 4.6% increase before 2001. These extra 100 000 jobs will signal a trend towards the P and P category.
- **Yorkshire and Humberside** – with 2m jobs in this region there is bias towards the C and SM, OEO and PMO categories. All other occupational groups are considerably lower in percentage terms than the UK average. Some 120 000 new jobs (5.9%) are expected to come into existence between 1993 and 2001. The P and P and the M and A categories will be the main beneficiaries.
- **East Midlands** – the East Midlands has considerably more C, SM and PMO workers in its 1.7m total. There are lower percentages for all other categories. With a massive increase of 9.1%, 160 000 new jobs are expected to be created between 1993 and 2001. The P and P category would increase by at least 33%.
- **West Midlands** – the 2.15m jobs in this area are mainly in the C, SM and PMO categories. With a 120 000 job increase forecast before 2001, this represents a 5.7% growth rate. As with many other regions, the P and P category is expected to increase the most.
- **South West** – with just less than 2m people employed, there are interesting imbalances which favour the M and A and the Pro categories. As a result of deindustrialisation in the area, the PMO category is significantly lower than the average. Some 200 000 new jobs are expected to be created between 1993 and 2001. This is the largest growth rate, at 10%. Principal beneficiaries would be the M and A and the P and P categories.
- **East Anglia** – with just 900 000, jobs there is an imbalance towards the OEO and PMO categories. All other occupational groups are under-represented. Despite this, East Anglia hopes to enjoy the second fastest growth in the UK between 1993 and 2001 at 9.7% which will mean 90 000 new jobs. It is expected that the P and P category will be the main growth area.
- **Greater London** – with 3.4m jobs there is an imbalance towards the M and A, Pro, APro and C categories. Other more manual occupations are under-represented. With just a 6% expected growth rate, this will still mean 210 000 more jobs. It is in the more dominant categories that exist already that additional growth will occur.
- **Rest of South East England** – this area, which includes the whole of the South East except Greater London, has a work force of 4.5m. Being greatly influenced by London, M and A and C categories are still dominant. This region is expected to have a growth rate of 8.6% amounting to 390 000 new jobs, but again the largest beneficiary would be

the M and A category. However, the biggest proportionate growth would be in the P and P occupational areas.

If we now turn our attention to the EU and the general trends in Europe, we can find the following information. We have covered the main European competitors as well as examples of the minor ones. Although there may be some dispute regarding our classification of major and minor competitors, we have covered all of the countries to the same level of detail. In this section we will look at:

- *Germany*
- *France*
- *Italy*
- *Spain*
- *The Netherlands*
- *Belgium*
- *Denmark*
- *Portugal*
- *Greece*
- *Eire*
- *Luxembourg*

The first four countries are, in our own estimation, the major competitors to the UK. We have not included any of the former Eastern Bloc countries at this stage, since their economies are largely in chaos and they are not, as yet, very serious competitors.

We have listed all of the main areas of specialisation. The letter in brackets after the type of product or service refers to the following:

(a) agriculture
(m) manufacturing
(s) services
(e) energy

We begin our European tour with Germany.

Germany

Growth in Germany has been rather moderate. Inflation rates and budget deficits have been acceptable, with unemployment comparatively low. For Germany, however, the unemployment rate is still unacceptably high in its terms. In the former GDR, for so long part of the Soviet Union, the government has had to put billions of DM into restructuring the economy and supporting the unemployed. With this massive reinvestment, the climb out of the recession was slower.

Main areas of specialism:

- *construction (s)*
- *electrical engineering (m)*
- *mechanical engineering (m)*
- *car manufacture (m)*
- *metal goods (m)*
- *chemicals (m)*

France

French industries have become more competitive and much more active in the export field. Although the recession did affect the French economy, the effect was not as deep as in other European countries and it is expected that France will be in a better position once the long-term effects of the recession wear off.

Unemployment has always been quite high – on average around 10%; at worst 12%. Despite the fact that output has increased, the unemployment figures remain stubbornly high. The labour market is quite rigid, coupled with the fact that the education system leaves something to be desired. There is particularly high unemployment among the many unskilled workers.

Main areas of specialism are:

- *tourism (s)*
- *engineering (s)*
- *data processing and office machinery (m)*
- *car manufacture and parts (m)*
- *aerospace (m)*
- *nuclear and hydroelectric power (m)*
- *electrical equipment (m)*
- *food (m)*
- *wine, brewing, soft drinks and water (m)*
- *pharmaceuticals (m)*
- *wool (m)*
- *dairy products (a)*
- *livestock (a)*
- *fruit and vegetables (a)*

Italy

Italy suffers from a marked difference between the north (industrial based) and the south (mainly agricultural). The Italian government's support for local industries and its attempts to tackle unemployment have put considerable strain on the economy.

Main areas of specialism are:

- *tourism (s)*
- *design and fashion (s)*
- *cars and motor bike manufacture (m)*
- *textiles, leather, footwear and clothing (m)*
- *furnishings (m)*
- *jewellery (m)*
- *machinery and machine tools (m)*
- *electrical goods (m)*
- *wire and cables (m)*
- *food (m)*
- *wine (a)*

Spain

Spain has suffered from high inflation and high unemployment problems. The key to success must be the control of the labour costs, otherwise they will be unable to withstand the competition of the single market.

Main areas of specialism are:

- *tourism (s)*
- *car manufacturing (m)*
- *oil refineries (m)*
- *electrical goods (m)*
- *wire and cables (m)*
- *food and drink (m)*
- *footwear and clothing (m)*
- *textiles (m)*
- *rubber products (m)*
- *wine (a)*
- *olive oil (a)*
- *fruit and vegetables (a)*

The Netherlands

The Netherlands was hit the hardest of all of the EU member states during the recession. The high social security expenditure has led to:

- *high levels of labour cost*
- *high taxation*

These two major costs seriously affected profits during the 1970s and 1980s. Despite this, the inflation rate is one of the lowest in the world. Other advantages are:

- *a strong currency*
- *a good geographical location*
- *very competitive world-wide*

In short, The Netherlands is one of the best placed of the minor competitors to take advantage of its position and relative strengths in the light of an end to the recession.

The main areas of specialism are:

- *transport (s)*
- *communications (s)*
- *trading services (s)*
- *business services (s)*
- *chemicals (m)*
- *telecommunications (m)*
- *electrical goods (m)*
- *food processing (m)*
- *ship building (m)*
- *dairy products (a)*
- *horticulture (a)*

Belgium

Belgium's growth rate and output are fairly average in European terms. It does have high labour costs and regional differences in terms of priorities and wealth.

Although Belgium is having to deal with a crushing level of debt, it too has the advantage of its geographical position in Europe.

The main areas of specialism are:

- *administration (s)*
- *transport (s)*
- *distribution (s)*
- *banking and insurance (s)*
- *chemicals (m)*
- *food and drink (m)*
- *car assembly (m)*
- *wool and cotton (m)*
- *carpets and textiles (m)*
- *glass (m)*

Denmark

Denmark has a rigid labour market, with low wage rates, but its social security costs are very high. This is as a result of the fact that unemployment is unacceptably high.

The main areas of specialism are:

- *transport (s)*
- *distribution (s)*
- *trading services (s)*
- *pharmaceuticals (m)*
- *machinery (m)*
- *medical equipment (m)*
- *ship building (m)*
- *plastics (m)*
- *fishing (a)*

Portugal

With a rather poor quality economy in the past, Portugal joined in 1986. This has meant that it is a major recipient of EU development money. Portugal has been able to restructure its industrial base and streamline its government's involvement in the economy through administrative reform.

The main areas of specialism are:

- *tourism (s)*
- *textiles, clothing and footwear (m)*
- *food processing (m)*
- *ceramics (m)*
- *wire and cables (m)*
- *paper (m)*
- *wine (a)*

Greece

As a result of poor growth and the general low quality of the economic base, Greece has been a major recipient of EU funding.

The main areas of specialism are:

- *shipping services (distribution and transport) (s)*
- *tourism (s)*
- *cement (m)*
- *clothing and footwear (m)*
- *textiles (m)*
- *wool (a)*

Eire

Eire did not have a solid industrial base, but since the 1980s this has been addressed and there has been a lot of work undertaken to attract inward investment. The economy has shifted significantly away from being agriculturally dominated to become a mixture of services and manufacture.

Eire has one of the worst records for unemployment in the EU. It has a high population growth that is not helping this problem.

The main areas of specialism are:

- *office and data processing equipment (m)*
- *telecommunications (m)*
- *medical equipment (m)*
- *pharmaceuticals (m)*
- *wire and cables (m)*
- *dairy products (a)*

Luxembourg

Luxembourg has suffered from deindustrialisation and a loss of its former core industries. Since the late 1980s the economy has begun to pick up and the country has developed into a major centre for financial services.

The main areas of specialism are:

- *banking (s)*
- *insurance (s)*
- *trading services (s)*
- *business services (s)*

UK Finally, we will look at the UK in the same manner as we have considered the other countries.

The growth rate of the UK is the lowest of the member states of the EU. The service sector has expanded well, at the expense of manufacturing and primary sector activity. The recession hit the UK very hard and caused a very high level of unemployment. The UK economy still has very serious structural problems.

The main reasons for these weaknesses are that:

- *the UK economy is very prone to inflation*
- *there has not been a very high investment in research and development*
- *savings are low*
- *there are considerable regional differences in terms of unemployment, investment and quality of infrastructure*
- *the UK industrial base produces largely low value products that are prone to competition from overseas*
- *investment in the public sector has been low, patchy and unsustained*
- *without a flourishing public sector, there is little support for the private sector*

On a positive note, there has been considerable external investment in the UK from Japan and other countries such as Germany (in the form of BMW's purchase of Rover for example). This has substantially modernised certain areas of the industrial base. One of the difficulties is that the recoveries seen in recent years are not based on really firm improvements, things could go badly wrong once again.

The main areas of specialism are:

- *banking, insurance and financial (s)*
- *business services (s)*
- *trading services (s)*
- *chemicals (m)*
- *pharmaceuticals (m)*
- *aircraft (m)*
- *office machinery and computers (m)*
- *telecommunications (m)*
- *publishing (m)*
- *electrical plant and machinery (m)*
- *brewing and soft drinks (m)*
- *oil products (e)*

1.3.3 Compare working conditions for employees in different organisations

1.3.4 Present results of investigation into employment, or comparison of working conditions

Compare working conditions

Working conditions within an organisation can differ, depending on an employee's department, site or rank. Factors which may differ include the technology used, the physical surroundings or the number of people with whom the employee works. Furthermore, individuals' qualifications and skills differ, as do the ways in which these are used in the context of a specific job. Obviously, the way in which individuals are paid and how much they are paid is controlled by the organisation's policy, and government legislation may also have an impact on conditions. Individuals' training requirements and needs may differ, as may their opportunities to gain new qualifications and training.

The basic physical working conditions are governed by health and safety rules. In addition, it has long been accepted that employees work much better if the employer takes note of the following:

- *that the workplace is well lit*
- *that the workplace is kept at a constant temperature, regardless of the weather*
- *that the workplace is pleasant and well decorated*
- *that efforts are made to encourage health and fitness and to reduce sickness*
- *that the hours worked can be flexible to take account of employees' external commitments*
- *that the workforce receives regular training and the opportunity to gain qualifications*
- *that the acquisition or use of skills is rewarded either financially or in terms of improved promotion prospects*
- *that with age, additional payments are made to encourage experienced workers to stay with the organisation*
- *that trade unions are recognised and there is a regular dialogue with them*
- *that, above all, pay and conditions should be attractive and competitive*

Having said all of this, there is a vast difference in how the points are adopted by individual employers. The physical working conditions of an individual in an administrative job are very different from an individual working on the factory floor in industry. The former will enjoy relatively luxurious conditions, perhaps with carpets, window blinds, comfortable seating and a clean environment. In a factory, you may find a completely different set of conditions. The environment may be dirty and noisy, the employee may be on his/her feet all day, the job may be physically demanding and the hours long.

Examination of the nature of jobs in the different sectors of industry will show a wide variety of working conditions. Industrial working conditions could pose the following questions:

- *Where is the work?*
- *Is the work outside or inside?*
- *Is the environment hot or cold?*
- *Does the employee work on his/her own?*
- *Is there much opportunity for contact throughout the day?*
- *Do the hours differ?*
- *Is there a requirement to work shifts?*
- *Is the environment clean?*
- *Should the employee have regular health checks?*
- *How safe is the job?*
- *How physically demanding is the job?*
- *Is there a risk of injury?*
- *Does the employee have to wear protective clothing?*

Individual activity

Time: 1 hour

PC 1.3.3
C 2.2
IT 2.1
IT 2.2
IT 2.3

Assess the working conditions in the following occupations:

- a butcher
- a sales representative
- a sales assistant in a shop
- a nurse

When you have considered all of the above occupations, choose one in particular and word process a report on your findings and opinions.

Travel to work (time, cost)

An individual employee's ability to switch from one job to another is largely dependent upon his/her experience, skills and training. Clerical workers, for example, have highly transferable skills. In many respects, administrative work, although the function of the organisations may be different, is essentially the same. Equally, a builder is not restricted to the construction of homes. To a large degree the skills employed in such construction work are the same, regardless of the building involved.

Those individuals which have particularly specialist or unique skills may find it significantly more difficult to obtain alternative employment. They may need expensive retraining before they can be considered for alternative employment.

If individuals consider that they are neither qualified nor experienced to undertake alternative employment, or if the incentive to move is not sufficient, then certain organisations or industries may experience labour shortages. In this respect, the organisation must turn to existing employees and encourage them to consider retraining programmes.

Particularly in economic situations where individuals are unwilling or unable to consider being 'mobile' because they fear the risk of making an expensive move which might not actually work, the organisation may have to resort to more drastic methods of attracting employees. One would think that in situations where there is high unemployment certain employees would be very easy to recruit. This may be the case for semi-skilled or unskilled workers. However, when we consider skilled employees, an attractive pay and 'perks' package may have to be offered to encourage them.

In times of low unemployment, an organisation is faced with having to compete with other organisations for a relatively small number of available potential employees. Again, as is the case with the more skilled workers in times of high unemployment, the employer must offer significantly better pay and conditions in order to attract new staff.

Physical conditions, hours of work, pay (wages, extra payments), safety and job security

The use of non-standard contracts has come about as a result of the economic recession experienced in recent years. In addition to this, organisations have had to cope with an increasingly competitive international market, and as a result there has been a level of uncertainty regarding the demand for their products and services. To this end, fixed short-term contracts have become quite common in order to allow the employer to make only a short-term commitment to the employee. In this way the employer is able to increase or decrease employee numbers as a quick response to changes in demand.

Fixed short-term contracts of employment

Termination of a fixed short-term contract is normally regarded as dismissal in legal terms. However, providing both parties agree to exclude the employee's right to redundancy payment (assuming that the fixed term contract is for two years or more), and also to waive the right for compensation for unfair dismissal (providing the contract was for over one year), this means that fixed short-term contracts are flexible and attractive to both employer and employee.

In essence, fixed short-term contracts not only provide the employer with the opportunity to respond to short-term fluctuations in demand, but also to deal with projects or tasks on a one-off basis, or to bring in specialists to carry out a particular function. Areas which have significantly increased their use of fixed short-term contracts are:

- *health*
- *education*
- *distribution*

In fact, most public sector organisations find that the fixed short-term contract allows them to reduce their long-term commitments in the knowledge that their potential future budgets may not be wholly predictable.

Long-term contracts

Having said that fixed short-term contracts are finding considerable favour with some employers and employees, long-term contracts are still the norm. These open-ended contractual agreements form the most common basis which establishes the relationship between the employer and the employee.

There have been some changes and clarifications made which act as a guide to employers in the formulation of contracts of employment.

Pay

The changing nature of contracts obviously has an impact upon the pay received by the employee. One of the more obvious impacts is that the employee is only paid for hours worked. While this arrangement may be beneficial to the employer, it does mean that the employee cannot predict his/her income beyond the short term. The nature of these new contracts may mean that the employee has only guaranteed work for limited periods of time. These work periods may be punctuated with considerable amounts of unemployment. While flexible working conditions and their relationship to pay may allow the organisation to budget more accurately for particular contracts or projects, the employee is faced with the prospect of having to seek work elsewhere. For the employee, this makes it very difficult to plan any long-term financial commitments, such as a mortgage or a loan. Without guaranteed work and the pay associated with it, financial institutions would be unwilling to risk significant loans.

Benefits

While the majority of benefits are protected by government legislation, there is something of a grey area relating to part-time or casual workers. Broadly speaking, they are disadvantaged in the sense that they may not be entitled to sick pay or holiday pay. Short periods of work may equally not be sufficient to qualify for statutory benefit payments by the DSS or, indeed, the Unemployment Benefit Office. The specifics of these benefits are as follows.

Holiday pay

In comparison with all other major European countries, the UK has possibly the most meagre level of both public holidays and annual statutory leave entitlement. In fact, under current legislation, there is no annual statutory leave entitlement in the UK. The only other European country which does not have statutory annual leave entitlement is Italy.

In the European league table of holiday entitlement and public holidays, the UK is firmly bottom (*see* Table 1.2). Spain leads the table with a total of 38 days (25 days minimum annual leave plus 13 public holidays). The vast majority of countries, if we include both annual leave and public holidays, give in excess of 25 days. This leaves the UK's 8 public holidays, plus annual leave entitlement on a rather low, but sliding scale, dependent upon years worked.

Organisations have taken advantage of the high rates of unemployment in order to institute relatively low holiday pay entitlements. Indeed, part-time workers, temporary workers and those on fixed short-term contracts may find that they have no paid holiday entitlement at all.

Employees, particularly those working on an hourly-rate basis, have to decide between the cost of working and the consequent loss of leisure time as against the payment received for that work. This is an example of opportunity cost, as, if the employee works extra hours they lose leisure time but, conversely, by taking leisure time they lose wages.

The Social Charter, as proposed by the EU, was intended to improve working conditions and to attempt to harmonise them throughout Europe. The UK not only requires its employees to work longer hours (an average of 43.6 hours per week) but, as we have said, offers far less paid holiday entitlement.

Sick pay

Employers have to pay a minimum amount of sick pay to employees aged 16 or above, if they have been off sick for more than four consecutive days. Statutory Sick Pay (SSP) is paid by the employer just like normal pay. The employer is required by law to keep records of absences due to sickness and the payment of SSP for inspection by inspectors from the Department of Social Security.

Maternity pay

Although not strictly speaking sick pay, we should include Statutory Maternity Pay here. There are fairly strict rules governing the payment of this benefit.

Maternity pay and leave varies between the different countries of the EU. Perhaps the most generous country is Denmark, which allows leave of six months for both parents. In the UK there is no entitlement for the father to claim paternity leave unless the employer is sufficiently enlightened and prepared to allow this benefit.

Obviously, considering the enormous pressure on the UK's budget, steps have been taken not only to attempt to reduce sick pay and maternity payments, but also to ensure that payments are not made in error or fraudulent claims made.

In 1993 an investigation was undertaken by a House of Commons Watchdog Committee, under the supervision of the then Social Security Secretary, Peter Lilley. The investigation discovered that there were some 70 000 errors in the payment of Statutory Sick Pay and Statutory Maternity Pay. The total cost of this was in excess of £250m. This amounted to nearly 30% of all payments. The payment of SSP and SMP costs the UK something in excess of £1bn per year.

Redundancy

The vast number of redundancies in the latter half of the 1980s and early 1990s brought many problems to the UK. Long-term unemployed, middle-aged former employees swamped the job market just as employers froze recruitment and employment prospects. The consequent effects on health, law and order, not to mention marriages, proved to be an increased cost which the UK had to fund. This form of unemployment is both disastrous to the individual and to the economy in general. There are strict rules and regulations governing termination of employment and whether it is redundancy, as well as redundancy payments themselves.

Many organisations employed the last-in, first-out system to identify potential redundancy candidates. This is a reasonable way of approaching the problem, but employers should also be aware of the employee's skills, length of employment service, performance and many other factors.

Personnel units within organisations were inundated with requests for counselling by individuals selected for redundancy during the mid-1980s to early 1990s. Working closely with both local and central government agencies, they attempted to find alternative employment for the redundant individuals. Retraining was essential as the individuals in most cases needed to acquire or improve their skills in order to match the local job market.

Redundancy packages which, in effect, encouraged individuals to accept either voluntary redundancy or early retirement, were fairly attractive. The lump sums involved often ran into many thousands of pounds, with the prospect of also receiving pension enhancements which would further buffer the drastic effect of unemployment. Many individuals reinvested, in some cases unwisely, in businesses of their own, only to discover that their new business was not able to survive the recession. Organisations paying out redundancy payments are entitled to rebates which may encourage them to offer more generous lump sums and enhanced pension benefits.

One of the implications of changing working conditions is that employees are expected to be far more flexible in their approach to work and availability for work. Principal areas included in this are hours worked, location of the work, work space available, multi-skilling needs and job sharing opportunities.

Table 1.2 European employment law – a comparison of rights and responsibilities

	Contract of employment	*Dismissal*	*Grievance*	*Redundancy*	*Working hours*	*Equality*	*Trade unions*
Austria	Salaries paid in 14 instalments. After 5 years contracts may be terminated with 6 months' notice.	Reasons include: disloyalty, disobedience, competing (privately) with employer.	If unfairly dismissed up to 3 months' wages to be paid.	Details must be given to Labour Authority, including age, sex, responsibilities and qualifications, for appraisal.	Working Time Act states hours not to exceed 8 per day or 40 per week. Even with overtime, hours must not exceed 50 per week.	Equal Treatment Act covers sexual discrimination, and covers all areas of work. Employer must prove discrimination did not occur.	Only one trade union body is recognised – Austrian Federation of TUs. This organisation is responsible for collective agreements.
Belgium	Includes a probationary period (1–12 months). No written contract is required by law.	Providing notice is given, either party may terminate the contract.	Under the Belgian law on employment contracts no reason is required for dismissal.	Formula includes: length of service difficulties in finding a new job, age, job role and salary.			
France	Can be written or oral. If these contradict one another, then the situation most favourable to the employee is taken. Also may include a trial period.	Reasons include: incompetence, long-term illness, age, retirement, gross misconduct, economic problems.	Whether personal or economic reasons for dismissal, employee may ask for an industrial tribunal to hear the case.	Certain protection for older employed with families or for single parents and disabled. Also redundant employees have priority if employer recruits within a year.	Normal working week is 39 hrs, although employees can work for up to 46 hrs per week for a 12-week period.	In 1983 new laws covered sexual discrimination and restrictions relating to family status in all aspects of work.	Five main nationally recognised bodies to undertake collective bargaining. Employer must supply meeting rooms if over 200 employees are union members. Shop stewards allocated paid time.
Germany	Usually written, normal contractual obligations. 18 days' minimum holiday entitlement. Payment is made in 13, 14 or 15 instalments.	Long notice periods, specified usually in contract of employment. Normal dismissal reasons.	Heard in the employment court. Total compensation does not usually exceed DM 36 000.		Mainly 35 hours per week. Also working day must have regular breaks. Prohibits work on Sundays or public holidays.	Federal law forbids discrimination. Violation means automatic fines and compensation.	When collective agreements are made, the Federal Minister of Labour regards them as 'binding'. All employees (regardless of TU membership) are bound by them.
Greece	Includes a 2-month trial period. Normal contractual obligations. Salaries paid in 14 instalments.	Phased dismissal procedures. Also includes temporary dismissal.	Employee can challenge validity of dismissal, etc. If not legal then employee can demand reinstatement and back pay.	Providing legal compensation is paid, although employer must take into account seniority and family commitments.	Usually 40 hours per week. Employer may require employees to 'overwork' an extra 8 hours with higher rate of pay.	No discrimination allowed on the grounds of sex, race, religion, etc.	Collective agreements made locally or nationally. Trade union officials legally protected. Court of Arbitration called in if dispute is unprovable; then judgment is legally binding on both parties.

Eire	Very comprehensive legislation covering contracts. Reasonably long notice periods.	Wrongful dismissal outlawed. Statutory compensation of up to 104 weeks' pay.	Claims made through either Rights Commissioners or Employment Appeals Tribunal. Complex legislation.	If employee has worked for at least 104 weeks, then compensation is due. No rules regarding choice of redundant employees.	Covered under Conditions of Employment Act and Protection of Young Persons (Employment) Act.	Many laws, including Anti-discrimination (Pay) Act, Employ-ment Quality Act, and Promotion of Equality Employment.	Industrial Relations Act 1990 required pre-strike ballots, and establishment of Labour Relations Commission (covering conciliation and advice).
Italy	Oral or in writing. Fixed-term contracts last a minimum of 5 years. Also includes trial period.	Normal reasons, but does not protect the over 60s, those in trial period, housekeepers and executives.	Claims through arbitration boards if up to 22 months' pay.	Complex, but may entitle employee to up to 80% of salary or to be considered 'early retired'.	Normally no more than 8 hours per day, 48 hours per week.	Comprehensive, particularly in relation to sex, equality and the disabled.	Not normally recognised, but nearly always consulted.
Luxembourg	In writing and in duplicate. All other normal contractual obligations. Long notice periods.	By law, employee must be interviewed before dismissal. Otherwise usual reasons apply.	Court of appeal hears complaints and imposes judgments.	Usually for economic reasons.	Standard 40 hours over 5 days. Overtime must be agreed by the Minister of Labour.	Law considers that equality is expected. Minimum salaries apply regardless of sex.	Collective agreements run for 6 months or more. Trade unions recognised and must be part of negotiations to make a collective agreement.
The Netherlands	Maximum 2-month trial period; fairly simple contract of employment.	Employment controls cannot be terminated without a permit from the district labour office.	The National Court will settle blame and require compensation be paid. This is called a 'golden handshake'.	Employment contracts can be terminated by mutual consent and agreement of the Judge of the Court.	Dutch Act on employment states maximum 15 hours to be worked overtime.		Quite powerful collective bargaining agreements are made legally by the Dutch Ministry of Social Affairs and Employment.
Portugal	Normal contractual obligations. Written contract required for temporary or for permanent work. 15–30 day probation period.	Notification of reasons within 30 days. Trade union must be informed.	If deemed unfair, employer pays salary from dismissal date to date of court hearing.	Normally one month's salary for each year or part-year worked.	Normally 8 hours per day, 48 hours per week, or for clerical staff 7 hours and 42 hours.	Legislation covers sex discrimination, the disabled and students.	Both worker committees and trade unions, the latter involved in industrial actions, etc. Strike notice required.
Spain	Written or oral. All main contractual obligations. Variable trial periods.	'Serious and blameworthy non-fulfilment by employee'. Normal reasons apply.	If dismissal is unlawful, then the employer makes a payment of 45 days' pay per year employed or may have to re-employ.	Normally 20 days salary per year worked.	Normally 40 hours per week. No more than 80 hours' overtime per year paid at 17.5% usual pay.	Statute of Workers covers sex, race, marital status, religion, politics and trade union membership.	Key role in collective bargaining. Trade unions seen as vital to economic prosperity. Collective agreement legally binding.
UK	Usually written, particularly in the case of redundant employment (13 weeks maximum and in writing).	Many legitimate reasons, including misconduct, capability or any other 'substantial' reason.	Employee may use an industrial tribunal. Maximum rewards vary, but between £6000–£10 000 or up to 52 weeks' pay.	Complex calculation. Dependent upon years worked and rate.	No limitations except for those under 18 or in specific occupations.	Unlawful to discriminate in term of gender, marital status, race, membership of trade union.	Collective agreements not necessarily legally binding. Individuals, particularly, not bound by collective agreements.

Career opportunities and training opportunities

Organisations risk failure if they do not appreciate the need for constant reappraisal of their use of technology. Equally, if employees are unwilling or unable to adopt new working practices, the same net result may occur.

Many organisations have embraced the use of computers and information technology, regardless of the type or function of the organisation. In retailing, for example, the availability of the electronic point of sale system has revolutionised retail selling and stock control. It was viewed with considerable suspicion by employees and organisations themselves before they realised the benefits it offered. Rather than simply reducing the number of employees (after all, items do not have to be individually priced any more), employees are now free to undertake a wider variety of tasks and more interesting activities.

It is perhaps in the field of communications that technology has had the greatest impact. The flexibility and swiftness of telecommunications, in particular, has enabled organisations to collect, store and evaluate information effectively and efficiently.

For manufacturing organisations, technology has enabled them to reduce their costs of production and institute Just-in-Time methods of stock control (which means that they do not have to hold large quantities of stock as they are able to produce finished goods very quickly). This has been coupled with the introduction of robotics on the production line, further reducing the need to disrupt employee working patterns in order to fulfil rush jobs.

With any change in working conditions there may be a need to train, retrain or refresh individuals' understanding and knowledge. Factored into the overall implementation

Fig 1.17 A personal computer with a touch-sensitive screen

plan should be a rolling programme of training. Obviously, dependent upon the nature of the change in working conditions, more or less training will be involved. In the field of health and safety, particularly relating to new legislation, significant amounts of training may be required. If, for example, individuals are required to wear protective clothing or maintain equipment, then this may have a significant impact upon the productivity for a short period of time.

If new equipment or machinery has been installed to be used in the manufacturing process, again significant retraining may have to be undertaken. It is often the case that the suppliers of new equipment include in their quotation to the purchasing organisation a basic training programme for all operators or users of the machinery.

Use of new technology

Many organisations may have to consider radical restructuring as a result of the need to introduce new technology into their day-to-day routines or production processes. As we have said earlier, if an organisation fails to introduce technology at a time when their competitors are doing so, then they risk falling behind in the market. Obviously, employees will be required to embrace the new technology as it is introduced and may have to accept new structures and working practices.

It is, perhaps, in the field of administration that information technology has had the greatest impact. Organisational structures have had to be seriously overhauled, with many traditional administrative posts being made 'redundant' as a result of the introduction of desk top technology. In the past, in any organisational structure, you would find copy typists and other more routine processing posts which are now replaced by word processor operators using machines with the facility to store, retrieve and amend documents by simply using single key strokes.

Telecommunications have enabled organisations to streamline their structures and allowed remote sites to be in direct contact through audio, visual and text communication systems.

Organisational structures have also been affected in relation to production, with the introduction of automation and robotics. This has meant that many of the routine and repetitive production jobs have disappeared, making the organisational structure in this area of the business less complex.

The introduction of new technology does have some short-term problems for an organisation. They may find themselves in a position where they are unable to find or attract sufficiently experienced staff. Indeed, if the technology is sufficiently new, these new staff may not exist. In this situation, a forward-looking organisation will have appreciated this concern and have taken steps to institute retraining programmes.

New skills can also be identified as opportunities for individuals to embrace a new occupation, providing they are aware of the technological advances. In some respects, this proactive approach can ensure that the individual is well placed to take advantage of short-term skills shortages. An organisation will be only too happy to acquire the services of such individuals, albeit for a relatively short time.

Even in the most mundane forms of occupation, technological advances may not be the only reason for new skills development. Simple changes in procedure may not in the organisation's terms require significant re-skilling of their employees. However, in

Fig 1.18 Robots applying spots of adhesive to a car bonnet

practice any such implementation of new procedures will involve a certain level of retraining. In these cases, both the organisation and the employee need to be flexible. The organisation should be patient and allow the employee to 'catch up' with new developments and the employee should be prepared to spend time and effort in acquiring these new skills and knowledge.

Increasingly, as we have mentioned earlier, the multi-skilling of employees can be a solution to short-term potential skill shortages. These adaptable and flexible employees should be able and willing to adopt new procedures and learn to use new technology.

PC 1.3.3
C 2.1

Group activity

Time: 15 minutes

As a group, try to assess the importance of the reasons for change in working conditions as detailed above. Which of the reasons do you consider to be of the greatest importance? Try to reach some consensus within the group.

Element 1.3 Assignment

PC 1.3.1–4
C 2.1
C 2.2
C 2.3
C 2.4
IT 2.1
IT 2.2
IT 2.3

In this assignment you will be looking at the different types of employment in the UK and more widely in the rest of the EU. You will be expected to analyse the differences between two regions of the EU, including the UK. You will have to do a considerable amount of research, but the sources that we have mentioned in this Element should prove to be a good start for you.

Task 1 PC 1.3.1

Identify and describe the seven main types of employment. These should include the following:

- full time
- part time
- permanent
- temporary
- skilled
- unskilled
- self-employed

You should present your summaries of these types of employment as a word-processed document.

Task 2 PC 1.3.2

Word process a summary which analyses employment information about two EU regions, one of which should be the UK. You should include a graph which shows the percentage of individuals employed, addressing the following:

- the gender of the employed
- the age of the employed
- the sector in which they work

You should also include a description and analysis which looks at the reasons why there may have been shifts from one sector of the economy to another.

Task 3 PC 1.3.3

In a word-processed short report, describe and compare the working conditions of two individuals that work for different organisations. You should particularly consider the following:

- their hours of work
- their career opportunities
- their training opportunities
- their use of new technology

Task 4 *PC 1.3.1*

In the final part of your assignment, you must prepare to undertake an oral presentation. This should be supported by visual aids. It should focus on two different EU regions and include the following:

- the percentages of individuals employed
- the employment opportunities in both regions

Notes

You will find the following sources of information very useful when tackling the assignment:

- the Economic Development Unit (which can be accessed via your local authority)
- the TEC (Training Enterprise Council) or LEC (Local Enterprise Council) which covers your region
- the Chambers of Commerce operating in your region

UNIT 1 Revision questions

1 What is meant by the private sector of the economy?

2 What is meant by the term 'limited liability'?

3 How is a partnership set up and run?

4 Give three major decision makers of an organisation.

5 What is meant by franchising?

6 Why does the government interfere in the running of the economy?

7 Who are the decision makers in a public corporation?

8 What is meant by the primary sector?

9 What is meant by the secondary sector?

10 What is meant by the tertiary sector?

11 What are the major differences between a planned economy and a free market economy?

12 Ignoring profit, give three other objectives of a private company.

13 What is meant by privatisation?

14 What is meant by nationalisation?

15 How does a wholesaler differ from a retailer?

16 Which transportation system is the cheaper in terms of insurance: sea or air. Why?

17 Identify three major differences between a private limited company and a public limited company.

18 Identify three advantages enjoyed by a partnership over a sole trader.

19 What is the difference between a multinational and an international organisation?

20 Give three advantages of being part of a co-operative organisation.

21 What do you understand by the term 'multiple'?

22 What do you understand by the term 'multinational'?

23 What do you understand by the term 'conglomerate'?

24 Give three main resource requirements of a manufacturing business.

25 What is an enterprise agency?

26 Give three location criteria for a financial services organisation.

27 In your own words, explain the term 'market share'.

28 What figures would you need to consider when determining market share?

29 How do the needs of a customer and the wants of a customer differ?

30 In terms of location, how do a manufacturing organisation and a service organisation differ?

31 What is the average size of an organisation in terms of employees?

32 For a food processing organisation, located in a remote area, list three transport considerations.

33 Give two reasons for superstores being located in out-of-town sites.

34 Identify three areas currently receiving government help and incentives to attract businesses.

35 What particular services would a shipbuilding organisation require?

36 What particular services would a book printing organisation require?

37 Which do you think gives a better indication as to size of organisation: the number of employees, or their market share? Give two reasons for your answer.

38 How might a local authority attract businesses into an area?

39 What are the advantages of a business locating in an area which already houses organisations in a similar business activity?

40 What are the major differences between part-time and temporary employment?

41 What is the average working week in terms of hours for a full-time employee in the UK?

42 Identify six physical working conditions in a manufacturing organisation.

43 Identify six physical working conditions in an administrative organisation.

44 List three items appearing on a contract of employment.

45 How soon does a contract of employment have to be issued to a new employee?

46 What is meant by vocational training?

47 What is meant by non-vocational training?

48 List four available sources of incentives for organisations to locate in particular areas.

49 List three natural resources commonly found in the North of England.

50 Identify two manufacturing industries commonly found in the South West of England.

UNIT 1 End test questions

Focus 1 – Business organisations

1 A public limited company is an organisation which:
- **a** is owned by shareholders
- **b** is owned by the government
- **c** has shares sold on the Stock Exchange
- **d** provides services free of charge to those in need

2 Which of the following is a feature of a sole trader?
- **a** there is only one employee
- **b** it is owned by more than one person
- **c** it is owned by one person
- **d** it only produces one type of product

3 Which of the following is an example of a franchise operation?
- **a** a charitable organisation
- **b** a business which sells the right to trade under its name to businesses in different locations
- **c** a co-operative organisation
- **d** an organisation which is owned by several people

4 A private limited company is an organisation which:
- **a** makes a profit for its shareholders
- **b** is owned by the government
- **c** is a charitable organisation
- **d** is a co-operative organisation

5 Which of the following organisations is non-profit making?
- **a** a multinational organisation
- **b** a wholesaler
- **c** a charity
- **d** a sole trader

6 What are the minimum and maximum numbers of partners allowed in a partnership?
- **a** 2–3
- **b** 2–20
- **c** 2–10
- **d** 2–5

Focus 2 – Industrial sectors

7 Identify which of the following organisations is not in the private sector.
- **a** Sainsburys
- **b** British Telecom
- **c** Dixons
- **d** British Coal

8 How many of the following are primary sector industries?
- i) coal mining
- ii) gold mining
- iii) waste disposal
- iv) forestry

- **a** One
- **b** Two
- **c** Three
- **d** Four

9 The tertiary sector of industry includes businesses which:
- **a** manufacture goods
- **b** sell goods
- **c** build vessels
- **d** grow vegetables

10 Which of the following businesses is located in the secondary sector?
- **a** car sales
- **b** car manufacture
- **d** car servicing
- **d** car insurance

Focus 3 – Business locations

11 The best location for a garden centre would be:
- **a** a town centre
- **b** near a port
- **c** near a source of raw materials
- **d** on the edge of a large town

12 A location on the edge of town would be an ideal location for:
- **a** a power station
- **b** a newsagent
- **c** a depot for a wholesaler
- **d** a large chemical plant

13 An organisation has 5 factories based around the UK, one in Greece, and it has recently opened a new factory in Italy. This type of organisation can be described as:

a regional
b national
c European
d multinational

14 What is the difference between a multinational and an international business?

a one is a group of foreign businesses; the other is not
b one has foreign directors; the other does not
c there is no difference
d one produces and sells in many countries; the other just sells

Focus 4 – Markets

15 What does market share mean?

a the fact that several organisations have the whole market
b a shop contains several smaller businesses
c the percentage of the total market controlled by an organisation
d two or more businesses agreeing to help one another

16 A car manufacturer will aim to gain the biggest market share. In relation to its competitors, this means that it will try to:

a produce more cars than its competitors
b sell more cars than its competitors
c make more models than its competitors
d sell more expensive cars than its competitors

17 Which of the following would be used to decide whether there is a need for a product?

a telesales
b new production techniques
c market research
d point of sale material

Focus 5 – Products

18 Which of the following is a service?

a the production of cars
b the building of houses
c banking
d forestry

19 Which of the following is a manufacturer?

a an insurance broker
b a typewriter technician
c a hairdresser
d a furniture maker

20 In order to find out their customers' opinions about their products, an organisation would issue:

a a leaflet advertising goods
b a questionnaire
c information regarding their after-sales service
d information regarding their customer service

21 A manufacturer of clothing should begin to develop their range of winter clothes when?

a April
b October
c December
d August

Focus 6 – Types of employment

22 Which of the following could best be described as seasonal employment?

a full time
b part time
c temporary
d occasional

23 Which of the following could best be described as casual employment?

a full time
b part time
c temporary
d occasional

*Questions 24–26 below share answer options **a** to **d**.*

The main types of employment are:

a self-employed
b full time
c temporary
d part time

Which of the following are likely to be in which category?

24 The manager of a large retail outlet.

25 A builder.

26 A bar attendant working three evenings per week.

Focus 7 – Working conditions

27 Which of the following must be given to the employee by the employer?
- **a** details of social club membership
- **b** details of the profit and loss of the organisation
- **c** a contract of employment
- **d** a copy of all organisational documentation

28 Who is responsible for health and safety regulations?
- **a** the employer
- **b** the employee
- **c** both the employer and the employee
- **d** the insurance company

29 Potential hazards within the work place would normally be covered by which of the following pieces of legislation?
- **a** the Health and Safety at Work Act
- **b** the Consumer Protection Act
- **c** the Sale of Goods Act
- **d** the Trade Descriptions Act

30 An employer must provide an employee with which of the following?
- **a** suitable protective clothing
- **b** an organisational chart
- **c** details of new machinery to be purchased
- **d** details of new employees

Unit 2

PEOPLE IN BUSINESS ORGANISATIONS

Element 2.1
Examine and compare structures and working arrangements in organisations

Element 2.2
Investigate employee and employer responsibilities and rights

Element 2.3
Present results of investigation into job roles

Element 2.4
Prepare for employment and self-employment

Element 2.1
Examine and compare structures and working arrangements in organisations

Performance criteria

A student must:

1 describe **organisational structures**

2 produce organisational charts showing **departments**

3 describe the work and explain the interdependence of **departments** within business organisations

4 identify and explain **differences in working arrangements**

5 explain and give examples of **reasons for change** in working arrangements in one business organisation

Range

- *Organisational structures*: hierarchical, flat, matrix
- *Departments*: research & development, production, purchasing, accounting, human resources (personnel), marketing, sales, administration, computer (IT) services, customer services, distribution (logistics)
- *Differences in working arrangements*: in terms of: team working, centralised, de-centralised, flexible (shift, flexi-hours), contracts (fixed term, permanent), workbase (office, factory, shop, outdoors, home, mobile)
- *Reasons for change*: productivity, quality assurance, competition, technology

2.1.1 Describe organisational structures

There are many factors which influence the organisational structure of a business or enterprise. In order to appreciate the important demands which an organisation must fulfil, we must look at private and public sector organisations separately.

Private sector organisations

Factors which affect private sector organisations include:

1 **The number of employees** – in effect the actual size of the organisation.

2 **The type of premises used** – a multi-site or split-site organisation with a number of different branches would need to be organised in a radically different manner from an organisation which is based in a single building

– an organisation which is regional, national or international will base its organisational structure around logically grouped employees.

3 **The type of business**

- *Primary sector* If the organisation is in the primary sector, it is likely to be organised in such a way as to allow the efficient processing of the raw materials, and so may be based around a single mine, forest or quarry.
- *A manufacturing organisation* may either carry out all its processing procedures on a single site, or may need to transport partly-finished goods to other specialist sites. Organisations in this case may be based on the single factory unit, or a cluster of factories which contribute towards the finishing of a product.
- *Distribution organisations* tend to be organised around a regional, national or international framework. Depending on the bulk of goods being distributed, the organisational structure will be complex in certain geographical areas and more simple in others. In other words, if the organisation is busy in one area, its size and complexity will reflect this. As with many organisations, good communications between the regions is vital and a separate part of the organisational structure may concentrate on dealing with this area.
- *In the retailing sector* the obvious organisational structure is that of the branch. However, many functions of the business are carried out centrally. These services tend to be of a managerial, financial or buying nature, which allows the individual branches to concentrate on the selling process.
- *Professional services* tend to operate on the basis of a number of specialist individuals who are assisted by a variety of support staff. Often these support staff are drawn from a 'pool' of clerical and secretarial employees.

4 **The number, type and company size of the clients may have a bearing on the organisational structure.** If the organisation deals with only a handful of clients, then the structure need not be overly complex. On the other hand, if it is dealing with millions of retail customers, then the demands on the structure may be greater.

5 **The past structure of the organisation and its history may be a good or bad influence on how it is structured.** An old-fashioned organisation which has successfully managed to survive for many years may not see the need to change its structure. It may not

appreciate the benefits of reorganisation and may be structured in such a way as to prevent the possibility of growth or adaptation to new demands.

6 **The current structure of an organisation can be a positive or negative influence on the day-to-day running of the business.** If the organisation has recently undergone changes, it will be unlikely to adapt to further changes without encountering considerable problems.

7 **Future needs of an organisation should directly influence its structure.** The need constantly to react to changing demands, diversify into new areas and respond to changes in legislation are all strong reasons to consider how the organisation is structured.

PC 2.1.1
C 2.1
C 2.2
C 2.3
AN 2.1
AN 2.2
AN 2.3

Group activity

In pairs, research a local organisation belonging to the private sector. Your main aim is to look at the organisational structure and try to draw up an organisation chart. You may also wish to look at the next group activity on page 110 as you may be required to look at the job functions of various employees in that activity.

It may be useful for you and your partner to consider any work experience, Saturday work or vacation work you have undertaken in the past.

Your chart should include as many individual employees as possible. It would also be useful to indicate on the chart the hierarchy of the organisation, showing where decisions are made and who implements them.

When you have completed your chart, compare this with other charts drawn up by other members of the group.

Public sector organisations

1 *The duties and responsibilities* of the organisation will directly affect the way in which it is structured. The more diverse and complex its operations, the more complicated the structure will be. It may also be required by law to provide certain additional services (e.g. an information office) and monitoring services to keep a constant check on spending and budget control.

2 *The geographical extent* of the organisation's responsibility will not only affect the size of the organisation, but also its structure. From the smallest parish to the organisation responsible nationally for delivering a range of services, we can see some basic similarities, but obviously the former is far less complex than the latter. Other types of organisation which can be identified by their size are borough, district, town, city, county and region.

3 *The ever-changing government policies* that impact upon the running of public sector organisations may well influence the structure of the organisation. In recent years, Rate Departments transformed into Community Charge Departments, then into Council Tax Departments, meaning rapid reorganisation, retraining and redeployment of staff.

4 *The amount of income* that the organisation has, which may come directly from central government or from payments made by the public, will determine the complexity of the structure. In cases when much of the finance is collected by the organisation itself, large departments may be solely responsible for collection of money. In addition, the

organisation must have other departments which oversee the services provided to the public.

5 *Technological change* has had a general impact on all types of organisation. Many have developed complex and sophisticated computer systems in order to handle as many of the routine tasks as possible. The availability of computers and their relative fall in price has made them accessible to even the smallest types of public sector organisation.

6 *The public* makes many more demands on public sector organisations than in the past. One of the most significant is the public's interest in how and why decisions are made on its behalf. Public sector organisations must therefore be ready, willing and able to provide a wide variety of information instantly and on demand. Public Relations Departments and Liaison Officers have become common in nearly all public sector organisations. Meetings are nearly always open to the public, with information packs available on request.

7 As in the private sector, public sector organisations are finding it increasingly difficult to operate in isolation. Many factors which influence the decision making in a private organisation also apply to the public sector. Important decisions may have been made nationally or internationally that public sector organisations cannot ignore, and therefore the structure needs to be flexible enough to cope.

8 Some public sector organisations may have direct contact with the public. Those which provide goods, services or advisory assistance will need to devote part of their activity to this area. Those which do provide these types of services are similar in many ways to either private sector manufacturing or retailing organisations. A great many public sector organisations, however, only have minimal direct contact with the public.

Group activity

PC 2.1.1
C 2.1
C 2.2
C 2.3
AN 2.1
AN 2.2
AN 2.3

This is a similar task to the previous one. Remaining in the same pairs, first identify a public sector organisation in your local area. Then try to draw up an organisational chart along the same lines as the one which you completed for the private sector organisation. In all probability this chart for the public sector organisation will be more difficult to complete. There may well be many more employees, departments and functions to consider. If necessary, you may have to draw up additional charts to show the structure of particular departments and how they inter-relate with other departments.

Again, try to show where decisions are made and who must implement them. Once you have done this, compare your private sector chart with this public sector one. You will notice that there are many more layers of decision making in the public sector chart than in the private sector chart. Why do you think this is so?

Types of organisational structures

As we have seen, the structure of an organisation will vary, depending on the nature of a number of factors:

1 *The size and nature of the market in which it operates*
2 *The type of business in which it is involved*
3 *The need for the maintenance of good communications*

4 *The size of the organisation*
5 *The number of branches/outlets/sites*
6 *The type and number of clients*
7 *How much it is affected by government legislation*
8 *The impact of new technologies*
9 *The nature and extent of its responsibilities and obligations*
10 *Its past and current structure*
11 *Its future plans*
12 *The complexity of its business activity*

Before we concentrate on the activities of each individual department, division or unit of an organisation, we must first look at the overall nature of the structure

Individual activity *Time: 25 minutes*

Try to put in ranking order the 12 points made above. Give yourself 10 minutes to think about this. When you have completed this task, compare your list with those of the rest of the group. Try to agree a common ranking order.

PC 2.1.1
C 2.1
C 2.2

Hierarchical structures

The best way to understand what a hierarchical structure looks like is to imagine a pyramid. At the top of the pyramid are the owners or major decision makers of the organisation. If we look further down the pyramid, the shape of the organisation broadens as more employees are involved in that level. At the base of the pyramid will be the majority of the employees and below them are the customers.

Responsibility, power and authority are all much greater at the top of the pyramid than at the bottom. Decisions flow down the pyramid affecting a succession of layers of employees.

This form of structure can also be referred to as 'pecking order' as the higher up the pyramid you are as an employee, the more power and authority you have. Equally, we can see that the lower down the pyramid you are, the less influence you have on the organisation as a whole.

The reason for this hierarchical structure is that important decisions need to be made by those who have expertise and experience along with enough authority to make sure that a decision is implemented. Those at the top of a pyramid take all the credit for success, but also bear the consequences of failure.

Typically, a structure would begin with directors at the top of the pyramid making decisions for heads of departments below to pass on to middle managers, who would then tell the junior members of staff to implement them. The higher up individuals are in the pyramid, the less likely they are to understand how things are implemented. They may just have an idea of overall strategy and base their decisions on information received via the various layers below them. Each time information passes from layer to layer, the relative importance of what has been said may change. It is therefore likely that those at the top of the pyramid will have a distorted view of the organisation and how it really works.

For those at the bottom of the pyramid, the directors will seem remote, unable to understand the organisation's needs and unwilling to change decisions which may adversely affect the day-to-day running of the business.

The main advantage of this structure is that each layer sees the organisation in its own peculiar way. Each layer will have different opinions, priorities and interpretation of overall organisational policy (*see* Fig 2.1).

Flat pyramid structures

Flat structures have reduced the number of layers in the hierarchy (*see* Fig 2.2). The theory behind having less layers in the pyramid is that decisions can be made quickly and efficiently. Each layer is able to communicate easily with the other layers and this avoids the danger of becoming 'bureaucratic' (see below). This simpler, flatter structure is generally found in organisations operating from a single site where directors and other decision makers are readily available for consultation and guidance.

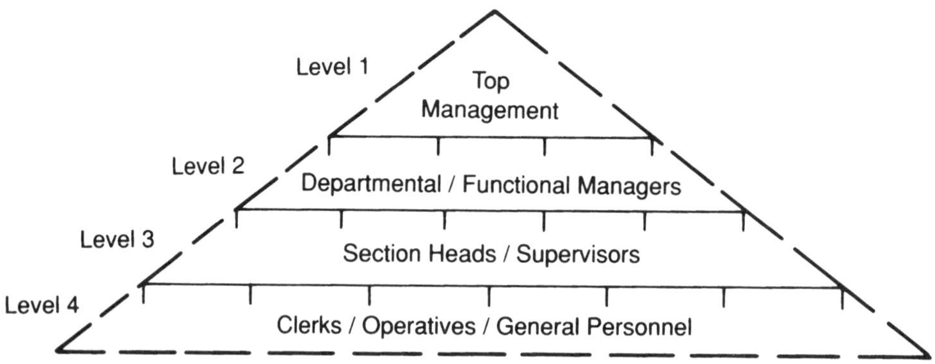

Fig 2.2 The flat pyramid

Steep pyramid structures

In this version of the hierarchical structure, there are many layers of management (*see* Fig 2.3). The reason for this may be that the organisation operates in several locations and needs to duplicate the administration in order to function efficiently. Alternatively, the nature of the business may be very complex, requiring the processing of many documents such as orders, messages, pieces of information or complaints, with checking and authorisation taking place at a number of levels.

Because the structure is multi-layered and complicated, those further down the pyramid find it difficult to understand how and why decisions are made and the organisation may find it impossible to ensure that employees follow through 'corporate decisions' (general statements of policy and procedures). The organisation may also suffer from being 'bureaucratic'. This means that decisions must pass through so many layers that they take a very long time to put into operation, and the systems designed to help implement them become more complicated than they need to be.

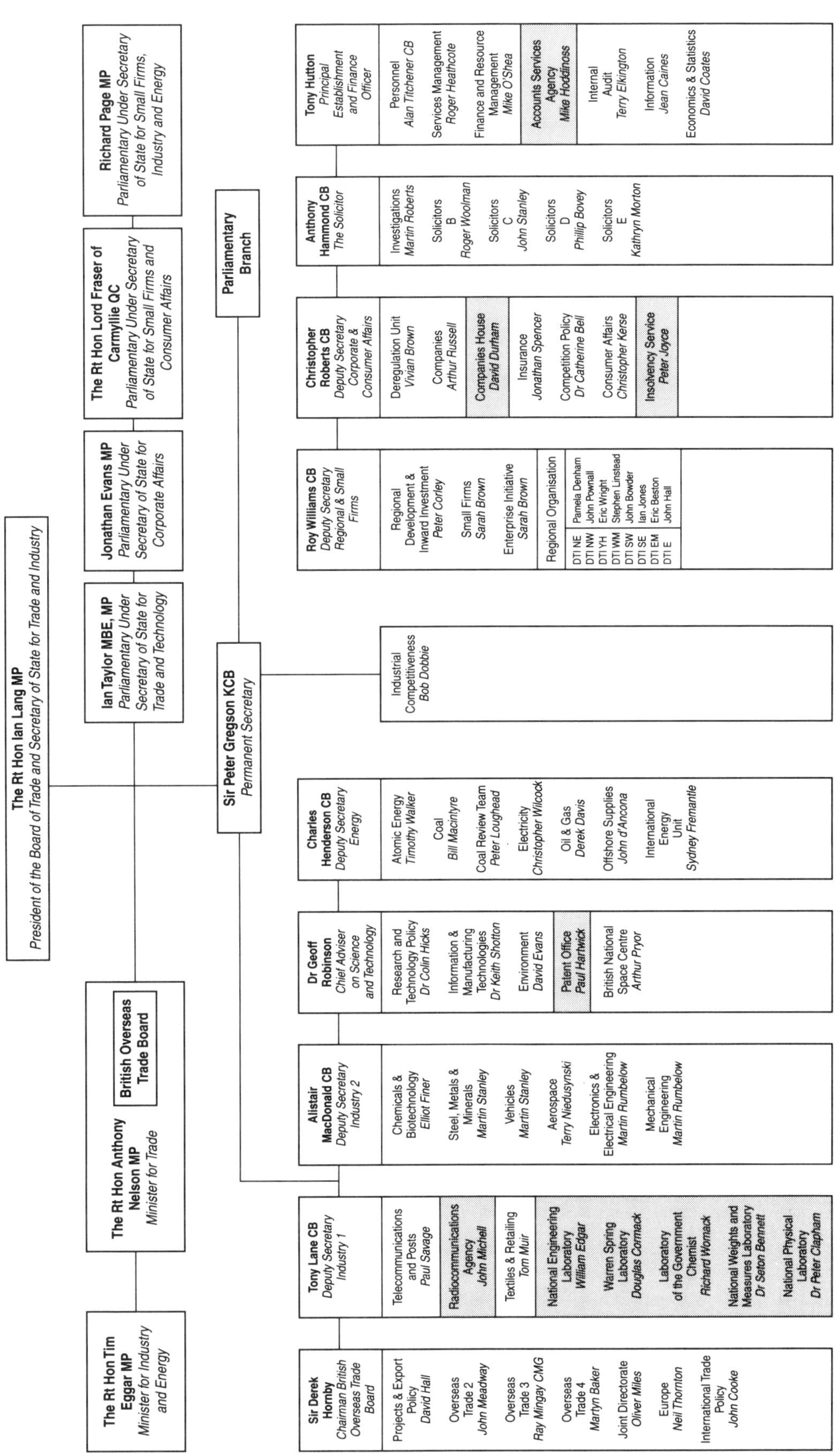

Fig 2.1 The DTI's organisation chart

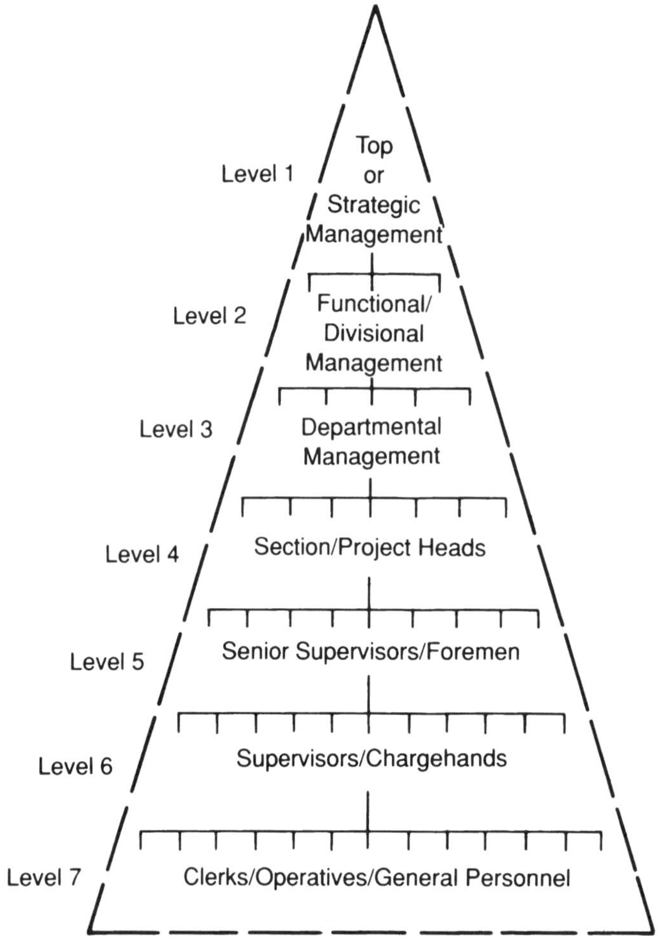

Fig 2.3 The steep pyramid

Cone structures

In recent years, some major organisations have recognised that relying on a pyramid structure has prevented quick and necessary decisions and change from taking place. This new cone form of structure is known commonly as 'decentralisation'. This is the exact opposite to having centralised services which assist individual branches or sites. Each part of the organisation that carries out a distinctly different function in the organisation is given a level of autonomy. This means that each is allowed, up to a point, to make decisions for itself without the permission or consent of the directors or the central office. This allows each sub-organisation to be more flexible with regard to its own needs and customers. It does not have to wait for central office to consider any points of concern which have been passed on to it. Most typically the structure consists of a central 'holding' company. (A holding company is the owner of several companies, which, while interested in the profits and decisions made by its companies, does not meddle in the day-to-day business.) The holding company has devolved (passed down power and authority) responsibility to each company forming part of its group.

Line management structures

As we have seen, a typical hierarchy in an organisation consists of a number of layers, through which power, responsibility and authority are delegated. This process is known as Line Management (*see* Fig 2.4). In other words, each person knows to whom they are responsible and from whom they should take instructions. A typical example of this would be the Sales Director who is responsible for supervising the Sales Manager, who, in turn, directs the operations of the Regional Sales Manager. The Regional Sales Managers have authority over their own sales personnel.

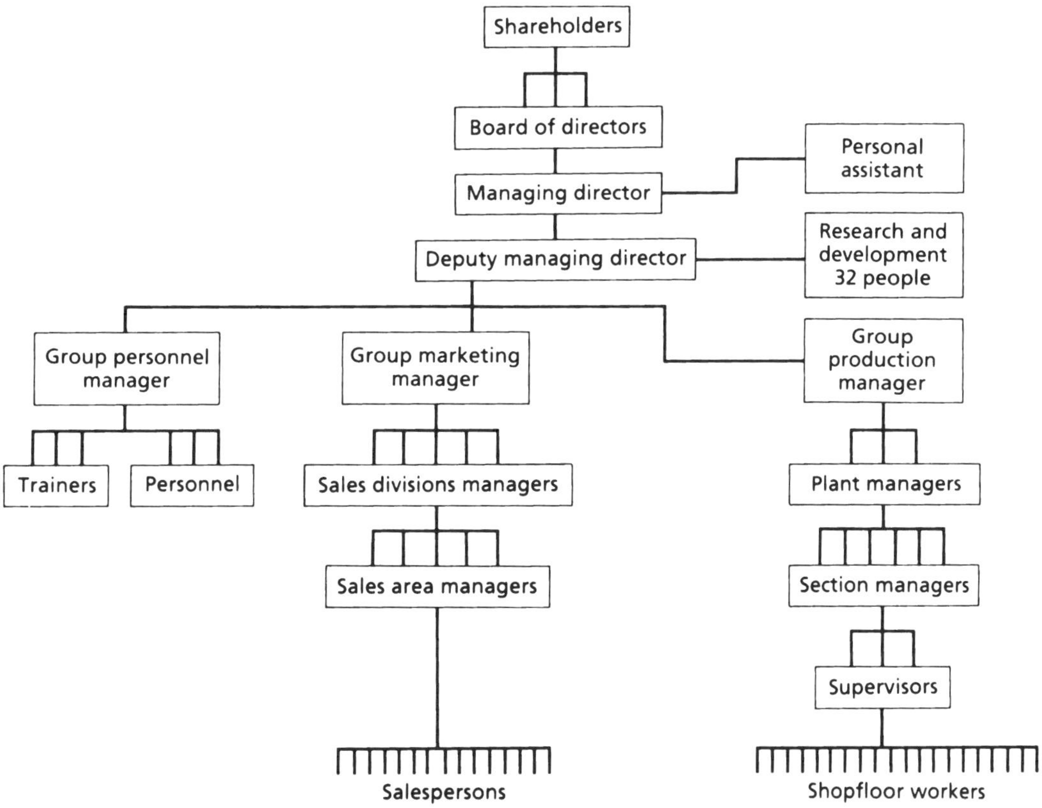

Fig 2.4 Typical hierarchical structure of an organisation
(Adapted from *Understanding Business*, A Norman, P Norman and P Short, Pitman Publishing, 1993)

Matrix structures

We can identify two main versions of this type of organisational structure. These are known as staff management structure and line and staff management structure. We will look at these in turn.

Staff management structure

This type of structure refers to individuals who carry out a specialised function within the organisation. In a typical retail outlet there will be a line management structure which can trace authority from the directors at central office right down to the sales assistants.

However, certain members of staff are not directly part of this line. The personnel department, for example, does not have day-to-day authority over the branches but does get involved in matters relating to personnel when needed. Equally, the marketing department, which again may be based centrally, will be carrying out functions which do not require reference to the branches. Generally speaking, a staff relationship would best describe the liaison between employees in the organisation that are not part of the direct line of authority. This is a form of matrix structure.

Line and staff management structure

In reality, most organisations have a mixture of both line and staff structures. This can also be described as a matrix structure. It particularly suits larger organisations with a number of different sites and complex production/sales operations. The departments which make up the staff side of the organisation tend to service the various lines of authority. In other words, they have responsibilities and authority which span across a number of lines of authority and provide a specialist service. Good examples of this are the warehouse, the buying department and the personnel department.

PC 2.1.1

Individual activity *Time: 30 minutes*

Returning to your two organisational charts, try to match the charts against the structures which have just been covered. You may find that they do not necessarily have all the characteristics of one of them. In fact, they may be a mixture of two or more. Now choose one of the structures above and try to reorganise your charts to fit this.

2.1.2 Produce organisational charts showing departments

2.1.3 Describe the work and explain the interdependence of departments within business organisations

We have taken these two performance criteria together since you will only be able to produce the organisational charts once you have understood the role of the departments which may make up the organisation.

Before we do this, it would be a good idea to investigate why certain organisations choose to be structured in one way or another.

If we look at the most simple structure of an organisation we begin with the person who works on their own. This person would obviously be responsible for everything that the organisation does. Someone, for example, who set up a mail order business would be responsible for buying in products, designing the catalogue, getting it printed, carrying out market research to find the kind of person that would buy the products, researching a mailing list, sending out catalogues, taking orders, despatching them, dealing with any correspondence, paying bills, banking cheques, doing the accounts and many other things.

In this situation the individual who is running the business is at the centre of everything.

The larger the organisation, the more need there is for people to specialise in a particular area. Good examples are bank managers, solicitors and accountants. All of these people have specialist skills. All of these people can take some of the responsibility off an individual business person's shoulders.

As a business expands it needs to employ people, some part time; some full time. As it expands, the person who set it up has to think about how to do this. The business needs to be organised in the best possible way in order to meet the objectives that have been set for it. A definition is needed for what individuals do, and precisely what departments are responsible for. Who will supervise the employees? Who should tell them what to do? Where does everyone fit into the organisation? And who is ultimately responsible? This is known as the division of labour and specialism.

The division of labour involves breaking down into clearly defined specialist tasks the process of producing things or providing services. The fact is that if the process is broken down into these separate tasks then production can actually be increased. Instead of one person trying to do everything, everybody who works as part of the production of goods or services will specialise. Specialism means being more efficient.

Group activity

PC 2.1.2
PC 2.1.3
C 2.1
C 2.2
C 2.3
AN 2.1
AN 2.2
AN 2.3

Consider the organisation where you are studying, working in pairs in an attempt to discover the level of specialism of the teaching staff. You will find that some of them concentrate on particular subject areas, while others are involved in a range of different topics.

Construct a series of pie charts which illustrate the amount of time each member of the teaching staff spends on particular subject areas. Colour code the pie charts so that you can easily see who is involved in which area. When you have done this, show the pie chart to the staff member(s) involved and obtain feedback from them as to whether they consider themselves to be specialist or not.

Advantages and disadvantages of specialisation

Advantages	*Disadvantages*
■ Resources can actually be concentrated where they are needed the most	■ Specialisation can often lead to doing a very boring job. Simple repetition of the same task day in day out demoralises people and they can become less efficient
■ If the worker becomes more efficient at doing a particular job they become more skilled	■ Specialisation is always dependent on how good or efficient the specialists in the previous task were. If they are not as efficient or as fast at every stage of the production this can cause bottlenecks
■ Specialisation allows greater output. This means that each item produced is produced cheaper because the labour involved in producing it is less for each unit	■ There is a tendency in specialisation for workers to become little more than machines. This in turn could lead to a loss of skill
■ If people specialise then they can pass on their skills and experience to others and help them become more efficient	■ Specialising actually reduces a worker's ability to adapt to change
■ Specialising will hopefully bring a better standard of living. By specialising, talents can be developed and traded with other people	■ Those that specialise have only got a narrow view of the product or service which they are actually producing. If someone makes something from start to finish they have got a greater overview and can help make things more efficient in the long run
■ A specialist can do a job well rather than lots of jobs badly	

Many organisations are constructed in a formal way. The organisation needs to reflect the kind of activities for which each worker is going to be responsible, and it also needs to see exactly what each worker is responsible for.

Departments

Departmentalisation is the process by which certain functions that an organisation carries out are grouped logically under a particular manager. There are usually four ways of grouping employees or what organisations do:

1 *By what they produce, known as the product*
2 *By their function, or what they do for the organisation*
3 *By process, which means how they do it, for example by geographical area, such as by having various regional offices*
4 *By type of customer, for example if they deal with other business organisations, or with retail outlets*

This leads us to look at another form of organisational structure and that is the Division by Function. As we saw above, one of the most common ways of organising the structure of the business is to look at exactly what employees do. Every organisation has its own way of structuring the functions that it carries out and some of the more common ones follow. (*See* Figs 2.5 to 2.12.)

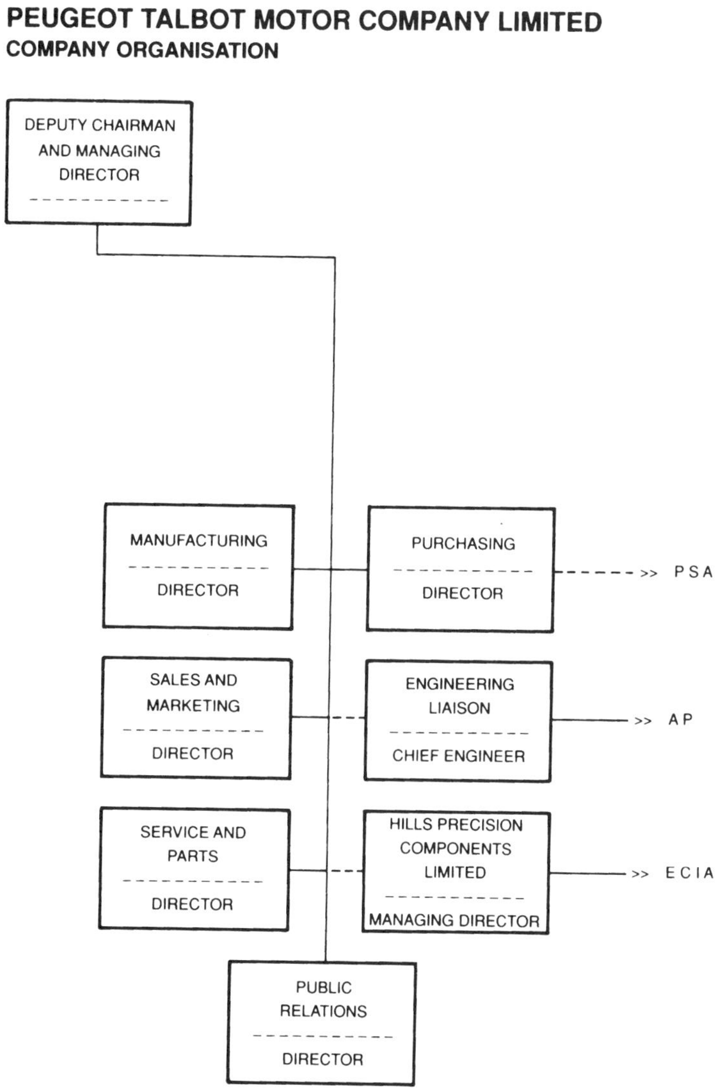

Fig 2.5 Peugeot Talbot's company organisation charts illustrate the value of departmentalisation and specialisation

PEUGEOT TALBOT MOTOR COMPANY LIMITED
MANUFACTURING

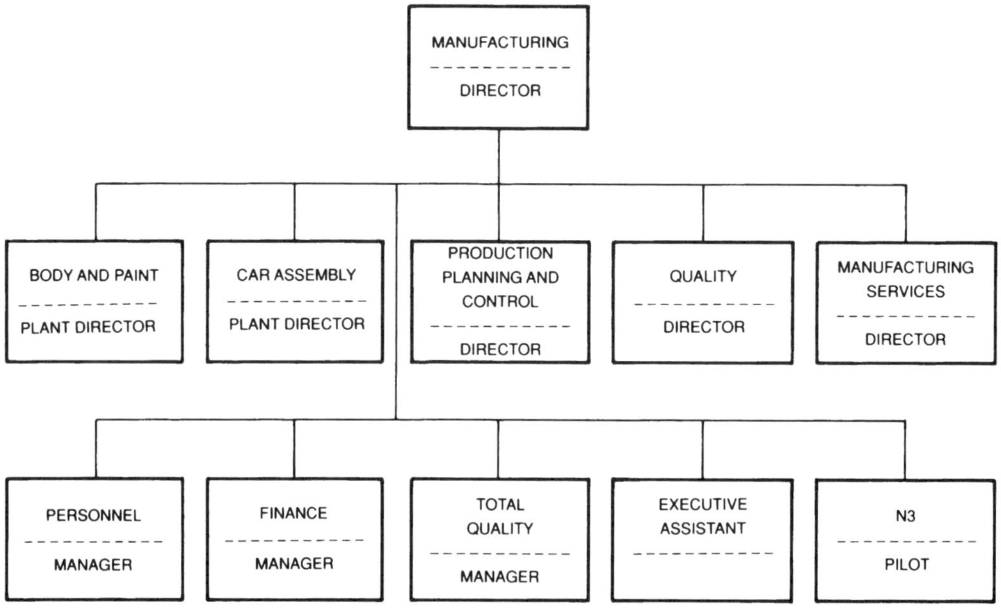

Fig 2.6 Peugeot Talbot – manufacturing division

PEUGEOT TALBOT MOTOR COMPANY LIMITED
SALES AND MARKETING

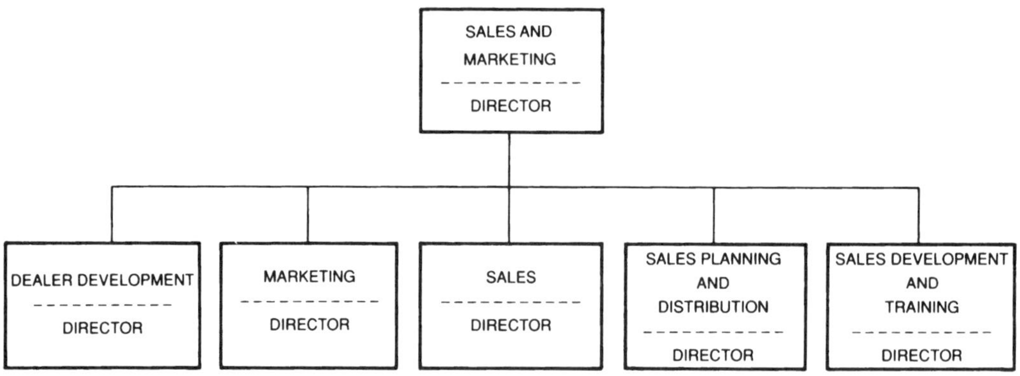

Fig 2.7 Peugeot Talbot – sales and marketing division

PEUGEOT TALBOT MOTOR COMPANY LIMITED
SERVICE AND PARTS

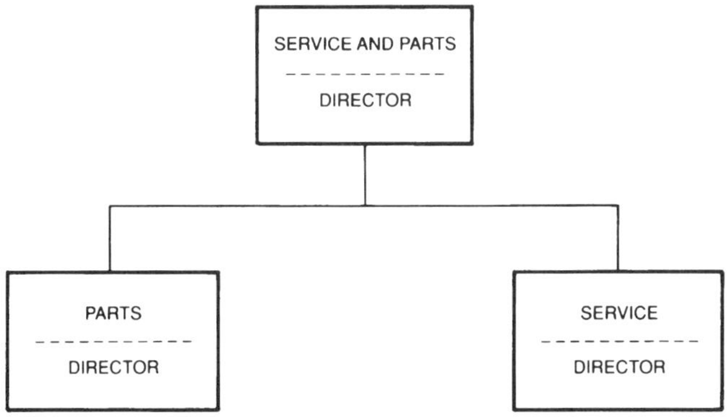

Fig 2.8 Peugeot Talbot – service and parts division

PEUGEOT TALBOT MOTOR COMPANY LIMITED
PURCHASING

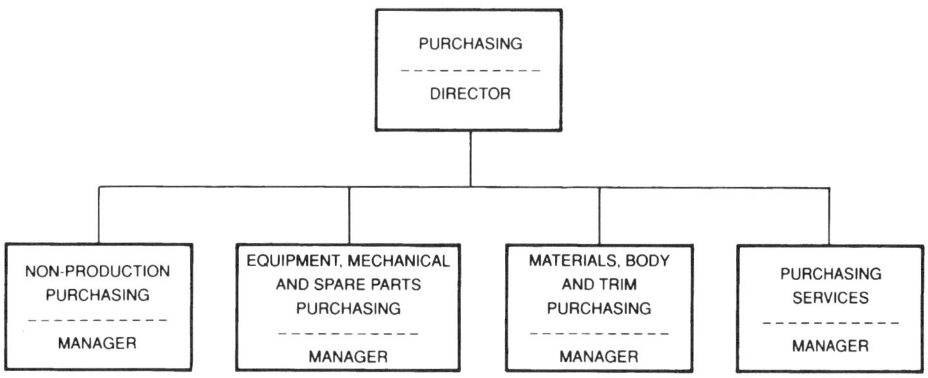

Fig 2.9 Peugeot Talbot – purchasing division

PEUGEOT TALBOT MOTOR COMPANY LIMITED
ENGINEERING LIAISON

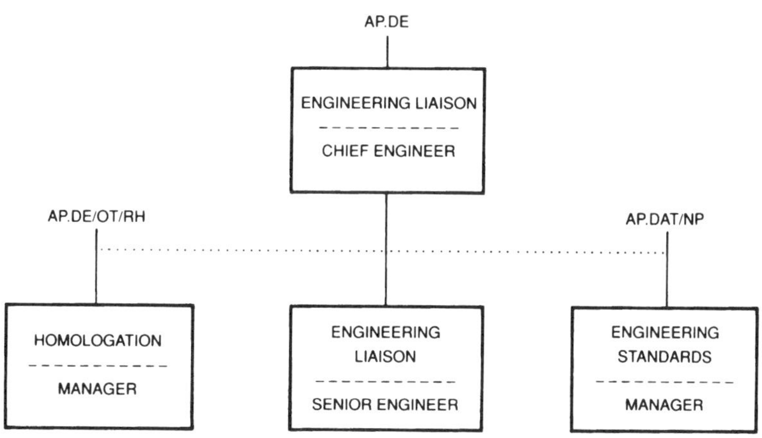

Fig 2.10 Peugeot Talbot – engineering liaison division

HILLS PRECISION COMPONENTS LIMITED

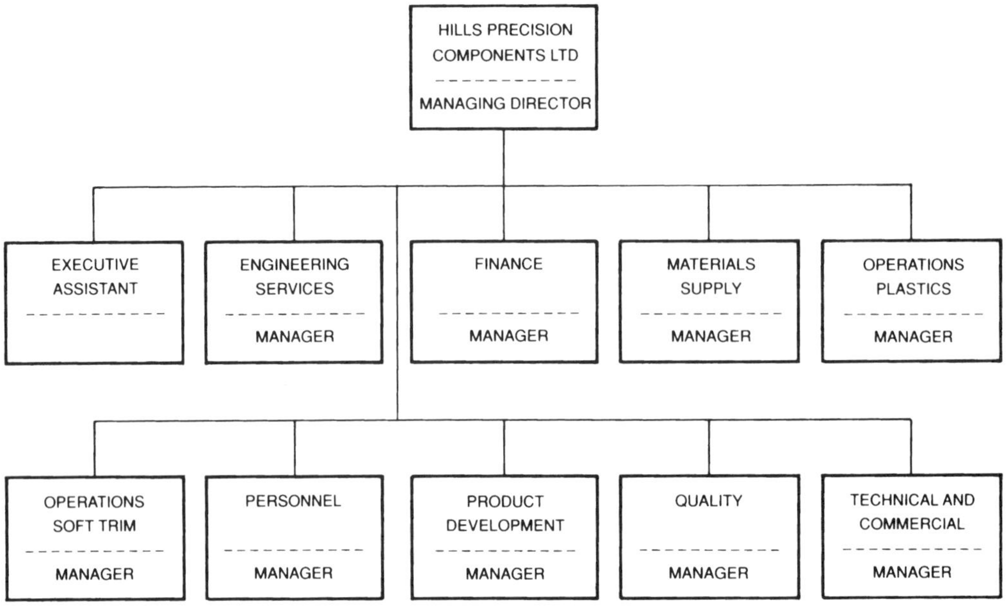

Fig 2.11 Peugeot Talbot – Hills Precision Components Limited

PEUGEOT TALBOT MOTOR COMPANY LIMITED
PUBLIC RELATIONS

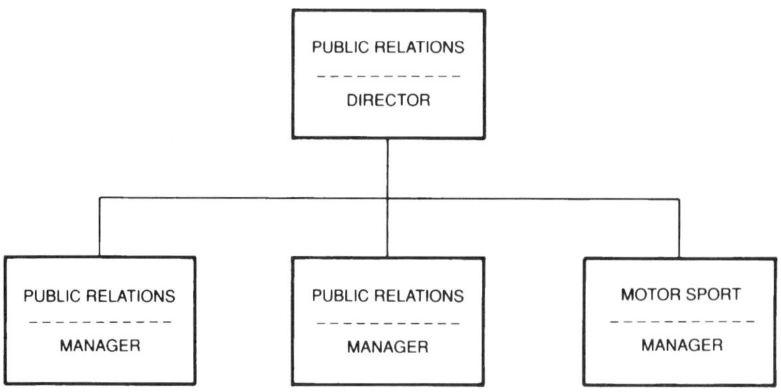

Fig 2.12 Peugeot Talbot – public relations division

Research and development

Working closely with the marketing department, which is keeping a constant check on competitors' products and services, the R & D department may be informed of the need for a new product. Equally, it may be developing new products or ranges of products in its own right.

The main function of the R & D department is not only to design new products, but to work out the most efficient and logical method of producing them. It will, after a number of exhaustive tests, pass on its designs and proposed methods of production to the production department itself, which will then be responsible for putting the new product into production.

Routinely, the R & D department will test random samples of products being manufactured to ensure that they comply with the quality standards set by the organisation, as well as with government legislation. In some organisations this function is separated from the R & D department and called the 'Quality Assurance/Control Department'.

The R & D department will also test competitor's products to see how they have been manufactured and whether the organisations' products compare favourably to them. Additionally, it will keep a close eye on the technological advances made within its area to see if the design and production processes used can be improved.

PC 2.1.2
PC 2.1.3
AN 2.1
AN 2.2

Individual activity

Time: 30 minutes

With reference to your organisational charts, you may have discovered that neither organisation you looked at has a Research and Development Department. If they have, calculate the percentage number of employees engaged in these activities. What kind of research and development is carried out in this department? If you have discovered that they do not have an R & D department, what benefits could the organisations obtain from the setting up of a department to deal with research and development?

Production

The production department is involved in all functions which revolve around producing the goods or services for the customer.

This department will monitor levels of wastage to ensure the most efficient use of resources. It will also check the cost of raw materials and parts purchased to make sure that profit margins are maintained.

As new products are developed, and technology changes, the production department will be responsible for purchasing all the necessary plant and equipment required, as well as organising the production process.

In consultation with the sales department, the production department must make sure that it can manufacture or supply customers with the quantity required at the time requested. The tight monitoring of production levels means that the production department should know how long it would take to produce enough products to fill a particular order. Advanced planning and close liaison with the sales department is vital as deadlines must be met.

Regardless of how many units of production are being produced, the production department is also responsible for the maintenance of quality. Each product must meet a number of strict quality standards and must to all intents and purposes be exactly the same every time. Periodically, products will be randomly selected from the production line and tested by either the R & D department or the Quality Assurance / Control Department.

A good production department will monitor methods of production used by all major competitors and allied industries and take steps to implement any useful methods of production used elsewhere.

Increasingly, as production becomes more automated, the production department will also have to design computer programs which can handle the new processes.

PC 2.1.2
PC 2.1.3
C 2.1
C 2.2
C 2.3
AN 2.1
AN 2.2
AN 2.3

Individual activity *Time: 1 hour*

Again, your organisations which you charted may not necessarily produce physical goods. If they do, calculate the percentage of employees engaged in this activity. Look at the turnover of the organisation involved and divide this number by the total number of employees in the production department. This will give a very crude idea of how productive each employee is. Compare your total with those of other members of your group and see whose organisation is the most productive.

If your organisation does not have a production department, then try to identify another department which fulfils a similar function. It may not necessarily be called a production department, but may produce something which the organisation then sells. Why do you think this department is not called a production department?

Purchasing

A purchasing department would be responsible for assisting the other departments within the organisation in ordering and buying the goods and services required. This is an important function, as the purchasing department will have to ensure that it is buying in raw materials, components or consumable items (such as stationery) at the most competitive prices available. In addition, it will have to make sure that the goods are being supplied at the correct time so that they arrive when required by the other departments.

The purchasing department would keep a stock of catalogues and price lists from suppliers. When production staff receive a purchase requisition (a request to purchase) from one of the other departments or individuals within the organisation, they would research the various suppliers until they found the right product, at the right price, with the right delivery. We deal much more with the purchasing process in Unit 4, Elements 4.1 and 4.2.

Group activity *Time: 20 minutes*

PC 2.1.2
PC 2.1.3
C 2.1
C 2.2

Thinking about your two organisations, in pairs discuss whether the organisations you have chosen have a purchasing department. How many employees are involved in this department? If neither of your organisations has a purchasing department, try to assess who is responsible for the buying in of materials, components or services for the organisation.

Accounting

The accounts department supervises all matters involving finance. Again computers and calculators are used extensively. It is often the case that an accounts department is split up into two further sections:

1 The day-to-day accounting procedures are handled by the financial accounting section. Essentially this keeps track of all incoming and outgoing cash or credits.
2 On the other hand, the management accounting section concentrates on analysing the figures and trying to predict possible future income and outgoings.

In detail, the accounts/finance department will record and monitor the following:

- *sales*
- *purchases*
- *manufacturing costs*
- *running costs (lighting, heating, etc.)*
- *dividends to shareholders*
- *payment of salaries and wages*
- *departmental and organisational budgets*

At all times, the accounts/finance department must know whether the organisation is operating at a profit. This is achieved by checking that revenue from sales is greater than costs. The directors, shareholders and senior managers will need to have instant access to this information. This is presented in various forms, such as balance sheets and profit and loss accounts. We look at these in more detail in Unit 4.

The department is also responsible for maintaining records of financial transactions required by law, e.g. the payment of tax, National Insurance and pension fund arrangements.

Individual activity *Time: 20 minutes*

PC 2.1.2
PC 2.1.3

Following on from the work carried out regarding the purchasing department, calculate a similar percentage for this area of work. Also try to find out whether the organisations carry out all of the accounts and finance functions themselves or whether some tasks are undertaken elsewhere by other organisations.

Human resources (personnel)

The main function of the personnel department is the recruitment and organisation of individuals required for the various functions required to run the organisation.

This primary responsibility is achieved through a close monitoring process which begins with the selection of potential employees, continues through promotion and training of existing members of staff, to the termination of employment (by retirement, redundancy, staff leaving to go elsewhere and those who are asked to leave).

Close liaison is maintained with all other departments to identify the various training needs of staff. This may include the induction of new employees (telling them about the organisation), additional training (perhaps to cope with new technology) and retraining (e.g. when a job has been replaced by a new process and the employees have been re-deployed to a new area).

The personnel department maintains all records relating to employees, including holiday entitlement, sickness records, qualifications and experience, salary, pension contributions and entitlements, and confidential reports from line managers. Some of this information is very useful in identifying training needs, as well as matching existing staff to new vacancies within the organisation. Much of this information is of a confidential nature, and is restricted by the Data Protection Act, which we will consider later.

A further useful function of this information is to provide background for confidential counselling of employees. This will take account of any welfare or social difficulties employees may be experiencing.

The personnel department is the main negotiator for the organisation in matters relating to trade unions and employee associations and general problems regarding pay and conditions of employees.

In many medium to large organisations a wide range of social activities and facilities is provided. The personnel department is responsible for running these, which may include such things as subsidised catering, sports and social clubs, non-trade union employees' associations and season ticket loans.

Any organisation which truly values its key personnel will take all the steps necessary to ensure that they are happy and contented in their work. If these key employees feel that they could achieve a higher salary, better working conditions or a wider range of fringe benefits (e.g. company cars, better pension schemes or reduced rate mortgages), then they will be seriously considering leaving the organisation. The personnel department is responsible for monitoring and expanding the total package offered to employees and ensuring that it is better than that of competitors.

PC 2.1.2
PC 2.1.3
C 2.1
C 2.2
C 2.3

Individual activity

Carrying on from the previous tasks, again calculate the percentage of the employees engaged in the human resources area of the organisation's activities. In the role of Assistant Personnel Manager, you are responsible for organising the induction schedule for new employees. What do you think would need to be included in such a schedule? Imagine that you have four new employees starting work in one month. Each of these employees will be working in different

IT 2.1
IT 2.2
IT 2.3

departments of the organisation and will receive specific training from these sections.

Draw up a general organisational training schedule, ensuring that it covers all the aspects required. Word process your document and take copies using the photocopier.

Marketing

The main function of the marketing department is to try to identify customer requirements. There is also an element here of trying to predict customer needs into the future.

The marketing department works very closely with the sales department, and it is important that the two communicate well.

The starting point for most marketing functions is to carry out extensive research on a particular market to try to discover exactly what consumers want, where they want it, how much they want to pay for it, and the most effective way of getting the message across. This is known as the 'marketing mix'. We will look at this in more detail later.

The marketing department needs to work closely with the R & D department and the production department in developing attractive and saleable products. This will also include the constant updating of existing products to cater for changes in taste and demand.

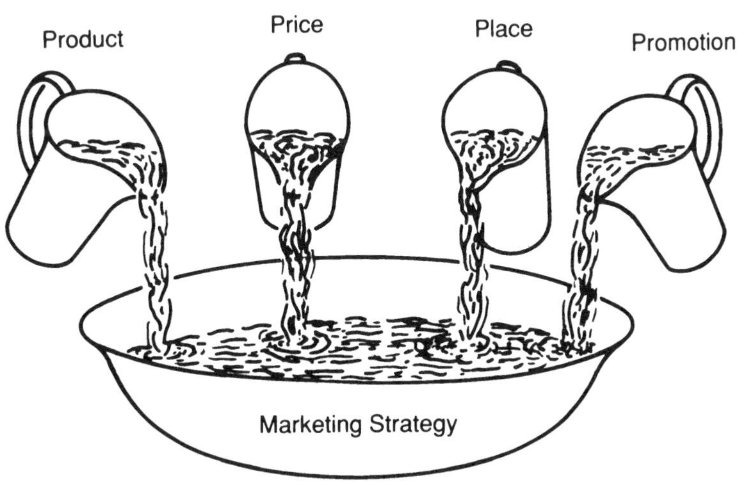

Fig 2.13 The marketing mix

One of the more obvious responsibilities of the marketing department is the design and development of advertising ideas and marketing campaigns. This design and development process will take account of the needs of the sales department and any other interested area of the organisation.

As a part of the regular market research procedures, the marketing department will monitor changes in trends and fashions relating to its customers. Some information is readily available as statistical tables published by the government, but much information must be researched as required by the organisation itself.

Individual activity

Time: 30 minutes

PC 2.1.2
PC 2.1.3
C 2.1

As in the tasks related to other departments of the organisation, calculate the percentage of employees engaged in the marketing area of the organisation's activities.

In the role of Marketing Manager, where would you look for changes in customer trends and fashions? What use do you think you could make of this information? Discuss this in small groups.

Sales

The sales department's main responsibility is to create orders for goods and services. Many organisations employ a large sales force, which may be based either on a local level, in the case of retail stores, or, in the case of organisations which supply other organisations, on a regional basis.

The greater the emphasis on selling to individual customers, the larger the sales force, and those organisations which rely on heavy advertising to stimulate interest in their goods or services can have a relatively small sales team.

In terms of organising the efforts of the sales employees, the sales department will draw up a detailed sales plan which will include targets to be met by each area or region of the sales force. It will also include in this plan the level of profit that can be expected from each and every product.

Working closely with the marketing department, the sales department will regularly supply sales information regarding sales levels, activities of competitors, and requests from customers for new or improved products. The sales force compiles the raw data about its sales figures on a weekly basis, and this will be interpreted by the Sales Manager, who will then pass it on for analysis by the marketing department.

In order to stimulate sales, the sales department will develop a range of 'point of sale' (POS) materials (this will include posters, leaflets and boxes with the company logo) and other promotional materials.

Individual activity

Time: 40 minutes

PC 2.1.2
PC 2.1.3
C 2.1
C 2.2

Work out the percentage of employees engaged in the sales area of activity from the organisations you researched.

In the role of a sales representative, try to map out a typical working week, assuming the following:

- **you are only required to be present on the organisation's premises for two hours per week**
- **your customer list extends to over 200 organisations**
- **the sales area for which you are responsible is roughly one-tenth of the UK**
- **your normal travelling time (i.e. time spent driving from customer to customer) is around 20 hours per week**

- your normal visiting time per customer is approximately 20 minutes
- you are required to spend around one and a half hours per day on paperwork
- you are usually on the telephone for approximately one hour each day (you have a car phone – but remember you are not supposed to use the phone while driving)

Compare your weekly timetable with those in the rest of your group.

Administration

Most organisations have a central administration. The main function of an administration department is to control paperwork and to support all the other departments by servicing their needs for secretarial work – filing, mailing, handling data, etc.

As offices have become more used to using computers, administration departments have shrunk in size because many of the tasks carried out by them can now be carried out simply at the desk top with a networked computer. We will look at this in more detail later.

One of the more common functions that is still carried out by an administration department is that of organising office services. The manager in charge of office services is responsible for training, advising departments about how their space should be organised, supplying equipment and stationery, and setting up an effective communications system within the organisation, which obviously includes the telephones and the mailing.

The administration department will also provide a centralised purchasing service for office supplies and storage. It also operates as a 'pool' of business stationery and corporate materials, e.g. memoranda and letterhead paper, and will co-ordinate the mass printing of stationery. Allied to this it will control the large central photocopying facilities, providing a fast and efficient reprographic facility, which may include photocopying, collating and binding of documents.

Traditionally, administration departments are responsible for arranging insurance for the organisation and the monitoring of leasing agreements (cars, equipment and premises).

PC 2.1.2
PC 2.1.3

Individual activity *Time: 20 minutes*

Using the information that you have gathered from the organisations in the previous activities, try to work out in percentage terms how many employees work in the administration department of the organisation.

Computer (IT) services

The information technology / computer services department will have responsibility for computing (both hardware and software), maintenance of databases, telecommunications, and other technological office developments.

As most organisations are now incorporating computers into almost everything they do, the number of information technology / computer services departments that can be considered to be truly separate is diminishing.

The information technology / computer services manager must not only be aware of new developments in technology, but must also know how to use them. The department will also supply all support and guidance to help others too.

PC 2.1.2
PC 2.1.3
AN 2.1
AN 2.2
AN 2.3
IT 2.4

Individual activity *Time: 30 minutes*

For the computers and software available in your institution, draw up a chart which shows the responsibility for the purchasing, maintenance and training related to this information technology.

Do not forget also to calculate the percentage number of employees engaged in activities related to information technology in your two organisational charts.

Customer services

Increasingly, organisations have recognised the value of not only responding to customer needs by adapting or expanding product ranges, but also of employing particular staff whose sole responsibility it is to liaise with the public and the media.

The customer relations department is the main point of contact for customers who have complaints about the product or service supplied by the organisation. The smooth, efficient and courteous response to customer complaints is a key feature in making sure that the organisation's reputation is maintained. You will often see a short sentence on products which states that, if you have any problem with the product, simply to return it to the manufacturer. This is an offer in addition to the legal requirements that a product must be fit for the use for which it was intended and this has gone a long way to enhance an organisation's reputation for being fair.

A public relations department traditionally was the main way in which the organisation passed on news and information to the media and other interested parties. In recent years, this role has been expanded to include close contact with the public. Requests for information about the organisation and its operations are dealt with by the public relations department, which has developed a range of booklets and other materials for this purpose. Particularly in the field of education, many larger organisations have also developed teaching packs and other educational literature for supply on request.

It is the public relations department which writes press releases and product news to be distributed to extensive mailing lists of newspapers, magazines, journals and specialist organisations. The public relations department will also advise members of their organisation's management as to how they should respond to questions from the media, and provide specialist support for conferences and seminars.

PC 2.1.2
PC 2.1.3
C 2.1
C 2.2
C 2.3
IT 2.1
IT 2.2
IT 2.3

Individual activity

Time: 1 hour

Carrying on from the previous tasks, again calculate the percentage of the employees engaged in this area of the two organisations' activities.

In the role of Public Relations Officer of a road haulage company, you must prepare a statement to the public via the press, covering the following issues:

- **new EC regulations state that the present limit of haulage vehicles has been increased from 38 to 44 tonnes**
- **your vehicles will still have to use their present routes through a number of small villages**
- **in consultation with the local authority, you have discovered that there are no present plans to build a by-pass to avoid these small villages**
- **you have already received a number of complaints from local residents regarding noise, damage to property and diesel fume pollution**
- **although you do not rely on local businesses or local residents as clients of your road haulage business, it is company policy to maintain and develop good community relations and to avoid any bad publicity**

You should word process your statement to the press and then present this to the remainder of your group who will take the role of the local press and residents. You should be prepared to answer any questions which they may wish to pose.

In many of the larger organisations throughout the UK a Community Projects Department has been set up with a responsibility to ensure that the local community is made aware of exactly what the organisation is doing. In some organisations this responsibility is carried out by a public relations officer. Other areas in which the department is involved are liaison with other local businesses, close contact with the local education service and maintaining an effective environmental policy.

WOOLWORTHS IN THE COMMUNITY

Woolworths has always recognised the importance of putting something back into the communities in which it trades. This commitment is expressed through a wide range of activities. The enthusiasm with which Woolworths staff support worthy causes at both local and national levels has helped the company towards outstanding achievements in this field.

It was the company's proven track record which led Comic Relief to choose Woolworths as the high street focus for its Red Nose Days in 1989 and 1991, which raised over £40 million for famine relief in Africa and help for the homeless in Britain.

In recent years Woolworths company-wide appeals have generated over £500,000 for Help a Child to See (1989) and National Children's Homes (1990) through a combination of store-based and regionally co-ordinated events. In support of these campaigns Woolworths staff have climbed Britain's tallest mountains, covered thousands of miles on sponsored walks and organised countless Fun Days to encourage customers to contribute towards these causes.

Track and field athletics in the shape of the Young Athletes League became part of Woolworths community involvement in 1990. The company committed £700,000 over three years to help The YAL provide 20,000 youngsters from over 200 athletics clubs, with invaluable experience of competitive

athletics. And in 1991, as a result of Woolworths support, The YAL launched its first competition for girls.

Finally, the company's support for the YAL nationally saw individual Woolworths staff forging close links with local youth athletic clubs. The clubs received regular publicity through their local stores.

At the start of 1992 Woolworths

Fig 2.14 Woolworths values the local communities in which it trades and believes in putting something back into the community

adopted Barnardo's as the focus for its national fund-raising drive. This effort complements the company's successful sponsorship of Barnardo's Champion Children Awards – the longest established and most prestigious awards for British children – which recognise achievements in seven categories including bravery, music, sport and triumph over adversity.

But this is not the whole story of Woolworths support for good causes. At Christmas and Easter staff and customers in each of the company's stores are invited to nominate a local deserving cause to receive a giant box of chocolates or a giant Easter egg.

These are specially made by Woolworths suppliers to be raffled. The exercise raises an estimated £100,000 every year.

In addition to these activities schools are an important year-round focus for Woolworths.

For thousands of youngsters Woolworths provides their first work experience whether as Saturday assistants or on short work-experience placements while still at school.

Managers are often invited to give careers talks or conduct mock interviews and stores regularly provide prizes for school fetes.

Fig 2.14 continued

PC 2.1.2
PC 2.1.3
C 2.1
C 2.2
C 2.3
IT 2.1
IT 2.2
IT 2.3

Individual activity

Carrying on from the previous tasks, again calculate the percentage of the employees engaged in this area of the organisations' activities. Your organisations may not have a community projects department, but working in pairs, in the role of Community Projects Manager, you should consider the following request made by your board of directors:

- **the board wishes to donate £10 000 to a deserving local cause**
- **it would like you to identify at least five possible causes which would benefit from such a donation**
- **it would prefer the donation to be given to an organisation within an area of five miles from the site of the organisation**
- **it would like to receive as much publicity as possible in both the lead up to, and immediately after, the donation has been made**
- **it would consider a split donation, but to no more than two different organisations**

Prepare your findings in the form of a word processed report, which must include a brief section on each of the proposed organisations that you have chosen to nominate. You should also give reasons why you have chosen each of the organisations. In your recommendations you must offer your suggestions as to the organisation you feel is most deserving.

Distribution (logistics)

We should identify two distinct departments which are involved in this area of the organisation's activities. The first is the stores and warehousing function, and the second is the distribution or transport department itself.

The stores or warehouse

The stores or warehouse has the responsibility for safely housing a variety of the organisation's property. This may take the form of products ready to be sold, various packaging materials, part-finished goods or raw materials, presently unused or unwanted equipment and machinery, and bulk amounts of stationery and corporate materials.

This service department must keep a careful check on the stock levels of all items for which it has overall responsibility, and should inform the relevant department should stocks begin to approach their minimum stock level.

Individual activity

Time: 20 minutes

PC 2.1.2
PC 2.1.3
C 2.2
C 2.3

Carrying on from the previous tasks, again calculate the percentage of the employees engaged in this area of the organisation's activities.

In the role of the Warehousing Manager, draw up a list of essential equipment which you would expect to find in the warehouse. In order to help you consider this role, assume that the warehouse receives at least two lorries full of goods inwards per day and distributes via the Royal Mail at least 100 packages per day. You may also like to consider how many employees you would need in order to carry out all of the tasks involved.

The distribution or transportation department

The main function of the distribution or transportation department is to co-ordinate the organisation's transport needs. This will include the purchasing or leasing of vehicles (company cars, etc.) and servicing and maintaining delivery vehicles.

As an integral part of this transport service, the department will have to maintain records such as insurance, vehicle registration, road tax, service records, and leasing and purchasing agreements.

In situations where an organisation provides a delivery service to the customer, it is essential that the most efficient and cost-effective routes are used. This is increasingly done with the aid of computer packages, specifically designed for this purpose.

As with most departments, when training or retraining needs are identified, the distribution/transport department will liaise with the personnel department to organise training programmes.

Fig 2.15 Mobil's automated warehousing at Birkenhead
(Photographs courtesy of Mobil Oil Company Limited)

PC 2.1.2
PC 2.1.3
C 2.2
IT 2.4

Individual activity

Time: 20 minutes

Carrying on from the previous tasks, again calculate the percentage of the employees engaged in this area of the organisations' activities.

As we have mentioned, distribution departments are increasingly using computer packages. What type of software package do you think would be of assistance to them? How could they make use of such software packages as part of their day-to-day operations? You should consider this question in groups of three.

PC 2.1.1
PC 2.1.2
PC 2.1.3
C 2.1
C 2.2
C 2.3
IT 2.1
IT 2.2
IT 2.3

Group activity

Working in pairs, now collate all of the percentages that you have calculated regarding the organisational structure of your two chosen organisations.

Your first task is to present this information in the most suitable format, with the emphasis on ease of reference.

Your second task is to consider the decision-making process within your two organisations, taking the following points into account:

- How many people are involved in the initial decision-making process?
- How many layers of management must a decision pass through before being acted upon?
- Can the organisation plan effectively and ensure that any decisions are actually implemented?
- How does the structure affect the quality of the decision making (you should think about this in terms of the negative effects a decision made at the top of the organisational structure has upon those at the bottom of it)?
- How does the structure of the organisation affect the speed of decision making?
- How likely is it that decisions, which have been made by the hierarchy, will be changed beyond all recognition by the time they reach the rest of the employees?
- If the organisation has a number of senior decision makers, how is responsibility for decision making organised?
- In order to make sure that a decision is implemented, the decision maker needs both power and authority. Are there any decision makers within your organisation that lack either power or authority? How do they operate?

Your findings should be presented in the form of a word-processed formal report.

2.1.4 Identify and explain differences in working arrangements

Differences in working arrangements

In this performance criteria we will be looking at the different working arrangements within organisations that either:

- *are as a result of the structure*
- *mean that the organisation needs to be structured in a particular way*

Specifically, we will be looking at the different ways in which individuals work. There are variations of the standard contract of employment. It is no longer the case that the majority of the work force is employed on a 'Monday to Friday, 9–5' basis. The demands of the employer have changed and this has meant great changes in the way in which employees are expected to work.

Team working

It is rare to find individuals within organisations who work on a solitary basis. Regardless of the position of an individual within an organisation, they will, at some time or another, on a day-to-day basis, have to involve, rely on or delegate to another person.

Teams work in a variety of different ways. Every individual has a number of traits or characteristics which determine the way in which they will be prepared to involve themselves and contribute to the team's activities.

Teams have been recognised as being one of the more useful ways of improving the overall amount of work that employees do. By working as a team they have company, more ideas and are motivated to work harder by seeing others working harder.

This team-working idea has been tried successfully by a number of organisations. It has been borrowed from Japanese organisations, which have been using it for many years. They have noticed that their employees work far harder if they are in a group. The group, or team, spur one another on and the individuals in the team do not want to let the rest of the team down.

Team working has meant that many organisations have had to abandon their old organisational structures and adopt a more flexible approach. The matrix structure, which we have looked at already, offers the greatest hope of being able to encourage the formation of teams.

Centralised

There are two different ways of looking at centralised structures, both of which will have an impact on the working arrangements:

1 **Centralised services** – this version of a centralised structure involves the reorganisation of key services to provide for the organisation as a whole. Central control means that the service should be more efficient, as well as attempting to keep costs down.
2 **Centralised decision making** – in larger organisations, it may be a preference to concentrate command and decision functions in a few individuals. They will be supported by a variety of employees and will be responsible for all decision making. It is often the case that these organisations are more traditional ones, or rely on the expert knowledge of a handful of individuals.

The main advantages of a centralised organisational structure are that:

- *the organisation can make decisions quickly, using a specialist staff*
- *larger discounts can be obtained by centralised purchasing*

De-centralised

In recent years, some major organisations have recognised that relying on a traditional structure has prevented quick and necessary decisions and change from taking place. This new form of structure is known as decentralisation. This is the exact opposite of having centralised services which assist individual branches or sites. Each part of the organisation is allowed to make decisions for itself without the permission of the directors or the central office.

Advantages and disadvantages of decentralisation

Advantages	*Disadvantages*
The main advantages are that:	The main disadvantages are that:
■ local decisions can be made by local managers	■ the organisation can be difficult to supervise and control
■ individuals can learn about the management process	■ there may be conflict between different parts of the organisation
■ the head office can concentrate on the strategic decisions	■ unless the policies are clear, the decisions made can be in conflict with the organisation's overall strategy.
■ there is a greater overall freedom in decision making.	

Flexible (shift, flexi-hours)

There is a large number of variations in the hours worked by employees. We can identify two of the main ones and two other less common ones.

Shifts

Shift working, or the working of non-standard hours, has long been an accepted method of ensuring that either the production process is 'manned' at all times, or that individuals are available to provide essential services on a 24-hour basis.

Shift working is essential in such occupations as the emergency services. It is obvious that the fire brigade, police force or ambulance service, for example, could not operate on a 9–5 basis.

In manufacturing, where shift work is again an accepted way of working, the production process requires this form of working. If the manufacturer employs flow production, for example, then it is essential that the production line is manned at all times. There may be additional payments made to employees working unsocial hours. In some cases, employees may be required to work for a number of days and then, after a short break, work for a period of nights. Alternatively, the contract may require the employee to work a mixture of days and nights.

Flexi-hours

Flexible working arrangements, such as flexi-time, allow some 2.5 million people to take advantage of the opportunity to arrange their working hours to suit both themselves and their employers. Normally, employees will be expected to work during a core time – usually 10 a.m. to 4 p.m. – but they can then choose to make up the balance of the hours at some point between 8 a.m. and 6 p.m. Alternatively, employees may choose to work longer hours for a short period of time and thus 'build up' days off.

The two less common versions of flexible working patterns are:

1 **Compressed working weeks** – certain organisations choose to close early on Fridays, or perhaps close on Fridays altogether. This means that employees work longer hours between Monday and Thursday. This can prove to be a good arrangement since the organisation can concentrate its business activities on four full working days which are fully staffed by all employees, who have the advantage of enjoying an extended weekend.
2 **Compressed annual hours** – certain employees will find that their contracts simply stipulate the number of hours they will be expected to work throughout the year. With such arrangements, they may be able to work extremely long hours for short periods of time (providing this does not breach legislation) and then be able to benefit from long breaks at the end of these work periods.

Contracts (fixed term, permanent)

The use of non-standard contracts has come about as a result of the economic recession in recent years. In addition to this, organisations have had to cope with an increasingly competitive international market. Fixed short-term contracts have become quite common in order to allow the employer only to make a short-term commitment to the employee. In this way, the employer is able to increase or decrease employee numbers as a quick response to changes in demand.

Fixed short-term contracts not only provide the employer with the opportunity to respond to short-term fluctuations in demand, but also to deal with projects or tasks on a one-off basis, or to bring in specialists to carry out a particular function. Organisations which have increased their use of fixed short-term contracts are:

- *health*
- *education*
- *distribution*

In fact, most public sector organisations find that the fixed short-term contract allows them to reduce their long-term commitments, as their budgets in the future may not be predictable.

Although fixed short-term contracts are finding considerable favour with some employers and employees, long-term contracts are still the most common. These open-ended contractual agreements form the most usual basis in establishing the relationship between the employer and the employee.

Workbase (office, factory, shop, outdoors, home, mobile)

The variety of different workbases common in most businesses is largely dependent upon the nature of the work and the need to be in a specific place at a specific time.

We should not see working in an office or a factory as the traditional type of workbase. Before the beginning of the industrial age, most individuals worked either from home or outdoors. The type of work available was different, so the workbase was different. Today it is impossible to carry out a number of different jobs in the confines of the office or factory. Many individuals spend their time either alone, or in small groups, moving around or permanently outdoors.

We shall try to look at the different sorts of job related to each of the categories mentioned above, but we are sure that you can come up with others that would be equally as good examples.

Office

Many of the departments which we have talked about in this Element are office-based. The main reason for this is the ability of the organisation to control all of its activities either on one site or on a collection of sites in different locations. Increasingly, we shall see that many of these activities could be carried out at home, due to improvements in information technology and communications.

Factory

We all think of a factory as being a large concern that involves quite complicated machinery and processes. This may not necessarily be so; some factories are relatively simple in their design and the activities that are carried out there.

For the most part, the factory is the place where goods or products are made or processed. There are good reasons for this, mainly relating to the fact that the organisation can, again, concentrate its resources in one place and be able to control what is happening. This is particularly true if the production involves complicated activities.

Shop

Traditional retailing is still quite a large employer in the UK and throughout the world. There are large numbers of employees working in retail outlets selling a variety of different products and services.

In recent years there has been a move away from traditional retailing that has been made possible by improvements in information technology and communications. Home shopping is now quite popular and it is possible to purchase a wide range of different products and services by telephone.

Organisations have also moved into the 'direct selling' area which involves making telephone calls to the potential customer and trying to convince them to purchase a product. An alternative to this is called 'canvassing', where the organisation attempts to convince the potential customer that a representative should be allowed to visit them at home.

All of these new forms of selling have had an impact on the more traditional shop or retail activities.

Outdoors

There are a number of very obvious types of job that could not be undertaken under cover. These include the following:

- *farming and agriculture*
- *building work*
- *construction of roads and other forms of transport network*
- *window cleaning*
- *deliveries*
- *services such as police work, fire brigade and ambulances*

Home

As we mentioned earlier, this form of work is becoming popular once more. People have worked in their home for hundreds of years. The most common forms of home-working have been in the clothing or assembly business. Home-workers would be paid a fee for each unit (product) that they completed.

In recent years, it has been possible to include more complex and technical activities at home. Telecommunications and information technology now allow an individual to undertake computer work or data processing within their own homes. Through this new 'networking' the employee is as valuable and contactable as an employee sitting in an office somewhere. The big advantage is that the employer does not have to pay for the office space.

Mobile

Aside from the fact that many individuals are happy to move around the country looking for work in their particular area of expertise (such as construction or building), there are a number of employees and self-employed who do not have a particular 'base' from which to work. Among these are:

- *sales representatives*
- *auditors*
- *car repairs and service (e.g. AA)*

- *milk delivery persons*
- *other delivery persons*
- *van and truck drivers*
- *removals persons*
- *consultants*

Individual activity *Time: 15 minutes*

Referring to the workbases of employees, identify at least five different occupations that could be undertaken at home or on a mobile basis. Compare your list with those of the rest of the group.

PC 2.1.4
C 2.1
C 2.2

2.1.5 Explain and give examples of reasons for change in working arrangements in one business organisation

Reasons for change

This performance criteria forms an integral part of the Element assignment. We can, therefore, only make some general points since we do not know the nature of the organisation that you have chosen. It should be remembered that you will only have to look at one of the following considerations in the Element assignment, but you will be required to know about the others in a little detail. The considerations to look at are:

- *productivity*
- *quality assurance*
- *competition*
- *technology*

As we have said, we will look at these in general, so that you can use the comments as a guideline in your own investigations.

Productivity

Any business must operate in a manner in which it addresses the needs of the customer. The organisation must ensure that it uses its resources in the right way. Furthermore, the organisation needs to ensure that it has a sufficient number of employees who are experienced, qualified and well trained. The production process itself should be as efficient as possible, as also should be the layout of the premises. Productivity is measured by considering the total output of the organisation and the number of employees involved. The main methods of doing this include the following:

1 Encouraging the employees
2 Motivating the employees
3 Analysing output levels
4 Analysing the number of employees needed to do the work
5 Analysing machinery and equipment requirements
6 Monitoring quality
7 Continually analysing production processes and methods

Quality assurance

The implementation of a strong quality assurance policy can involve the following:

- the idea that quality is not just related to the physical production of the product; quality assurance policy must be taken up by the whole of the organisation
- fixing in the minds of all individuals working for the organisation that the quality assurance refers to them and everything that they do
- that any system which supports quality assurance also supports the individuals in their attempts to produce quality work
- that there is a commitment to continual quality improvement across all areas of the organisation
- that quality should be measured in terms of what the customer wants, their needs and requirements
- that new technology should be used as quickly as possible

Competition

It can never be predicted exactly what the competing organisations are up to in terms of developing new ideas or using new methods of producing things. An organisation, in order to keep up, must always pay attention to what is happening in the rest of the industry. This may require the organisation to consider the productivity, the quality assurance or the use of new technology. You will find full details of these in the rest of this performance criteria.

Since the actions of the competition can so drastically affect the organisation, it may be the main purpose of a particular individual to assess these actions and keep a close eye on developments worldwide. This is a complicated task, as the organisation cannot predict where or when the major competition will emerge or who it will be.

If the organisation can identify a competitor as having a distinct advantage, it may seek to copy their competitor's structure, working arrangements or some other feature. This can be a good idea sometimes, but can often lead to the copier experiencing difficulties because they may not understand exactly how their competitor has implemented these changes. In the short term, at least, the organisation copying a competitor will be disrupted during the changeover period.

Technology

Organisations which fail to take account of the need to look constantly at their use of technology will risk failure. Equally, if employees are unwilling or unable to adopt new working practices, the same result may occur.

Many organisations have adopted the use of computers and information technology. In retailing, for example, the availability of electronic point of sale has revolutionised retail selling and stock control.

It is, perhaps, in the area of communications that technology has had the greatest impact. The flexibility and speed of telecommunications, in particular, has enabled organisations to collect, store and evaluate information effectively and efficiently.

For manufacturing organisations, technology has enabled them to reduce their costs of production. This has been coupled with the introduction of robotics and automation on the production line.

Element 2.1 Assignment

PC 2.1.1–5

As you may have gathered, throughout this Element you are expected to look at the organisational structures of two different organisations. You will also have to consider the departments which make up the organisations. In relation to this, you will be required to compare the working arrangements of the organisations. Finally, you should also consider team working in the organisations and identify how certain factors have caused changes.

Task 1 PC 2.1.1–2

Identify two businesses and draw up an organisational chart for each of them. Your choice of organisations should include a hierarchical structure and a flat or matrix structure. These organisational charts should show the departments within the organisation.

Task 2 PC 2.1.3

Using the organisational charts as a basis, describe the interdependence of the departments within the organisation and briefly explain each of the departments' main functions.

Task 3 PC 2.1.4

Write a short report which compares the working arrangements in the two organisations. You should pay particular attention to team working. In relation to this, you should explain why team working was introduced in one of the organisations and how it works.

Task 4 *PC 2.1.5*

Finally, prepare a short summary which investigates one of the following factors in relation to one of your chosen organisations:

- productivity
- quality assurance
- competition
- technology

You should focus on how one of these factors has caused change to the working arrangements or structure.

Notes

Your tutor should be able to provide you with case study material for your two organisations if you cannot obtain information from outside your college or institution. Some organisations may be willing to help, but you may not be aware of their organisational structure before contacting them. The danger here is that they may all have a similar structure.

Element 2.2
Investigate employee and employer responsibilities and rights

Performance criteria

A student must:

1 explain the **benefits of employer and employee co-operation**

2 describe **ways to resolve disagreements**

3 explain **employer rights and responsibilities**

4 explain **employee rights and responsibilities to their employers**

Range

- *Benefits of employer and employee co-operation*: survival of the business, improved employee commitment to the business, improved efficiency
- *Ways to resolve disagreements*: trades union negotiation, legal representation (ACAS [Advisory, Conciliation and Arbitration Services], industrial tribunals, European Court of Justice)
- *Employer rights*: employees' compliance with terms of contract, employees' compliance with health and safety regulations; disciplinary action; legal representation (ACAS [Advisory, Conciliation and Arbitration Services], industrial tribunals, European Court of Justice)
- *Employer responsibilities*: to explain business objectives, to offer and facilitate training, to implement equal opportunities legislation at work (Sex Discrimination Act, Race Relations Act, Equal Pay Act), to comply with health and safety regulations, remuneration (pay, deduction of income tax, payment of National Insurance, pension deductions if in contract)
- *Employee rights*: remuneration, employer compliance with terms of contract, health and safety at work, equal opportunities at work (Sex Discrimination Act, Race Relations Act, Equal Pay Act), legal representation (ACAS [Advisory, Conciliation and Arbitration Services], industrial tribunals, European Court of Justice)
- *Employee responsibilities*: to meet the terms of the contract, to meet health and safety regulations, to meet the objectives of the business, to meet customers' needs, to maintain quality standards

2.2.1 Explain the benefits of employer and employee co-operation

Benefits of employer and employee co-operation

This Element may give you the idea that the relationship between employers and employees can be somewhat difficult at times. Indeed, you may think that they are always in conflict with one another. There are times, of course, when this is the case. In the main, however, the employer and the employees co-operate to achieve their own goals (which are often different), but use the functions and the success of the organisation for this purpose.

We will begin our look at the relationships between employers and employees in the most positive light. The first performance criteria in this Element looks at the benefits of co-operation to both sides.

Survival of the business

It is obviously a good idea that, to some extent, both sides co-operate to make sure that the business is able to survive. There are enough pressures and competition outside the organisation to make this job difficult, without having to deal with constant problems within the organisation.

It is in neither party's interest to allow the organisation to get into a position where it cannot compete with other organisations because of internal problems. It is sometimes very difficult to keep the differences that will arise to an acceptable level. If either party allows disagreements to get out of hand, then the organisation may face severe difficulties.

If the organisation intends to remain profitable, then the co-operation and understanding of both parties is essential. Disputes will occur, but these need to be solved with the minimum of fuss and disruption. If the production or services offered by the organisation are affected by disputes, then there is a danger that customers will go elsewhere to find that product or service which they require.

There have been a number of examples in the past that have caused the failure of a business, or in some cases the whole of the industry. Perhaps the most famous was the coal disputes and strikes of the 1980s. In this case, the miners were concerned about safety, pay and the danger of the mines being closed. In the event, many of their fears actually happened. The owners (which were then the National Coal Board, a public sector organisation) refused to negotiate with them and bussed in other non-striking miners to the pits to carry on the work. They also took the opportunity to close some of the pits that were not making enough money. The dispute ended with the coal miners losing everything that they had fought so hard to defend. Within a few years, the majority of the pits had either been privatised or had been closed. The number of miners in work now is a fraction of the number working in the 1980s.

Refusing to negotiate is just one way of dealing with a dispute. It is much more common that the two parties will get together and try to thrash out a solution to the problem. As we will see in the next performance criteria, there are a number of different ways of trying to resolve a dispute.

Improved employee commitment to the business

If the employer and the employees can enter into an agreement about how they can help the organisation to be successful, then this partnership will bring great benefits.

We will now look at the particular ways in which an organisation can attempt to gain employee commitment. Many organisations realise that employees are valuable in terms of their work. They have largely ignored their ability to offer specialist knowledge which could help the organisation. To this end, some employers have started schemes aimed at using these skills.

There are various forms of employee representation and consultation. Some organisations have formed a joint consultative committee in which employees are given the opportunity to involve themselves in the organisation's decision making. These committees hold regular meetings at which decisions made by the management are relayed to the workforce for discussion. Another form of employee consultation is known as employee participation. This includes the following:

- **Employee briefing sessions** – where the employees are given useful and relevant information regarding the objectives of the organisation.
- **Quality circles** – where the employees meet on a voluntary basis to discuss their work and how systems and procedures may be improved.
- **Transfer of responsibility** – when employees take on some of the management-related decision making.
- **Worker directors** – where employees attend meetings of the board of directors. In the rest of Europe this idea has proved to be very successful in improving the quality of decision making at board level. It also gives the board the opportunity to hear the views of the work force at first-hand rather than relying on the management.

PC 2.2.1
C 2.1

Group activity *Time: 20 minutes*

How do you think these forms of employee consultation have improved the workforce's commitment to the organisation? Discuss this as a group.

Teamwork

Employees rarely work in an organisation on their own. Often teams are created in order to bring together the skills of individuals. Organisations will spend considerable time and effort in order to make sure that the teams created are able to be efficient. Teams are able to generate a high degree of commitment, not only to themselves but to the organisation. One of the particular problems with regard to teamwork is that the teams often do not want to be split up after the task has been completed. We will be looking at teamwork in much more depth in the next of the performance criteria of this Element.

Share ownership

In recent years, employers have recognised that a degree of ownership on the part of the employee will mean much greater dedication, productivity and motivation. Organisations which use this form of participation include Marks & Spencer plc and the John Lewis Partnership.

The issue of shares is usually worked out by looking at the number of years an employee has been working for the organisation.

Quality circles

A quality circle is a discussion group which meets on a regular basis to:

- *identify quality problems*
- *investigate solutions*
- *recommend suitable solutions*

The members of the quality circles are ordinary members of the workforce and may include an individual with specific skills. Quality circles aim to use knowledge from the factory floor, as well as giving employees the opportunity to show their knowledge and talents in terms of problem solving.

Job security

Job security, is the belief that the job is guaranteed for the foreseeable future. Employers have recognised that a lack of job security can mean poor motivation and morale. Although it is difficult to guarantee that a job will last for the foreseeable future, employers are keen to stress that so long as the organisation continues along its projected course, then the job will be secure.

Improved efficiency

This implies that the organisation needs to make the most of the effectiveness and efficiency of the workforce to reduce costs. It is a good idea to make sure that the working conditions are such that the workforce positively responds to the environment and remains highly motivated.

2.2.2 Describe ways to resolve disagreements

Ways to resolve disagreements

Procedures are necessary for the many cases that arise in relation to the following:

- *the breaking of an organisation's regulations or codes of practice*
- *the breaking of government regulations or codes of practice*
- *times when an employee believes that he or she has been wronged or ill-treated*

In many cases, potential disputes may be resolved without having to involve any of the following:

1 Trade unions
2 Staff associations
3 ACAS
4 Industrial tribunals
5 Court action

Many other forms of negotiations seek to avoid the employee having to turn to industrial action.

Trades union negotiations

Trade unions and staff associations become involved (generally) in such areas as:

- *negotiations*
- *new developments within the organisation*
- *disciplinary and grievance procedures*

It should be remembered that, although organisations like trade unions and staff associations do become involved in negotiations, these should still be considered as 'internal' negotiations. It is only when the trade union feels it is necessary to ask for assistance from its regional office or headquarters that negotiations take on a more serious nature.

The basic role of trade unions and, indeed, staff associations is to negotiate on a collective basis. There will be accepted procedures which will outline the way in which negotiations take place.

Legal representation (ACAS, industrial tribunals, European Court of Justice)

ACAS (Advisory, Conciliation and Arbitration Services)

ACAS is an independent organisation that offers employers, trades unions and individuals the opportunity to obtain unbiased assistance in relation to disputes. ACAS is recognised by employers and employees alike as being a valuable and reliable source of assistance.

In an arbitration situation, the two sides will turn to ACAS when they feel that they have exhausted the options open to them. ACAS will listen to the two parties involved and consider their arguments and will then provide a solution which both parties must accept. It is a rule that before they begin the arbitration process both sides agree to abide by the decision made.

On the conciliation side, again, ACAS will listen to both sides of the argument and attempt to resolve the situation by encouraging those in dispute to move closer to one another's point of view.

Industrial tribunals

Industrial tribunals are made up of individuals who have specific knowledge of employment law. The chairperson of a tribunal is either a barrister or solicitor with at least seven years' experience. The other members of the industrial tribunal include two 'lay' people (individuals who do not have a specific allegiance to either employers or employees). These 'lay' people are either nominated by the CBI (Confederation of British Industry) or the TUC (Trades Union Congress). The members of the tribunal all have an equal say and decisions are made by majority verdict. Industrial tribunals are somewhat more accessible than other courts. By simply filling in a form, an individual need not resort to the professional assistance of a solicitor, or, indeed, have any representation at the hearing. The tribunal does not take place in a courtroom and all of the usual complications that are associated with courts are avoided.

As there are no court fees, it is inexpensive to take a case to an industrial tribunal.

Normally, an industrial tribunal is involved in complaints regarding unfair dismissal. The ex-employee must first ask ACAS to decide whether the case needs to be taken to an industrial tribunal. Once a complaint reaches an industrial tribunal, around one-third of complaints are upheld. Although this may seem to indicate that employers tend to 'win' more often than not, lessons still need to be learned by the employers who have allowed the complaint to go as far as an industrial tribunal.

Individuals who have had their complaints supported by an industrial tribunal are entitled to compensation, reinstatement or re-engagement.

In the event that an employer or employee makes an appeal on a point of law made by an industrial tribunal, then they can be referred to the Employment Appeals Tribunal.

The Employment Appeals Tribunal (EAT) consists of a High Court Judge and two lay people. It is the role of the EAT to confirm or reverse the findings of an industrial tribunal. In some cases, an appeal may be made to the Court of Appeal or to the House of Lords. The House of Lords is the highest court in the UK.

The European Court of Justice

The European Court of Justice was created to help enforce the following:

- international law
- European Community law
- other customary law

The European Court of Justice has the final say in cases which involve EC law in particular. In this respect, the Court of Justice can be seen as the final court of appeal if all other actions have failed. Usually the House of Lords will itself refer the case to the Court of Justice if it does involve EC law. In recent years, the Court of Justice has become involved in many other areas of law, employment law being just one of these.

2.2.3 Explain employer rights and responsibilities

Employer rights

The success or failure of an organisation will largely depend upon the balance struck between the employer and the employee.

Employers are very dependent on the people who work for them. In nearly all functions it will be these people who represent the interests of the organisation. Just how these people react to the requirements of the organisation, and how they respond to a variety of conflicting needs, are of crucial concern.

The relationship between employer and employees is not left solely for the two parties to agree upon. There is a range of laws which govern the relationship. Equally, just as the employee should be protected from abuses, so too should the employer. We will look at this aspect of the relationship later. Nevertheless, the employee does have a range of responsibilities that will be taken on when accepting employment.

We will first look at the employee's rights and responsibilities. Essentially, these fall into six major categories which cover most of the aspects of the relationship with the employer.

PC 2.2.3
C 2.1

Group activity *Time: 15 minutes*

Before reading any further in this section, in pairs try to think of at least three rights or responsibilities of both the employer and the employee. Compare your list with the rest of the group.

Employees' compliance with terms of contract

The employee has a responsibility to the employer to work in a loyal, conscientious and honest manner. The employee is also expected to accept any reasonable and legal directions from superiors. In essence, this means adhering to the terms of the employee's contract of employment. As we have seen, the contract of employment can be a very detailed document and is considered to be a legally binding contract once both parties have signed. By law, all employees must have received a contract of employment within 13 weeks of beginning employment. The employer is required to exercise a duty of care over employees, provide sufficient work for them to do, pay the employee at due times and maintain a number of records on behalf of the employee. These will include:

- *PAYE deductions*
- *National Insurance contributions*
- *pension scheme contributions*

The employer must take care when advertising a job, as it is considered to be the beginnings of the formation of the contract of employment. Once a candidate for a particular job accepts employment on the basis of the advertisement details, then much of the contract of employment has already been decided. Before the employer finally accepts a candidate as an employee, references will usually be taken up. If the prospective employer receives unfavourable references about the candidate, then they are quite within their rights to withdraw the job offer. In reality, just how the employer interprets the content of a reference is open to question.

A contract of employment is really like any other contract. It gives both parties rights as well as obligations. The contract, as we mentioned earlier, identifies formally what was really agreed during the interview or selection process. Normally, a contract of employment will contain the following, either directly, or by inference:

1 The employer will pay wages
2 The employer will provide work
3 The employer will pay any reasonable losses or expenses incurred by the employee in the course of their work
4 The employer will provide a reference if required by the employee
5 The employer will provide safe working conditions and working practices
6 The employer will not act in such a way as to breach the trust and confidence given by the employee
7 The employer will provide necessary information relating to the employee's work, pay, conditions and opportunities
8 The employer will always act in good faith towards the employee

In addition to the obvious obligations the employee may have, he/she will also be expected to:

- act in good faith towards the employer
- account for any cash received from other sources (this is to make sure that the employee does not accept bribes or fees in pursuit of their normal activities from external organisations)
- keep trade secrets confidential
- obey any reasonable orders and give faithful service to the employer

Employees' compliance with health and safety regulations

Just as the employer must take heed of the requirements of the important series of Acts regarding health and safety, so must the employee. Employees may suffer harm or injuries which are not necessarily the fault of the employer.

If an employee is negligent and causes injury to himself/herself or to another person, then the employer may be in a difficult position. The employee may claim that it was not really his/her fault. As long as the employer provides safe working conditions, then apart from accidents caused by negligence, there should be no real concern here. We will look at the employer's role in preventing accidents later.

Another possible area of concern is when an employee deliberately puts someone else's life in danger. Depending on the circumstances, the employee could find themselves not only dismissed, but the subject of criminal or civil proceedings.

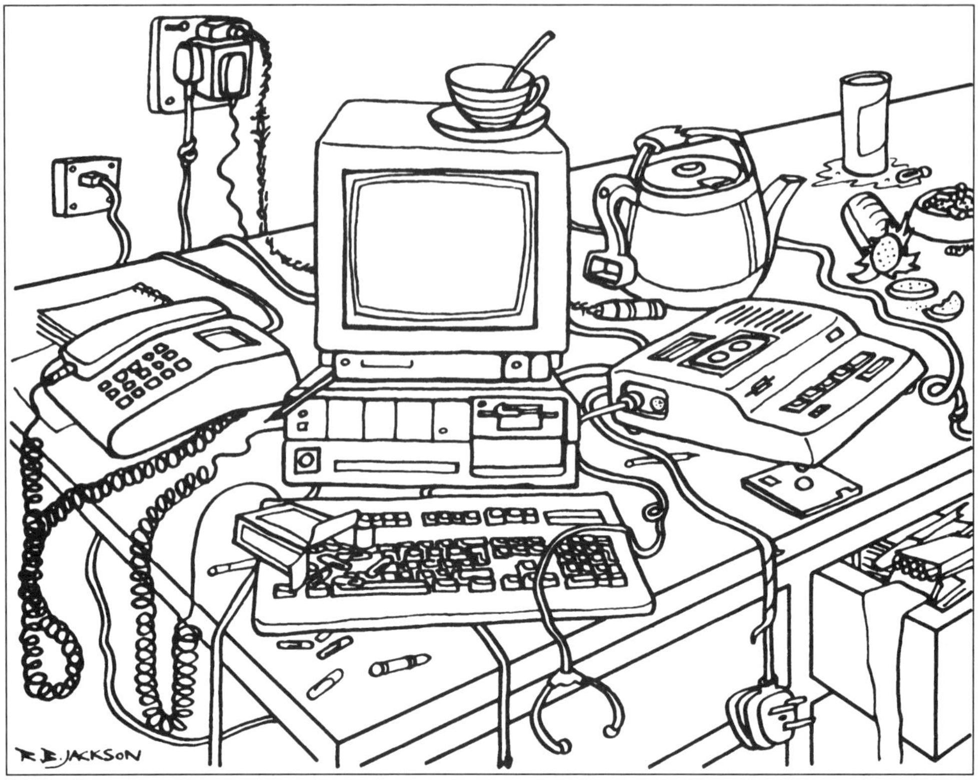

Fig 2.16 Health and safety hazards

PC 2.2.3
C 2.2
C 2.3
IT 2.1
IT 2.2
IT 2.3

Individual activity

With reference to the legislation detailed later in this Element, compile a Health and Safety report based on the institution in which you are carrying out your studies. You should highlight any potential dangers and compare these with any preventative procedures already in place. It would be useful to talk to the person who has responsibility for health and safety and to consult any documentation they may be able to supply.

Your report should be word processed.

Disciplinary action and legal representation (ACAS, industrial tribunals, European Court of Justice)

The contract of employment, between the employer and the employee, inevitably must cease at some point. Often, but not always, this is related to disciplinary matters. The key part is that one or other of the parties who signed the contract of employment has broken it. The employee may not be dismissed without good reason. Let us look at the reasons for dismissal relating to the employee breaking the contract.

DISCIPLINARY NOTICE

COMPANY NAME AND ADDRESS

Classification of Warning	Tick as appropriate
VERBAL WARNING	
WRITTEN WARNING	
FINAL WRITTEN WARNING	

Employees Name: .... Date and Time of issue: ....

Issued by: .... in the presence of ....

Warning issued as a result of a disciplinary meeting held on ....

DETAILS OF OFFENCE:-

EMPLOYEES EXPLANATION:-

FUTURE ACTION REQUIRED FROM EMPLOYEE:-

THE EMPLOYEE has been informed of:-

(a) The right to be accompanied by a Friend or Colleague (who is also an employee of the Company) at all stages of the disciplinary procedure.

(b) The right to appeal, in accordance with the Company's Appeal Procedure against any warning.

Signed by person issuing: ....

Signed by Receiving Employee: ....

Fig 2.17 Proforma disciplinary notice. Note the multi-purpose nature of the form

Dismissal

This basically means that the employer is terminating the contract of the employee for a particular reason, usually relating to their behaviour or conduct. The employer has to give the employee notice of the intention to dismiss them. In some cases, the dismissal may be instant, but this is usually restricted to very serious matters.

If the employer puts the employee in such a position as to make it impossible to stay with the organisation, this is known as constructive dismissal. Courts have found in favour of employees who have been put in this position by the unfair attitudes and actions of the employer. Such examples would relate to:

- *changes in wages, without informing the employee*
- *changes in the location of the job, without consultation*
- *changes in duties required, without negotiation*
- *changes in job descriptions, without negotiations*

In all of these examples, the employer has decided, on their own, to change certain conditions of work. In some cases, this will break the original contract of employment. Sometimes, an employee may resign as a result of a series of events. In these cases, an industrial tribunal would look carefully at the series of events and decide whether this is constructive dismissal.

Some of the breaches of the contract of employment may refer to sexual harassment or discrimination on the grounds of race or colour (for further details please see relevant Acts later in this Element).

All contracts are a matter of interpretation, and we will look at this aspect shortly.

Unfair dismissal

The right not to be unfairly dismissed from your job is a very important one. The laws relating to this prevent employers from thinking that they have the right to hire and fire as they see fit. It is, however, a very complex issue. Whether an individual employee qualifies in claiming that they have been unfairly dismissed is a much argued subject.

Generally speaking, for an employee to qualify for a claim for unfair dismissal, the following requirements have to be met:

1 The employee must have worked for the employer, as a full-time member of staff, for at least two years
2 If a part-time worker, working eight hours a week or more, the employee must have been in employment for five years
3 The individual must not be of pensionable age
4 Police officers cannot claim unfair dismissal even though they may qualify in terms of service
5 Individuals who are only paid by receiving a share of the profits are exempt
6 Employees who work for the organisation outside the UK are exempt
7 Employees on fixed-period contracts are exempt (it will expressly state this in their contract of employment)
8 Members of the armed forces are also exempt on service grounds

In cases of dispute between the employer and the employee, ACAS will assist and attempt to resolve the conflict (*see* page 150). The person working for ACAS will try to get the two parties to agree rather than having to resort to the courts for a settlement.

Causes of dismissal

There will nearly always be a reason for an employer dismissing an employee, whether the reasons are right or wrong. There are essentially five main reasons:

1 **Capability and qualifications** – these two reasons relate to the employee's fitness or competence to do the job. In this sense capability means skill, health, physical or mental ability. Qualifications, on the other hand, refer to the academic, technical or professional qualifications relevant to the job. Capability is an easier reason to define and explain. Basically, if the employee is shown to be incompetent or shows serious errors of judgement, then the employer has grounds for dismissal. Qualifications can

be more complicated. If the employee is taken on by the employer on the basis that he/she must achieve a certain level of qualification, and then fails to, the employer may dismiss the employee.

2 **Redundancy** – if the employer closes down the business, or part of the business, some or all of the employees may no longer be needed. In such cases, the employer must consult the employees, and must have fairly selected those to be made redundant and offered them alternative employment if available. There are always ways around this problem of redundancy. For example, the employer could freeze recruitment and redeploy the existing employees, or reduce the number of hours which all of the employees work.

3 **Misconduct** – this is a very wide area, and includes the following:

- *absenteeism* – where an employee is away from work too often
- *lateness* – where an employee constantly turns up late for work
- *insubordination* – where an employee refuses to carry out instructions from a superior
- *incompetence* – where the employee shows on several occasions the inability to do the job
- *immorality* – where the employee behaves in a way that is unacceptable, perhaps sexually or morally
- *breaking safety rules* – where an employee endangers his/her life or the lives of others by not taking heed of the safety rules, perhaps deliberately
- *theft* – where the employee has stolen the property of the employer

In reality then, the employer can identify a number of reasons for dismissal due to misconduct. This may mean that an employee who is having an affair at work, or an employee wearing offensive badges or T-shirts, or, indeed, an employee involved in questionable activities outside the workplace could be dismissed under misconduct guidelines.

4 **Statutory contraventions** – this reason for dismissal relates directly to an employee doing something which breaks a legal requirement. Good examples of this would be a lorry driver who is banned from driving due to drink-driving or even an employee who works for a butcher and grows a beard! (This would be against hygiene and food legislation.)

5 **Other reasons** – this broad area includes all other reasons not covered above, and is therefore a difficult category to describe. Examples would include gradual deterioration in the output or performance of an employee, or in certain cases, the sexuality of the employee.

Fairness and dismissal

The employer really needs a valid reason for dismissing an employee. The employer must not single out an individual because of their sex (for women, they have the right, of course, to be pregnant). If the employer chooses to dismiss an employee on the grounds of their sexuality, then there would have to be very strong reasons to link sexuality with the requirements and nature of the job. The employer's conduct must be fair towards the employee. In one particular case, all of the employees were dismissed from a shop after stock had been disappearing over a number of months. A tribunal held that the employer could not do this as there were insufficient grounds to dismiss all of the employees when perhaps only one of them was the culprit. The employer had not 'proved' the guilt of all employees.

Within the category of fairness, it would be safe to assume that the following are 'fair' reasons for dismissal:

- *sexual harassment of other employees or customers*
- *racial harassment of other employees or customers*
- *wilful destruction of the organisation's property*
- *negligence*
- *long-term bad timekeeping*
- *sleeping at work*
- *gross insubordination*
- *inability to do the job that the employee was appointed to do*
- *fraud including the falsification of records*
- *inability to do the job as the employee is under the influence of alcohol*
- *inability to do the job because the employee is under the influence of illegal drugs*
- *fighting – when the employee has assaulted another person on the premises of the organisation*
- *unauthorised entry to confidential computer records*

On the other hand, unfair dismissal may relate to the following:

- **Race** – an employer cannot dismiss an employee on the grounds of the employee's race
- **Religion** – an employee cannot be dismissed on the grounds of his/her religious beliefs
- **Sexual discrimination** – an employer cannot dismiss an employee because they are a homosexual or a lesbian, unless it affects the standard of the work, or the individual is sexually harassing other members of the workforce
- **Pregnancy** – as we have already said, a woman cannot be dismissed because she is pregnant. However, if the pregnancy affects her ability to do the job in total (e.g. a woman may be a labourer or have to carry heavy weights) then there are reasonable grounds
- **Criminal record** – if the employer finds out that an employee has a criminal record, but it does not relate to the job, then that employee cannot be dismissed. However, some criminal records may relate to the job, such as fraud and accountancy! In this case, the employer is within his/her rights to dismiss the employee
- **Trade union membership** – an employee cannot be dismissed for being a member of a union

Disciplinary procedures

The approved disciplinary procedure, as recommended by ACAS, should be both fair and impartial. It includes the following features:

1. that all stages of the procedure should be written down as a record of events
2. that copies of the procedures should be available to all employees
3. that the employer should clearly state who is involved
4. that the employer should clearly state who operates the procedure within the organisation
5. that the employer clearly states what kind of disciplinary action will be taken in particular types of disciplinary matters
6. that the employee has the right to have a friend, colleague or trades union representative present during all disciplinary interviews
7. that in most cases, apart from really serious matters, an employee is not dismissed for a first 'offence'

8 that the employee does have the right to appeal against a decision made by the employer
9 that all proceedings should be administered in a fair way
10 that the employee should not be unfairly discriminated against throughout the whole process

Normally, the actual disciplinary procedure would work along the lines shown in the following checklist.

Stages in a normal disciplinary procedure

1 **Verbal warning** – if the employee's conduct, behaviour or performance does not reach suitable and acceptable standards, then they will be given a formal verbal warning. This is the first official stage of the proceedings, and will not last forever, providing the employee reaches acceptable standards. If the employee does so, then he/she will not move on to the next stage, and the matter will be dropped.

2 **Written warning** – if the employee persists with the same behaviour that resulted in their receiving a verbal warning, or if the 'offence' is serious enough, then a written warning will be issued. This is usually written by the employee's immediate supervisor.

The written warning details the complaint against the employee, and clearly states exactly what the employee must do to remedy the situation. The warning will also state how long the employee has to 'mend' his/her ways. If the employee persists, then inevitably the next stage of the procedures will occur. Again, if the employee complies with the requirements of the written warning, then the matter will be dropped. The employee may also appeal against this written warning through the usual channels.

3 **The final written warning or suspension** – if the employee continues to fail to improve his/her conduct, behaviour or performance, then normally a final written warning will be given. If the conduct has been sufficiently serious, the employee may automatically be given a final written warning, rather than go through the first few procedures. Just as the written warning gives details of the complaint and a stern warning that dismissal is imminent should there be no satisfactory improvement, so too does the final written warning.

As an alternative, the employer may wish to suspend the individual for a maximum of five days without pay. This is known as 'disciplinary suspension'.

4 **Dismissal** – the final stage in the disciplinary procedure is dismissal itself. To reach this point, the employee must have had to fail all the requirements as laid down in the written warnings. The employee's most senior but related line manager will make the decision to dismiss the employee. The employee will be given a written statement which includes the reasons for their dismissal and the date of termination of employment. Further, it will say how the employee may appeal.

5 **Appeals** – if an employee chooses to appeal at any stage in the disciplinary procedure, that employee must inform his/her superior within two working days. The manager will consider the appeal. However, the manager's decision is final. The manager may choose to uphold the decision to discipline the employee, but may not increase the severity of the action taken against the employee.

It is recommended that all disciplinary matters should be considered at length and that employees should have the right to state their side of the argument. As we have said, all disciplinary meetings or interviews should take place in the presence of a trades union official or a colleague.

Normally, an employee is given two verbal warnings, followed by a final written warning before they are dismissed. It should be remembered that the disciplinary code of the employer must be reasonable and fair. If an employee thinks they have not had sufficient opportunity to state their case, then they may choose to refer the matter to an industrial tribunal.

Employers are not legally obliged to follow the above disciplinary process, but many have nevertheless done so. After all, employers are unlikely and unwilling to face the disruption and expense of an industrial tribunal.

Industrial tribunals

Industrial tribunals were set up by the government as a kind of court. They are there to try to obtain an agreement between the employer and the employees and have the power to demand reinstatement of the employee or to award financial compensation if the former is not practicable. Over the years, industrial tribunals have heard matters arising from many of the laws and regulations detailed later in this book.

PC 2.2.3
C 2.1
C 2.2
C 2.3
IT 2.1
IT 2.2
IT 2.3

Group activity

Time: 1.5 hours

In pairs, in the role of Personnel Manager, draw up a disciplinary procedure which details the following:

- **reasons why disciplinary action may be taken**
- **the grievance procedure**
- **the appeals procedure**

You should try to present this information in the form of a flow chart and to indicate the government legislation, where necessary.

This information and flow chart should be in the form of a confidential memorandum, and will form the basis of a staff handbook to be issued at a later date. Your memorandum should be word processed.

Employer responsibilities

As we will see in this section of the Element, the employer has a wide range of responsibilities. Many of these are legally-based and must be carried out. Other responsibilities may relate to things that the employer does in order to make the organisation run smoothly: keeping the employees informed about what is going on and the direction in which the organisation is going is just one of the employer's responsibilities.

As you will see in the next section, many of the responsibilities of the employer are related to making sure that procedures are followed and that fair treatment is given throughout the organisation to all employees. In this section you will also find all the employment legislation which relates to working conditions, equality, and health and safety. We have already mentioned these in passing in the first part of this performance criteria, and will return to them later when we look at the employee's rights and responsibilities in the next performance criteria.

To explain business objectives

Obviously, it is in everyone's interests to identify the exact business objectives of the organisation. In addition, business objectives can differ from time to time. Objectives are the medium to long-term targets which help the business to achieve its 'mission statement'.

There are numerous methods of ensuring that the employees know about the current business objectives. It is advisable that the organisation ensures that the true picture and statement of objectives is made. Organisations will employ some of the following to ensure that this vital communication system, which is relaying perhaps constantly changing business objectives, is passing on the information to the employees. These include:

- *staff meetings*
- *newsletters*
- *company newspapers*
- *bulletin boards*
- *noticeboards*
- *E-mail*
- *press statements*
- *corporate videos*
- *letters sent direct to all employees*

An organisation which fails to ensure that its employees are told of any key changes in company policy or objectives may find itself working 'against' the employees. It is also a good idea to try to clarify the business objectives in order to prepare the employees for any possible training and development. An organisation which is able to look ahead and, to some extent, predict its business objectives is an organisation which will find that employees know what will be expected of them.

To offer and facilitate training

Training basically falls into four separate categories, which are:

1. **on-the-job training** – which refers to training carried out while at work
2. **off-the-job training** – which refers to training carried out at a location other than the workplace
3. **part-time training** – which refers to the 'mode' of training itself. This category includes day release, evening classes and short courses
4. **full-time training** – which refers to short-term or even long-term training courses which take the employee out of the workplace for an extended period

Most organisations run special courses, either at the workplace or in an alternative location. It is usually key employees who are chosen to attend these courses and they are then expected to pass on the knowledge they have acquired to the rest of the members of their work teams.

Many people start their careers with few or no qualifications. Most individuals will have at least some basic understanding of English or Mathematics, but it is only when they begin to consider what their career goal may be that they realise they should start to gain qualifications which will help them achieve their goal. Depending on the time and effort put in, individuals can slowly progress in their collection of qualifications. At the same time, particularly if the individual is in work, he/she will be gaining additional responsibilities as a result of the qualifications he/she has achieved.

Whether we are looking at training or qualifications, we must make two more important points which relate to the nature of the course of study, and concern whether it is vocational or non-vocational.

1 **Vocational training or qualifications** are those which relate directly to the job or job area. It does not matter whether the individual is in work or not, since the programme should be designed to offer the learner the opportunity to practise the type of skills required for a particular job. This has become a very popular area, much supported by employers, who see this as the only useful and relevant way of preparing individuals for work within industry, commercial services or technology.

2 **Non-vocational courses** In some respects, you would think that the non-vocational course is the complete opposite to a vocational course. This may not necessarily be the case. Typically, a course which falls into this category will not have a direct relevance to a particular job and may be more general in nature. Non-vocational courses may be academic and provide a wide range of knowledge. Individuals who have followed such courses will need to undertake further training to learn how to put into practice the knowledge they have gained on their academic course.

Group activity *Time: 20 minutes*

PC 2.2.3
C 2.1
C 2.2

In pairs, using the following sources of information, prepare a short list which should include at least five vocational and non-vocational courses:

- **your college library**
- **your local library**
- **your careers office**
- **your careers officer (if you have one)**

To implement equal opportunities legislation at work (Sex Discrimination Act, Race Relations Act, Equal Pay Act)

Even in these modern times, there are many individuals who are discriminated against on various grounds. Within employment, employees are protected to some extent by a series of laws and regulations, which we look at in some detail later. The main groups who suffer from discrimination are:

- *women*
- *ethnic minorities*
- *disabled*
- *those with an alternative sexual orientation*
- *the young*
- *the old*
- *certain religious groups*

Many organisations have adopted equal opportunities policies, although they are not yet required to do this by law. The Equal Opportunities Commission has designed a standard policy which employers can use. This covers a variety of different situations, and includes the following:

1. that to have an equal opportunities policy is a desirable thing
2. that it should be strictly adhered to
3. that all forms of direct and indirect discrimination are clearly defined
4. that the organisation states its commitment to equal opportunities and, further, states that it is in the best interests of the organisation and its employees
5. that all employees are made aware of the policy
6. that staff are trained to maintain the policy
7. that any preconceived ideas which employees may have regarding those who are subject to discrimination are addressed
8. that both recruitment and promotion is equal for all
9. that training is offered on an equal basis to all
10. that the employment contract does not inadvertently discriminate against anyone
11. that the organisation's facilities are open to all
12. that an individual is nominated to monitor the policy
13. that the policy is regularly reviewed and updated according to need
14. that any grievances relating to discrimination are dealt with in a prompt and fair manner
15. that no individual suffers victimisation in the course of their duties within the organisation

Group activity *Time: 20 minutes*

PC 2.2.3
C 2.2

Discuss the following statement as a group:

'An individual should not be protected by a series of laws and regulations. They should be able to stand on their own two feet.'

Sex Discrimination Acts 1975 and 1986

The Sex Discrimination Act 1975 covers discrimination on the grounds of gender. It is equally applicable to both males and females. The Act also covers discrimination relating to marital status.

The amended Act of 1986 extended protection against discrimination to employers employing five or less people. It also included for the first time employees working in a domestic capacity for private employers and employees working for professional associations.

Equal Pay Act 1970

This important act states that women performing a similar job to men should be treated in every way equally. This includes not only pay and conditions, but opportunity for promotion and recognition.

Race Relations Act 1970

This very complicated piece of legislation aims to protect individuals against discrimination on the grounds of race, colour, nationality, national origin or ethnicity.

The Rehabilitation of Offenders Act 1974

Individuals who have criminal convictions need not necessarily mention these on their job application forms or during interviews. Some convictions, after a certain period of time, are considered to be 'spent' (no longer applicable). If an employer subsequently discovers that an employee has 'spent' convictions and decides on dismissal, this is illegal.

Disabled Persons (Employment) Act 1958

An employer with 20 or more employees must employ a minimum of three registered disabled persons. Certain organisations can obtain an exemption certificate due to the hazardous nature of their work. On the other hand, certain organisations are required to give disabled persons priority in selection and recruitment, e.g. electronic switchboard operators, etc.

To comply with health and safety regulations

In general, the health and safety requirements with which any employer must comply are:

- *to provide a safe working environment*
- *to provide adequate welfare facilities*
- *to ensure entrances and exits are safe*
- *to ensure equipment and systems used are safe and regularly serviced*
- *to make sure that items needed for use in handling or storage are safe*
- *to make sure that dangerous or toxic materials are housed in safe containers*
- *to provide instruction, training or supervision regarding working practices and materials used*
- *to ensure that all accidents are rigorously investigated and the causes promptly dealt with*

If legal requirements are broken by either employers or employees, in effect one side or the other has been negligent.

PC 2.2.3
C 2.3

Individual activity *Time: 45 minutes*

Identify a particular health and safety concern of your own choice. Create a simple flowchart which describes the actions to be taken in the event of this health and safety matter occurring.

Many laws, directives and other forms of legislation relate to health and safety. We identify all of the main ones in this section, but you will find that there are a great many specific laws relating to very particular situations and hazards in the workplace.

The Factories Act 1961

This Act covers a wide range of different organisations, focusing on the use of machinery. The key features of this piece of legislation are:

1. The employer must provide toilet and washing facilities.
2. Premises should be adequately heated and ventilated.
3. The employer must make sure that floors, stairs and passageways are not obstructed in any way.
4. All floors should have a non-slippery surface.
5. Potentially dangerous machinery should be fenced off to protect employees.
6. The employer must ensure that there are adequate fire escapes, well signposted and regularly maintained.
7. Fire doors themselves should never be locked or obstructed.

The Offices, Shops and Railways Premises Act 1963

This act concentrates on conditions within shops and offices and provides a number of clear guidelines to the employer, including:

1. In work areas, the temperature must never drop below 16°C.
2. The employer must ensure that there is an adequate supply of fresh air.
3. Following on from the Factories Act 1961, this legislation states that the employer must provide enough toilet and washing facilities in relation to the number of staff. The employer must also make sure that there is hot and cold running water as well as soap and clean towels.
4. Again, following on from the Factories Act 1961, this legislation states that an employer has to provide suitable lighting wherever employees are expected to work or move around.
5. The employer must ensure that there is at least 12 square metres of working space per employee.

Health and Safety At Work Act 1974 and EC Directives on Health and Safety

Before this Act, employees had been protected against hazardous working conditions under a number of different pieces of legislation. HASAWA aimed to bring together and extend the protection of employees under a single Act. The main points were:

1. State general duties of an employer across all types of industry and commerce.
2. Create a system by which HASAWA could be enforced (by the Health and Safety Executive and local authorities).
3. The formation of the Health and Safety Commission which aimed to help employers understand the regulations and develop codes of practice.
4. The Act was backed up by imposing a series of legal duties on employers, who ran the risk of criminal proceedings being taken against them if they failed to follow these requirements.
5. The imposition of minimum safety regulations and improvements to the working environment were introduced.

The work of HASAWA has been followed up by a number of EC Directives covering such areas as safety signs at work, employees handling hazardous materials, and guidance regarding avoidance of major hazards.

New regulations and codes of practice are being designed continuously and now cover nearly all work activities, both in the private and public sector. Steps are now being taken to cover any gaps in the legislation, and to make it easier to understand and implement.

Management of Health and Safety At Work Regulations 1992

This major piece of legislation aims to provide a systematic and well-organised set of guidelines in relation to health and safety. They include the following:

1. Employers are required to assess any potential risks employees may have to face and take preventative measures to cope with them.
2. This risk assessment must be continually monitored by a group of employers working closely with at least five employees.
3. Employers are required to employ specialists whose sole responsibility it is to implement the preventative measures, as well as providing information for all other employees within the organisation.
4. Employers are further required to carry out regular screenings of their employees to make sure that they have not suffered from any ill-effects as a result of carrying out their duties. If appropriate, any health hazards which have been identified should be addressed immediately.
5. Employees who have been given the duties of Safety Representatives should be regularly consulted, provided with time and space to carry out their investigations, and given the authority to act on them.

Health and Safety (Display Screen Equipment) Regulations 1992

This Act is designed to protect employees who spend considerable amounts of their working hours in front of a computer screen. The main points of the legislation are:

1. Employees must receive sufficient breaks from the screen.
2. Work should not be repetitive and the employee should be given a variety of tasks.
3. Basic safety requirements must be satisfied as regards the screen itself and the design of the keyboard, as well as the shape and height of the desk and chair being used.
4. Regular eye tests must be provided by the employer and, if the employee needs special spectacles in order to carry out their tasks, they should be provided by the employer.
5. Efficient lighting should be provided in the room where the employee is using the computer, as should proper ventilation.

Provision and Use of Work Equipment Regulations 1992

This Act covers all equipment from major production line machinery to hand-held tools. The legislation requires employers to:

1. Take into consideration how and where equipment will be used, and choose the least hazardous methods of production.
2. Ensure when purchasing equipment that it conforms with any applicable EC Safety Directive.
3. Ensure that employees are given sufficient information to use any equipment safely. Where appropriate, training and retraining should be offered.
4. Ensure that all equipment is regularly serviced.
5. Ensure that potentially dangerous machinery has appropriate guards to prevent injury.
6. Ensure that when using hazardous materials protection is available.

7 Be responsible for ensuring that work is carried out in an environment which has sufficient light.
8 Display any relevant warnings regarding potential dangers.

Manual Handling Operations Regulations 1992

These regulations were implemented to assist in the avoidance of unnecessary injury at work. This Directive covers lifting, pushing, pulling, carrying and moving objects at work, and offers advice as to the correct manner in which these should be carried out.

Personal Protective Equipment at Work Regulations 1992

The term 'personal protective equipment' includes life-jackets; harnesses; head, hand and foot protection; glasses and goggles; and clothing designed to be visible at all times and in all conditions. The Directive states that the protective equipment must be fit for the purpose for which it is intended, as well as actually fitting the employee. The equipment must conform with EC regulations and it must be suitably stored, regularly cleaned and replaced if defective. In addition, employees must be trained in the correct use of the equipment.

PC 2.2.3
C 2.1

Group activity *Time: 30 minutes*

In pairs, in the role of Personnel Manager, or Health And Safety Officer, say which of the following situations relate to the Acts as detailed above:

1 **A word processing operator has complained of constant migraines since being issued with a new computer.**
2 **There has been a complaint regarding noxious fumes in the factory.**
3 **The temperature in the office has dropped to 10°C.**
4 **It has been rumoured that an employee has a criminal record of which you are officially unaware.**
5 **A female member of staff has been receiving sexually abusive telephone calls at work. Investigations have shown that the calls have been made from another extension within the organisation.**

Remuneration (pay, deduction of income tax, payment of National Insurance, pension deductions if in contract)

In the majority of cases, people work for pay. This may be in the form of:

- *wages, paid weekly, sometimes in cash*
- *salary, paid monthly, either by cheque or by bank transfer*
- *commission, paid on performance, usually measured in sales volume generated by the individual*
- *bonuses, paid according to whether specific targets have been met*
- *performance related, an additional payment related to the individual's commitment beyond their usual job*
- *profit related, linked to the overall profit made by the department or organisation as a whole*

Whatever the form of remuneration, the employer is essentially paying the employee for their time and effort. Some would say that employers are 'buying' a piece of the employee's life. This is true to some extent but we will see that this is a two-way relationship.

There are, of course, some individuals who do not work for remuneration. These would include the following:

- charity workers
- volunteers
- individuals who 'trade' their skills and time in return for someone else's expertise

In the majority of cases, an employee would, quite rightly, expect a fair day's pay for a fair day's work. The key to this equation is two-fold:

- *the employer must be able to place a 'value' on the employee's time and effort*
- *the employee must have a clear idea of what his/her time and effort are worth*

If the two parties can agree, then this relationship should be a relatively easy one. In many cases, however, the two parties radically disagree. This can form the basis of conflict in the future. In such circumstances, the employer may find the only option is to pay the amount the employee demands. This might be because there is a shortage of skills and expertise. On the other hand, and far more commonly, it is the employee who finds it impossible to get the payment he / she believes is fair, as there are too many people with the same skills and expertise chasing too few jobs on offer.

PC 2.2.3
C 2.2
C 2.3
C 2.4

Group activity

In the past, many people operated on a barter system rather than receiving payment for goods or services. In pairs, research the barter system and try to work out when it really went out of fashion. Why do you think this was? Is there a place for it today? Compare your findings with those of the rest of your group.

Deduction of income tax, National Insurance and pension contributions

In relation to the employer's responsibility for deducting income tax and National Insurance contributions from employee's pay, we can see the employer as being tax collectors on behalf of the government. It would be impossible for the government to try to collect taxes from individuals directly. The government relies on the employer to make the correct deduction and then to pass this on to either the Inland Revenue (in the case of income tax) or the Department of Social Security (in the case of National Insurance contributions). It is the responsibility of the employer to ensure that this money is sent on to the relevant government department, since the employee has no direct contact with either organisation unless it is to make an enquiry about their tax code or the amount of National Insurance contribution that they are paying.

- **P60** The Inland Revenue will produce a yearly P60 form for each employee, which details the salary or wage total for the year, together with the income tax and National Insurance paid. This acts as a record for the employee to make sure that the deductions made by the employer are the same as the totals detailed on the P60.
- **P45** The P45 form details the tax code, which, in effect, tells the employee how much

they can earn before they are taxed. This amount is known as the personal allowance. The personal allowance varies according to circumstances. A married person will have a higher personal allowance than a single person, for example.

- **National Insurance** Each individual has a National Insurance number (which is shown on the pay slip). This is the reference number that you can quote if you need to make an enquiry. The payment of National Insurance entitles the individual to sick pay, maternity pay and a pension at retirement age.
- **Pensions** On the question of pensions, many organisations offer a company pension scheme that requires the employee to make regular contributions out of their salary or wages. Again, the deductions will be detailed on the pay slip and will usually be a regular amount each time. Pension schemes tend to be:

  1 **Contributory** – which means that the employer also makes a payment into the pension scheme on behalf of the employee each month or week.
  2 **Non-contributory** – which means that the employer does not make a payment and all of the pension payments are the responsibility of the employee alone.

To comply with other legislation

We have identified all of the major types of legislation that relate to equal opportunities and health and safety. In this additional section, we will look at the remaining pieces of legislation that must be complied with by the employer.

Employment Protection Act 1975 and Employment Protection (Consolidation) Act 1978

The original Act, substantially amended in 1978, covers the main features of a contract of employment. In addition, it requires employers to provide a contract of employment within 13 weeks of commencement of employment. We have looked at contracts of employment in much more detail earlier in the book.

Employment Acts 1980–90

Since 1979 successive governments have taken steps to limit trade union power. The main points of each of the laws are as follows:

1980 Picketing (attempting to prevent other employees, customers, deliveries, etc., from entering or leaving the premises during industrial action) was restricted to the premises involved in the dispute and none of the other organisation's premises. The Act also restricted 'blacking' (employees refusing to handle goods from an organisation whose employees are in dispute). It also became illegal to sack an employee who refused to join a trade union. Before this, certain occupations required compulsory membership of a trade union (known as a 'closed shop'). These closed shops were further restricted by the law requiring 80% of employees to agree that a closed shop should exist.

1982 This law restricted the reasons for an industrial dispute being called in the first place. The reasons had to be related directly to employment matters and could in no way be political. A more damaging part of the Act, as far as trade unions were concerned, was that they could now be sued by employers for any loss of business to other organisations as a result of industrial action.

A trade union's funds were now open to seizure by the courts to pay for damages.

Following on from the restrictions made on closed shops in 1980, the law stated that trade union members must vote as to whether closed shops should continue.

1988 For the first time, individual trade union members were given the right to take their union to court to prevent industrial action. This only applied when the union itself declared there should be industrial action, and a ballot had not been taken. Union members were also protected under this law against disciplinary procedures for not having taken part in industrial action. Employees could now work for organisations which had closed shops, and not join the union, in the knowledge that they would keep their jobs.

1989 This amendment Act required employers to provide some form of document which stated the terms and conditions under which an individual is employed. This is not a contract of employment, and does not have all its details.

1990 This Act outlawed the dismissal of an individual who refused to join a union. Secondary action (union members taking industrial action in support of other union members) was made illegal. Unions became responsible, legally and financially, for any unofficial industrial action taken by members. All industrial action had to be approved by a majority of members in a secret ballot. Any union members involved in unofficial industrial action could be singled out by the employer and dismissed.

Trade Union Act 1988

This Act clearly stated that all industrial action must be agreed in advance by a majority of union members in a secret ballot.

EC Directive 'An Employer's Obligation to Inform Employees of the Conditions of Employment Relationship' 1991

The most important feature of this EC Directive is a change to the nature of the contract of employment. Employers are now required to provide a range of information, as detailed below, within two months, instead of within 13 weeks as before.

- *The location of the work*
- *The job title*
- *The type of job (by categories)*
- *A job description*
- *Paid leave entitlements*
- *Hours of work*
- *Collective agreements made organisationally/nationally*

This is the first stage of a comprehensive range of legislation designed to ensure that employees throughout the European Union have an employment contract, and know exactly what is required of them. The intention is also to treat employees working on a part-time basis as equal to full-time employees in most respects.

Trade Union Reform and Employment Rights Act 1992

This law was designed to assist the rapid creation of jobs by clearly stating exactly what an employer has to provide for the benefit of the employee. This includes a written statement which covers the employee's main conditions of employment (pay, holiday entitlement and hours worked).

Female employees are entitled to take 14 weeks' maternity leave in the knowledge that their job is secure for them to return to, should they desire to do so after the pregnancy.

Employees who have responsibility for ensuring that health and safety regulations are adhered to, and find themselves in a position where their employers have broken those regulations, are protected under this law from having the employer take action against them.

Focus study

Rights and responsibilities

One of last year's Level 2 students recently started a new job. It seemed to be just what Rachel was looking for. She loved to work with people and was always happiest when she was busy. MacMillans Estate Agency in the high street had selected her from no less than 20 other applicants. It was true that her job was not exactly glamorous at the moment, but the potential was there to learn and to gain valuable experience.

Her official job description was that of a Trainee Sales Negotiator. In effect, though, she found she was the office dogsbody! 'Photocopy this, Rachel!' 'Get me a sandwich, Rachel!' 'No, I don't want to talk to him; take a message, Rachel'. Frankly, after just a month, it was getting her down.

Rachel had been brooding about the whole problem for the entire weekend. Somehow she managed to pluck up the courage at least to walk to Mrs MacMillan's office door. Mrs MacMillan seemed to be an understanding type of person, but always too busy to give Rachel anything other than a smile. The promise of training had never materialised. Rachel was just left to pick things up as best she could. She hesitated in the corridor outside the door, then suddenly found herself gently knocking on the varnished wood.

'Come in', she heard. 'Oh, it's you, Rachel. What can I do for you? I hope this won't take long. I need to see a client across the other side of town in half an hour.' Rachel obviously looked embarrassed, confused and disillusioned. Mrs MacMillan picked up the telephone and rang through to the front office to rearrange her meeting.

'Sit down. What's wrong?'

Firmly, Rachel replied, 'I have decided to pack this job in.'

'What? You have only been here a month! I thought that you were happy. You seem to fit in OK. I have got lots of plans for you in the future. I think you would make a great Sales Negotiator,' protested Mrs MacMillan.

'I just haven't got a clue what I am supposed to do. No one tells me anything. No one really talks to me. If I do something wrong, they just shout at me. I just can't handle it any more,' Rachel poured out.

Individual activity *Time: 2 hours*

PC 2.2.3
C 2.1
C 2.2
C 2.3
C 2.4

Having read the situation in the focus study above, try to answer the following questions and solve the problems posed:

1. **Should Rachel have waited this long before seeing Mrs MacMillan?**
2. **Should the company have offered Rachel some training before throwing her in at the deep end?**
3. **Whose fault is the situation? Mrs MacMillan's or Rachel's?**

After some discussion with Rachel and the other members of the organisation, Mrs MacMillan decided to take Rachel under her wing and train her personally. In the role of Mrs MacMillan, how would you organise this training programme? What do you think Rachel needs to know before being left to her own devices?

Working individually, prepare a draft training programme on behalf of Mrs MacMillan to ensure that Rachel is fully informed about office procedures and communication with staff and clients, and is aware of what to do in circumstances when she cannot personally handle an enquiry.

2.2.4 Explain employee rights and responsibilities to their employers

Employee rights

As we have seen, the employer takes on a number of responsibilities in relation to the employee. If the relationship between the employer and the employee is to be successful and mutually beneficial, then employees need to accept responsibilities themselves. The employees are, of course, protected in terms of their rights by the legislation that we have looked at already.

In this performance criterion we will focus on the employees' rights and responsibilities. In other words, the employees' legal protection and the responsibilities that they have towards their employer.

Remuneration

Remuneration is the level of payment for a particular job. Normally, the level of payment is calculated to ensure the following:

- that it attracts suitable staff
- that it retains staff for a considerable period of time
- that it motivates staff by offering a reasonable payment package, or the ability to earn extra payment related to individual or organisational performance

- that it helps towards the general objectives of the organisation, in terms of competitive rates of pay and linking pay increases and bonuses to overall organisational performance

As we have already said in the previous section, an employee can reasonably expect to be paid for their labour, payment being at the times stated in the contract of employment.

Employer compliance with terms of contract

The employer must take care when advertising a job, as the advertisement is considered to be the beginning of the contract of employment. Before finally accepting a candidate as an employee, the employer will usually take up references. If the employer receives unfavourable references about the candidate, then the employer is quite entitled to withdraw the job offer. In reality, just how the employer interprets the content of a reference is open to question.

A contract of employment is really like any other contract. It gives both parties rights as well as obligations. Normally, a contract of employment will contain the following commitments, either directly or by inference:

1 The employer will pay the employee a wage / salary.
2 The employer will provide work.
3 The employer will pay any reasonable losses or expenses incurred by the employee in the course of his / her work.
4 The employer will provide a reference if required by the employee.
5 The employer will provide safe working conditions and practices.
6 The employer will not act in such a way as to breach the trust and confidence given by the employee.
7 The employer will provide necessary information relating to the employee's work, pay, conditions and opportunities.
8 The employer will always act in good faith towards the employee.

Group activity *Time: 20 minutes*

What do you understand by the phrase 'breach of trust and confidence'? Discuss this as a group.

PC 2.4.4
C 2.1

Health and safety at work

Employers are under a duty to ensure that reasonable care is taken to provide their employees with:

- *a safe place of work*
- *safe working methods*
- *training in health and safety practice*
- *safe equipment*

Obviously, it is hard to establish the nature of reasonable care. It is not usually sufficient that the employer simply provides a safe system of work. The employer must make sure that these systems have been fully put into effect. If, for example, the law requires that all employees use safety equipment while using machines, it is the employer's responsibility to make sure that the safety equipment is actually used. The employer cannot simply claim that the employees were told to use the safety equipment, or that someone was told to make sure this happened.

PC 2.2.4
C 2.1

Individual activity *Time: 10 minutes*

Individually, try to define the term 'reasonable care'. What do you think this means? Compare your definition with those of the rest of your group.

Equal opportunities at work (Sex Discrimination Act, Race Relations Act, Equal Pay Act)

As we have already addressed the main points of equal opportunities elsewhere in this Element, we will focus on the activities of various organisations that monitor equal opportunities and serve as a point of contact for assistance, should an employee encounter any discrimination.

Focus study

Equal Opportunities Commission

The Equal Opportunities Commission was created to ensure that the Sex Discrimination Act and Equal Pay Act were used within the workplace.

The EOC has the power to carry out investigations and, if they are satisfied that an unlawful act has happened, they can then issue non-discrimination notices which require the discrimination to cease.

The EOC has the power to require any individual to provide information or attend hearings to give evidence.

The EOC also has the power to help individuals prepare and conduct complaints in either courts or tribunals.

As well as their investigations, the EOC makes recommendations to the government regarding the operation of existing law.

The EOC also takes legal proceedings in its own right against individuals or organisations.

The EOC is involved in research and educational work relating to equal opportunities.

Fig 2.18 **A Short Guide to the Equal Opportunities Commission**

Group activity

Time: 30 minutes

PC 2.2.4
C 2.1
C 2.2

What is sex discrimination? There are two kinds of discrimination:

1 **Direct discrimination** – which involves treating a woman less favourably than a man because she is a woman.
2 **Indirect discrimination** – which favour one sex more than another for unjustifiable reasons.

Try to think of examples of direct and indirect discrimination. If you were the EOC, how would you identify them? Think of examples in pairs, write them down and swap your examples with another pair. Look at the examples of discrimination and work out the best way you could sort out the situation.

Focus study

Equal pay

Some twenty years have passed since the Equal Pay Act came into operation. Women still on average earn only 79 per cent of men's full-time hourly earnings. They tend to cluster in 'women's jobs', often undervalued and underpaid. Women provide the bulk of part-time workers, with low pay, and fewer opportunities for overtime or bonus earnings.

Focus study

Racial equality

The Race Relations Act came into force in 1977 and applies to discrimination before and after that date. The Act defines two kinds of racial discrimination; again, we can identify these as being direct or indirect.

Direct racial discrimination occurs when an individual treats another individual less favourably on racial grounds. The term 'racial grounds' covers the following:

- colour
- race
- nationality
- ethnicity
- national origins

Indirect racial discrimination can be best described as an individual requiring specific conditions to be satisfied as a result of being a member of a particular racial group. It is unlawful for an employer to discriminate in relation to employment.

Legal representation (ACAS, industrial tribunals, European Court of Justice)

Again, earlier in this Element we have covered the procedures and legislation which relate to legal representation. The employee would normally have to resort to legal representation only if the situation has got sufficiently out of hand and the employer is refusing to discuss the situation. It is usually the following causes of dispute which mean the employee needs to seek legal help:

- *disagreements over disciplinary procedures*
- *wrongful dismissal*
- *disputes over pay*
- *disputes over working conditions*
- *disputes relating to behaviour*

Group activity

Time: 15 minutes

Can you think of any other reasons why an employee may have to resort to legal measures to resolve a problem with his/her employer? Discuss this as a group.

PC 2.2.4
C 2.1

Trade union membership

Although trade unions have been the subject of a range of legislation to restrict their activities, the primary need for their existence still remains.

In effect, there are four different types of trade union, but the distinction between them is becoming increasingly less obvious.

Craft unions

These are the earliest type of trade union, which were formed for craftsmen who had received an apprenticeship. Craft union membership consists of individuals who work with the same basic range of skills. They are still relatively powerful, since they control the number of skilled craftsmen entering the workforce. Craft unions restrict their membership by having very strict entrance qualifications and charging high membership rates.

It is still the case that you cannot work in a particular field unless you are a member of a specific union.

Fig 2.19 Trades Union Congress meeting

Industrial unions

Traditionally, these unions were formed to cater for all employees (regardless of grade and job) within a particular industry. Good examples are the National Union of Mineworkers and the National Union of Railwaymen.

Occupational unions

Contrary to industrial unions, the occupational unions recruit from a wide range of different industries, but always from the same occupational group. A good example of this type of union would be the National Union of Public Employees, which recruits manual workers from hospitals, councils, schools and colleges.

General unions

Initially, these unions were for those individuals not covered in the three categories above. The first general unions concentrated on unskilled workers, offering a wide range of benefits for relatively low subscription rates. General unions have thrived in recent times as new industries have emerged and older, more traditional skills-based ones have declined. Often, these general unions are the result of several smaller, more specialist unions merging with one another.

Whatever type of union is involved in the workplace, the basic functions remain the same. A union exists to protect and promote the interests of its members. It essentially does the following:

- *acts as a pressure group, which promotes the interests of its members*
- *acts as a pressure group, which protects the position of its members*
- *acts as the main instrument of bargaining with the employer*

All unions are formed and financed by the members. They are run by full-time officials, voted or appointed in place by the members. Unions are independent of the employers; they do not rely on them for funding. The union must also organise its own facilities and not count on the employers offering space within their own premises.

Trade unions carry out a multitude of different tasks in looking after their members' interests. Some major functions include:

- *Protecting the wages of members, particularly in times of recession*
- *Negotiating the working hours required by the employer*
- *Negotiating the working conditions of the employees*
- *Monitoring health and safety*
- *Providing a range of benefits, including pensions, sick pay, unemployment pay and injury benefits*
- *Representing the interests of the members in times of dispute with the employers*

In addition to these tasks, unions undertake a number of political duties relating to employment. They will actively negotiate with the Government and Opposition parties to further the cause of their members.

With a few notable exceptions, all employees are entitled to join a trade union and take advantage of the benefits, both in terms of protection and facilities offered.

PC 2.2.4
C 2.1
C 2.2

Group activity

In groups of three, identify at least 10 unions which operate in your local area. You should also find out which type of union they are and what kind of employee they represent.

Compare your list with those of the rest of your group.

Employee responsibilities

Just as the employer has a number of responsibilities, so too does the employee. Although we have covered many of these aspects already in this Element, we will be addressing some more specific responsibilities which relate to:

- *the contract of employment*
- *the health and safety regulations*

- *the meeting of the organisation's objectives*
- *the meeting of customers' needs*
- *the maintenance of quality standards*

To meet the terms of the contract

As we have seen so far, the employer has a number of duties towards the employee. This can be seen very clearly in the contract of employment. This really formalises the relationship and is seen as a legally-binding document for both the employer and the employee. A contract of employment should formulate all of the following points:

1. **Job role** – what is the precise nature of the job?
2. **Job title**
3. **Pay details** – how the employee is paid; frequency of payment
4. **Additional payment details** – such as which salary / wage scale the individual will be placed on, when overtime can be undertaken, and how bonuses and commission may be earned
5. **Start times and finishing times of work**
6. **Total number of hours worked per week before overtime**
7. **Number of paid days off for holidays, etc.** Also are there any restrictions on when these may be taken?
8. **Sick leave details**, duration and entitlement to sick pay and maternity leave
9. **Pension schemes** – with details of contributions made by the employer and employee
10. **Grievance procedure details** – who is the Grievance Officer and the processes of the grievance procedure itself
11. **Period of notice to be worked/given**
12. **Number of weeks' or months' notice required** (by either side) in the event of resignation or termination of employment

In addition to these legally required details, the employer may wish to inform the employee of the following:

- *rules and regulations to be followed by employees*
- *codes of behaviour expected of employees*
- *the nature and availability of sports, social and welfare activities offered*
- *a full organisational chart so that the employee identifies where he/she fits into the overall scheme of things*

Just as the employer will be expected to fulfil any obligations as set out in the contract of employment, so too will the employee.

The employee will be expected to comply with all of the aspects of the contract of employment and, furthermore, will be required to accept responsibility for his / her actions at work.

Confidentiality is important, and the employee should take care not to release any information of a sensitive or secret nature to the media or to competitors.

	OVERTIME, CASUAL SHIFT ALLOWANCE, TRAVELLING TIME AND ADDITIONAL FLEXITIME CLAIM FORM						Week Ending:
Shift Worker *(Delete as appropriate)* Permanent Casual	Room No.	Pay Grade	Flexitime Borer No. if claimed	Name	Initials	Cost Centre	Pay No.
	Dept:			Home Address			

OVERTIME AND CASUAL SHIFT PAYMENT CLAIM

	Attendance Time From	Attendance Time To	Time claimed as Flexitime	Shift Worker Tick if Rest Day Worked	Hours and Twelfths Claimed for overtime: Hours	1/12	For office use: M/A	Pers
SUN			X			/12		
MON						/12		
TUE						/12		
WED						/12		
THUR						/12		
FRI						/12		
SAT			X			/12		
TOTAL						/12		

NUMBER OF HOURS AS TIME IN LIEU	MON-FRI	SAT	SUN	
FOR ACCOUNTS USE ONLY			ACCUM 102	TTC OCC

NOTE: All time claimed above to be in hours and one twelfths (e.g. 2 3/12) and attendance time in terms of twenty four hour clock

1 In the event of any discrepancies found subsequent to the payment of this claim, I agree to repay any overpayment which has been made

2 I understand that my Flexitime records will be updated from the above information

3 I acknowledge that any employee who makes a false statement renders himself herself liable to disciplinary action and prosecution

SIGNED CLAIMANT .... PG .... Date ....

BNFL 5938 (6/86) (Monthly Paid)

SPECIMEN

TRAVELLING TIME CLAIM

		Travelling Time Outside Working Hours From	To	a Total Time Hrs Mins	b LESS: Normal Home/Office Travel Time	c Time Claimed as Flexitime	d = a − b − c Net Travelling Time Claim
SUN	Morn				X	X	
	Eve						
MON	Morn						
	Eve						
TUE	Morn						
	Eve						
WED	Morn						
	Eve						
THUR	Morn						
	Eve						
FRI	Morn						
	Eve						
SAT	Morn				X	X	
	Eve						
TOTAL							

FOR ACCOUNTS USE ONLY	Initials	Accum 28N	Code 320	Var N	TT Hours

NOTE: Travelling time from to to be in terms of twenty-four hour clock (e.g. 18 22) Columns a-d must be expressed in hours and minutes (e.g. 3 24)

1 The amount of travelling time is reasonable and was made in the proper performance of duty

2 The hours of work are correct and were authorised and performed with proper supervision other than in exceptional circumstances

SIGNED CERTIFYING OFFICER .... PG .... Date ....

Fig 2.20 BNFL's multi-purpose form for overtime, casual shift allowance, travelling time and additional flexitime claims

PC 2.2.4
C 2.1
C 2.2
C 2.3
IT 2.1
IT 2.2
IT 2.3

Group activity

In pairs, using the above guidelines, try to design a draft contract of employment. This document should be word processed, and blank spaces should be left for the company's name, employee's name and any other specific details.

To meet health and safety regulations

An employee can quite rightly expect to work in conditions that are neither hazardous to life or health. The central piece of legislation that protects the employee, and gives the employer strict guidelines to which to adhere, is the Health and Safety at Work Act 1974 (this has been covered in much greater detail earlier). It essentially sets out that the employee must work in an environment that is healthy, safe and considers the welfare of the individual. The employer is ultimately responsible for any hazards or accidents which may be caused by not taking note of the legislation. Very heavy fines may be incurred if the law is broken.

Safe working conditions include many of the more obvious dangers to employees, but employees need to be aware of the potential hazards and not create any of their own.

Sometimes, situations occur where a health and safety hazard puts employees in danger. In other cases, due to lack of attention, or perhaps fooling about or bad behaviour, a health and safety problem may arise. The employer will, obviously, take a dim view of behaviour that may cause an accident or hazard. It could be the case that the employer would usually take disciplinary action in these situations.

To meet the objectives of the business

It is the employer's responsibility to attempt to inform their employees at each stage when the business objectives are altered. This will be done by using forms of internal communications such as newsletters, posters and notices.

As an employee, it is difficult to respond to the needs of the organisation if not told about the organisational objectives. Broadly speaking, the employee should be aware of the basic organisational objectives as it is probable that these aims do not change.

To meet customers' needs

The organisation must inform its employees about the following, in order to help employees to understand customer needs.

- *Why will the customer buy?*
- *What does the customer want?*
- *What are the benefits and features of the organisation's service?*

In relation to the product itself, the employee must know the following:

- *What is the appearance of the product?*
- *What is the product made of?*
- *What colours are available?*
- *How is it packaged?*
- *What is the speed and reliability of delivery?*
- *How does the organisation deal with faults?*
- *How frequent are maintenance visits (if applicable)?*
- *What quality levels are desired?*
- *How does the price compare to those of its competitors?*

Regular training and staff development is obviously required in order to ensure that the organisation's employees are not only up to date with product availability, but know intimately the characteristics of the products currently available.

To maintain quality standards

Quality standards can be measured by looking at the following:

- *The appearance of the product*

- *The packaging*
- *The reliability*
- *The performance*
- *The service offered (before, during and after the sale has been made)*

It will be the responsibility of the employee to make sure that all reasonable care is taken to maintain the quality standards required by the employer. Many organisations offer additional bonuses if the quality levels are maintained or improved.

Many organisations have quality audits aimed at maintaining high quality standards. Obviously, the nature of this monitoring process is largely dependent upon the type of business involved. Some ways of doing this are:

1 Measuring the speed and reliability of response to customers' enquiries
2 Maintaining a strict rule on the number of 'rings' before the telephone is answered
3 Ensuring that administrative procedures are in place to record any customer complaints and to monitor these regularly

Element 2.2 Assignment

PC 2.2.1–4
C 2.1
C 2.2
C 2.3
C 2.4
IT 2.1
IT 2.2
IT 2.3

In order to show that you understand the requirements of this Element, it is necessary to put together a report which focuses on co-operation, disagreements, rights and responsibilities.

Task 1 *PC 2.2.1*

For the first part of your report, you should explain the benefits that have been enjoyed in a named business organisation as a result of employer/employee co-operation.

Task 2 *PC 2.2.2*

Using the same organisation, now detail how disagreements have been resolved. You should focus particularly on the involvement of trade unions or courts.

Task 3 *PC 2.2.3–4*

In the final part of your report you should now identify at least *two* examples of employer and employee rights and responsibilities. The examples should pay particular attention to the effects of legislation on these rights and responsibilities.

Notes

Your tutor may have to provide you with a case study if you are unable to obtain the permission from an organisation upon which to base your investigation of rights and responsibilities.

Your report should be word processed.

Element 2.3
Present results of investigation into job roles

Performance criteria

A student must:

1 identify and describe individual's **job roles** at different **levels** within organisations

2 explain the **benefits of team membership** in performing job roles

3 identify **activities** performed by individuals at different **levels** within organisations

4 identify **tasks** in job roles

5 present results of investigation into job roles

Range

- *Job roles*: director, manager, supervisor, production operative, support staff
- *Levels*: senior, middle and junior
- *Benefits of team membership*: achievement of objectives and targets, awareness of the needs of team members, improved commitment to job role
- *Activities*: human resourcing, producing (goods or services), accounting, administration, selling, marketing, distributing, providing customer service, cleaning, security
- *Tasks*: routine (planning, decision-making, problem solving, setting targets, achieving targets), non-routine (dealing with emergencies or accidents)

2.3.1 Identify and describe individual's job roles at different levels within organisations

This whole Element requires you to look in some detail at one particular organisation. You will need to be able to gain access to some fairly detailed information about this organisation. You may find that your tutor will provide you with a case study or information pack on a particular organisation which should contain the majority of the information that you will need.

Job roles

Having identified the different types of structure of organisations, employer and employee responsibilities, and legislation relating to employment, we will now look at the specific job roles of individuals within an organisation. We will begin by looking at the senior members of an organisation. The following points should be borne in mind throughout all these explanations of job roles:

- *The employer has clearly identified exactly what the employee should do.*
- *At the same time, the employee is well aware of what is expected of him/her by the employer.*
- *The employer, and the employee too, are confident that the employee is capable of doing the job. If not, then whatever steps need to be taken must be taken to ensure that the employee can perform to the best of his/her ability.*

There are a number of key phrases that we will use continuously in describing exactly what the individual job roles are:

- *Authority* – can the individual command others to carry out tasks? In other words, does the individual have any real power?
- *Accountability* – to whom is the individual responsible? How many superiors have responsibility for that individual?
- *Responsibility* – what exactly are the tasks or duties related to the job?
- *Rights* – what should the individual reasonably expect from the employer? What should the employer reasonably expect from the employee? This has already been looked at in much greater detail earlier in this book

Director

The Managing Director is the most senior member of the Board of Directors. In some cases, the Managing Director is also the Chairperson (also sometimes known as Chair, Chairman or Chairwoman) of the organisation. It is the role and responsibility of the chairperson to preside over every meeting of the board.

The main roles of the Managing Director are:

- *To exercise all the powers and duties of a director*
- *To exercise power and responsibility in the name of the rest of the board on a day-to-day basis*

The board itself will have agreed certain guidelines of conduct and policy to which it will expect the Managing Director to adhere.

The Managing Director is chosen by the other members of the board, who will be looking for an individual with a number of important qualities. Among these may be the following:

- *Wide business experience*
- *A proven track record of success*
- *The ability to make the right decisions under pressure*
- *To answer for any decisions made and stand by those decisions*
- *To be accountable to the board and ultimately the shareholders (the board itself is answerable to the shareholders)*
- *A clear idea of the policies and objectives of the organisation and the ability to work towards the fulfilment of these objectives*
- *Excellent communication skills and the ability to be a good ambassador for the organisation in a variety of situations*

The Managing Director is responsible for the implementation of policy formulated by the board, and represents the board at all times. To some extent, the Managing Director has to interpret the wishes of the board, and develop a clear programme of organisational objectives. Furthermore, the Managing Director must be aware which key members of staff can be relied upon to follow through his/her policy decisions to a successful completion. At all times, the Managing Director must keep the board informed of any problems, decisions or crises of which it should be aware.

PC 2.3.1
C 2.1
C 2.2

Group activity *Time: 20 minutes*

Working in groups of three, in the role of the Board of Directors, draw up a list of qualities you would be looking for in a Managing Director. Compare your list to those of the rest of the group.

Depending on the type of organisation, there must be at least one director. In the case of private companies, there need only be one, but a public company requires a minimum of two. A directorship has a dual function, that of direction itself and, of course, management. The main difference between these two functions is that direction tends to relate to longer-term aims, while management concerns the day-to-day decision making (*see* Fig 2.21).

Direction is essentially the implementation of the board's policies. If a director is an Executive Director, this means that he/she is full-time and has responsibility for a particular part of the organisation. On the other hand, a Non-Executive Director may be part-time and may concentrate on a particular aspect of policy in which he/she is experienced.

Management by executive directors is, as we have seen, related to day-to-day decision making. Many executive directors find it very difficult to separate the direction and management roles. They may have a good grasp of the nature of the organisation's policies, and have a clear idea as to how these may be achieved. Unfortunately, day-to-day decision making may mean that the executive director has to make decisions at odds with organisational policy. One way around this problem is to organise the Board of Directors

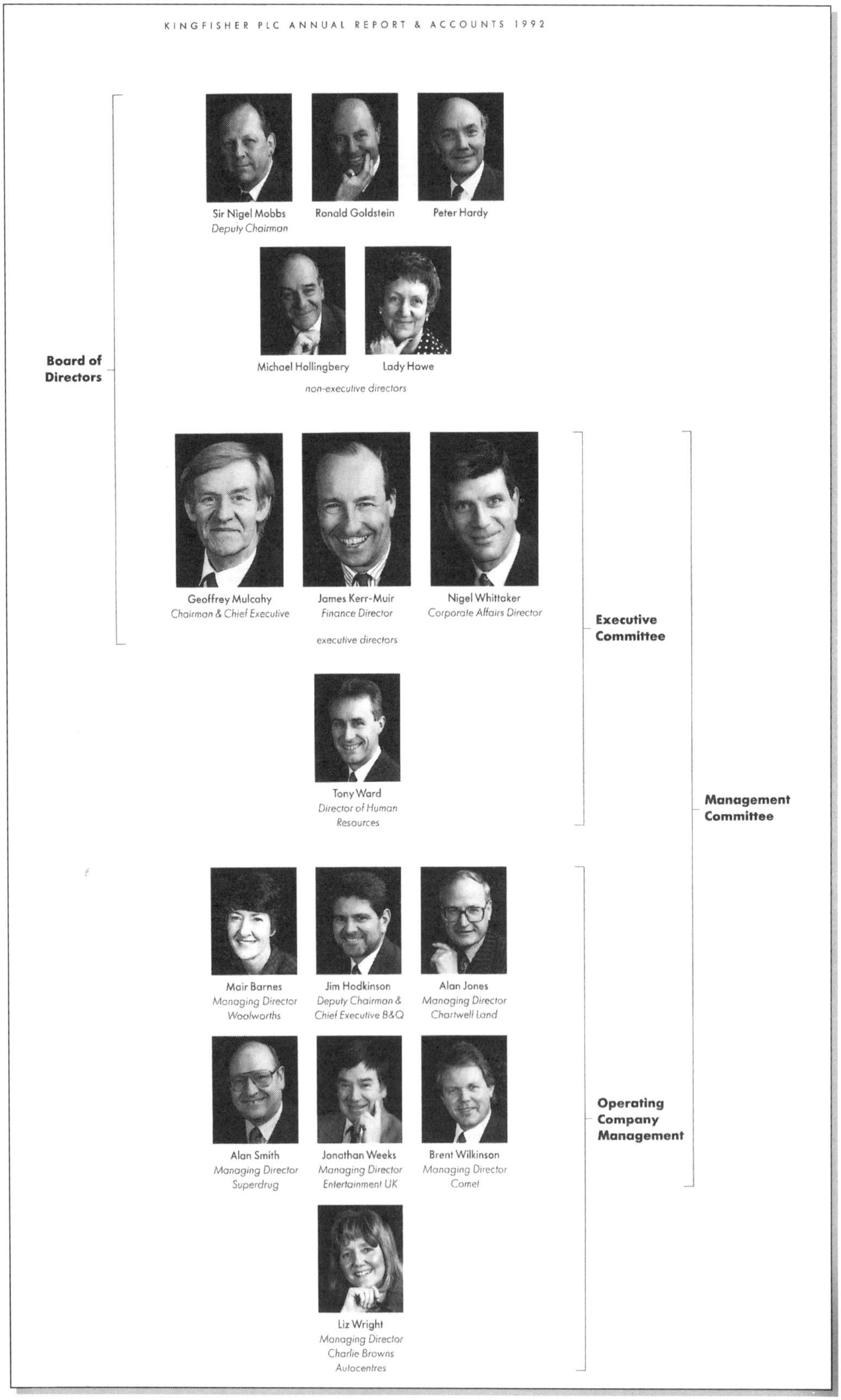

Fig 2.21 The organisational chart of key decision makers at Kingfisher plc

into two separate units. Board members will serve on one or other of the units (with the exception of the Managing Director, who will serve on both). One unit of directors will deal with overall policy and the other unit will concentrate on day-to-day implementation of policy. In this way, any conflict between policy and management of decision making is avoided.

The main duties of a director are:

- *To exercise power and authority in good faith and for the benefit of the organisation*
- *To put aside personal interests and always consider the organisation first*
- *To endeavour not to be casual or off-hand when managing the affairs of the organisation*

These duties essentially mean that a director should display care and skill at all times. Obviously, non-executive directors who have been included on the board for their experience and expertise in a certain area are expected to be even more professional in their conduct on behalf of the organisation. At the same time, these non-executive directors may not have had the skill or expertise of being a board member. In such cases, they are often assisted by an employee who can guide them as to the processes and procedures required of them.

Group activity *Time: 20 minutes*

PC 2.3.1
C 2.1

Consider this statement and discuss it with the other members of your group:

'The only useful director is one who spends all of his/her time involved in the company's business. Part-time directors are worthless and can walk away from problems, leaving the full-time directors to sort them out.'

The Company Secretary

Both public and private limited companies are required by law to have a Company Secretary. Essentially, this is an administrative post. Depending on the size of the organisation, the Company Secretary may have a variety of different duties. The most common duties are:

- *To keep all records, as required by law, which includes keeping a register of members of the organisation, plus minutes of board meetings and other directors' meetings*
- *To keep all of the organisation's legal documents and the 'seal' secure. The seal bears the organisation's name and registration number*
- *To arrange the organisation's and directors' meetings*
- *To ensure that information, as required by law, is sent to the Registrar of Companies*
- *To enter into legally-binding contracts on behalf of the organisation*

Group activity *Time: 15 minutes*

PC 2.3.1
C 2.1
C 2.2

In pairs, make a list of legal documents for which you think a Company Secretary should be responsible. Compare your list with those of the rest of your group.

The Auditor

Annually, there is a legal requirement to look into the financial affairs of the organisation. This is undertaken to ensure that any facts or figures relating to finance made by the organisation are true and accurate. This auditing is done mainly for the benefit of the shareholders.

It is usual for the auditors to be a professional organisation, not related in any way to the organisation being audited. Only registered auditors can carry out auditing work and there are a number of limitations regarding who may act as an auditor for an organisation:

- *The auditor must not be an officer or servant of the organisation being audited*
- *Equally, an auditor may not be the partner of, or employed by an officer or servant of the organisation*
- *This exclusion of officers and servants extends to any subsidiaries of the organisation and their employees and partners*
- *Finally, any individual who has any relationship with the organisation being audited is also excluded*

The auditor, having been appointed, looks at two main areas. First, the organisation's accounts; and, second, what the organisation has said to its members in relation to these accounts.

PC 2.3.1
C 2.1
C 2.2

Individual activity *Time: 15 minutes*

In the role of an auditor, which documents would you expect to be given open access to when completing the audit? Make a list and compare this to those of the rest of your group.

Manager

Below the level of director, are a number of layers of managers. It is the duty of a manager to undertake tasks and duties as delegated to them by a director. In effect, it is the manager who takes responsibility for the day-to-day decision making and implementation of organisational policy. A manager will be accountable to a director, and ultimately to the board and shareholders via any other managers senior to him/her.

A manager would usually have a far better working knowledge of the organisation than a director. It is therefore the case that directors tend not to interfere with basic decision making and are happy to delegate their authority to the various levels of management.

The exact duties of a manager are totally dependent upon the level of responsibility, the department for which they are responsible, and the exact nature of the organisation to which they belong. We shall look at specific management job roles at a later stage.

PC 2.3.1
C 2.2

Group activity *Time: 10 minutes*

As a group, discuss the following statement:

'Managers are the ones who do all the hard work. Directors just grab the glory, but blame their managers if things go wrong.'

Supervisor

Supervisors tend to be the next tier down in the organisational structure below managers. They are team leaders or organisers of specific projects or functions of the organisation. It is difficult at times to see the exact difference between a manager and a supervisor. Perhaps it is easier to think in terms of the actual managerial responsibilities involved. Supervisors tend to deal with day-to-day tasks. Supervisors do not necessarily have wider managerial responsibilities. They will usually answer to a manager who takes on these functions.

Particularly in industrial organisations, supervisors are fairly common. They have responsibility for specific functions of the production process and have relative independence in their choice of the deployment of employees to achieve success.

In an office environment, a supervisor will tend to have responsibility for ensuring that all individuals have been allocated sufficient work, that the work produced is of an acceptable standard and that the secretarial duties fully support the other operations of the organisation.

PC 2.3.1
C 2.1

Group activity *Time: 20 minutes*

As a group, try to identify the main differences between a supervisor and a manager. In the role of an employer, try to decide whether you think it would be better to give an individual the job title of 'manager' instead of 'supervisor'.

Production operative

The term 'operative' is a relatively new one which is applied to a wide variety of different job roles. Perhaps the main feature of these is some form of manual labour. Strictly speaking, the term 'operative' refers to the operation of machinery or equipment. More recently, this term has been adopted to include many non-manual activities. Indeed, if you go into a fast food outlet such as McDonald's, the counter staff are referred to as operatives.

Support staff

This job title infers a junior role in the organisation. A member of the support staff would help a more senior member of staff. Typically, we would find the word 'assistant' attached to job titles, for example: 'shop assistant', 'catering assistant', 'administrative assistant', 'clerical assistant', 'editorial assistant' and 'personal assistant'. These are all examples of support staff.

Despite the fact that these job roles may not appear to be particularly important in an organisation, the mere fact that the more senior member of staff needs an assistant means that the individual fulfilling this role is also a vital member of staff. Many managers who have personal assistants working for them would find it impossible to do their jobs without one.

Levels

The jobs which people actually do within an organisation are clearly dependent upon three major criteria:

1 *The size of the organisation*
2 *The type of the organisation*
3 *The function of the organisation*

Perhaps a good starting point in trying to assess exactly what a job entails is to try to discover what an organisation needs. Once this has been done, jobs can then be designed to fulfil the various functions required by the organisation. However, things are not always this simple. The majority of organisations have evolved over a number of years and the jobs undertaken by individuals working for them have changed as well. In fact, many jobs have expanded to incorporate other duties different to those originally intended to be done.

The result of this change is that some employees find themselves extremely overworked, while others cope well with the tasks required of them; yet others still are underworked (perhaps because technology has replaced the bulk of their original duties). An organisation which allows such an imbalance of work to persist will find that it may well adversely affect the smooth running of the organisation.

The solution appears to be simple, but is not often taken advantage of. Each time an individual leaves a job, there is an opportunity to evaluate exactly what the job entails and assess whether certain duties can be merged or reallocated elsewhere. A normal course of action in the more progressive-thinking organisation is that of job review and evaluation. This process aims to look in detail at each job role and see if any features of the job need to be changed to take account of developments in working practices, new or different demands, and technological breakthroughs.

The smaller the organisation, the more complex each individual employee's job may be. Employees may have to be capable of carrying out a wide variety and number of unrelated duties. The owner of a small business will not only be a managing director, but may have to cope with recruiting, training and promotion of employees, to supervise all aspects of the organisation's operations, and to work out wages and other financial requirements. This individual will rely on a small number of employees to carry out their duties largely unaided, but will be able to turn to a number of professionals to cope with certain complex situations. Good examples would be an accountant, bank manager or solicitor.

In the case of larger organisations, different functions of that organisation tend to be split into distinct areas. These will include many of the departmental divisions looked at earlier in the book. It would be useful to look at the various layers of management and authority before considering these divisions in detail:

- *Directly below the level of director are the senior managers. In consultation with the directors they will set any necessary policies or procedures to achieve the organisation's objectives. These senior managers, as we have mentioned previously, may well be executive directors.*
- *The task of implementing organisational policies and procedures is left to the middle managers. On a day-to-day basis they will liaise with the senior managers, in order to clarify organisational objectives, and with the supervisory managers, who are directly responsible to them.*
- *The managers who deal directly with the workforce are known as supervisory managers. These are responsible for ensuring that tasks, as directed by the middle managers, are carried out promptly and efficiently.*
- *The individuals who make up the bulk of the organisation are the workers. Alternatively, these may be referred to as subordinates. It is their role to actually deal with the job in hand. They are often simply called 'staff' to make a distinction between all types of managers and these employees.*

It is commonly held that there are effectively only five different types of job related to the skills required to carry them out, as follows.

Professional

This category includes solicitors, accountants, dentists, doctors and architects, all of whom display a certain degree of specialist knowledge of a given area. In recent years, although many professionals might strenuously disagree, new professionals can be said to have joined this group. They are in the main related to new areas of work, as opposed to the more traditional professions. Examples of these would be computer analysts, personnel managers, marketing executives and a wide variety of business consultants.

Managerial

This category is a very wide one but essentially features managerial and supervisory posts. Some occupations which we have already mentioned as being professional can also be referred to as managerial, such as personnel directors and marketing managers.

Technical

This relatively recent category of occupational type (although ever since there have been machines this group has existed) essentially refers to those individuals who are responsible for the setting up and maintenance of machinery and technological equipment. Within this category we will find computer programmers, television cameramen and sound recordists, and production-line technicians.

Administrative

This category is also a fairly wide one, which includes any job that could be considered clerical or administrative. Typical examples are secretaries, receptionists, word processor operators and switchboard operators.

Manual

Essentially, this group covers all manual workers who operate various types of equipment or machinery. It is further broken down into three sub-sections, which are:

- *Skilled* – in this sub-section we would find tradespeople such as carpenters, plumbers, bricklayers and roofers or tilers. It is usually the case that members of this sub-section belong to a guild or association for their specific trade.
- *Semi-skilled* – in this sub-section we would find workers who have not been fully trained in a particular trade, but who have been trained to operate the equipment or machinery they use regularly for their job. Typically, skilled manual workers' assistants or 'mates' would be found in this category.
- *Unskilled* – in this sub-section we would find workers who are not trained for a specific job and fulfil the role of labourer, factory operative, warehouse packer or cleaner.

PC 2.3.1
C 2.1
C 2.2

Group activity *Time: 15 minutes*

In pairs, write down all of the occupations undertaken by your family and friends. Now try to place them in one of the categories given above. Which of the categories covers most of the occupations? Compare your findings with those of the rest of your group.

2.3.2 Explain the benefits of team membership in performing job roles

Benefits of team membership

In this brief performance criteria, we will look at the benefits that can be enjoyed by the employee's membership of a team.

We should always consider that many opportunities present themselves to be part of a team within a business's activities and that some of these teams are somewhat less formal in the sense that individuals merely co-operate and help one another without actually being called a 'team'.

We should not ignore this point as it is rare to find employees working in an organisation on their own. It is much more often the case that teams are created, either formally or informally, to carry out specific tasks. A team is basically a group of individuals or operatives working together towards a single common objective. When working as a member of a team, people need to know which members of the team have the power and authority – in other words, who is actually directing the efforts of the team. In this case, it is common to find a supervisor fulfilling this role. To be a successful team member, a number of skills are required, which include:

- *the ability to communicate*
- *an understanding of the objective of the task*
- *being fully trained to carry out a variety of roles within the team*

Employers have recognised the advantages of team building and many have been prepared to pay for residential training programmes aimed at improving team-building skills.

Achievement of objectives and targets

Being able to achieve something as an individual is obviously a very desirable thing. Achieving an objective or target as a team member has its own advantages and sense of success or accomplishment. Co-operation, as we have already discussed, is the key to successful teams.

With any achievement there should be some form of recognition. This may take a variety of different forms such as bonuses, publicity, certificates or some other type of incentive reward.

The ability to complement an individual's skills and expertise with a matched group of other employees is the key feature in ensuring that the team operates well as a group and will achieve success.

Clear objectives and targets are the obvious beginning in establishing the level of achievement. To this end, a particular project, set within a specified time period, will often be the way in which the employer assesses the achievement itself.

Awareness of the needs of team members

We can approach this factor in two different ways:

1. Is the employer aware of the needs of the team members and has the employer taken steps to ensure that the team members receive sufficient support?
2. Do the individual members of the team understand the motivations of the other members? Each individual may have different needs that should be addressed. What are they?

Full support needs to be given by the organisation in terms of:

- *information*
- *resources*
- *time*
- *administrative support*
- *guidance*
- *clear setting of the objectives*

Support also needs to be forthcoming from the individual members of the team towards their colleagues. This would include the following:

- *An understanding of what motivates the other members of the team*
- *An understanding of the strengths and weaknesses of other team members*
- *An appreciation of the differing levels of support each member of the team will need to carry out the task*
- *An understanding and appreciation of the other duties and responsibilities of team members that may get in the way of the task in hand*

Some individuals are good 'team players' and they will not need a period of adjustment to get used to the functions of the team. Others will need support and guidance, not to mention understanding and patience, from the other members of the team while they get themselves mentally prepared for the task.

Improved commitment to job role

If individuals can see positive benefits to both themselves and the team by working as a member of a group, then this can form the basis of highly-motivated employees.

Commitment to any job role will only be as great as the degree to which the individual recognises that his/her activities are valued by either the organisation or other team members.

If we consider that the previous two factors, achievement and the addressing of needs, are the foundations of success, then if they are addressed, the individual (and the team) will operate much better. They will accept their role and not see the activity just in terms of what is expected of them. They will exceed the requirements of the task only if they know that they will be recognised as having a part in it.

If we consider the normal type of teamwork, where individuals routinely operate as a group, then a certain degree of mutual understanding would be a good idea. This understanding extends to each individual being aware of the exact role they (and the other members of the team) will be expected to adopt. For some there will be the satisfaction that a task has been completed well, and for others the smoothness of the co-operation and joint activities will be sufficient.

In the case of teams which are established for a particular project, it is wise for the organisation to state clearly the roles of each individual. This will include making clear what each individual's responsibility actually is within the team exercise.

2.3.3 Identify activities performed by individuals at different levels within organisations

Activities

In looking at this performance criteria, we have attempted to identify many of the key roles that will be found in organisations. You should be aware of two factors in reading what follows:

- *Not all of these roles or job titles necessarily exist in all organisations. There will be a different emphasis, depending on the nature and size of the organisation*
- *Some of the job roles are more senior and demanding than others*

In most cases, we have covered the job roles in order of seniority. A number of the layers or levels of employee are merged in some organisations. In others, they may use a slightly different description of what, in the main, is the same job role.

Human resourcing

The personnel manager

The personnel manager is ultimately responsible for the recruitment, retention and welfare of all staff. In this role the personnel manager will be involved in the designing of job descriptions and job specifications, the interview process, any training required by employees, handling staff problems, and preparing any necessary documentation relating to termination of employment, for whatever reason. The personnel manager will monitor and fulfil any staff development requirements. He/she is the first and main point of contact with the management structure in trade union negotiations. The personnel manager will also be involved in the co-ordination of staff facilities such as catering, sport, leisure and social activities.

The assistant personnel manager

The assistant personnel manager deputises for the personnel manager in various situations, and has regular duties delegated to him/her. They are usually the first point of contact for employee problems and individuals enquiring about possible vacancies within the organisation. The personnel manager and the assistant personnel manager between them offer a confidential counselling service to all employees. The assistant personnel manager is also responsible for the maintenance of comprehensive staff records.

Clerical assistants

Routine personnel duties, such as the maintenance of staff records and work logs, are carried out by clerical assistants in the personnel department. Various duties are delegated to them by either the personnel manager or the assistant personnel manager and it is essential that these are carried out with confidentiality always in mind.

PC 2.3.2
C 2.1
C 2.2
IT 2.1
IT 2.2
IT 2.3

Group activity *Time: 30 minutes*

Working in pairs, assume the role of assistant personnel manager. You have been asked by the personnel manager to draft the details of a job advertisement for your organisation. The post to be filled has the following features:

- **job title - cleaner**
- **hours - 0700–0930 daily (except Sundays)**
- **payment - £2.73 per hour**
- **previous experience preferred**

Use a word processor to make the advertisement look as attractive as possible.

Producing (goods or services)

Production manager

The production manager's responsibility is for the manufacture of products to the correct specification, quality, price and safety levels. Production managers tend to be quite technical people, who understand the production process intimately. They will work closely with the research and development manager, as well as the sales manager. It is the production manager's role to turn new product ideas into finished products and supply the regular needs of the sales department.

Assistant production managers

These will be given the responsibility by the production manager to oversee the smooth running of the various production lines. They will work in close co-operation with the production line managers to ensure that production levels and product quality are maintained in relation to demand. The assistant production managers will be technically competent and may have a good working knowledge of the machinery.

The buyer

The buyer is required to purchase sufficient stocks of raw materials and components to enable the production lines to run efficiently. The buyer must be able to predict demand for all raw materials, components and machinery by close examination of past, present and projected sales figures. An essential duty of the buyer is to obtain all items at the best possible prices. The buyer may be able to negotiate favourable extended credit terms from regular suppliers. The buyer will also be responsible for making sure that all items ordered are received in good time.

Production line manager

The production line manager is responsible for the smooth running of a part of the production department which produces a single product or product range. The production line manager will be given quotas (amounts) to achieve by the production manager or assistant production manager and will have to organise his/her staff to meet the required deadlines.

Production line supervisor

It is the production line supervisor's responsibility to deploy the members of his/her work team to the maximum possible effect. The supervisor will monitor the performance of both the work team and the machinery, and regularly report to the production line manager regarding any potential problems. This supervisor is the main point of contact between the employees and the management structure of the organisation. In the event of potential problems with the machinery, this supervisor will liaise with the service engineers.

Service engineers

It is the service engineer's role to ensure that any defects or breakdowns in machinery within the production department are swiftly and efficiently dealt with. The service engineer will inform the production manager and the relevant production line manager regarding any need to close down a production line for the purposes of maintenance, service and cleaning. The service engineers need to keep a stock of basic components in order to repair machinery on the spot.

Production line operatives

Depending on the type of production employed by the organisation, the production line operatives are responsible for either a repetitive task or a series of related tasks. Many production lines have been developed so that only routine duties need to be carried out by humans. In these cases, production line operatives tend merely to feed the machines with raw materials and components and do not actually take part in the production process itself. In situations when the production is less automated, production line operatives are involved in the production of goods to completion. Many organisations run their production lines continuously and therefore require their production line operatives to work shifts.

PC 2.3.2
C 2.1
C 2.2
C 2.3
C 2.4

Group activity *Time: 1.5 hours*

In the role of production manager, and working in pairs, design a timesheet for use on the factory floor by production operatives. The production operatives are paid on piece-work only, and up to this point you suspect there have been a number of false claims for work carried out. The total number of products finished is much smaller than the claim total. Try to design a system which would eliminate this problem. Compare your form with those designed by the rest of the group.

Accounting

Company accountant

It is the company accountant's responsibility to maintain an up-to-date record and analysis of income and expenditure. The company accountant will have a number of accounts specialists working in the department, who will be monitoring various financial aspects of the organisation. At any time, the company accountant may be asked for detailed information regarding the financial status of the organisation, and must be able to respond immediately. There are a number of legal and statutory requirements that an organisation must fulfil and it is the responsibility of the company accountant to ensure that all of these obligations are met. The company accountant is directly accountable to the Board of Directors for his/her actions and decisions.

Accountants

A variety of accounts specialists are employed by organisations to carry out specific monitoring and analysis of financial data. These accountants will oversee the flow of data received regarding sales, purchases, running costs and other expenses. In addition, they will provide essential accounting information such as gross profit, net profit, turnover and relative profitability of different areas of the organisation. In larger organisations they may keep track of the performance of investments in other organisations and regularly monitor the financial strengths and weaknesses of subsidiary companies.

Credit controller

This member of the accounts staff will monitor the orders placed by customers and the payment history of customers in order to establish their reliability as payers. Each customer will have a set credit limit (rather like an agreed bank overdraft) and the credit controller will endeavour to make sure that customers do not exceed this limit. In cases of late payment or non-payment of invoices, it is the credit controller who will contact the customer in question in an attempt to secure payment. The credit controller will take into account how long the customer has been purchasing from the organisation and may well look back into the past to see if there have been any previous problems with regard to payment.

Accounts clerk

An accounts clerk carries out the routine day-to-day accounting duties, as directed by either the chief accountant or senior accountants. This may involve either manual figure work, or the use of the increasingly popular range of accounting computer software. It is usually the accounts clerk's role to prepare figures for analysis by the more senior accountants. In some organisations, one duty of an accounts clerk is to maintain and issue petty cash (cash for small items of expenditure by staff) to those who request it, on the presentation of a validly-signed voucher (this will be discussed further in Unit 4).

Payroll clerks

Working closely with the personnel department, the payroll clerk is responsible for ensuring that the correct wages or salaries are paid to every member of staff. The payroll clerk must be familiar with income tax and National Insurance and pension scheme contributions. Depending on the size of the organisation, the payroll clerk may have to undertake these tasks manually or, in a larger organisation, may be assisted by a software package. In some organisations where the wages structure is complex, or is related to performance and output, this job may not be as straightforward as one might imagine (*see* Fig 2.22).

Individual activity

Time: 45 minutes

PC 2.3.2
C 2.1
C 2.2

In the role of an accounts clerk, what action would you need to take should the following arise:

1. **You are processing a cheque which has not been signed.**
2. **You receive petty cash vouchers which do not correspond with the attached receipts.**

Having completed your list of actions to take, compare and discuss with the rest of your group.

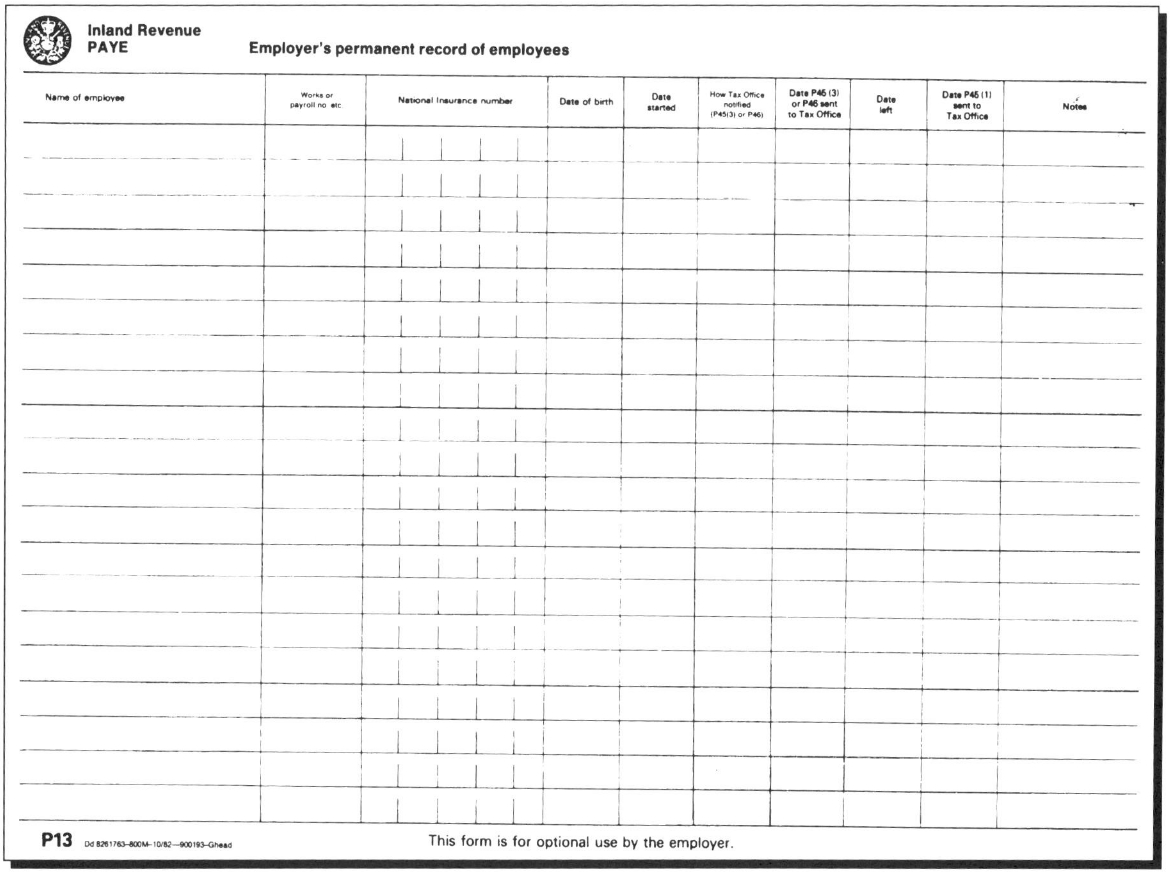

Inland Revenue
PAYE

Employer's permanent record of employees

Name of employee	Works or payroll no etc	National Insurance number	Date of birth	Date started	How Tax Office notified (P45(3) or P46)	Date P45 (3) or P46 sent to Tax Office	Date left	Date P45 (1) sent to Tax Office	Notes

P13 Dd 8261763–800M–10/82—900193–Ghead

This form is for optional use by the employer.

Fig 2.22 A P13 form which details the employer's record of employees. Issued by the Inland Revenue for PAYE records
(Crown copyright)

Administration

Chief administration officer/office services manager

Overseeing all major functions of the department, allocate work received from other departments (and routine administrative duties) and carry the responsibility for the smooth running of the department.

Secretariat supervisor

Allocating and monitoring all work carried out by the secretaries, audio typists, shorthand typists, word processor operators and typists.

Word processor operator

Under the guidance of the secretariat supervisor, the word processor operator will undertake work from a variety of different sources and will be responsible for its presentation and safe storage (on disk or hard copy) and for ensuring that any deadlines related to the work are met.

Secretary

The secretary usually works directly for one or more managers. It is the secretary's responsibility to ensure that any information in the form of messages, memos, letters, reports, etc, is brought to the attention of the manager. In addition, a secretary will also be responsible for routine letters and notetaking, on behalf of the manager, as well as keeping track of all the manager's diary commitments (and sometimes the manager's personal diary too!). The secretary may also arrange meetings on behalf of the manager. At all times the secretary will ensure that only relevant information and individuals who really need the time of the manager are brought to his/her attention. A secretary's skills may include the capacity to use audio tapes, word processors and shorthand.

Audio typist

Responsible for working for several people in the organisation, possibly based in a 'pool' with others doing similar work. The audio typist's duties will include typing from audio tapes which have been prepared by various individuals and ensuring that this work is completed to the given deadline, in a neat and accurate way.

Shorthand typist

Also working for several individuals within the organisation, the shorthand typist will take dictated notes from the manager and will have the responsibility of transcribing them and typing up the document in a neat and accurate way. A shorthand typist is usually present to note the decisions taken at any company meetings.

Typist

Involves the typing of routine documents within the organisation. To a great extent this role is gradually being taken over by word processor operators, as increasingly organisations are tending to buy word processors rather than typewriters.

Messenger

Involves the distribution of both internal and external documents. The role is particularly useful in organisations which have a number of closely situated sites, or in situations when the organisation's customers are located in the immediate vicinity. Messengers are still used in the City of London. However, many functions of the messenger have been replaced, with the availability of facsimile machines, modems and electronic mail.

Records supervisor

Responsible for ensuring that all necessary documents are safely, securely and accessibly stored. Despite the fact that technology has substantially reduced the need to store vast amounts of paper documents, there are many reasons why organisations still prefer to have hard copies of documents available for inspection. Upon receiving a request for information, the records supervisor will instruct a records clerk to retrieve and deliver the required documentation.

Records clerk

Allocated work by the records supervisor. Responsible for retrieving the required information and ensuring its safe delivery by internal mail, personal delivery, or by a messenger. The records clerk will also take note of who has requested the information, the date of the request and the date of return. This 'Out' card is completed in order to keep track of the documents and ensure their safe return.

Librarian

Responsible for acquiring and maintaining resources relevant to the organisation's activities. These may take the form of books, reports, periodicals, newspaper cuttings, etc. This resource is then available to all members of the organisation who may need to research into a specific area related to their work. It is the librarian's task to ensure that the information is as up-to-date as possible and that all staff are aware of its availability.

Mail room supervisor

Responsible for the handling of all internal and external mail. The office is commonly known as the post room. This location acts as a central collection point for letters, packages and parcels. These may include mail to any part of the world as well as internal mail or bulletins. The various pieces of mail will either be collected by a mail room assistant, or delivered by various individuals from within the organisation. It is the mail room supervisor's responsibility to make sure that all outgoing mail is weighed, franked (stamped to show the postage) and made ready for collection by the Post Office. The mail room supervisor will also note (for internal cost allocation) the postage totals for each department within the organisation.

Mail room assistant

Working under the direction and instruction of the mail room supervisor, the mail room assistant may carry out a variety of different tasks:

- *Collect mail from the various departments*
- *Deliver mail received each morning to the relevant person(s). Before this can be done, the mail needs to be sorted and perhaps re-routed to another site*
- *Weigh, frank and put outgoing mail into the correct Post Office bag ready for collection or delivery to the Post Office*
- *Note postage costs of each department and ensure that the mail room supervisor has up-to-date figures for these*
- *Ensure that the Post Office leaflets kept in the mail room are current*

Telephone/switchboard supervisor

Since many organisations rely heavily on the internal and external telephone system, this key post is vital to the smooth running of most operations. The supervisor ensures that all telecommunication needs are met and that the switchboard system is capable of fulfilling the demands of the organisation. In addition, the supervisor will make sure the switchboard is constantly staffed and, at times when the organisation is closed for business, that an answerphone can record incoming calls, or can give useful information to callers.

FOR: **FROM:**

OF: DATE:

TEL: FAX: TIME:

TAKEN BY:

TELEPHONED ◯ PLEASE RING BACK ◯ RETURNED YOUR CALL ◯ WILL RING BACK ◯ WOULD LIKE TO SEE YOU ◯ URGENT ◯

Fig 2.23 A telephone message form as used by Mercury Communications

Switchboard operator

In many cases, a customer's first contact with an organisation is via the telephone. It is therefore most important that the switchboard operator answers the calls swiftly and is helpful and responsive to the caller. A good switchboard operator will instantly know exactly who the caller needs to speak to (despite the fact that the caller may not ask for a named individual) and will know from memory the extension number of most members of staff.

PC 2.3.2
C 2.2

Individual activity *Time: 30 minutes*

Draw up an organisational chart showing the operations of an administration department which includes all of the above posts.

Indicate on this chart who has responsibility for decision making.

Selling

Sales manager

This job entails the co-ordination of the organisation's sales efforts. The sales manager is usually located at the organisation's head office, with an administrative staff who monitor the performance of the various national, regional and area sales managers and teams. In positions such as this, a considerable amount of the salary is related to sales performance. Periodically the sales manager will visit the members of his/her sales team in the field (in the area where they are working) to assess their effectiveness and to keep in touch with current customer demands.

Assistant sales manager

Deputising for the sales manager, this individual will take on a range of sales-related responsibilities and may often be the first point of contact for the various members of the sales force. It will be the assistant sales manager's role to help the sales manager formulate the sales policy of the organisation.

National sales manager

In larger organisations, there is a need to co-ordinate the sales efforts on a country-by-country basis. National sales managers are usually given considerable freedom to formulate a sales policy which is the most effective for the country in which they operate. Normally, a national sales manager will have a wide knowledge of the country in which he/she works and may even be a national of that country. Other organisations may not have national sales managers, as they may have entered into an agreement with a local company which will represent the interests of the organisation in that country or area.

Regional sales manager

Just as different countries have their own peculiarities, regions within a country also have theirs. Different sorts of industry and commerce tend to cluster around particular towns or cities. The regional sales manager will have an intimate knowledge of the needs of these businesses, which may be different from the national needs. The regional sales manager will be located within the region for which he/she has responsibility and will be required regularly to analyse any changes in the local economy which may affect sales.

Area sales manager

Working under the direction of the regional sales manager, an area sales manager will be responsible for a part of the region. In some cases, this may mean a single city or county. Again, a good working knowledge of the needs of the area is essential in co-ordinating the sales effort. The area sales manager will regularly accompany sales representatives when they visit customers and be able to offer on-the-spot advice and guidance.

Sales representatives

These individuals form the backbone of the sales team. Constantly on the road, visiting both existing and potential customers, they will be in direct contact with their area sales manager via mobile or car phones. Since the bulk of their salary is directly related to the sales they generate, they are always under pressure to meet their targets in order to achieve their bonuses. The image of the sales representative in their company car, is easy to visualise. In reality, they may be very well trained sales people, with an expert knowledge of their field and extremely useful to their customers. They are, after all, the first point of contact and may well become a useful 'partner' in building up a business.

Tele-sales assistant

Working from central, national, regional or area offices, tele-sales assistants will not only take direct telephone orders for goods and services from the customer, but will also receive regular orders from the sales representatives. Operating with up-to-date lists of customer contacts from the sales representatives, they will attempt to gain new sales or arrange for one of the sales representatives to visit the business. They will be particularly well trained in telephone skills and have any useful information to hand via a desktop computer.

MERCURY RESIDENTIAL SERVICE

PIN CODE (AUTHORISATION CODE) AND MERCURY TELEPHONE ORDER FORM 1/93/6654

FILLING IN THIS FORM

1. Please use a ball point pen and use BLOCK CAPITALS.
2. Please complete a separate form for each exchange line at which Mercury 2300 is to be used. Additional forms can be obtained from Mercury Customer Assistance.
3. Please **return this top copy to us** in the envelope provided and **keep the yellow Customer Copy** for your reference.
4. Please allow 7-10 days from receipt of order for delivery.
5. **If you have any queries** about this form or any aspect of Mercury service, please contact **Mercury Customer Assistance by dialling 0500-500-194**, or write to: **Mercury Customer Assistance**, P.O. Box 49, Birmingham B1 1TE.

MERCURY USE ONLY

Order No. ______
Sales Ref: ______
Customer Billing No: ______
AC Ref No: ______
A/C Manager: ______
Dealer's Name: ______

1 PIN CODE

Address at which PIN Code is to be used

Contact Name ______ TITLE Mr/Mrs/Miss ______ INITIALS ______

Job Title BUSINESS ONLY ______

Company Name BUSINESS ONLY ______

Address ______

POSTCODE ______

Telephone No. (incl. STD Code) ______

If you are an existing BT ex-Directory Telephone Subscriber please tick this box ☐

The principal use of this Telephone number is for:

Residential use from my home ☐ Business use from my home ☐ Business use from my office ☐

Billing Address, if different ______

ATTENTION OF ______

Telephone No. (incl. STD Code) ______

PIN Code Annual Charge £11.75*

2 CALL CHARGE OPTIONS

Please tick the box for the call charging rate you require

Basic ☐ I agree to be charged at Mercury's Basic 2300 Service Rate.

Frequent Caller Programme (Scheme C1) ☐ I agree to be charged at Mercury's Frequent Caller Programme Rate. In order to join the Programme I agree to pay a quarterly fee of £5* plus VAT in advance in respect of this account. This charge is in addition to my call charges and annual PIN Code charge. To subscribe to the Frequent Caller Programme, I agree to pay this account by Direct Debit and enclose the Direct Debit instruction supplied with this form.

PLEASE NOTE

3 BILLING OPTIONS (please tick boxes as required)

Do you require monthly or quarterly billing? MONTHLY ☐ QUARTERLY ☐

COST CENTRE CODES By keying in a code number - either 2 or 3 digits - before dialling each and **every Mercury** call, businesses can allocate calls to different jobs, or residential users can see who is responsible for which call. A separate summary of cost centres will be provided with your bill.

Would you like Cost Centre Codes? (See note above) NO: ☐ YES: 2 DIGITS ☐ 3 DIGITS ☐

4 MERCURY TELEPHONE(S) REQUIRED

Model No.	Colour:	Total No. required	Cost of each (Incl.VAT)	**Total Cost** (This will appear on your first bill)
GPT Connect 1+	Grey		**£34.99***	**£** :

IMPORTANT – PLEASE NOTE: The Customer's attention is particularly drawn to the provisions of Condition 33.3 overleaf relating to the obligation on the Customer to notify Mercury immediately of possible misuse of PIN Code as more precisely set out herein. Customers are advised that the warrant provisions relating to security and confidentiality of the PIN Code set out in Condition 35 overleaf apply only if and to the extent that the Customer uses telephone equipment that Mercury considers is secure and confidential to access the Mercury Service. Mercury's Service Literature or Mercury Customer Assistance will identify such equipment within this category for the purposes of such warranty.

Mercury, and other members of the Cable and Wireless Group of Companies, may be able to offer you information on other services and equipment. With your agreement we will use your details contained herein for this purpose. If you would prefer us not to do so please tick here. ☐

SEND NO PAYMENT WITH THIS ORDER. YOUR CHARGES WILL APPEAR ON YOUR BILL

5 SIGNATURE

7244

Signature ______ Date ______

Name ______

Job Title BUSINESS ONLY ______

Mercury COMMUNICATIONS

A Cable and Wireless Company. Registered in England No. 1541957. Registered Office: New Mercury House, 26 Red Lion Square, London WC1R 4HQ. VAT No. 232 3037 10.

***Correct at time of going to press and liable to variation without notice. VAT at 17.5%. August 1992.**

Fig 2.24 Mercury Communications application form for residential telephone installation

Invoice clerk

The role of the invoice clerk is to process all orders generated by either the sales representatives or the tele-sales team. Essentially, the documents produced will form both a list of required products for the warehouse to despatch and also a record for the accounts department of products sold. The invoice clerk will be in regular contact with the warehouse to ensure that the sales team is aware of the stock levels of each product.

Individual activity *Time: 45 minutes*

PC 2.3.2
C 2.2
IT 2.1

In the role of the sales director, prepare a memo which answers a note from the personnel department. The note states that at the end of the month you will lose the services of your invoice clerk. Your memo should state your reasons for wanting to keep this individual and it should be word processed.

Marketing

Marketing manager

Marketing managers are responsible for planning, organising, directing and controlling the marketing efforts of the organisation. Increasingly, they are professional individuals who are well versed in formulating a marketing plan which is workable within the limitations of the organisation. In effect, they are responsible for establishing the organisation's marketing objectives (known as the strategy) and deciding how the overall objectives may be achieved (known as the tactics). All organisations have a 'corporate image', which means that everything the organisation produces, from letterheads to finished products, has the same overall look. The marketing manager will decide exactly how the corporate image relates to each and every aspect of the organisation.

Assistant marketing manager

Deputising for the marketing manager, and co-ordinating the efforts of each of the product/brand managers are the main responsibilities of the assistant marketing manager. It will be their role to implement the marketing strategy across all aspects of the organisation and to ensure that the corporate image is consistent.

Product/brand manager

A product manager is responsible for co-ordinating the marketing plan relating to a single product. A brand manager, on the other hand, may be responsible for a range of products which have the same brand name. In both cases, the individuals will have to organise all activities relating to their product(s), including advertising, sales promotions, launches, re-launches and packaging.

Marketing research analyst

Millions of pounds are spent each year on marketing research. Nearly 10 per cent of the retail price of every item is spent on marketing research alone. Marketing research is the systematic collection and analysis of data which looks specifically at the customer's attitudes, needs, opinions and motivation, and anything which influences these. In order to minimise the risks involved in launching a new product, the organisation needs to know as much as possible about the potential customer, competition and any other factors which may affect sales. This specialist will use existing statistical data, as well as commissioning new market research if required.

Advertising manager

An advertising manager will be responsible for co-ordinating the advertising budget of the organisation. Working in close co-operation with various other members of the organisation, the advertising manager should be able to identify the best media for the advertising of the product. Additionally, the advertising manager will negotiate with magazines, newspapers, radio and television companies to achieve the best possible price for advertising. In many organisations, the advertising manager's function is taken over by an outside advertising agency which places and co-ordinates all advertisements.

Promotions manager

There is a narrow line between the responsibilities of a promotions manager and an advertising manager. Essentially, the promotions manager will co-ordinate all other marketing strategies apart from advertisements. These will include special offers, competitions, trial offers, money-off vouchers, point of sale material and exhibitions.

Distributing

Distribution manager

This manager is responsible for the design, running and maintenance of a cost-effective method of ensuring that products reach their correct destination, in a suitable state, at the right time. The distribution manager works in close co-operation with the sales department, which informs the distribution manager of orders placed by customers, as well as expected delivery dates. The distribution manager tends to control the operations of the warehouse and all storage facilities. When information is received from the warehouse manager that levels have reached the reorder level, the distribution manager gives this to the production department.

Transport manager

The transport manager's responsibility is to maintain and run the fleet of delivery vehicles which service the distribution requirements of the organisation. He/she will liaise closely with the distribution manager, the warehouse manager and the sales department. The transport manager is also responsible for keeping service records and vehicle registrations, as well as any related insurance for the fleet. He/she also negotiates any leasing or purchasing agreements relating to vehicles. The transport manager directly co-ordinates the efforts of the drivers, vehicle service engineers and the administration staff within his/her department.

Warehouse manager

The warehouse manager is responsible for the smooth running of the warehousing facilities of the organisation. He/she will co-ordinate all warehouse staff in an effort to ensure that goods, both inwards and outwards, are dealt with in a quick and efficient manner. The warehouse manager will design the storage facilities in such a way as to enable easy access to the most used items. He/she must also keep a close eye on the stock levels of all stored equipment, products, components and raw materials.

Fig 2.25 An example of BNFL's commitment to enhance the organisation's public image

Drivers

The drivers are directly answerable to the transport manager, who issues them with delivery rounds. In certain cases, particularly in larger organisations, there may well be a need to have regional distribution points which will have small warehousing facilities and attached drivers/delivery men or women.

PC 2.3.2
C 2.2

Group activity

There are many rules and regulations which control the operations of a driver. Working in groups of three, try to find out as many laws and restrictions as you can which relate to drivers. Compare your findings with those of the rest of the group.

Providing customer service

The public relations officer

The public relations officer is responsible for fostering a good relationship with the media, in the hope that they will consider giving the organisation both editorial space and favourable news reporting. The public relations officer maintains a comprehensive database of media contacts, from which extensive mail shots will be made. He/she is also responsible for the writing of press releases, and for producing a range of booklets and leaflets concerning the operations of the organisation.

The customer relations officer

While the public relations officer is concerned with media and news coverage, the customer relations officer concentrates on existing and potential customers. He/she responds to customer enquiries, providing a range of information packs on request. In addition, the customer relations officer also co-ordinates activities within the community projects department. In cases where a customer has a serious complaint about the products or services of the organisation, the customer relations officer will be available to assist in the solving of any problem.

PC 2.3.2
C 2.1
C 2.2
C 2.3
IT 2.1
IT 2.2
IT 2.3

Individual activity

In the role of a customer relations officer, write a letter in response to one received from a customer complaining that their car was broken into and their radio cassette stolen while parked on the premises of your organisation.

It is company policy to point out that there are notices clearly visible which state that you take no responsibility for damage or theft from vehicles while parked on the premises.

Your letter should be word processed and in the correct business format.

WOOLWORTHS DISTRIBUTION NETWORK

Satellite communications and computerised ordering are key to today's distribution network.

The company's two distribution centres supply the chain with 64 million products each year.

The efficiency of the distribution network was recently recognised by the British Standards Institute.

In 1992 Woolworths became the first retailer to be awarded British Standard 5750 for its Distribution Quality Management system.

Continuous monitoring and spot checks by distribution personnel ensure these standards are maintained and that techniques and systems are continually updated.

Running an all year-round operation from its two centres at Swindon and Castleton, distribution aims to make delivery to a store within 48 hours of receiving an order through an electronic messaging system. Speed and accuracy are crucial to the success of the operation which works to achieve an error rate of less than half of one per cent.

During 1992 a new transport fleet was introduced and it is estimated that drivers will cover eight million kilometres a year. The new fleet not only helps to further improve the speed and efficiency of distribution, but by using more fuel-efficient vehicles, reduces the environmental impact of the operation.

BSI REGISTERED FIRM

WOOLWORTHS

***Fig 2.26** Woolworth's two main distribution centres supply some 64 million products to their stores per year*

News from BUAV
campaigning to end animal experiments

British Union for the Abolition of Vivisection, 16a Crane Grove, London N7 8LB.
Press line: 0171-607 9533. Fax: 0171-700 0252.

PRESS RELEASE WEDNESDAY 1 MARCH

EUROPE SAYS NO TO PATENTING ANIMAL LIFE

Britain's leading anti-vivisection organisation, the British Union for the Abolition of Vivisection (BUAV), today (Wednesday 1 March) welcomed the European Parliament's rejection of a new European law which would have given the 'green light' to the patenting of genetically engineered animals. The 'patenting' Directive was rejected by 240 to 188 votes, with 23 abstentions, at its third and final reading. The Directive now falls. Dr Malcolm Eames, BUAV's Head of Information & Research, states:-

"Today's vote is a major victory in the battle against the genetic engineering and patenting of animals. The European Parliament should be congratulated on the stand it has taken against the patenting of life. Having seen the defeat of its flagship legislation, the European Commission must now urgently reassess it's uncritical support for genetic engineering to ensure due respect for animal life."

The BUAV will now be vigorously pursing its formal legal challenge to the only existing European animal patent, which was granted under the European Patent Convention (Europe's existing patent law), in the Harvard Oncomouse case. This test case will now be heard at the European Patent Office, in Munich, in November.

ENDS

For further details contact:
Dr Malcolm Eames **0171 607 9533 (Press Line)**

Fig 2.27 BUAV's company policy is constantly to inform the Press as to any interesting development regarding the organisation

The community projects officer

Many organisations, having recognised the need to form a closer relationship with the local community, have appointed a community projects officer. In several respects, the duties of this individual are somewhat similar to those of the customer relations officer. However, the community projects officer tends to concentrate on the immediate locality. He/she will organise, with the assistance of other local organisations, a range of activities in order to heighten the public's awareness and appreciation of the organisation. This may take the form of sponsoring local events, financing community projects, or offering the organisation's facilities to local groups.

Computing

Departmental manager

It is the responsibility of the departmental manager to provide a round-the-clock and comprehensive service back-up for the organisation's computing and data processing requirements. Within his/her area of influence, the manager will co-ordinate the design of computer programs to manipulate data for the various departments.

Assistant departmental manager

Under the direction of the departmental manager, this assistant manager will be responsible for acquiring and maintaining all computer software and hardware. In order to carry out this task, he/she will delegate various aspects to specialist managers. In co-ordination with the departmental manager, the assistant departmental manager will ensure that sufficient support is given to all computer-based communication systems within the organisation.

Data processing manager

This manager will maintain a detailed record of the organisation's stored information, which will be constantly updated and always accessible. The manager will also ensure that sensitive information is protected from access by an unauthorised person. On a regular basis, the data processing manager will also make sure that back-up copies have been made of all computer data stored and that these are kept in secure and fireproof locations.

Computer services manager

The computer services manager will keep a constant overview of new developments in order to inform the departmental manager of more efficient ways of storing and manipulating data. It will also be the computer service manager's responsibility to install and maintain new or updated versions of software as they become available. Further, the manager's team of servicing engineers will regularly check all of the organisation's computer equipment. In some organisations, this service function has been bought-in from computing service specialists.

Computer programmers

These specialists will write computer software programs specific to the needs of the various departments, so that information may be processed and analysed according to changing requirements.

Computer operators

These individuals will be responsible for the inputting of data and the manipulation of existing information at the request of various departments within the organisation. Routinely, they will update information from a variety of sources, deleting or modifying as required. Increasingly, organisations have become more reliant on computer-based information and will need constant access to reliable and contemporary data.

PC 2.3.2
C 2.1

Group activity *Time: 20 minutes*

Discuss the following statement:

'Computers have taken the human factor out of too many business decisions.'

Researching and developing

Research and development co-ordination manager

It is the responsibility of this manager to co-ordinate the development of products and services to prototype (sample or model) level. All products and services must be rigorously tested before they are put into production and offered to the customer. The individual who will fill this post is likely to be a technical expert within a specific field. He/she will be aware of the technological requirements and any production problems related to these. Normally, this manager will be given clear instructions as to the organisation's requirements for a new product or service, but will have to work very closely with the production manager in order to develop a product which the organisation is capable of producing.

Researchers

Once the departmental manager has been given a brief to develop and test a new product or service, researchers will investigate all aspects of this product or service. They will refer to any scientific reports which relate to the area of interest, as well as investigating competitors' products. In effect, they will produce a report which offers a series of alternatives from which the developers can work. This report will also be circulated to any other interested person in the organisation.

Product/service developers

These individuals are specialists in their own field. They will have been chosen for their knowledge and ability to apply their skills. It is their responsibility to work from the information given to them by the researchers and to develop a working version or versions of the product. This product will then be subjected to exhaustive testing to ensure that it meets the requirements of the organisation, safety tests and the needs of the customer. At all stages of the development, the production department will advise the developers of any production considerations.

Cleaning

Cleaning supervisor

All organisations, whether or not they have a constant flow of visitors, need to ensure that the premises are kept as clean and tidy as possible. Organisations which have sensitive technological equipment may even need to ensure that the work areas are as dust-free as possible. The cleaning supervisor will allocate cleaning staff according to the demands of each particular work area. Periodically, floors and windows may need to be given special attention and may require specialist equipment/subcontractors to carry out the necessary work.

Cleaners

A cleaner is usually given a particular area of the premises for which to be is responsible. The main cleaning duties will include emptying of bins, clearing away of empty boxes and packing materials, vacuuming and dusting, and routine general cleaning duties. Specialist cleaners may be employed to sanitise telephones, clean word processors with anti-static sprays, and clean carpets or polish floors.

Security

Head of Security

Most larger organisations now realise that it is essential that their buildings are made secure. This is in response to the threat of theft, damage or trespass. The Head of Security will monitor the security of the site(s) and implement procedures aimed at excluding unauthorised individuals from entering the building(s). Some organisations have a more acute problem. For example, nuclear or other power generators (which need to prevent possible deliberate tampering); organisations which carry out animal experiments (animal rights' activists would like to gain entry to seize documentation and free the animals); or organisations that feel they have sensitive or confidential information and so would not wish their building(s) to be entered by unauthorised individuals.

Security Officer

Usually working on a shift system, security officers do carry out an important role in maintaining the security of the buildings and the site. Since thieves tend to use the night as a principal aid to their illegal entry, there is a need for security guards or officers to be present at all times of the day and night.

2.3.4 Identify tasks in job roles

2.3.5 Present results of investigation into job roles

Tasks

We will first make the distinction between the duties and responsibilities as found in the employee's job description, or as part of the contract of employment, and the tasks that will need to be carried out on a daily basis.

The further distinction we will make is that some of these tasks are routine in the sense that they are daily activities, while others are non-routine, such as various emergencies or accidents.

In order to be a successful employee, or a successful manager, you need to display a wide range of different skills. In this sense, if you are a computer programmer, we are not necessarily talking about your skills in computer programming. We are looking at more basic skills, such as decision making, managing your own time, deciding whether you need to delegate tasks to anyone, your problem-solving skills, how you would manage problems like conflict with other individuals, how you would manage stress, if you can set targets, and how you achieve them.

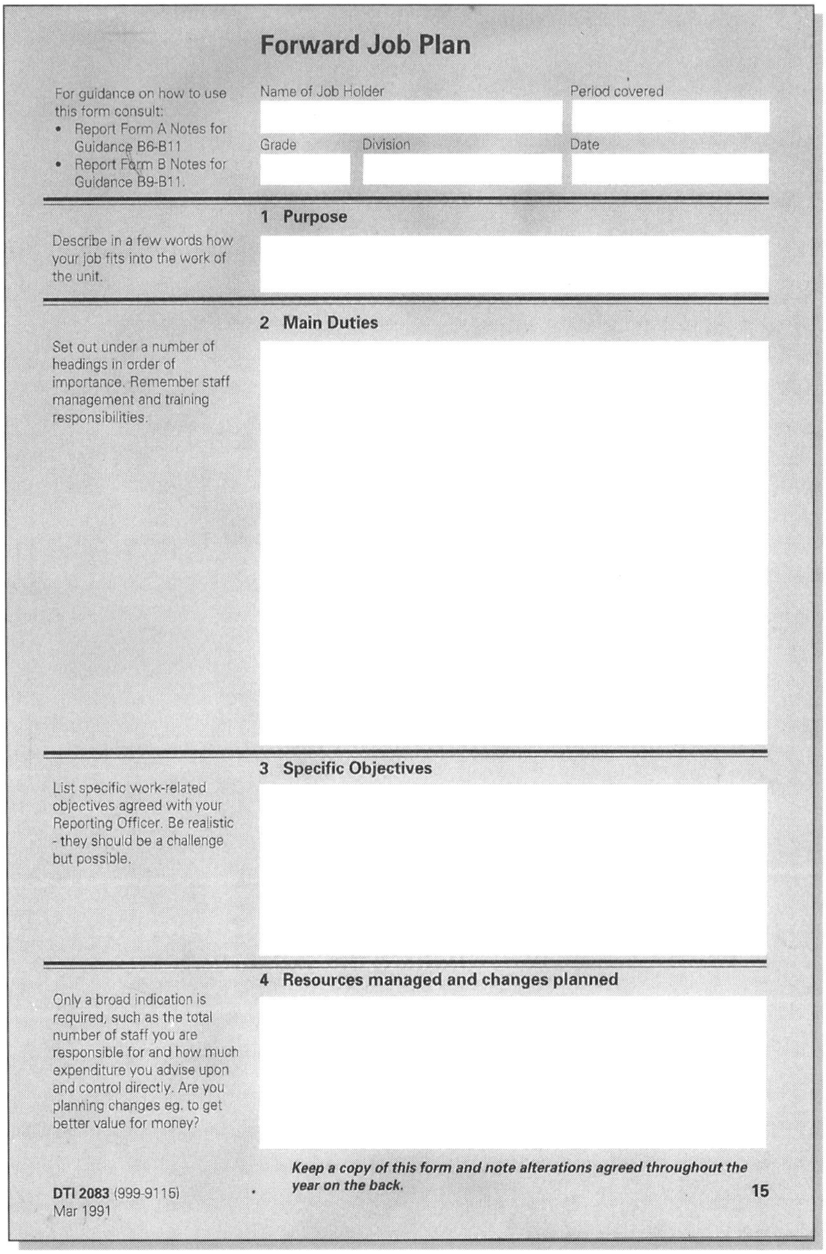

Forward Job Plan

For guidance on how to use this form consult:
- Report Form A Notes for Guidance B6-B11
- Report Form B Notes for Guidance B9-B11.

Name of Job Holder

Period covered

Grade

Division

Date

1 Purpose

Describe in a few words how your job fits into the work of the unit.

2 Main Duties

Set out under a number of headings in order of importance. Remember staff management and training responsibilities.

3 Specific Objectives

List specific work-related objectives agreed with your Reporting Officer. Be realistic - they should be a challenge but possible.

4 Resources managed and changes planned

Only a broad indication is required, such as the total number of staff you are responsible for and how much expenditure you advise upon and control directly. Are you planning changes eg. to get better value for money?

Keep a copy of this form and note alterations agreed throughout the year on the back.

DTI 2083 (999-9116)
Mar 1991

15

Fig 2.28 The DTI's forward job plan aims to focus employees' efforts to attain special objectives

Routine (planning, decision-making, problem solving, setting targets, achieving targets)

Planning

Most of us, if we are honest, would admit that we do not really stop to make a decision about how we are using our time. We may get into a pattern of life or a pattern of working and just continue to take it from day to day, basically being content to let things go on as they are. So what does managing time, or time management actually mean? Here are some variations on definitions:

- *Making better use of the time that you have*
- *Getting more done in the time that you have got*
- *Only to concentrate on important things and to ignore things that are irrelevant*
- *Take control over the time itself and allocate particular amounts of time to things*
- *Spend more of your time on what is important*
- *Try to avoid getting into the situation where you have to rush things at the very last minute*

Planning itself means taking more control over how we spend our time and trying to make a sensible decision about how we are using time. There are three major causes of bad time management:

1. **Crisis management** – this is where people avoid making decisions about anything until they absolutely have to. In turn, this causes stress and we will look at this later.
2. **Priorities** – if you make yourself too available to other people, they will constantly interrupt you. They have their own priorities; you should have yours. By allowing other people to control how you spend your time, you will find yourself in a situation where you are constantly behind with your work, causing unnecessary stress and mistakes.
3. **The treadmill** – this is when you have got behind with your work. You are making no real attempt to catch up on your work, but always working a few days or a few hours behind. Again, this causes stress, but more importantly it causes frustration, not just for yourself, but for those who work with you. It also does not give you an opportunity to take advantage of situations as they arise, because you miss them. There are some ways of getting out of this:
   - *To clarify your own goals*
   - *To choose your own priorities and to stick with them*
   - *To make decisions at the right time instead of putting them off*

So how do you make time work for you? There are two basic tools which a good employee or a good manager will use:

- *A diary for long range planning, and to make a note of any appointments you may have*
- *To make a list – this will help you plan day by day, week by week, month by month. First get into the habit of making a daily list, and then checking your progress against that list at midday and at the end of the day*

The next step is to identify any tasks that you have which have a deadline. Essentially there are two sorts of deadline: a fixed deadline is when something has to be completed by a certain time; a natural deadline is when something has to be done before something else can be done after it. So a progression of different things have to be tackled in a particular order.

1 The first stage is planning, whether you use a diary or list. These should help to jog your memory as to what you have to do to keep track of several jobs at once, deciding how long you need to spend on something, deciding in what order to do things and how to plan your next step in a series of tasks.
2 The second stage is to order these plans. Some things that you may need to do are urgent; others are important. Put them into some sort of logical order.
3 Third is to realise that plans cannot always be achieved and not to get frustrated about them if you have not managed to achieve them.
4 Fourth is the ability to deal with regular disruptions of your plans. Establish which individuals are going to waste your time, and try to avoid them. Also try to work around things which take up a large amount of your time. Allocate them only the time they need.
5 Fifth, consider using a time log. This consists of a daily or weekly planner where you meticulously note exactly how much time you are using on a particular task. The information that it contains can help you to get an idea of time management and whether you need additional training or assistance or resources to carry out the tasks with which you are expected to cope.

PC 2.3.4
C 2.1
C 2.2

Individual activity

Individually, keep a diary of your activities for a week. At the end of the week review the entries and answer the following questions:

1 How many hours, on average, do you devote to your studies?
2 How many hours, on average, do you devote to your leisure activities?
3 How many hours, on average, do you spend sitting in front of the television?
4 Can you identify any times during the week when you managed your time badly?
5 Can you identify any times during the week when you managed your time well?

Compare your weekly diary of activities with those of the rest of the group.

Now, draw up an action plan for yourself, to help you use time more efficiently.

Decision making

To be a good manager or supervisor, or for that matter an employee, you need to be able to make decisions easily. The more senior the position you hold within an organisation, the more decisions are likely to fall on your own shoulders, and the more decisions will have to be made by you on behalf of other people. The lower down the organisation, the less decisions you will have to make of a very important nature. All the same, however, they may very well be important decisions; after all, successful decision making will make your life easier or lack of success will make it much, much harder.

It is generally accepted that decision making goes through five particular phases:

1 Deciding on your aims and exactly what you want to achieve by making the decision.
2 Looking at the various strategies or options you may have in overcoming the problem and making the decision.
3 Choosing the best option that is available to you. This may mean trading off perhaps the cheapest way of doing something for the most efficient way of doing it. In other cases, it may mean choosing the least difficult way of doing it, or the way that takes you the least amount of time.

4 Actually implementing the decision. Having decided on the course of action, you then need to follow it through – knowing, of course, that you could always change your mind if this particular way of solving the problem turns out to be ineffective.
5 Looking back at what you decided to do and assessing whether you made the right decision and whether, given a similar set of circumstances in the future, you would choose the same way again. Perhaps you would not.

Problem solving

This skill is at the heart of any good employee, whether they be a manager or clerk. It is an essential feature of problem solving to be able clearly to identify the problem facing you, and then to consider all possible options to cope with the problem. Perhaps to order them in your own mind or in consultation with others. To consider which will be the most appropriate of the solutions you are offering to the problem, and then to move into the decision-making process which we looked at earlier.

Problem solving is a difficult skill. In many cases people will not even realise that there is a problem which needs to be solved. It is only when the problem emerges and is in danger of seriously affecting their work that people recognise the problem is there.

Problems need not necessarily be big ones. They can be simple problems such as not having enough staff on a particular shift, or running out of stationery, or the telephone system breaking down. Whichever kind of problem we are considering, solutions have to be arrived at in a swift and efficient manner. In order to do this, as we have said, a manager or employee needs to be good at decision making. They may also need to be good at managing their own time in order to be able to devote necessary time to problems as they emerge. Equally, they may have to be willing to delegate responsibility for solving a problem to another person who is adept at coping with that particular kind of situation.

Setting and achieving targets

Several years ago, a particular management technique was designed which aimed to try to assess and monitor how targets and objectives were set. This became known as management by objectives and results. It is not so popular now, but still some of the ideas behind it are very useful to think about. How is a target set?

- *Design a plan of action which can be easily followed*
- *Ensure that you have enough information to work with*
- *Make sure that you do not substantially change your original plan while you are trying to achieve it*
- *Ensure that communications are good between anyone involved in trying to achieve the plan*
- *Ensure that employees involved in trying to achieve the objective are sufficiently motivated and have a clear idea of the organisation's overall objective*
- *Try to make sure that problems outside your control do not adversely affect your move towards achieving the objective*

Having said all of this, some of the problems which will get in the way of achieving an objective are, by their very nature, beyond your control. It may mean that no matter how carefully you have planned and organised all the factors to help you achieve the objective, there may still be problems that will arise which are insurmountable.

In reality, then, setting and achieving objectives boils down to just four main considerations:

Section 3 Assessment of Aspects of Performance

Performance rating

1 Outstanding

2 Performance significantly above requirements

3 Performance fully meets normal requirements of the grade

4 Performance not fully up to requirements; some improvement necessary

5 Unacceptable

Reporting Officer's Assessment

See Guidance Notes C14–29 and Note 1 on page 8

3.1 Give a rating for aspects of performance. Comments would be helpful. Write "not applicable" against any aspect of performance not tested by the job.

	1	2	3	4	5	Comments
Accuracy						
Output						
Quickness on the uptake						
Reliability						
Willingness to take responsibility						
Supervision of staff						
Relations with others						
Oral expression						
Written work						
Figure work						
Application of skills						

Overall Performance

3.2 Give a rating of 1 to 5 (using the performance rating scale as described in Section 3.1).

See Guidance Notes C30–52

Important

3.3 If you have given a 4 or 5 marking for Overall Performance explain what action has been and will be taken to improve the Job Holder's performance and attach a copy of the written warning(s) you have given.

See Guidance Notes C44–52

3.4 Comment if you wish on any features of the Job Holder's performance not already covered and make any general comments you feel add to your overall assessment.

See Guidance Note C53

➤ **Reporting Officer to pass report to Countersigning Officer**

The Job Holder has worked for me for ________ years ________ months

Signature ________________ Telephone number ________

Name in CAPITAL LETTERS ________________

Grade ________________ Date ________

Countersigning Officer's comments on Performance Assessment

3.5 Refer to how much and what is seen of the Job Holder's work. Indicate whether you endorse the mark for overall performance in section 3.2 and how far you agree with the rest of the Reporting Officer's assessment.

See Guidance Notes D8–10

4

Fig 2.29 Pages from the DTI's staff appraisal form – note performance rating

1 That you should be determined to see the plan through
2 That you should be prepared to negotiate with all individuals involved in trying to achieve the objective
3 That you should constantly monitor progress towards the objective, making adjustments as and when required and putting in extra resources as necessary
4 That you should consider adjusting your overall plan should there be significant problems in achieving the objective in the first place

PC 2.3.4

Individual activity

Consider the diary that you kept in the previous activity. Choose one aspect of time management which you know you are not very good at. Set yourself a realistic target relating to that aspect of your life. Promise yourself that you will do your best to reach this target and to show a great improvement within the next month. As a further incentive, promise yourself a small reward for having achieved this target. You may also wish to deny yourself something should you fail!

Non-routine (dealing with emergencies or accidents)

Some people at work will carry out a series of non-routine activities. They will have to be more adaptable than those doing routine tasks, as the demands of each day will differ greatly. These individuals will not be able to predict the demands upon them with any great accuracy. On a single day they may have a series of meetings or tasks to perform without prior notice or instruction.

Routine functions of an office can be easily organised through the establishment of systems to handle them. An office organised in this way will base its procedures upon previous experience and will know with considerable accuracy the demands that will be placed upon it. In situations when an individual or department must carry out a non-routine function, they must be able to rely upon a separate series of procedures to support them. It may be the case that a support system has to be created for that specific purpose.

Sometimes a member of staff may be absent from their routine duties because they are on a course or a period of training. In such cases another member of staff will have to deputise for them and would be carrying out their duties. For the member of staff who is deputising, this would mean that they are carrying out duties which are non-routine for them.

In addition to the non-routine duties that may have to be carried out by individuals within an organisation, there is a possibility of some extraordinary occurrence for which they should also be prepared. Such occurrences might include the following:

- *emergencies* – such as a fire, a bomb threat or a raid
- *accidents* – to individuals working for the organisation, or to visitors

In order to deal with such non-routine emergencies and accidents, the organisation will have to make sure that its staff are prepared. Although such occurrences may never actually take place, it would be wise to carry out a series of 'practice runs' so that all members of staff likely to be involved in such an occurrence would be sure of their role. An organisation would try to ensure that its staff are prepared by carrying out the following with regard to an emergency related to fire:

- **Fire drills** – these should take place at regular intervals
- **Display fire procedure notices** – so that each room has a notice displayed which shows the correct exit route in the case of a fire
- **Display clear and prominent exit signs** – so that there is no confusion when leaving the building in a hurry
- **Install a fire alarm system**, including emergency lighting should the power fail during an emergency
- **Ensure that sufficient and suitable fire extinguishers are in place** throughout the building(s)
- **Ensure that fire doors are always kept clear** and that exits are not blocked in any way
- **Ensure that all staff are aware of the fire procedures** of the organisation and all their exit routes in case of an emergency

When considering an emergency such as a bomb threat or a raid, the organisation should again carry out a series of training sessions for its staff so that they know exactly what to do should such an emergency occur. It should nominate a series of personnel who should be contacted should any such emergency happen and there should be strict guidelines set out regarding the way the organisation should deal with the incident.

Accidents can happen at any time to anybody. In order to ensure that the organisation is equipped to deal with such non-routine occurrences, the following should be in place:

- A health and safety officer should be nominated to try to ensure that there are no obvious dangers to either personnel or visitors to the organisation
- The organisation will have several members of staff (depending on the size of the organisation) trained in first aid at work. This qualification ensures that the individual(s) are capable of administering first aid to any casualty until professional help arrives
- First-aid boxes will be placed in prominent places around the organisation's building(s) and they will be regularly inspected and replaced by a specified individual
- An accident report book or form will be completed each time an accident does occur. This will help the health and safety officer to monitor the type of accident which is occurring and try to ensure that this hazard is dealt with before it is repeated

PC 2.3.4
C 2.1
IT 2.1
IT 2.2
IT 2.3

Individual activity

Time: 1.5 hours

Assess the comparative amounts of time spent by the following individuals on routine and non-routine tasks:

- **An accounts clerk**
- **A receptionist**
- **A shop manager**
- **A tele-sales assistant**

Present your findings in the form of a pie chart for each individual, using computer software to produce this information.

Element 2.3 Assignment

PC 2.3.1–5
C 2.1
C 2.2
C 2.3
C 2.4

In order to show an understanding and application of the performance criteria in this Element you will have to investigate job roles, tasks and activities. It may be the case that you will be able to use a 'real life' example if an organisation will allow you to investigate job roles. If not, your tutor should be able to arrange a case study for you.

Task 1 *PC 2.3.1, 2.3.3*

Summarise the job roles within one organisation. You should describe the day-to-day activities and tasks of the job roles. You should also indicate the extent to which the job is enhanced by teamwork.

Your choice of job roles should be made with regard to the need to identify job roles at different levels (senior, middle and junior).

Task 2 *PC 2.3.2, 2.3.4–5*

Prepare and present an oral assessment of the following:

- a detailed description of a single job role
- an identification of the tasks, activities and duties relating to that job role
- an identification of a routine problem-solving task
- an identification of a non-routine task (which can be in response to an emergency or a potential accident or hazard)

Element 2.4
Prepare for employment or self-employment

Performance criteria

A student must:

1 identify **types of employment and self-employment**

2 identify **opportunities** for employment or self-employment

3 select **information** from relevant sources which applies to identified employment opportunities

4 **analyse skills** for employment or self-employment

5 discuss own strengths and weaknesses in relation to skills for employment or self-employment

Range

- *Types of employment and self-employment*: paid (private, public sectors), voluntary; own business (family business, business start-up, enterprise scheme, partnership, franchise)
- *Opportunities*: local, national, international
- *Information sources*: Job Centres, media (newspapers, TV, radio), careers offices, employment agencies, Federation of Self Employed, banks, TECs (Training and Enterprise Councils), charitable organisations
- *Analyse*: in terms of: own skills achievement, ways to develop and improve skills
- *Skills*: working with others, working independently, time management, decision-making, problem-solving, planning, information seeking, evaluating, communication, application of number, information technology, occupational skills

2.4.1 Identify types of employment and self-employment

Types of employment and self-employment

Many people consider starting their own business, but this is not always practical. Also, many organisations do not necessarily employ people on a full-time basis. There are, therefore, a number of choices and restrictions that must be considered before embarking on the writing of a plan for employment or self-employment.

We intend to begin this Element with an investigation into the potentials of employment and self-employment, starting with a brief look at the different types of employment.

Paid (private, public sectors)

This is perhaps the most common form of employment in the UK. Large numbers of individuals work either for the private or public sector. Paid employment involves being actually paid for the hours or duties which you carry out for or on behalf of an organisation. We can identify the following versions of paid employment:

- *Full-time* – this means that a working week of 35 or more hours is undertaken by the individual in return for a wage or salary.
- *Part-time* – this means individuals undertake work for part of a week. The line between part-time and full-time is a little blurred, but it can be assumed that part-time workers are those who work for less than 25 hours per week.
- *Permanent* – this is a sub-category of full-time and part-time work. It means that regardless of the number of hours the individual works, the post they hold is of a permanent nature.
- *Temporary* – this is another sub-category of both full-time and part-time work. Normally the individual would work on a fixed-term contract basis and they would know that their employment is secure during that period.
- *Seasonal* – this is a variation which could include full-time and part-time employment. Seasonal workers would be employed during periods of high business activity and during holiday periods, when the permanent employees are on vacation but the organisation still requires the work to be carried out. In the same way, additional members of staff may be needed during such periods as the run up to Christmas if increased demand requires the organisation to have more people working for it.
- *Casual* – this type of employment, which can sometimes take the form of a limited number of hours worked on an as-and-when-needed basis, is normally paid by the hour or by the day. This is one method of employing people that does not need the organisation to make them a long-term commitment. Casual workers could be employed to undertake specific projects or tasks or they may be employed only during periods of high demand. It is usually the case that casual workers are paid quite low rates and they are asked to undertake jobs which the permanent employees feel are beneath them.

Voluntary

Non-profit-making organisations, for example charities in the voluntary sector, such as Greenpeace, Friends of the Earth, the Terence Higgins Trust and Oxfam, often employ voluntary workers. These charities work on the basis that the income they generate should be passed on to the charitable cause (after running costs and administration have been deducted). For this reason, there are always some opportunities for both unpaid and paid employment. When we think about unpaid work, a number of charities have local retail outlets where they sell a range of second-hand, recycled or 'fair trade' goods. In this instance, the shop managers may be paid, but the shop assistants are often employed on a free voluntary basis, although they could receive travel expenses. The voluntary sector has become more aware recently that if it is to prosper and support the charitable activities which it finances, it has to become more professional in its approach. While, in general terms, the pay scales and opportunities offered by voluntary organisations may be limited when we compare them with consumer-based organisations, many managers, administrators and marketing specialists begin their working lives in voluntary organisations.

Own business (family business, business start-up, enterprise scheme, partnership, franchise)

In this part of the Element we will be looking at the types of employment that you may be able to consider. Knowledge of the variety of different types of work may prove to be very valuable in helping you to plan for the future.

Family business

A lot of individuals who run small to medium-sized businesses actually began their business lives as either part of a family business or a new business or as a result of a government enterprise scheme.

Working for a family business can, of course, have its benefits. The individual can be protected from the major business pressures which a self-employed individual would have to face. At the same time, the individual may be required to work longer hours and for less pay than in other forms of work. It is a tradition for parents to pass their businesses on to their sons or daughters. As the parent takes a gradual 'back seat' in terms of the decision making and day-to-day running of the business, the son or daughter will have to be prepared to cope alone. Despite the fact that parents may be prepared to pass their business on to their children, there is always the question of continued interference from them. This can cause considerable problems.

This is not to say that inheriting a family business is a bad thing. After all, much of the hard work in establishing a business has already been done. Developing the business and choosing a new direction or setting new objectives for the business offers the son or daughter a good opportunity to prove themselves.

Business start-up

Business start-up, or the establishment of a new business, means a different set of potential problems and opportunities. There is a need for a lot of forward planning and forecasting before starting a business of your own. There is no limit to the possibilities for starting your own business; the only limit is in your own ability to convince potential lenders that your business plan will work and that your business has a reasonable future. Good relations, particularly with the bank, or other lenders, is, of course, important. Again, the success or failure of the business will largely rest upon the individual's ability to use his or her skills to the benefit of the business. Starting up a new business is very much a question of being able to learn as you go along. No amount of training, development or advice from other people can ensure that the individual is ready to tackle unexpected problems. As we will see towards the end of this Element, it is advisable for individuals intending to start up in business to evaluate their own strengths or weaknesses in several different skills in order to establish that they are capable of running their own business.

Banks, in particular, are very keen to support new businesses, provided it can be shown that the business is a viable venture. It is in the bank's own interest to establish good relations with the business at the beginning of its life, as the owner of the business could remain with the bank as a customer for a considerable amount of time.

Enterprise schemes

Government enterprise schemes can be accessed usually via the local Training and Enterprise Council. We will be looking at certain types of government enterprise schemes in Element 2.4.3. These allowances or grants aim to help the individual financially for a particular period of time without that individual having to take money out of the business. The different forms of support can be tailor-made to suite the circumstances of the individual. The individual will have to show the ability to put together a business plan which can convince the TEC that the business will work. In each area there are different names for the government enterprise schemes and, indeed, in some areas, particularly those which are assisted or urban programme areas, there may be an even greater variety of grants. Local authorities, in their role as local government, also offer advice regarding grants, premises and loans. The loans tend to be cheap and available particularly to younger individuals.

Partnership

Entering into a partnership may be a good alternative to the risk of beginning your own business. It is important that an individual thinking about this course of action should look at the history, assets and business prospects of the partnership. As a partner you are liable for the debts of that partnership. In practice, this means that you are responsible for making sure that bills are paid and you may have to cover the other partners' shares if they fail to pay. It is also wise to find out whether the other partners have enough assets that can be realised to cover their share of any debts. If a partnership has a history of unpaid bills, then that particular partnership should be ruled out. It is also a good idea to establish whether you can get on with the other members of the partnership. Since you will be making decisions which will affect the future of all the other partners, a good working relationship is of great importance.

It is normal to have a solicitor draw up a partnership agreement, or to have a look at a partnership agreement which has been prepared by the existing partners. This is a good idea since another view on the partnership would be very valuable.

Franchise

Franchises offer the opportunity of starting your own business with a greater chance of survival than in other circumstances. The first three years of a new business's life are the most dangerous. Franchises have a much better record of surviving these vital three years than any other form of new business.

It goes without saying that the individual who decides to buy a franchise will have to pay a price for it. It may be a lump sum as well as paying an amount per year to the person who provided the franchise. It may also involve being tied up with the purchasing of products or services from the franchisor. The franchisee will not be able to benefit from shopping around for better prices. The franchisor charges a percentage of sales per year, leaving the remainder of the profit (if any) to the franchisee.

2.4.2 Identify opportunities for employment or self-employment

Opportunities

In this performance criteria we will be looking at the particular types of opportunities that are available to you locally, nationally and internationally. You should never think that your employment prospects are limited to jobs which are a bus ride away.

As you will discover, having a qualification from the UK is a very great advantage when you look at jobs overseas. UK qualifications are considered to be of a very high quality and are much admired by many countries. Also remember that you will not only have the knowledge needed for a great many jobs, but you will also have the skills required to carry out the jobs.

The performance criteria are very practical and we cannot really predict what kind of employment you might be looking for. Neither can we predict whether you would seriously consider a job overseas.

The Element assignment requires you to identify at least three employment or self-employment opportunities. By carrying out this student activity you will have prepared quite a lot of the groundwork to finish the Element assignment.

It would be a good idea to look at the next performance criteria before you carry out your research into employment or self-employment prospects. The next performance criteria looks at the best sources of information to find employment or self-employment opportunities.

Individual activity

In order to cover the performance criteria of this section of the Element, you will need to identify at least three different employment or self-employment opportunities.

PC 2.4.2
C 2.1
C 2.2
IT 2.1
IT 2.2
IT 2.3

You should consider the following:

- local prospects
- national prospects
- international prospects

You may choose any mix of the three categories, or may focus on just one of them if you wish.

You will need to provide a word-processed summary for each of the job opportunities. This should include the following:

- source of information (e.g. job advertisement, article or careers information)
- actions required by you to make an application for the job

You should keep the information from this student activity to be included in your Element assignment.

2.4.3 Select information from relevant sources which applies to identified employment opportunities

This performance criteria is designed to help you to identify the sources of information that you will need to consider in assisting you to find suitable employment or self-employment. Obviously, not all of the sources will be of use to you. This will depend upon your ideas of what you wish to do in the future. We have investigated all of the sources of information and noted how useful they might be and exactly how they could help you.

The addresses of these organisations can normally be found in the telephone directory. If you contact your local Careers Office or your local TEC, they should be able to pass on to you the names, addresses and telephone numbers you will need. The local Job Centre is also a very valuable source of information about the services offered by other organisations.

Remember that you will need to make contact with some of these organisations in order to complete your Element assignment.

Information sources

Job Centres

Job Centres are the UK's largest employment organisation. Through a Job Centre it is possible to gain access to a wide variety of services. It should be noted that, at the time of writing, many of these services are under review. Indeed, it is widely believed that the government will reorganise this service and the range of help that it offers.

Job Centres are an ideal place to begin to look for a job. The available job vacancies are clearly displayed on cards and all you have to do is to write down the vacancies that you feel you are interested in and then take them along to the reception desk.

If you are unemployed, then the Job Centre will be able to help you in your job search and will attempt to 'match' you with one of their advisors. The client advisor will provide you with a 'Back to Work Plan'.

Fig 2.30 The Job Centre logo

The advisor is a good source of information, providing information about benefits which could be claimed and employment or training opportunities available in the area.

As we will see later in this Element, on television both ITV and Channel 4 cover a number of job vacancies. The ES Jobfinder provides a 24-hour a day Teletext service which shows a selection of the vacancies available, including those around the UK and abroad. In addition to advertising job vacancies, the ES also provides general help and services, including the listing of events in a particular area. All of the information contained within these services is regularly updated.

If you have been looking for a full-time permanent job for at least four weeks, then you will be entitled to claim expenses from the Travel to Interview Scheme. After three months, if you are still unemployed, you will be asked to return to see your advisor, who will review and update your Back to Work Plan with you.

Through the Job Centre, as a part of the Employment Department Group, there are several schemes and initiatives available, including:

- **Job search seminars** – which last for four days spread over five weeks and look at job interviews, letter writing, the compiling of CVs, making telephone calls, typing and other skills.
- **Job review workshops** – which last for two days and use a computer program to help you to match your skills to new areas of work.
- **Restart interviews** – which are designed to give the individual a fresh start and access to a number of specific services, including lists of jobs to apply for, a job interview (through job interview guarantee), a place on a training programme, the opportunity for temporary work and help to start your own business.
- **Job club** – this gives the unemployed person direct help on telephone and interview techniques, and access to telephones, newspapers and stationery (all free of charge).

These job clubs are organised by a leader who will also help the individual to prepare job applications.

- **Job interview guarantee** – which is a scheme that matches the right skills and qualifications against the employers' vacancies and guarantees the individual an interview for the job.
- **Job preparation course** – which will help the unemployed person to improve their interview techniques and look at their strengths and weaknesses.
- **Employment on trial** – which gives the unemployed person the opportunity to enter employment on a trial basis.
- **Work trial** – this lasts for up to three weeks and is a useful way of finding out whether you like the job. The employer has a real vacancy and this short trial period gives you the opportunity to have a taste of the job and for the employer to see whether he/she likes you. You will receive benefit during the work trial period, as well as receiving up to £5 per day for travel and £1.50 per day for meals.
- **Job plan** – this scheme lasts for five days and is a workshop which are designed to identify the unemployed person's strengths and weaknesses, and to encourage them to look at new options and to use a computer program to match their preferences with possible jobs.

Fig 2.31 The Job Seekers' Charter, which guarantees quality of service

- **Community action** – with an additional allowance over and above any other benefit the unemployed person may be entitled to, this scheme aims to get individuals involved in environmental and conservation issues as well as administration, caring and research projects.
- **Restart course** – this part-time two-week course aims to develop techniques to get back

to work, increase awareness of employment and training opportunities, understand the recruitment process and develop an individual plan of action.

- **Disability employment advisor** – this person will help those with a disability or health problem to find a job which will be suitable for them.

Fig 2.32 'Positive about disabled people' disability symbol

- **Job introduction scheme** – this scheme allows the individual to try a job for an introductory six-week period. The individual will be paid the normal rate of pay by the employer during the trial period.
- **Access to work** – particularly if the individual is disabled, or has a health problem, the access to work scheme can offer up to £21 000 over a five-year period to help find a job, keep a job, or improve career prospects.
- **Supported employment** – in the case of individuals who have severe disability, the supported employment scheme offers supported placements, access to the Re-employ Interwork and workshops.

A number of the above schemes are only available if the individual has been out of work for six months or more (in some cases three months). However, ex-offenders and ex-service personnel, or those with disability, will be entitled to be included on one of these schemes immediately. If the individual is returning to the job market after being away for more than two years, then he/she will also be able to gain instant access to the schemes.

1. The Employment Department Group's publication *Just the Job* (which is revised annually in order to accommodate changes in the schemes and initiatives) is a very valuable source of information for those seeking employment or self-employment. The Job Centres can claim that they have succeeded in finding jobs for around 400 000 people per year.
2. Another important service which is supplied by the Employment Department Group is the 'Career Development Loan Scheme'. This enables an unemployed individual to borrow money from Barclays Bank, the Co-operative Bank, Clydesdale Bank or Royal Bank of Scotland. It allows the individual to borrow between £200 and £8000 for up to 80% of any course fees. In addition to this loan, the individual can claim the full cost of any books, materials or other related expenses. Those who have been out of work for three months or longer can apply for up to 100% off course fees, as well as some living expenses if the course is full-time.
3. One other service which the Job Centre provides is the *Be Your Own Boss* advice and leaflets. There is a great deal of useful information regarding self-employment, entering into a partnership or co-operative, buying a franchise, undertaking commission-only jobs, and relevant training and professional advice. This service is provided in conjunction with TECs and LECs.
4. Euro Action is an annual event and promotion supported by BBC Radio 1 and the Employment Department Group. It focuses on the following:

- *student grants, loans, sponsorships and scholarships*
- *education and training*
- *job searches*
- *money management*
- *setting up businesses*
- *identifying opportunities in Europe*
- *education and training in Europe*
- *enterprise in Europe*

If you are considering a career in Europe, then Euro Action has some useful information.

5 The Employment Department Group, in association with the Overseas Placing Unit and European Employment Services produce a range of booklets entitled *Working in . . . .* Each of these booklets focuses on job opportunities and sources of information for all the major European countries.

Focus study

Job Centres

The Job Centres produce very useful information packs for those people interested in working in other countries. These packs include information on the following:

- finding work
- immigration and registration documents
- health and social security
- taxation
- employment issues
- accommodation
- education
- comparability of qualifications
- culture
- legal matters
- useful addresses
- reading
- a checklist

PC 2.4.3
C 2.1
C 2.4

Group activity

Time: 30 minutes

Assuming that you are interested in employment abroad, the following checklist will provide you with a useful guide to the matters you need to think about:

1. Find out whether you need a full UK passport or a visitor's passport
2. Find out the method and frequency of payments of any salary
3. Find out what travel arrangements need to be made
4. Find out whether the employer is prepared to pay these travel expenses or, indeed, make the arrangements for you

5 Find out about the availability of accommodation
6 Make sure that you have a form E111, which gives medical expenses cover
7 Find out if you need private health insurance
8 Make sure that you have enough money to last until you are paid
9 Make sure that you have saved enough money to pay for a return journey in the event of any emergency

Some of these points are quite obvious, but you should make sure that you know who is responsible for carrying them out. Although it will mostly be you in the end, other individuals or organisations will have a part in it. You should also consider whether you would be prepared to accept employment abroad without knowing some or all of the above information. You should discuss this point as a group.

Media (newspapers, TV, radio)

The different sections of the media offer various levels of help in obtaining information regarding employment. There are very few jobs advertised on the TV or on the radio. However, many independent television stations do not broadcast programmes in the early hours of the morning. Using a teletext-type service, they will show printed details on the screen of employment prospects and specific job vacancies in the region. Many of these job vacancies are provided by the Job Centres in the area, or they may be jobs available through agencies. It should also be noted that there are a number of programmes which relate either directly or indirectly to certain employment areas, particularly on BBC2 and Channel 4, which broadcast a number of programmes relating to specific occupations.

Newspapers and magazines provide the majority of advertised vacancies and job opportunities. The national press newspapers often have particular days on which they have advertisements for jobs in particular fields. Specialist magazines may be a useful source of information on occupations in their area. There are some free newspapers and magazines distributed at tube or train stations which provide an opportunity for employment and recruitment agencies to advertise their current range of vacancies. The local press may deliver free sheets to homes or publish local newspapers which can be bought from retail outlets, and these contain local job opportunities and vacancy details.

The majority of printed material such as newspapers and magazines can be researched at local libraries and Job Centres.

Careers offices

The careers offices can provide a service to both employers and potential employees. They establish a link between schools and colleges and employers. It is a good idea to ask for careers service advice as the advisor may be able to give you useful addresses, telephone numbers and contacts which may save you a great deal of time in researching. The careers service will also give advice regarding the qualifications needed for particular job areas and will help if you have an idea of the type of work you would like to do but are unsure of the specific job for which you should be applying. Careers advisors will visit schools and colleges and suggest suitable training and qualifications to individuals who are unsure of the route to take in order to become a suitable candidate for a particular job.

Employment agencies

Employment and recruitment agencies offer a wide range of advice to a potential job seeker in looking for full-time employment. Agencies also offer seasonal or part-time job opportunities. Although these two types of agencies cater for slightly different markets, their common aims are to match potential candidates or applicants with the requirements of the employer. Normally the agency would receive a percentage of the successful candidate's first year's salary in return for successfully placing the individual.

In the case of temporary workers, the employee, although working for an organisation, is not directly paid by it. The agency receives an hourly rate from the employer and the employee receives a rather lower hourly rate from the agency.

Many agencies, particularly in cases when the applicant has useful skills, will advise on the improvement of the individual's CV and interpersonal skills (such as interview technique). As such agencies are often part of a network of agencies, they offer an advantage to the individual because they can investigate the possibility of employment in areas other than the immediate locality.

Recruitment agencies usually have a city-centre location and may have associations with other recruitment agencies, but tend to look for applicants in a slightly different manner to an employment agency. While an employment agency may use the local press or their own shop windows, a recruitment agency will tend to use specialist publications as the main method of attracting potential candidates.

THE FEDERATION OF RECRUITMENT AND EMPLOYMENT SERVICES
FRES
REPRESENTING BEST PRACTICE

Fig 2.33 The Federation of Recruitment and Employment Services' logo
Any reputable employment agency will be a member of this organisation, which aims to set standards and ensure best practice. Some 3000 member offices operate in all sectors of industry

PC 2.4.3

Individual activity

Thinking about your own career intentions, try to identify any local or national recruitment agencies that would be able to assist you in some way. Also, consider at what point it would be a good idea to contact them. Do you think it would be best to wait until you need their help, or should you make an initial contact with them at this stage?

Federation of Self-Employed

The Federation of Self-Employed provides a network of regional and local groups to assist and support those engaged in self-employment. The organisation and its members provide a wealth of information and advice, based upon many years of experience.

Federation of Small Business

The FSB aims to assist the approximately 400 000 new enterprises which are established each year. With the financial support of Mercury Communications, the FSB is a leading campaign and pressure group. With nearly 60 000 members, it is concerned with bringing about changes in legislation, particularly in relation to the protection and promotion of small businesses. One of the key services which it offers is a 24-hour legal advice scheme. In its booklet *Getting Started in Business* the FSB offers valuable advice on a number of issues, including finance, tax, premises, marketing, customer care and problem solving.

Banks

Banks perform a vital role in the following areas:

- *Financial facilities, including current accounts, overdrafts, loans, leasing, factoring, and import and export assistance*
- *Specialist services, primarily for small businesses through Small Business Centres*
- *Free banking in the first year for new businesses*
- *Frank and objective advice and judgements regarding business problems*
- *Advice on such business matters as insurance*

Obviously the relationship which individuals are able to strike up with their bank and bank manager will have a bearing on their willingness to involve the bank in their business affairs. It should be noted that it is a good idea always to separate business and personal affairs so that one does not influence the other.

TECs (Training and Enterprise Councils)

There are 82 Training and Enterprise Councils (TECs) throughout England and Wales. Scotland has 22 Local Enterprise Companies (LECs). Both of these organisations offer training and support for small businesses in the interests of addressing the needs of the local community.

Each TEC and LEC has its own particular purpose. Generally speaking, the training opportunities they provide include:

- *Enterprise awareness events – these aim to alert potential new businesses to the demands and problems which could be associated with the setting up of a new business*
- *Specific business training aimed at assisting the setting up or development of a business*
- *Open learning skills programmes – business skill seminars on such topics as management and marketing*
- *Information and advice on the Investors in People programme*
- *Co-ordination and planning for small firms' training loans*
- *Training programmes for employees*

Fig 2.34 Norfolk and Waveney TEC's logo – one of over 100 TECs and LECs operating throughout the UK, offering training and support

TECs and LECs are also involved in the following business services:

- **Training access points (TAPS)** – which provide information about local and national training opportunities. These can usually be found in libraries and high street locations, as well as in TECs and LECs.
- **Counselling and advice** – TECs, LECs and Local Enterprise Agencies also offer advice to both new businesses and existing businesses. Through the services of a personal business advisor, a wide range of problem-solving advice is provided.
- **Consultancy** – the Enterprise Initiative Consultancy Scheme enables small businesses to employ consultants in specific areas. This service is also available through business links.
- **Investors in People** – based on the idea that training and development of employees is crucial in the successful development of a business, IiP is an initiative which helps businesses to address this consideration. Operating within national standards, the TECs and LECs offer guidance in this matter.

There are a number of other services and initiatives which are handled by the TECs and LECs, including:

1 **Business Development Centres** – which provide informal advice, information and guidance, as well as other business services. These may be contacted via a freephone number.
2 **Enterprise 2000** – which is designed to give specific help and support in starting your own business. It offers impartial advice from experienced business counsellors as well as seminars on marketing, finance, business administration and preparing a business plan.
3 **Target Training** – this offers specialist advice to match your specific ambitions and education. The scheme provides an allowance of £29.50 per week if you are 16 and £35

per week if you are over 17 during the training programme. You will be engaged in on-the-job training which is provided by an employer and a college (or training agency). The studies may take up to two years and there is every chance that you may be offered full-time employment by your employer.

4 **Business Development Fund** – this service provides information on everything you need to know in terms of financial support for your business. It has been primarily set up to help small to medium-sized businesses (those with up to 100 employees).

Charitable organisations

Charitable organisations offer the opportunity of both voluntary and paid work. Getting a full-time paid job for a charitable or voluntary organisation follows very similar lines to those you would expect in any other organisation. However, there are some differences, which may include the individual having to prove that he or she supports the purpose of the organisation.

Alternatively, charitable and voluntary organisations offer people the opportunity to do work (without pay) which could not only broaden their horizons, but also provide them with vital job skills and experience. It is quite common for individuals on leaving full-time education, to offer their services to a voluntary organisation. This use of their time and skills can be done while looking for employment or a self-employment opportunity. You will find a variety of voluntary organisations in both your *Yellow Pages* and via your local library. Many areas have a voluntary services bureau which acts rather like an agency, placing temporary workers, although, of course, no money changes hands.

Focus study

Voluntary Service Overseas

Voluntary Service Overseas (VSO) was founded in 1958 and sends volunteers to over 55 countries throughout the world. These individuals are sent abroad as a result of requests from governments or other relief and development agencies and non-governmental organisations. The VSO is open to anyone over 20 who is prepared to spend at least two years overseas. There are some restrictions, which include:

- No dependent children
- Willingness to work for a small allowance
- A full UK passport must be held
- The individual should be qualified
- The individual should have at least 18 months' experience

The VSO acts as a recruitment agency for overseas employers. As a volunteer, you are employed by an organisation in the country where you are working.

The UK headquarters of the VSO is in London and it has a 24-hour answerphone service.

Individual activity

If you might be interested in offering your services on a voluntary basis, contact the VSO and establish what qualifications and work experience you would need to have in order to be a volunteer. Your letter to the VSO should be word processed.

PC 2.4.3
C 2.2
C 2.4
IT 2.1
IT 2.2

Local Enterprise Agencies (LEAs)

There are over 400 LEAs throughout the UK which offer business advice and counselling to new or expanding businesses. They also offer extensive assistance in the formation of business plans. The LEAs have very good links with various businesses and organisations in the local area. They will be able to offer you either direct assistance or referral to an organisation which can provide that help. You can obtain the address and telephone number of your local LEA from a TEC, LEC or Job Centre.

The Prince's Youth Business Trust/Prince's Scottish Youth Business Trust

These organisations offer grants or low-interest loans to individuals between the ages of 18 and 29. They will also provide assistance to those who are having difficulties in raising finance from other sources. They provide advice, training and marketing opportunities to help new businesses.

Live Wire

This initiative, sponsored by Shell (UK) Ltd, offers advice and assistance to young business people. Part of this initiative is a competition held annually to reward excellence and achievement by young people.

2.4.4 Analyse skills for employment or self-employment

2.4.5 Discuss own strengths and weaknesses in relation to skills for employment or self-employment

These performance criteria aim to analyse and discuss your own skills in relation to your proposed employment or self-employment plans. We have put these two performance criteria together so that you can get a really good view of what you are good at.

Perhaps the best place to start is an analysis of your own general strengths and weaknesses. By doing this you may be able to begin to realise your own potential and limitations.

PC 2.4.4
PC 2.4.5
C 2.4

Individual activity

Time: 40 minutes

Answer the questions below, using the following responses:

always
sometimes
occasionally
never

1 Are you able to work long hours?
2 Do you find problems a challenge?
3 Can you come up with good ideas to get out of problems?
4 If you started a new business and it was struggling, would you be prepared to keep it going?
5 Are you able to keep going at something until it is completed?
6 Would you always put your own business before anything else, including your leisure activities and your family?
7 Are you always able to keep going and able to stick with a problem?
8 Would you always consider success to be measured in terms of how much money you make?
9 Would you be able to live under the worry of not being sure about your job or your income?
10 Do you consider yourself to be self-confident?
11 Are you able to take criticism?
12 Do you tend to ask for others to give you feedback on your performance in the hope that you can do something better next time?
13 Do you tend to believe that your success is dependent upon things you cannot control?
14 Do you tend to be a leader in certain situations?
15 Are you good at finding the right person or source of information to help you achieve what you want?
16 Do you have the ability to realise that in certain circumstances you may need help?
17 Do you set high standards for yourself?
18 Do you take risks rather than being cautious?
19 Are you healthy?
20 Do you have the ability to pass jobs on to others?
21 Are you able to identify important decisions as against unimportant ones?
22 Do others think of you as a survivor?
23 Do you find coping with problems a real difficulty?
24 Do you respect others' views and opinions?
25 When others express an opinion or offer advice and information, are you able to accept what they say?

If you have answered these questions with mainly 'always' or 'sometimes' responses, then you are probably suited to self-employment. If you have not answered these questions in this way, then what could you do to change yourself to meet the demands that you would face as a business owner?

Working with others and working independently

Decision making, problem solving and information seeking may be an important part of a job. In the case of individuals who are involved in a small business, they may be required to be the problem solver, decision maker and information seeker. In cases when the business is particularly small, two or more individuals may have to combine their talents and abilities to cope with certain projects or tasks.

The following student activity aims to assess whether you are more of a team worker than an independent worker.

Individual activity

Time: 20 minutes

PC 2.4.4
PC 2.4.5

You will need to respond to the following questions by stating one of the following:

I agree
I neither agree nor disagree
I disagree

1 I want to control the tasks and environment around me.
2 I want to be involved in everything.
3 I find it impossible to pass on a job to someone else.
4 I hate being uncertain about things.
5 I do not trust other people's ability to do a job.
6 I hate asking other people for favours.
7 I like to be alone when I have things to do.
8 I always check and change other people's work.
9 I would rather stop doing what I am doing than let someone else do what I think I should be doing.
10 I lose interest in a task if someone else interferes in what I am doing.

If you have agreed with the above statements, then you are much more of an independent worker than a team worker. If you have neither agreed nor disagreed with the statements, then you may be either unsure of what you might do in certain situations, or it may not actually worry you whether you are working alone or as a member of a team. Those that have disagreed with the majority of the statements should be fairly good team workers.

Time management

Time management involves not only other people, but also physical items such as paperwork, and other things. It involves the constant checking of what needs to be done. The following student activity attempts to analyse your time management potential.

PC 2.4.4
PC 2.4.5

Individual activity *Time: 20 minutes*

Try to answer the following statements with a '*true*' or '*false*' response:

1. **I have identified my strengths in relation to time management.**
2. **I have identified my weaknesses in relation to time management.**
3. **I know where and how I waste my time.**
4. **I know why I allow my time to be managed badly.**
5. **I am able to decide which tasks should be done first.**
6. **I can quickly process and decide on the importance of information.**
7. **I understand the reasons behind my time-wasting behaviour.**
8. **I can use a variety of different methods to manage my time.**
9. **I can cope with other individuals who may try to stop me from getting on with my tasks in hand.**
10. **I am able to control my time.**

If you have responded 'true' to the majority of these questions, then you have already begun to manage your time effectively. If you have a number of 'false' responses to these statements, then you may have to consider making stricter rules for yourself and others.

Decision-making and problem-solving

Decision making is an important skill that must be looked at by any individual within a business. We all make lots of decisions on a day-to-day basis, but we may not recognise them as such. There is no reason to believe that decisions in a business environment are any different to the choices and processes that you go through in making the decisions in your private life. Often the options available to you will either be more extensive than you are used to or may appear to be more extensive but are not so on closer examination. Again, we must refer back to our theme throughout this section of the Element. In other words, all of these skills are inter-related. Without having first decided *how* you will make the decision, *when* you will make the decision and *why* you will make the decision, you cannot expect to find yourself in a position to make that decision.

In terms of problem solving, which is to some extent a variation of decision making itself, you may be faced with a situation that requires an immediate response. Problem solving tends to be routed in 'here and now' rather than the more long-term decision-making problems. Many problems will arise without a great deal of notice. There are very many ways of handling such situations, but one of the most common forms of problem solving is still crisis management. An individual who is forced down this panic route will find themselves unable to plan or manage their time effectively, since they are constantly having to respond to often petty and relatively unimportant problems. If these problems are ignored, however, then they become much bigger than they need to be and so they require a decision to be made.

The following student activity aims to establish whether you are able to make effective decisions and solve problems.

Individual activity

Time: 20 minutes

Answer the following questions with either a *'yes'* or *'no'* response:

PC 2.4.4
PC 2.4.5

1 I can identify the nature and sources of problems before they happen.
2 I have already examined the possible solutions before I make a decision.
3 I have clear ideas that help me arrive at a solution.
4 I am able to compare possible solutions and choose the right one.
5 I can put into action and then monitor the results of my decisions.
6 I am able to assess a problem before it really becomes a problem.
7 I never make a snap decision.
8 I would rather think about the problem at length than risk making a wrong decision.
9 I do not find decision making stressful but it is challenging.
10 If I manage information correctly, then decision making is relatively easy.

If you have answered 'Yes' to the majority of the questions, then you have some grasp of the decision-making process and are reasonably able to solve problems. Alternatively, you may be somewhat over-confident and you should be aware of the potential dangers of over-confidence, in the sense that you may not be fully able to predict, process and make logical decisions. If you said 'No' to the majority of these statements or to some of them, then you are perhaps being a little more honest with yourself. There are only a few even highly-experienced managers who could claim that they always make the right decision and that they are invariably able to solve problems effectively.

Planning

Planning plays an important role in making sure that tasks are carried out at the right time. There are a number of different planning techniques. The following self-assessment should help you identify how good you are at planning ahead.

Individual activity

Time: 20 minutes

Answer the following questions *'yes'* or *'no'*:

1 Before setting a target I need to be aware of what is required.
2 In setting a target I am aware of the limitations of skills, resources and time.
3 I only set achievable targets.
4 Once a target has been set I will do everything within my power to ensure that it is achieved.
5 In certain cases, it is important to reassess the target if things have changed.
6 The review procedures should be part of the planning of target setting.
7 Reviewing progress should be on-going, with regular and systematic checks.
8 It is a good idea to use the skills of another individual to assist in the review of progress.

9 Reviewing progress can often throw light upon the reasons behind targets not being met.

10 In some cases, the review may require the target to be changed.

If you have agreed with most of these statements, then you show some idea of the importance of planning. If you were unsure about some of these statements, then you will need to look at the way you set targets and undertake a planning exercise.

Information seeking and evaluating

Following on from decision making and problem solving, the collection of information and the subsequent handling of it is yet another key skill to obtain. The information that you are able to obtain, handle and process will be vital in establishing your ability to communicate.

The following student activity seeks to investigate your information seeking and handling skills.

Individual activity

Time: 20 minutes

Again answer these questions with either a *'yes'* or *'no'* response:

PC 2.4.4
PC 2.4.5

1 I know what information I need.
2 I know from whom or from where I can obtain the information.
3 I do, of course, know why I want it.
4 I have a good idea of the timescale involved.
5 I have some requirements about the format in which the information should be delivered.
6 Once I have the information I know what I have to do with it.
7 I can look at the information and know what is valuable and what is useless.
8 I can process the information and present it in a more clear and logical manner.
9 Once I have tackled the information I can draw clear conclusions from it.
10 I also know the use of the information and to whom it should be relayed.

If you have answered these questions with a 'yes' response, then you have a fairly clear understanding of research, investigation and handling skills related to information. You should be aware, however, that in this slightly over-confident point of view you may have run the risk of overlooking some vital piece of information or discarded potentially valuable data by only giving it a cursory glance.
Alternatively, if you have a mixture of 'yes' and 'no' responses, or mainly 'no' responses, you should not consider yourself a failure in this respect. A cautious user of information and, indeed, a careful handler of information may see things that the more confident person could miss.

Communication

The use and development of communication skills is an important consideration when attempting to establish relationships with others. You will encounter a number of different sets of circumstances which may require you to assume certain standards of communication; at other times, you will need to display power and authority through your communication ability. By using the following student activity you may be able to identify some of your communication skills.

Individual activity

Time: 20 minutes

Answer these questions with a '*true*' or '*false*' response:

PC 2.4.4
PC 2.4.5

1 I can use a variety of communication methods, including body language.
2 I can listen effectively and display correct responses.
3 I am able to manage myself in the communication process.
4 I am able to control relationships through my communication.
5 I am able to cope with situations requiring both formal and informal communication.
6 I am able to use a variety of different questioning techniques when seeking information.
7 I am able to read the body language of other people.
8 I appreciate that communication is a two-way process.
9 I am able to communicate well in written form.
10 I am able to present information in a variety of different visual formats.

It will only be the most accomplished communicator who will be able to claim to display all of the above characteristics. If you have responded 'false' to a number of the statements above, then you should consider how these communication aspects may be improved.

Application of number

Regardless of your role, either in a business organisation as an employee, or as a self-employed individual, you will inevitably face a mountain of paperwork. You will encounter numerous pieces of data which will require some form of numerical processing. The successful manipulation of numbers or figures, in whatever format, is another skill that is closely related to other personal abilities.

The student activity below aims to assess not only your understanding of numerical manipulation but also your understanding of the importance of getting the answer correct.

PC 2.4.4
PC 2.4.5

Individual activity

Time: 20 minutes

You will need to answer the following questions with one of these responses:

fully experienced
somewhat experienced
a little knowledge
no knowledge

In relation to these responses we will not, of course, expect you to have actually carried out these tasks or displayed these skills in a 'real environment'. However, if you feel that you know the implications and procedures involved, you may answer that you are experienced.

1 Do you feel that you could keep sales and purchase ledgers and cash books accurately?
2 Do you think that you would be able to chase bad debts?
3 Do you feel that you have an understanding of cash flow?
4 Do you feel that you understand the techniques behind invoicing?
5 Do you feel that you understand the correct use of an overdraft?
6 Do you feel that you have the ability to present a request for a loan?
7 Do you feel that you could understand leasing?
8 Do you feel that you could understand the displaying of data?
9 Do you feel that you could cope with working out the financial needs of an organisation?
10 Do you feel that you could identify and analyse sources of long-term finance?

If you have claimed competence in the criteria above, then we must assume that you have had considerable work experience in the past. Alternatively, you may consider that the exercises and activities undertaken as a part of this course have been sufficient to prepare you for the real situations. Beware of this over-confidence. If you have, perhaps more commonly, felt that you cannot claim experience in all of these competences, then you should try to undertake some more exercises which address these numerical requirements.

Information technology

Increasingly, the use of information technology has affected all levels of business activity. It is rare to find an organisation which does not use information technology to assist in the streamlining and general efficiency of its work. While it is rare to find someone who is capable of understanding complexities of information technology that is not an information technology specialist, you should by now have a general ability to handle such equipment and systems.

The following series of questions attempts to address the specific information technology requirements of a normal business organisation.

Individual activity

Time: 20 minutes

PC 2.4.4
PC 2.4.5

You should answer these statements with either a '*true*' or '*false*' reply:

1 Most business organisations would achieve increased efficiency if they used information technology.
2 The use of fax machines, modems and e-mail improves both internal and external communications.
3 An organisation which has a number of computer terminals would be best advised to link them together via a network system.
4 Multi-task programs or software are those which bring together word processing, database and spreadsheet applications.
5 An organisation would be able to cater more effectively for their customers' needs if they held customer information on a database.
6 An organisation would benefit from an accounts software package which enabled it to produce an instant picture of its financial position.
7 All managers' decision-making and problem-solving tasks would be greatly eased if they had access to a management information system.
8 An organisation which holds considerable quantities of many different components or products would be able to improve the monitoring of its stock control levels by using a stock control software package.
9 The efficiency of a salesperson or sales representative who is employed to work outside the office would be improved by the issue of mobile phones or pagers.
10 An organisation which has a number of different sites throughout the world would be able to call together its senior managers at very short notice by use of videoconferencing.

These statements have looked at your views on the uses of information technology, but they have not sought to measure your ability to use it. You may not have been able to try videoconferencing, e-mail or mobile phones. Despite this, it is hoped that you have answered 'true' to all of the above statements. If you have answered 'false' to any of them, perhaps you do not yet appreciate the full value of the various information technology systems.

Occupational skills

Obviously, occupational skills refer to specific skills in relation to your chosen profession, career or vocation. You will need to understand that, in employment or self-employment, individuals have specific occupational skills which may vary. In general terms, we can address some of the more broad skills and knowledge by completing the following student activity.

Individual activity

Time: 20 minutes

PC 2.4.4
PC 2.4.5

You will need to answer the following questions with one of these responses:

fully experienced
somewhat experienced
a little knowledge
no knowledge

In relation to these questions it will not be expected that you have actually carried out these tasks or displayed these skills in a 'real environment'. However, if you feel that you know the implications and procedures involved, you may give the answer that you are experienced.

1. Would you feel confident in attempting to sell a product or service to a customer?
2. Do you feel that you could set your own goals and objectives?
3. Do you feel confident that you could select a suitable candidate for a particular job?
4. Do you feel that you understand legislation which relates to your chosen career?
5. Would you feel confident in having to handle the day-to-day decision making of a small business?
6. Do you feel confident that you could process customer enquiries and respond in an effective way?
7. Do you feel that you understand the effect that control of costs can have on profits?
8. Do you feel that you understand the requirements of the manufacturing process?
9. Would you feel able to introduce an effective stock control system?
10. If you identified a shortcoming in the administrative system of your business, would you feel confident in being able to suggest an effective alternative?

We have left these occupational skills rather vague since we cannot predict your chosen career intentions. These 10 questions relate to the overall management and administration of a business and highlight the wide-ranging skills that may be required.

Element 2.4 Assignment

PC 2.4.1–5
C 2.1
C 2.2
C 2.3
C 2.4
IT 2.1
IT 2.2
IT 2.3

In order to show an understanding of the range statements and your ability to cope with various research needs, this assignment is in a number of parts.

Task 1 *PC 2.4.1*

Interview at least *three* people in different types of employment. You should include their names, current employment, brief recent employment history and the skills that their type of employment needs. Your findings for the interview should be word processed in a short report format.

Task 2 *PC 2.4.2, 2.4.3*

Prepare a word-processed summary which describes local, national and international job opportunities and the supporting information collected from relevant sources.

You will already have carried out this task in the student activity given earlier in this section.

Task 3 *PC 2.4.4*

Create a chart which shows the skills that you will need for employment or self-employment. You should look at your own achievements and how you could improve and develop each skill.

Task 4 *PC 2.4.5*

Prepare yourself for an interview with your tutor which will look at your strengths and weaknesses. You should write a summary of the discussion and note when and where the discussion took place. This should be signed by the interviewer to validate your summary of the discussion.

UNIT 2 Revision questions

1 Give three features of a private sector organisation.

2 Give three features of a public sector organisation.

3 What is CCT?

4 Give three factors which might affect the structure of an organisation.

5 What is a hierarchical structure?

6 What are the features of a steep pyramid?

7 What are the features of a flat pyramid?

8 What is a cone structure?

9 What is line management?

10 What is the division of labour?

11 What is specialisation?

12 What is departmentalisation?

13 Give three functions of the administration department.

14 Give three functions of the accounts and finance department.

15 Give three functions of the sales department.

16 Give three functions of the marketing department.

17 What is staff management?

18 Give three functions of the production department.

19 Give three functions of the personnel department.

20 What is the difference between the public relations department and the community projects department?

21 What is remuneration?

22 State two potential hazards at work.

23 Give four items you would expect to find on a contract of employment.

24 What is a craft union?

25 Name three well-known general unions.

26 State three functions of a trade union.

27 What is negligence?

28 What is dismissal?

29 Give three reasons why an employee could be dismissed due to misconduct.

30 What is statutory contravention?

31 Give two examples of unfair dismissal.

32 What is the normal disciplinary procedure and its stages?

33 How soon must an employee appeal after dismissal?

34 What is meant by 'acting in good faith'?

35 What do you understand by a 'safe working environment'?

36 What is a Joint Consultative Committee?

37 What is a quality circle?

38 What is compassionate leave?

39 What are equal opportunities?

40 What is picketing?

41 What is accountability?

42 What is the difference between an executive and a non-executive director?

43 Give two important duties of a director.

44 Who, or what, is the Registrar of Companies?

45 What is the role of an auditor?

46 List three attributes of a good team member.

47 Give three occupations that could be considered as professional ones.

48 Give three occupations that could be considered as technical ones.

49 Give two examples of semi-skilled workers.

50 What is the difference between an audio typist and a shorthand typist?

51 What is the role of a company accountant?

52 What is the difference between a regional sales manager and an area sales manager?

53 What do invoice clerks do and in which department would you expect to find them?

54 What are the differences between strategies and tactics?

55 List at least five different forms of media that would be handled by a promotions manager.

56 What is the role of a data processing manager?

57 In which department would you normally find a buyer?

58 Who would be responsible for fulfilling staff development requirements?

59 What are the five phases of decision making?

60 What is meant by the term 'under delegation'?

UNIT 2 End test questions

Focus 1 – organisational structures and departments

1 Which of the following structures has the fewest levels of authority?
- **a** hierarchical
- **b** matrix
- **c** flat
- **d** geographical

2 Which of the following determines an individual's position in the structure of an organisation?
- **a** their power and authority
- **b** their pay
- **c** their holiday entitlement
- **d** their years of service

3 If the sales department receives an order, which of the following departments would have the responsibility for making sure that the order is delivered to the correct address?
- **a** the personnel department
- **b** the accounts department
- **c** the distribution department
- **d** the marketing department

4 Which of the following individuals would have responsibility for monitoring output of production workers?
- **a** the section manager
- **b** the managing director
- **c** the company secretary
- **d** the production manager

5 If the production department uses the raw materials and components to produce products, which of the following departments would organise the payment for these raw materials and components?
- **a** sales
- **b** distribution
- **c** finance/accounts
- **d** personnel

6 Which of the following departments usually provides the clerical support for all other departments?
- **a** marketing
- **b** sales
- **c** distribution
- **d** administration

Focus 2 – working arrangements

7 If an organisation has a number of different sites around the country, then this may be an example of:

a a decentralised organisation
b a centralised organisation
c a teamwork-based organisation
d a flexi-based organisation

*Questions 8–10 share answer options **a** to **d**:*

Employees work in a variety of different ways:

a flexi-time
b shift work
c fixed term
d permanent

Which type of working arrangement is best described by the following:

8 A pattern of work which may involve night duties.
a **b** **c** **d**

9 A contract which specifies a particular end date.
a **b** **c** **d**

10 The opportunity to work additional hours before or after a 'core' time.
a **b** **c** **d**

11 The place of work of an employee may be dependent upon the nature of the work itself. How would you best describe the work base of a chimney sweep?

a home
b mobile
c outdoors
d factory

Focus 3 – employer and employee co-operation and disagreements

12 What is meant by 'improved employee commitment'?

a the employees owing the employer money due to overpayment of wages
b the employees agreeing to negotiate over a problem
c the employer taking on more employees
d the employees entering into a full partnership with their employer

13 What is a quality circle?

a employees meeting on a voluntary basis to discuss their work and how it can be improved
b the employer calling the employees together to give them information
c employees attending meetings of the board of directors
d employers meeting with other organisations to discuss quality issues

14 What is meant by arbitration?
- **a** an independent third party listening to both sides of a disagreement and providing a solution
- **b** the activities of an industrial tribunal
- **c** the main role of a trade union
- **d** a production technique to improve quality

15 Which of the following is true regarding the European Court of Justice?
- **a** it is less important than the House of Lords
- **b** it is only concerned with employment law
- **c** it is the final court of appeal
- **d** it is only involved in EC law

Focus 4 – employer and employee rights and responsibilities

16 It is the responsibility of the employer to make a number of deductions on behalf of the government from an employee's wages or salary. Which of the following is not a legal deduction?
- **a** VAT
- **b** PAYE
- **c** NI
- **d** pension contributions

17 Which of the following are grounds for fair dismissal?
- **a** religion
- **b** gender
- **c** drunkenness
- **d** pregnancy

18 How soon should an employee appeal after dismissal?
- **a** 3 months
- **b** 7 days
- **c** 1 month
- **d** 6 months

19 When would an employee expect to receive a written warning?
- **a** if their behaviour was sufficiently serious
- **b** if they break company rules
- **c** if they are late more than once in one week
- **d** if they join a trade union without informing their employer

20 The following are different pieces of employment law. Which is incorrect?
- **a** Race Relations Act
- **b** Sex Discrimination Act
- **c** Equal Pay Act
- **d** Trade Descriptions Act

21 What is meant by the term 'remuneration'?
- **a** making sure that there is sufficient petty cash
- **b** an accounting term which refers to checking invoices
- **c** being paid for work carried out
- **d** the checking of a bank statement

Focus 5 – job roles, teams and tasks

22 Which of the following would not normally be a member of the board of directors?
- **a** managing director
- **b** company secretary
- **c** supervisor
- **d** director of personnel

23 Which of the following would not normally be a member of an accounts department?
- **a** a payroll clerk
- **b** a credit controller
- **c** a service engineer
- **d** a company accountant

24 A distribution manager in terms of his/her level within an organisation would normally be which of the following:
- **a** junior
- **b** middle
- **c** senior
- **d** director

25 Which of the following is not a non-routine task?
- **a** dealing with fire drills
- **b** dealing with emergencies
- **c** dealing with accidents
- **d** dealing with visitors

Focus 6 – employment and self-employment opportunities, information and skills

*Questions 26 to 28 share answer options **a** to **d**:*

The following are different types of employment
- **a** temporary
- **b** casual
- **c** full time
- **d** seasonal

Which type of employment is best described as:

26 An employee taken on during periods of high business activity.
a **b** **c** **d**

27 An employee working on a fixed-term contract basis.
a **b** **c** **d**

28 An employee working a limited number of hours and on an as-and-when-basis.
a **b** **c** **d**

29 Which major organisation sponsors the Live Wire Project?
a the Prince's Youth Business Trust
b the Department of Trade and Industry
c Shell (UK) Ltd
d the Department of Education

30 What does TEC stand for?
a Training Enterprise Council
b Training and Education Council
c Trade Enterprise Committee
d The Education Council

Unit 3
CONSUMERS AND CUSTOMERS

Element 3.1
Explain the importance of consumers and customers

Element 3.2
Plan, design and produce promotional material

Element 3.3
Providing customer service

Element 3.4
Present proposals for improvements to customer service

Element 3.1
Explain the importance of consumers and customers

Performance criteria

A student must:

1 describe the **effect of consumers** on sales of goods and services

2 identify and explain the **buying habits of consumers** with different **characteristics**

3 identify **trends in consumer demand**

4 produce graphics to illustrate the trends

5 explain **causes of change in consumer demand** for consumer goods and services

6 explain and give examples of the **importance of customers** to business organisations

Range

- *Effect of consumers*: create demand (weak, strong), cause changes in demand, stimulate supply of goods and services to meet demand
- *Buying habits of consumers*: types of goods and services, level of buying, frequency of buying
- *Characteristics*: age, gender, geographical, lifestyle (taste, fashion, preferences)
- *Trends in consumer demand*: past (short term, long term), future (short term, long term), increasing consumer demand, decreasing consumer demand
- *Causes of change in consumer demand*: money to spend (cost of living, earnings), confidence to spend, changing needs, changing wants, advertising
- *Importance of customers*: to income, to repeat business, to survival of business, for information, to contribute to profit

3.1.1 Describe the effect of consumers on sales of goods and services

Effect of consumers

Customers' needs, wants, desires and requirements change all the time. Anticipating what will be needed in the future is quite an art. The preliminary task of the organisation is to try to identify what the customers want and not what the organisation thinks that they want.

Overall market demand and customer demand are often beyond the control of the individual organisation. While the demand and the patterns of need generated by the public in any region or market are unique to that market, the underlying factors are the same. These factors are relatively easy to measure, as we shall see.

Create demand (weak, strong), cause changes in demand and stimulate supply of goods and services to meet demand

It is possible to categorise the main determinants of demand, or in other words the needs, under the following headings:

1 *Economic*
2 *Demographic*
3 *Geographical*
4 *Socio-cultural*
5 *Comparative price*
6 *Mobility*
7 *Government or legislative*
8 *Media communications*

Demand also responds to changes in the supply of products and services. Supply is an important determinant of demand and demand is an important determinant of supply. Let us return to the eight points that we have mentioned already and analyse their influence on the demand for products:

1 **Economic** – the influence of economic variables can be seen in countries that have enjoyed a growth in people's average disposable income. For the majority of the population, there has been a steady rise in the real value of their income. As a result, their disposable income has increased. If the population has a 10 per cent increase in their disposable income and this is matched by a similar increase in demand for a product, then the market is known as *income elastic*. If, on the other hand, the change in demand is less than the rise in disposable income, then the market is called *inelastic*. A typical example of an elastic market is the travel business. If people have more disposable income, then the number of people travelling abroad or going on holiday increases in proportion.

PC 3.1.1
C 2.1

Individual activity

Time: 20 minutes

If you were involved with an organisation that offers holidays abroad, which of the following would you consider to be important in the light of what you have just read?

- better-quality furnishings in hotels
- sound proofing
- better heating and ventilation
- better bathroom facilities
- bigger rooms
- better lighting
- better food on the plane

You have probably realised that all of these are important, but how would you rank these in order of priority, given that not all of these can be done immediately?

2 **Demographic** – this factor is far slower to have an influence on the demand and needs of the market than economic factors, but nevertheless it is not a factor that should be ignored. It includes the following:

- *the age distribution of the market*
- *the average household size of the market*
- *the composition of the household (i.e. the number of adults and children)*
- *the education level of the market*

3 **Geographical** – for populations living in the northern hemisphere, the weather effects have a great influence on the products and services demanded. This is particularly true of leisure activities and related products. Next to the weather is the size of the community in which individuals live. Large urban areas and suburban areas tend to generate more demand than the less populated and wealthy rural areas.

4 **Socio-cultural** – this is used to describe the broad trends in the attitudes which influence the motivation of the customer. The trends also have a wider implication if we consider that many of the core attitudes of individuals are held by the majority of the population. Luxury goods are a measure of an individual's status in society. By consuming relatively expensive products, individuals may perceive this as a measure of their worth in society. The full marketing implications of this factor have been exploited very well by businesses. The trend towards exclusive or comparatively expensive products is ongoing. There is still the fact that some products tend to be more expensive at certain times of the year and cheaper at others. A good example of this is the general availability of fresh fruit and vegetables at times during the year when, technically, they are 'out of season'. Individuals will still buy these products at a premium or higher price as part of their belief that this consumption reflects their life style and socio-cultural position in society.

5 **Comparative price** – price reflects the value to consumers in relation to their spending power. The concept of comparative prices is very complex and quite hard to predict with any hope of accuracy. Price is, without doubt, one of the principal determining factors of demand. Effective marketing can seek to exploit the comparative price factor. This is particularly true when we consider products that are competing with one

another across international boundaries. Within each country a different set of economic factors may determine the price that needs to be charged for a product or service. This is amplified by the fact that if the product is to be distributed outside the country, then it comes into contact with products that have been produced under very different economic conditions. Such economic influences will include the following:

- *inflation*
- *wage levels*
- *cost of raw materials*

Another aspect is that some organisations have a completely different attitude to the price that they will charge for their products, regardless of the fact that they are operating in the same market. This is when quality, craftsmanship, method of production and distribution come into the pricing considerations.

6 **Mobility** – the use of public means of transport inevitably declines as car ownership increases. Apart from non-leisure travel (such as for example much of intercity travel by road, rail and air), there are some important parts of the travel infrastructure that are determinants of the demand for a product or service. The general willingness of the individual customer to travel considerable distances to visit a particular outlet or location cannot be underestimated. The demand for factory shopping is so great that one company, based in Somerset, has reported that customers will travel from as far away as South Wales. Coach and bus companies have found many niches to exploit. Witness the number of day excursions to popular shopping centres and other attractions.

7 **Government or legislative** – although government and other regulatory factors will determine the legality and control over the production of certain products and services, organisations do attempt to lobby the decision makers if they believe that the legislation will adversely affect demand.

8 **Media communications** – this is the final consideration which has a powerful influence over the demand for products or services. Television-watching is far and away the most popular form of leisure activity. The average person in the UK watches some nineteen hours of television per week. The cumulative impact of so many hours of watching has to have an influence on the demands of the customer. The massive and continuous exposure to this medium alone will impact upon the consumption patterns and hence the demand for products and services.

At lower levels, the radio and the print media will have an impact on the demand too. Drawing attention to a particular product or service by advertisements may be one thing, but anticipating customer needs is another. Keeping a close eye on the activities (in terms of advertising and other promotions) is one useful way of anticipating the customer's needs. A truly successful organisation will take a rather more proactive approach. In this respect, the organisation will carry out market research on the impact and awareness factors stimulated by advertising in the media.

3.1.2 Identify and explain the buying habits of consumers with different characteristics

Buying habits of consumers

In business, as with almost any other area of life, the only really constant and dependable piece of information to work on is that things are always changing.

An increasingly important function of the marketing efforts of an organisation is to attempt to manage this change. This may appear to be impossible. How can an organisation 'manage change'? Surely, the nature of change itself means that much of it is unpredictable? At the very least, the organisation needs to identify the sources of the potential change and to have in place a series of measures or proposed policies to deal with them. This begins with an appraisal of the external factors that may influence the organisation. In other words, we are considering the changing environment in which the organisation operates, which includes the activities of the competition. It is vital that the organisation monitors this, since it needs to be sure that it can react more effectively and efficiently than its competitors, no matter what the changes may involve.

The formation of the strategies to be employed often begins with a PEST analysis. This form of analysis addresses the four major external influences on the organisation. These are:

1 **Political and legal** – where the organisation is affected by changes in legislation or government decision making. Equally, any form of instability may affect the smooth running of the organisation and its ability to respond in a meaningful way.

2 **Economic** – where the organisation is affected by the economic policies of the government of the country in which it is based. Also, world recession, such as the recessions that occurred in the 1980s and early 1990s, can determine how successful an organisation could be on the world markets. Other such factors which fall into this economic category are:

- *inflation*
- *economic growth or contraction in the country*
- *consumer consumption patterns*
- *the distribution of income within the country*
- *the protectionist policies adopted by other countries*

3 **Social** – where the organisation is affected by the nature of the society within which it operates. Typically, these factors will include:

- *demographic changes*
- *migration of people*
- *age of the population*
- *the population's culture*
- *social trends*
- *family size*

4 **Technological** – where the organisation is affected by developments in the manufacturing process. The net effect of these changes may influence such things as the cost-effectiveness of the current methods of production, particularly when comparing the process with that of the competitors.

Types of goods and services

Customers, obviously, demand that their requirements are met. They are always looking for benefits that a product or service can offer them. The key elements are:

- *having the right product available*
- *having the product available at the right price*
- *having the product available in as many places (outlets) as possible*
- *having the product in stock at all times, both in the warehouse and the outlets*

Customer expectations are a very difficult thing to measure. It is only through continuous market research and the monitoring of customers' reactions to the products and services that an organisation can begin to build up a profile of the customers' expectations. All organisations can identify the key expectations that relate to their particular area of business. Some of the expectations may include the following:

- *accurate and reliable information about the product or service*
- *prompt and courteous advice and feedback regarding questions about the product or service*
- *wide availability of the product or service*
- *consistency in the quality, style, colour or other standardised features of the product or service*
- *reliable and responsive after-sales service, maintenance or technical back-up after the purchase of the product or service*
- *good, competitive pricing structures that encourage the customer to return to the same organisation time and time again for the purchase of the product or service*
- *a consistent public image of the organisation that neither undermines nor embarrasses the customer*

PC 3.1.2
C 2.1

Group activity *Time: 40 minutes*

In pairs, try to think of some other basic customer expectations. Are these expectations fair? Does the customer expect too much from the supplying organisation? How much real effort should be expended by an organisation in ensuring that customers' expectations are met and often exceeded? Once you have drawn up a list of expectations, discuss the other questions arising from this with the rest of the group.

Level and frequency of buying

Typically, we can identify the repeat sales potential of the products offered by an organisation in terms of the nature of the buying habits of the customer. There are three main categories of customer in this respect. These are the primaries, the secondaries and the tertiaries. The classifications should not be confused with the industrial sectors of the economy, as they have a very different meaning. Let us look at the nature of these three different customer groupings:

1 **The primaries** – these customers form the hard core of the repeat sales. After some expense in actually getting the customer in the first place, the primaries are the main source of regular income. These are few in number, but very valuable to the organisation. These individuals invariably make repeat purchases, and as such these are the main reason for the organisation to offer customer incentives and loyalty rewards.
2 **The secondaries** – although there are more of these, the secondaries tend to be irregular purchasers and, as such, occasionally make repeat purchases. Again, this group is valuable and is usually the target of the advertising campaigns of the organisation.
3 **The tertiaries** – these are the majority of potential customers that do not purchase from the organisation very regularly at all. These individuals are often difficult to target in advertising terms, and not really interested in targeted sales promotions, seeming immune to many of the marketing techniques of the organisation. The best that the organisation can hope for is to convert these into secondaries.

Characteristics

The need to identify and attempt to satisfy the needs of consumers is central to the concept of marketing. To do this efficiently is important, and to do it more efficiently than competitors can be vital. In order to do this successfully, market research is used and the forecasting of sales. The single most important factor affecting marketing is that there are a number of different markets for a product. A market is fairly difficult to define, but broadly speaking there are three ways of describing what a market is.

- *First, it can be a physical or geographical place where services are sold.*
- *Second, the market can mean the actual demand for a specific product or service.*
- *Third, it can be a set of conditions which determine the price of a product or service.*

The most commonly accepted definition of a market identifies a group of people with needs, what their purchasing power is and what their buying power is. A further refinement is that this market is not just existing customers, but should include those who are potential customers.

In order to identify a target market, a number of different things must be looked at. The following six variables are known as demographic factors and are the basis of segmenting the total marketing into identifiable smaller markets. These are:

1 Age
2 Gender
3 Geographic and cultural
4 Neighbourhood
5 Lifestyle
6 Socio-economic

Age

This strongly affects the purchasing power of individuals. In the younger age group (18–24, for example) fashion, records, take-aways, magazines and newspapers tend to be big areas of purchasing. This is known as the youth market and is a specific target for certain products. Age is one of the most important considerations, even if it is the easiest one to research.

Fig 3.1 Marks & Spencer's neighbourhood stores provide local communities with a range of everyday products such as food, basic clothing and seasonal lines

PC 3.1.2
C 2.1

Group activity *Time: 30 minutes*

In pairs, assuming the role of marketing manager and his/her assistant, identify which you think would be the age ranges interested in the following products:

- **Children's toys**
- **Cans of soft drinks**
- **Beer**
- **Recipe books**
- **Black lipstick**

Compare your age ranges with those of other members of your group.

As a sub-division of age, education is proving to be an increasingly less useful way of segmenting the market. It is a rather crude measure based on the school-leaving age of the individual. It does not therefore take into account any further education beyond school. This classification tends to infer that those who stay in school longer have a tendency to read quality newspapers rather than the tabloids. Equally, these individuals are supposed to be more interested in the more worthy or informative television programmes than in game shows. This assumption will have a direct effect upon an organisation's choice of where to place its advertisements. One factor related to education may be true, which is that with a better education an individual may well earn a higher salary.

PC 3.1.2
C 2.1

Group activity *Time: 15 minutes*

As a group, discuss the following:

'A person's education has a lot to do with what they will and will not buy.'

Gender

This is again a straightforward and easy variable to measure, but it is very crucial. Certain products or services are specifically female-oriented. Products either do not cater for one sex in particular, or they are clearly slanted in the way they are advertised to one sex or the other. For example, drink brands which are aimed at males are distinctly different from those which are aimed at females. Even cars can be labelled 'women's cars' and their advertising reflects this.

PC 3.1.2
C 2.1
C 2.2

Group activity *Time: 20 minutes*

In pairs, list 10 products which could be considered to be solely of interest to males; list another 10 for females; and list a further 10 which would appeal to either sex.

Did you make any assumptions about products and gender? Discuss this with the rest of your group.

Geographical

Regional differences within a country, not to mention internationally, can be marked. Some of these differences may be traditional, or may be related to economic concerns (such as the unemployment rate).

PC 3.1.2
C 2.1

Group activity *Time: 15 minutes*

In pairs, try to identify any particular regional differences evident in your area. Are any products or services particularly popular compared to the rest of the country? Discuss your findings with those of the rest of the group.

Purchasing behaviour is strongly linked to the ethnic or religious background of the consumer. Consumers may have a variety of alternative tastes which need to be considered as separate markets.

Some of the principal considerations related to geographical and cultural differences are:

- *Taste* – preferences vary greatly. Some coffee manufacturers, for example, offer no less than 40 different versions of the 'same' product, as some countries may prefer a slightly smoother or a more bitter taste.
- *Colour* – in different countries, some colours are positively preferred or avoided. Australians have a preference for colours which are similar to their flora and fauna, in other words for browns and greens. Moslems dislike yellow as it is associated with Buddhists. Italians seem to love pale blue. In Thailand you would find it impossible to sell white false teeth, as many people enjoy munching betel nuts which turn teeth black!
- *Size* – Americans, for example, love to buy huge packs of consumer goods. They have a tendency to over-shop and will often buy in sufficient stock to last several weeks. In the UK the tendency is to buy supplies on a weekly or monthly basis. Therefore, UK pack sizes are smaller. In poorer countries, manufacturers may have to provide for substantially smaller purchases, as the customer tends to shop on a daily basis.
- *Intended use* – products vary from country to country, depending on what the customer wants from the product. Both the style and the design may have to change, particularly if the product is in constant use. In poorer countries, where a product may be considered an essential purchase it may have to be extremely durable.
- *Ergonomics* – this is linked to size, shape and weight of the potential user. It would be foolish to attempt to sell Volvo cars to a tribe of pygmies! It is certainly true that individuals vary in size, shape and weight across the world and this will have a bearing on whether a product is suitable.
- *Climate* – the climate may directly affect the efficiency of the product. If the effects of constant hot weather on soft plastic kitchenware were ignored, the manufacturer could find its sales literally 'melting away'.

PC 3.1.2
C 2.1
C 2.2

Group activity *Time: 15 minutes*

In pairs, make a list of all the countries you can think of. Against this list write at least one product which it would be impractical to try to sell to them.

Compare your list with those of the rest of the group.

Looking at neighbourhood is a relatively new measure of segmentation and is based on a system called ACORN (A Classification of Residential Neighbourhoods). It identifies some 38 different types of residential neighbourhood, according to their demographic, housing and socio-economic characteristics. The basic information is based on the Census of Population in Great Britain, which is carried out by the government every 10 years.

The classification breaks Great Britain down into units of 150 dwellings. The most common type of dwelling within the 150 is the classification to which that unit is given. This means that in areas which contain a mixture of flats and houses, only the most common dwelling will be noted. This system of classification is used extensively by direct mail companies, financial institutions, gas and electricity companies, TV rental firms, credit card companies, travel agencies, charities and political parties.

The ACORN system has proved extremely useful in the location of new retail outlets and the siting of poster hoardings.

PC 3.1.2
C 2.1

Group activity

Survey the immediate area in which you live. Under ACORN, your home would be classified under the most common type of dwelling in your area. Which is the most common type of dwelling in your area, and is your home typical? Discuss this as a group.

Lifestyle (taste, fashion, preferences)

Family size is a straight categorisation of one or two members, three or four members, five or more members. The size of the family simply determines the size of the pack they buy and the frequency of their purchasing. The family life cycle determines the stage which the typical family has reached, and directly affects their demand for products and their consumption rate. The basic problem with using the family unit as a measure of demand and consumption is that we assume that the majority of individuals belong to a strict family group. Increasingly, this is not the case.

PC 3.1.2
C 2.1
C 2.2

Group activity *Time: 20 minutes*

In groups of three, try to list all of the stages of a family's life cycle. You should be able to identify around seven different stages.

Social class is a mixture of both social class and income. Again, this is a rather crude way of categorising individuals. The social class in which a whole family is placed is related only to the 'head' of the household. It does not, therefore, take into account a second wage earner (in other words, women are ignored for the most part). The accepted way of categorising individuals by social class was established by the National Readership Survey. This classification consists of six categories which are shown below.

A	Higher managerial, administrative or professional
B	Intermediate managerial, administrative or professional
C1	Supervisory, clerical, junior administrative or professional
C2	Skilled manual workers
D	Semi-skilled or unskilled manual workers
E	State pensioners, widows, casual and low grade earners

These categories are also known as socio-economic groups, as they take into account both class and income. There are a number of problems with this categorisation, since, to a large extent, the boundaries between each socio-economic group are somewhat blurred.

PC 3.1.2

Individual activity

Time: 15 minutes

To which socio-economic group do the following belong:

1 Teachers
2 Dentists
3 Dockers
4 Refuse workers
5 Farmers
6 Writers
7 Students

As we have already discovered, consumers have a range of different needs and wants, as well as attitudes. A successful organisation must try to identify any trends which may be evident from existing statistics, or from research which it may carry out itself. There are, obviously, a number of different ways of obtaining these statistics, and, indeed, interpreting what they mean. Let us have a look at some of the more common sources of information and how they are used.

Individuals' life styles have changed over the years to such an extent that many older products are no longer relevant or wanted. Sometimes the changes are rapid, and at other times they may take two or three generations to emerge. When we refer to social trends, we are, in fact, referring to a vast number of changes in population, tastes, lifestyles, health consciousness and availability of technology. Some examples of the more dramatic changes are as follows:

- **Smaller families** – people tend to have less children than in the past. This may be for many reasons, including the availability of contraception, the availability of pensions rather than having the support of sons or daughters in old age, or the fact that women are tending to return to work after having children.
- **Health concerns** – people are far more aware of the hazards of poor eating habits and other ill-effects caused by drinking and smoking. Over 10 per cent of the population is now vegetarian, and many more avoid fatty foods and red meats. Similarly, less than one-third of the population still smoke, but a high percentage of this number are the young. Many people are concerned with maintaining or reducing their weight and, as such, restrict their diet to calorie-reduced foodstuffs. Drinking is still very popular, but by no means to the extent it has been in the past.
- **Leisure activities** – there is a huge range of leisure pursuits both indoor and outdoor, physical and non-physical, now available to the consumer. DIY, for example, is very popular and supports a large number of manufacturers and retailers. As far as magazines are concerned, it is hard not to find a magazine which relates directly to your leisure interest.
- **Sundays** – traditionally, most people attended Church on a Sunday. Although there has been some increase in Church attendance in the past few years, the vast majority of people prefer either to stay at home or to go shopping. Other religious groups have different special days. This has led to a great debate as to the nature of Sundays, in terms of whether they are still special days or simply another trading day. Many retailers have taken advantage of the government's confusion over the issue and despite local authority fines for opening, have done very good business on a Sunday.

Fig 3.2 Marks & Spencer aims to cater for all cultural needs, as well as trends and fashions

PC 3.1.2
C 2.1

Group activity

Time: 20 minutes

Working in pairs, can you think of any other social trends which we have not identified? Think about whether they have had any serious impact on demand for products and, if so, which ones?

Compare your findings with those of the rest of the group.

Good basic sources of information include the following publications:

- *Social Trends* (Central Statistical Office) – this publication gives substantial detail regarding the nature of the population, in terms of growth, numbers of people in different age groups and average debts of consumers by age and sex
- *Annual Abstract of Statistics* (Central Statistical Office) – this publication gives a wide variety of information regarding consumer spending patterns compared to previous years

Along with original research carried out by organisations, marketing specialists will attempt to predict the demand, or likely changes in trends and fashions, in order to be ready to provide the next big-seller.

PC 3.1.2
C 2.1
C 2.2

Group activity

As a group, see if your institution's library has either of the above publications. If not, try the local library. Individually, try to look at the book and write yourself a list of contents.

We have already mentioned the tendency for women to want to return to work after having children and this has led to some interesting changes in expenditure patterns. Growth areas relating to this factor include convenience food, microwaves, dishwashers and other time-saving items.

In relation to spending and income, we will find many other dramatic changes in the past few years. Many people have more disposable income (this is money left after tax, insurance, bills, rents and mortgages). In turn, this has given people the opportunity to indulge themselves socially and in terms of leisure.

Many people are in debt, although they would not necessarily consider themselves to be. Credit cards, store cards and charge cards are freely available and offer the consumer the opportunity to spend beyond their means. Although in the short term this increases sales for the retailer, at some point the bills must be paid. In this respect, credit cards are something of a mixed blessing.

Typical sources of information regarding income and spending patterns can be found in the *Monthly Digest of Statistics* (Central Statistical Office). This publication details wages, prices and expenditure by age, sex and region.

PC 3.1.2
C 2.1

Group activity

Time: 15 minutes

Consider the following statement and then discuss it within your group:

'You cannot judge how wealthy someone is just by looking at what they possess.'

We have already mentioned some changes in the nature of products and services generally bought by the family, but there are some other factors which can be considered.

- **Consumer durables** – over 90 per cent of households have a television. This is an enormous figure compared to the handful of TV sets sold only 30 or 40 years ago.
- **New technology** – televisions now have remote controls; video recorders have simplified programming capabilities; and microwave ovens have pre-set dials to cope with a variety of convenience foods. Other products now commonly found in the home are computers, CD players, dishwashers and answerphone machines. Some of these are relatively new but have established themselves very quickly as not only desirable but necessary.
- **Home ownership** – recent government policy has positively encouraged many people to own their own homes. Despite the difficulties that the recession and high interest rates have created, there are far more home owners now than in the past. This, in turn, has had an effect on family expenditure, creating the need for mortgage payments, endowment policy payments, additional insurance policies and funds for home repairs and improvements.
- **Holidays** – the availability of relatively cheap flights and accommodation abroad has radically changed the way people choose to spend their holiday time. Increasingly, hundreds of thousands of people prefer to spend their holiday breaks in guaranteed sun rather than risk the traditional rainy English holiday.
- **Children** – children have been specifically targeted by marketing departments of organisations in the course of promoting their products. Children's needs and wants have changed drastically over the years and, just as general fashions and trends have altered, so have those of the younger generation.

Typical sources of information regarding family expenditure can be found in the following publications:

- *Family Expenditure Survey* (HMSO) – this publication has information regarding the spending levels of people, and in addition it details what they are buying and how much they are buying.
- *General Household Survey* (Office of Population Censuses and Surveys (Social Division)) – this publication gives information about each household as regards age, sex and size of family.
- *Household Food Consumption and Expenditure* (HMSO) – this publication, published by the government, details consumer expenditure on food and drink.

Individual activity

Time: 30 minutes

Individually, construct a pie chart which shows what you think is the spread of expenditure of a family whose total take-home pay is £15 000 per annum. Compare your pie chart with those of the rest of your group.

PC 3.1.2
C 2.1
C 2.2
C 2.3
C 2.4

As we have already noted, the changes in consumer trends over the past few years seem to have become even more rapid. Products which were very popular in the past have disappeared and are little more than oddities which can be found in jumble sales and car boot sales. But why does a product become obsolete? What makes it popular one day, and unwanted the next?

People's lifestyles have changed and, with these lifestyle changes, their need for particular products and services. It is unlikely that the kind of products which you favour today will be of any interest to your children.

New technology, as we have already said, has played a large part in the changing attitudes over the years. We are now able to buy ever more sophisticated machines which take the boredom out of many day-to-day routines. Whether it is in the home, at work or at play, we can now turn to technology to help us get through the day. We are constantly looking for devices which can give us the maximum amount of free time to enjoy ourselves. Organisations realise this and are continuously designing new products which can help us achieve this goal.

Fig 3.3 Marks & Spencer keeps apace of both changes in fashion and trends, as well as lifestyles

Just as attitudes change, so do lifestyles. The availability of a vast range of foodstuffs and household products has enabled us to try an ever-increasing variety of new items. In retailing, there has been a steady move from local shops which stock a limited range of goods to enormous superstores with a bewildering array of products. This has meant that a family is unlikely to shop on a daily or even weekly basis and may prefer the convenience of shopping monthly. These superstores are open for much longer hours than ever before, making their facilities available seven days a week. The high street, once the centre of shopping activities, has been severely hit by our preference to shop 'out of town'. We will now find specialist shops and the occasional general store which, increasingly, are the only types of outlet that can survive in the high street.

PC 3.1.2
C 2.1

Group activity

In pairs, make a survey of your local high street. Try to identify the different kinds of shops under the following categories:

- **Independent retailers**
- **Local chains**
- **Regional chains**
- **National chains**
- **International chains**

For the second part of this task, try to find a person who remembers what the high street was like 10 years ago. Show them your findings and ask them how things have changed.

Families now have a larger proportion of their disposable income available for leisure activities. This has led to the growth of the DIY market, thousands of specialist magazines and an increasingly large range of sports equipment. Another factor that has assisted the growth of this area is the increased amount of leisure time as working hours have been steadily reduced over the years.

Returning to food and health issues, it is now believed that almost 10 per cent of the UK population is vegetarian, or almost vegetarian. Many more people control their diet with low-calorie foods. Periodic scares regarding food and health have reduced our intake of animal fats, eggs and red meats. At the same time, smoking has become reduced to less than one-third of the UK adult population. All of these changes have had drastic effects on retail outlets which had in the past relied on consumption of these items.

As we have already mentioned, technology has drastically affected our lifestyles, making many routine tasks much quicker to undertake. We no longer need to spend hours laboriously doing things by hand when a machine can do them in seconds.

PC 3.1.2
C 2.1
C 2.2
C 2.3
C 2.4

Group activity

Time: 1 hour

In groups of four, design a questionnaire that looks at the following areas of consumer preferences:

- **How many people have given up or are thinking of giving up smoking?**
- **How many people have given up or are thinking of giving up red meat?**
- **How many people choose to buy recycled products nowadays?**
- **How many people choose to buy cruelty-free products?**
- **How many people use lead-free petrol in their cars?**

WOOLWORTHS
INFORMATION

ENVIRONMENTAL POLICY

It is the policy of Woolworths to manage the environmental responsibilities in accordance with the following principles:

Management Responsibility
Environmental affairs within Woolworths are the responsibility of one named Board Director. The responsible Director is charged with ensuring that specific action plans are developed to implement the provisions of the policy.

Internal Communications
Environmental awareness will be raised by communicating environmental issues to staff at all levels as an integral part of the company's training programmes.

External Relations
Woolworths will communicate openly to the public and outside agencies about its environmental performance.

Woolworths will give careful consideration to all environmental claims on products to help customers make informed purchasing decisions.

Products and Packaging
Woolworths will keep informed about the environmental issues and legislation influencing the products it sells.

Woolworths will carry out a systematic review of internal packaging practices and will produce a series of guidelines to assist suppliers in fulfilling the company's aim of waste minimisation in product packaging.

Suppliers
Woolworths will demand high environmental standards from the suppliers of Woolworths own-label products.

Woolworths will incorporate environmental concerns into its standard quality assurance procedures for other products.

Woolworths will expect all suppliers to co-operate with the company in meeting established environmental objectives.

Waste Management and Recycling
Woolworths will review its arrangements for disposing of wastes in stores, offices and distribution centres.

The company will promote waste minimisation and ensure that all wastes transported off-site are disposed of in accordance with best practices.

Woolworths will take every opportunity to extend in-house recycling schemes and encourage suppliers to take their share of the responsibility for reducing waste and encouraging recycling.

Energy
Woolworths recognises it has a responsibility to minimise energy used in all aspects of its business operations.

Woolworths will continue to monitor its energy consumption and set practical objectives to achieve energy savings.

Siting and Design of Premises
Environmental impacts will be considered when refurbishments are planned.

Where Woolworths commission new premises, site selection will take account of local environmental sensitivities.

WOOLWORTHS ENVIRONMENT POLICY ACTION TAKEN TO DATE

In order to minimise the negative impact our products and business methods may have on the environment, Woolworths has taken a number of steps to support green issues, involving staff, suppliers and customers.

It is our policy to support any initiative of obvious benefit in the campaign to protect the environment. We will also continue to monitor and review new initiatives which may be of value in the future.

Plastic Bags
Extensive research has shown that bio-degradable bags normally include a proportion of starch in their composition. When the plastic is buried in the soil, micro-organisms attack the starch over a period of five to 15 years, the plastic breaks down into small pieces which form the basis of soil crumbs.

Fig 3.4 A Woolworths press release detailing the company's environmental policy

WOOLWORTHS
INFORMATION

There is concern over the long-term effects should these particles enter the water supply, and as a result of this investigation, Woolworths has ceased to use bio-degradable plastics in the manufacture of carrier bags.

Aerosols
In response to concern over the depleted ozone layer, Woolworths ensures that all aerosols stocked are CFC-free.

Animal Testing
None of the cosmetics sold by Woolworths have been tested on animals.

Harmful Chemicals – Horticultural Products
Woolworths has withdrawn from sale any product containing aluminium, mercury or lindane over the last three years. Any other weedkiller is only stocked if approved by the Ministry of Agriculture, Fisheries and Foods and the British Agrochemicals Association.

Policy Re: Unbleached Natural Fibres in Kidswear
Woolworths strives to stock children's clothing manufactured with natural fibres as far as possible, while taking into consideration practicality and cost to the consumer.

Petrol
All our company cars delivered since 1989 are ready-converted, and run on unleaded petrol, and our lorries run on diesel.

Guidelines to Suppliers
Woolworths is working closely with its suppliers to meet the company's environmental objectives. This is an on-going process and Woolworths continually monitors its progress. In turn Woolworths maintains regular communication with suppliers via bulletins and briefings explaining these objectives and informing them of any new initiatives concerning its protection of the environment.

Support to Environmental Charities
Woolworths stores stocked a special range of Christmas cards during 1990, the proceeds of which were donated to the World Wildlife Fund.

We do not currently support any environmental charity on a national level.

Waste/Recycling
With regard to waste and recycling, Woolworths takes every opportunity to extend in-house recycling schemes, and encourages suppliers to reduce waste and undertake recycling likewise.

We stock a wide range of products which are manufactured using recycled paper. An exclusive range of recycled stationery won Woolworths a House of Commons award for helping to conserve trees, and wherever possible recycled paper is used for the company's internal communications needs.

Waste paper bins are located in and around every Woolworths store. We are currently recycling paper at head office and Distribution Centres. We are also currently trialling the recycling of plastic wrap in selected stores. In addition, we are recycling cardboard in all stores thus promoting waste minimisation and ensuring that all waste transported off-site is disposed of with due consideration to the environment.

We are also currently recycling plastic cups at Head Office on a trial basis with a view to expanding the project to other offices.

From February 1992 our staff newspaper has been printed on recycled paper.

Cleaning Equipment
Woolworths encourages the use of recycled and CFC-free cleaning materials for both stores and offices as far as possible.

Store Design/Fixtures
Woolworths endeavours to consider any impact on the environment when refurbishments are planned, and local environmental sensitivities will be taken into account where Woolworths commissions new premises.

With due consideration to the environment, we ceased using wooden fixtures and fittings in 1990. The only wood used is for the trim on cash desks, from a sustainable source. The new floors are in fact made from vinyl tiles, and not wood.

Heat/Light Wastage
With regard to the conservation of energy, Woolworths endeavours to minimise energy used in all aspects of its

Fig 3.4 continued

WOOLWORTHS

INFORMATION

business operations. Its energy consumption is monitored on a store by store basis and practical objectives are set to achieve energy savings.

Within the last five years all sales area lighting has been converted to a more efficient scheme. This, together with the introduction of good housekeeping practices, has resulted in a saving of over £1 million.

Communication of Environmental Policy to Staff
Environmental awareness is raised by communicating the relevant issues and developments affecting the company to staff at all levels. This is achieved through a number of methods, including Woolworths News – the company's monthly in-house newspaper – and store and office briefings. Alerting staff to environmental issues affecting the company is also an integral part of the company's training programme.

Communication of Environmental Policy to the Public
Woolworths considers its campaign to support 'green' issues to be an important part of its communications programme, and endeavours to communicate openly to the public about its environmental performance.

Woolworths gives careful consideration to all environmental claims on products to help customers make informed purchasing decisions.

Smoking Policy
Woolworths has established a 'smoking policy' at its Head Office in London, whereby smoking will only be permitted in designated zones of the building. Counselling Care Sessions for those who wish to give up smoking have been made available. As with any retailer, smoking is not permitted by the staff or customers in the sales area of any store, although staff members are permitted to smoke if they so wish in canteens/rest rooms.

Fig 3.4 continued

3.1.3 Identify trends in consumer demand

3.1.4 Produce graphics to illustrate the trends

These performance criteria essentially refer to work you will have to undertake in the Element assignment. In this respect, we have only produced a short section on each of the range statements. Throughout the first of the performance criteria (3.1.3) we have used a focus study to illustrate the points that you will have to make in your own investigations.

Focus study

Canned fizzy drinks (1)

Coca-Cola dominates the canned fizzy drink market. The key market is the 16–25 age group.

Heatwaves can mean an increase of 20%–30% in demand. Businesses have noticed that even after the heatwaves are over the drop in demand stabilises at a higher level than before.

The non-cola brands tend to be impulse and flavour-related. The younger age groups tend to buy more volume, more impulse buys and are much more image-oriented.

Canned fizzy drinks bought – July 1994

	% of sample
Coca-Cola	51
Pepsi-Cola	27
Diet Coke	24
Tango	23
Lilt	18
Irn-Bru	17
Pepsi Max	13
Lucozade	11
6 others under 6%	

Trends in consumer demand

Relating to the focus study, we can see that demand for products such as fizzy drinks is influenced by the following factors:

- *changes in the weather*
- *impulse buying*
- *characteristics of the product (e.g. taste)*
- *image of the product*

PC 3.1.3
PC 3.1.4

Individual activity

Time: 20 minutes

Identify the main features in the trends in consumer demand for the following products:

- crisps
- high-sugar chocolate bars
- concert or festival tickets

Past (short term, long term)

Short-term trends in consumer demand refer to trends over six months or so. Long-term considers the trends over a 2–3 year period. Continuing our look at canned fizzy drinks, now try the next student activity.

PC 3.1.3
PC 3.1.4
C 2.2
C 2.2
C 2.3
C 2.4
AN 2.1
AN 2.2
AN 2.3

Individual activity

Time: 1 hour

Using the table in the first focus study, create a graph showing the percentage of the sample which bought a particular brand in July 1994. Having done this, now do a similar graph (or overlay it on to the existing graph) for the percentage of the sample that would have bought a particular brand at a different time of the year. Suggest reasons why you have changed the figures.

Focus study

Canned fizzy drinks (2)

We will now look at two other related tables which show:

1 Recall of brands advertised (the ability of the sample to remember a particular advertisement)
2 Advertising expenditure (the total (MAT – which means moving annual total) advertising spend on each brand over the year and the spending during July 1994)

These two sets of figures should show us how effective the advertising has been.

Recall of brands advertised – July 1994

	%
Coca-Cola	57
Tango	41
Pepsi Cola	27
Pepsi Max	18
Irn-Bru	16
Lilt	16
Tizer	11
Lucozade	9
Sunkist	9
18 others under 7%	

Advertising expenditure (£000s)

Brand	*MAT*	*July 1994*
Coca-Cola	5518	1025
Tango	4727	349
Lucozade	4652	656
Pepsi Max	4474	—
Pepsi Cola	3493	98
Sunkist	3266	365
Lilt	2195	711
Irn-Bru	1844	458
Tizer	1439	518

PC 3.1.3
PC 3.1.4
C 2.1

Group activity *Time: 15 minutes*

As a group, discuss the two tables in the previous focus study. Compare the advertising spending with the levels of recall. Which has been the most cost-effective and why? How have you come to this conclusion?

Increasing and decreasing consumer demand

As we have seen from our example running throughout these two performance criteria, the canned fizzy drinks market is highly competitive. Constant advertising and sales promotions are essential to maintain and expand the brand's market share.

PC 3.1.3
PC 3.1.4
C 2.1

Group activity *Time: 20 minutes*

As a group, try to come up with reasons that would cause:

- **An increase in demand for canned fizzy drinks**
- **A decrease in demand for canned fizzy drinks**

Sorry, but you cannot use any of the reasons that we have already mentioned!

Focus study

Canned fizzy drinks (3)

In this final part of our investigation into canned fizzy drinks, we have discovered the following data which look at what influences are in action when an individual chooses to purchase a product in this category.

Reason for buying brand

	%
It is my favourite	91
One usually bought	89
Wanted to try something new/different	37
Saw advertised on television	31
Someone I know told me it was good	29
It was cheaper than others	25
Money-off voucher	25
Saw it advertised on a poster	14
Saw it advertised in a magazine	12
Heard it advertised on radio	5
Prefer diet/low sugar	9

Again, the data is taken from a sample. It was based on nearly 300 recent buyers of canned fizzy drinks, aged 16–35.

PC 3.1.3
PC 3.1.4

Individual activity

Time: 40 minutes

In the role of the marketing manager for one of these brands of fizzy drinks, how would you address the following, and try to reorganise your advertising to get around these factors?

1. Buyers do not like the flavour
2. Buyers do not usually buy it
3. Buyers did not see the advertisement for it
4. Buyers prefer a low-calorie drink
5. Buyers wanted to try something different, but not your brand

Finally, the following table shows the ranking order of brands by calculating their effectiveness using the tables we have already looked at (= means this is the average figure).

Rank orders

	Advertisement recall	*Penetration*	*Annual spend*
Coca-Cola	1	1	1
Tango	2	4	2
Pepsi Cola	3	2	5
Pepsi Max	4	7	4
Irn-Bru	5=	6	8
Lilt	5	5=	8
Tizer	7	12	9

PC 3.1.3
PC 3.1.4
C 2.1
C 2.2
C 2.3
C 2.4

Group activity *Time: 30 minutes*

Looking at the last table, why do you think that Pepsi-Cola has managed to keep its third position despite the fact that it is fifth in advertising spending? Discuss this as a group.

3.1.5 Explain causes of change in consumer demand for consumer goods and services

Causes of change in consumer demand

The causes of change in consumer demand are very hard to predict. Indeed, there is a great deal of money to be earned from predicting such changes. Some of these changes are as a result of factors that we have already looked at, but there are some other vital considerations that need closer attention. An organisation continuously monitors consumer spending patterns to try to look ahead to potential trends. An organisation routinely analyses any available data. Sources of useful information are government departments, industry-wide statistical surveys, opinion poll companies and market research carried out by the organisation itself. In general, it will look at the following considerations as clues to what demand will be like in the future:

- *money to spend (including cost of living and earnings)*
- *confidence to spend*
- *changing needs and wants*
- *advertising*

Money to spend (cost of living, earnings)

The amount of disposable income available to a customer will vary according to a number of different sets of circumstances. Beyond the normal deductions which we all expect to pay, such as tax and National Insurance, we may have a range of other commitments to meet. When interest rates were high, mortgage payments rose. This in turn meant that the disposable income available to the homeowner dropped dramatically. During this period, retail outlets, in particular, suffered a drop in sales. Equally, when unexpected bills arrive we are left with reduced amounts of disposable income. The cost of living is represented by the Retail Price Index. The RPI is a good indicator of the costs to a normal consumer of a 'basket' of ordinary goods or products. In addition to this is the consideration of the price of other regular outgoings, such as the following:

- *Gas*
- *Electricity*
- *Telephone*
- *Mortgage*
- *Rent*
- *Council tax (formerly community charge and rates)*
- *Tax rate*
- *National Insurance contribution*

A slight change in the earnings of customers can, as we have seen, radically effect the demand for products and services. If a customer experiences a reduction in their earnings, then certain decisions will have to be made regarding their outgoings. We will look at this aspect when we consider confidence to spend. It is true to say that low income earners are more drastically affected by changes in their earnings than those on higher incomes. Low income earners with the majority of their income devoted to essentials have less opportunity to make choices about their spending patterns. The higher or middle income earners can make choices about their spending patterns, deciding whether to spend or save. It is this group that can more seriously affect the demand for a product or service.

Confidence to spend

As with the above consideration, the confidence to spend is linked to the customer being careful over exactly how much they think they can afford. During difficult times, individuals are more likely to try to save money rather than spend it on luxuries. With this in mind, retailers have taken to offering interest-free credit, extended credit terms and delayed payment schedules. These credit facilities have gone some way in allaying the fears of the customer with regard to long-term debt. Confidence to spend can only really be achieved during times when the economy itself is healthy, jobs are secure and there is a possibility of earning additional income (such as pay rises).

THE CARING CONTINUES . . .

FACING THE FACTS

We were the first major beauty company to react to the potential dangers of CFC gases. In 1978, we switched to natural pump sprays for fragrances. Since then all CFC propellants have been totally eliminated from all our sprays.

An example of our natural pump sprays

All Avon company cars run on lead-free petrol.

In June 1989 we were the first major cosmetic company to announce an end to animal testing of our products, the conclusion of a programme which began many years before to find consumer-safe alternatives.

"The 1990's will bring new challenges. We will continue to demonstrate our determination to meet the demands of an ever changing world, setting new standards for others to follow."

All recyclable waste paper and cardboard packing is collected, sorted and recycled. Our suppliers are pledged to buy only from mills using managed forests, ensuring trees used for avon cartons are replaced.

Successful energy conservation systems since 1986, have reduced oil consumption by 55% and electricity by 27%.

Avon are now marking plastic containers with an identifying symbol enabling them to be sorted for recycling, contributing further to waste reduction.

landscaping around our orthampton creates attrac- orking environment.

THIS PAPER CONTAINS STRAW PULP TO HELP OUR ENVIRONMENT

FRAME

AVON

Fig 3.5 Evidence of Avon Cosmetics' commitment to respond to changing customer needs and demands

Changing needs

The changing needs of a consumer may depend on a number of different factors, including some of the following:

- *Changes as the individual gets older*
- *Changes if the individual gets married*
- *Changes if the individual is responsible for children*
- *Changes according to the type of work carried out by the individual*
- *Changes relating to the area in which the individual lives*
- *Changes relating to technology and availability of technology*
- *Changes relating to the importance which the individual attaches to the product compared to all of the other items needed by the individual*

Changing wants

On the face of it, we would consider that wants are related to considerations involving trends and fashions. While this is true, we must not forget that individuals are constantly changing their ideas about what they would like, independently of the fads and fashions of other people. We all have to put things that we would like on a list of priorities. Some items in this list are always there, but there may be other things that seem to overtake them at certain times. This may be because we have long-term wants and short-term wants. In other cases, this may simply be related to the cost of the wants and how much we really do want them.

Advertising

The key role of advertising is to affect consumer demand for a product or service. Whether this is to stimulate a new demand or to increase demand for an existing product or service, the success of the advertising is generally measured in terms of its impact.

As we will see in the next Element of this Unit, there is an identified process that aims to:

- *Attract the attention of the potential customer*
- *Get their interest in the product*
- *Make them want (or desire) the product*
- *Make them do something about it (in other words, buy it)*

Again, as we will see in the next Element, different types of promotional materials are used to target specific markets and an experienced marketing manager will know which is the most appropriate for a specific task.

As we have seen earlier in this Element, the type of target audience will define the type of promotional activity. It may not always be useful to rely upon advertisements to attempt to target and influence a particular market.

WOOLWORTHS AND CUSTOMER CARE

Woolworths is committed to ensuring that staff offer the highest standards of customer care. Woolworths people are trained to be proficient and confident when dealing with customers, and to have extensive product knowledge.

This is summed-up in Woolworths Customer First Policy, "We serve ourselves best by serving our customers first" and implemented through the Customer First Skills Training Programme, which is the standard induction course for all sales staff.

The vast majority of customer enquiries are successfully resolved at store level, but to support the work of stores Woolworths operates a central Customer Relations Department from its Head Office.

By letter or phone, this department handles over 10,000 customer enquiries every year.

WOOLWORTHS

Fig 3.6 Woolworths' 'Customer First' policy aims to prepare all staff to meet customers' needs

3.1.6 Explain and give examples of the importance of customers to business organisations

Importance of customers

As we have seen, many products and services are affected to a greater or lesser extent by the following:

- *trends*
- *attitudes*
- *lifestyle*
- *fashion*
- *available disposable income*

Others may experience no changes at all. Those products which are at the leading edge of technology are often rapidly replaced by later technological developments.

There are some other reasons for the change in demand for a particular product or services, these include:

- **Whether the customer has confidence to spend available cash** – in other words, if a customer is unsure of their medium to long-term future within their job, they will be unlikely to wish to spend their money on items which are not essential. They must have the confidence of being secure in their occupation in order to risk large sums of money.
- **The cost of living** – this is calculated by the government by means of the Retail Price Index. This RPI monitors a standard group of goods on a monthly basis, checking any changes in costs and comparing them to prices charged in the past. From this figure the government is able to calculate inflation, as well as identify any unexpected jump in the price of a particular product. The RPI is also used to compare increases in wages, which it is argued should rise in relation to the RPI. If wages have not increased at the same rate as the RPI, then it is obvious that customers are unable to afford all of the items they had previously been buying before the RPI increased.

Group activity

In groups of four, find out details of the Retail Price Index over the last two years. Your task is to present this information in the most effective manner, using a computer.

PC 3.1.6
C 2.1
C 2.2
C 2.3
C 2.4
IT 2.1
IT 2.2
IT 2.3

Specifically, in this last of the performance criteria in this Element, we will be looking at the following:

- *The importance of customers to the organisation in terms of income*
- *The importance of repeat business*
- *The importance of customers as a source of information*
- *The importance of customers for contribution to profit*

To income

Generating income from sales or producing a profit for the organisation is always an enduring requirement for any business. Organisations cannot survive without ensuring that sales income exceeds the costs incurred. We have looked at this concept in other parts of this book. At this stage, we will restrict our comments to the more general aspects. Generating extra income does not necessarily mean that the organisation will achieve greater profits. Also, the profit motive is not always the driving force behind the move to increase sales income. In the short term the organisation may wish to try to increase its market share and this may require suffering lower profits for a short while. In having to make extra investment and, perhaps, needing to reduce the product's price, the organisation may gain extra market share, but not gain extra profits. There is also a balance to be considered. If the organisation tries to expand its operations too quickly, then it may face the problem of overtrading. In this instance, the organisation cannot find enough working capital to ensure that the immediate debts of the organisation can be paid when they fall due.

To repeat business

As we mentioned earlier in performance criteria 3.1.2, the notion of repeat business is vital to any organisation. It has been shown by research that as much as 80% of the sales income of an organisation can be derived from 10% of loyal customers. In keeping these customers happy, the organisation needs to ensure that customer service is maintained at a high level (*see* Fig 3.7). In this respect retention (as this is called) can be expensive, but far more cost-effective than trying to gain new loyal customers.

Continued contact and help is the key to this retention goal. Customer satisfaction is very important since it has been said that a loyal customer is the organisation's best advertisement, but a dissatisfied one is the worst sort of public relations (*see* Fig 3.8).

To survival of business

At the heart of this consideration is performance measurement. There are many sophisticated ways of performance measurement which aim to alert the management to possible problems. Some of the ways in which problems can be identified at the earliest point include:

1 *Expense and revenue deviation charts* – these show the sales quotas required and the expense budgets for particular sales regions. They will show quota attainment, expense attainment, and poor or good performance

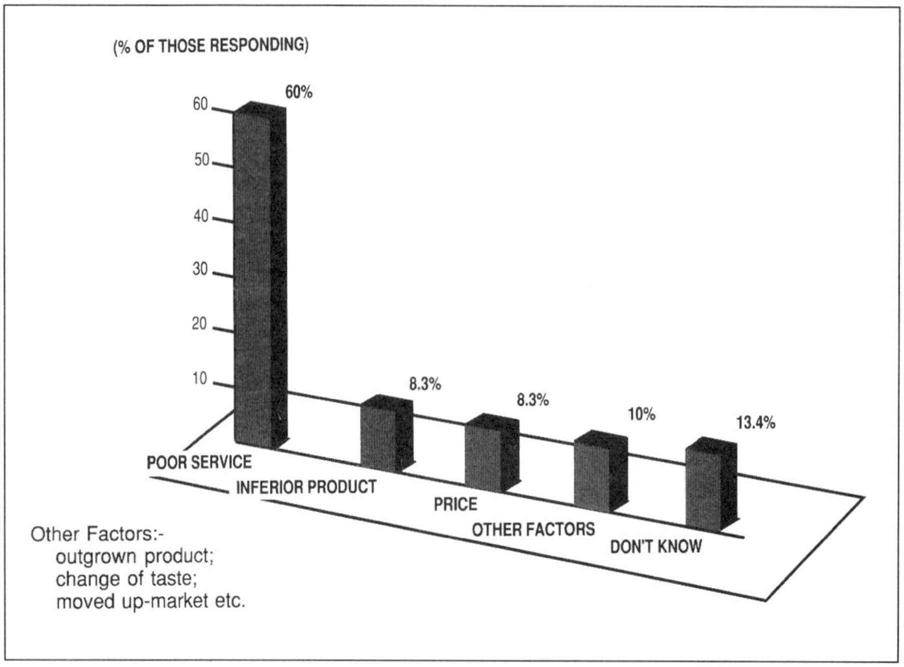

Fig 3.7 Why customers switch to the competition
(Courtesy of Peugeot Talbot)

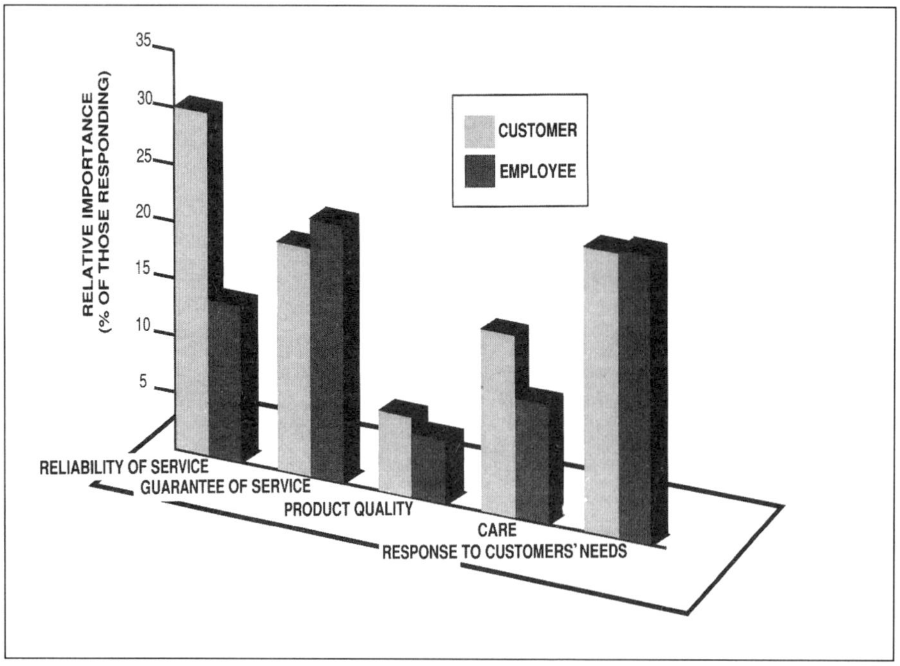

Fig 3.8 The importance of customer satisfaction
(Courtesy of Peugeot Talbot)

2 *Ratio analysis* – the expense and revenue deviation charts could be used to calculate ratios. However, there are several other methods which involve ratios and percentages:

- *expense to sales ratios*
- *gross profit to sales ratios*
- *percentage of goods sold at discount*
- *percentage of returned goods*
- *ratio of back orders to current stocks*
- *salesperson turnover, i.e. number of salespersons joining and leaving the organisation*
- *bad debtors ratios*

Cross-ratio analysis will also reveal a number of interesting and significant factors.

For information

As we have seen, the importance of customers as potential sources of valuable market information is of great interest to organisations. In this respect, the continual sampling of customers and asking their opinions is very valuable. Specifically, customers would be asked about the following:

- *Quality of the product*
- *Features of the product*
- *Price of the product*
- *Comparisons with competitors*
- *Product ideas*

Group activity

Time: 10 minutes

As a group, identify other types of information you could seek from customers.

PC 3.1.6
C 2.1

Focus study

Importance of customers

Tinned and packet soups are fairly regularly advertised on TV. The top brands, such as Batchelors and Campbells, have boosted their advertising spend to take advantage of Heinz's decision to stop its TV advertising.

Despite the decision that Heinz has made, the present division in market share exists:

Heinz	69%
Own label	28%
Batchelors	21%
Sainsbury's	16%
Campbells	13%
Batchelors' Cup-A-Soup	13%
Knorr	8%
Baxters	5%

The reasons for customers choosing to purchase a particular brand of soup is rather interesting. These include the following:

- The customer always bought a particular brand 86%
- The customer was tempted by the packaging 25%
- The customer wanted to try a new brand 23%
- The customer wanted to buy a cheaper brand 20%
- The customer saw the brand advertised on TV 13%
- The customer bought as a result of recommendation 11%
- The customer had a money-off coupon 10%
- The customer was sent a money-off coupon in mail 9%
- The customer saw the brand advertised in a magazine 7%

Given that 90% of the advertising spending for all brands goes into TV advertising and magazines take a mere 8%, there does not seem to be a significant difference in the percentages that encourage customers to buy a particular brand.

Soup is one of the 'low risk' purchases which means that customers are willing to try different brands because the unit price is low.

In 1993, Heinz spent over £1m in 'above the line' advertising. In other words, this was their spending on consumer media such as TV, magazines and newspapers. The fall to just £30 000 in 1994 should have given the opportunity for other manufacturers to take some of Heinz's market. Other brands did increase their advertising spend at the same time. Campbells increased spending by 33% and Batchelors by 35%.

PC 3.1.6
C 2.1

Group activity *Time: 30 minutes*

Having read the focus study on soup brands, what lessons can be learnt from it? What could the soup manufacturers do with this information? How valuable is it for planning purposes? Discuss these considerations as a group.

To contribute to profit

As we have already mentioned in the section which looked at the importance of customers to the income of the organisation, we can note the link between income and profit. If we bring in the repeat business factor, the importance of profit is all the more amplified. If the organisation is to ensure that profitability is maintained, then income, repeat business and profit margins all need to be addressed.

Element 3.1 Assignment

PC 3.1.1–6

This Element focuses on the ways in which consumer buying power creates a demand for a product or service. It should be noted that individuals with low incomes are less able to influence demand than those with a higher spending power. You should also remember that there is a connection between demand and the subsequent supply of products and services.

Task 1 PC 3.1.1

Produce a word-processed summary which describes the ways in which consumers can create demand. You should also identify one product and one service and show how change in demand has stimulated the supply.

Task 2 PC 3.1.2

In a word-processed summary, identify *three* changes in buying habits over the past few years. Describe the consumer's characteristics and suggest why their buying habits have changed.

Task 3 PC 3.1.3–5

Using graphics (either manual or computer generated), show how consumer trends have changed the demand for *three* products. Also produce a word-processed explanation of these changes in demand and suggest how demand may change in the next 2–3 years.

Task 4 PC 3.1.6

Produce word-processed notes on why customers are:

1 A vital source of income for business
2 A vital source of repeat business

You should produce these notes with examples.

Notes

You can find useful sources of data by looking at the media (CD-ROM) or government-produced statistics.

Element 3.2
Plan, design and produce promotional material

Performance criteria

A student must:

1 identify and give examples of **types of promotions** used in marketing goods and services

2 describe **constraints** on the content of promotional materials

3 **plan** to produce **promotional materials** to promote particular goods or services

4 explain the **purpose** of the planned promotional material

5 design and produce promotional materials and use them to promote goods or services

6 **evaluate** how successful the promotional materials were in achieving the stated purpose

Range

- *Types of promotions*: point-of-sale, advertisements (posters, radio, newspaper, magazines), sponsorship, competition
- *Constraints*: legal (Trade Descriptions Act, Sales of Goods Act, Consumer Protection Act), standards (Trading Standards Office, Advertising Standards Authority)
- *Plan*: time, people, materials, equipment, cost
- *Promotional materials*: advertisement, sponsorship, competition
- *Purpose*: to communicate a message to an audience, to create sales, to influence customers' perception, to provide information
- *Evaluate*: effectiveness in communicating to audience, effectiveness in creating sales, influence on customers' perceptions, effectiveness in providing information

3.2.1 Identify and give examples of types of promotions used in marketing goods and services

Types of promotions

A good advertisement tries to put over the message as clearly and accurately as possible without actually diverting the attention of the audience to the advertisement itself. It is the message that is centre stage and not the advertisement.

No one has really been able to get this mix right every time. There are many examples of advertisements which have done so; they are the exception rather than the rule. Here are a few pointers to help get the balance right:

1 The first and most obvious factor to consider is the amount of exposure that the advertisement gets. The concept of 'threshold' maintains that unless an advertisement is shown enough then people will simply forget it. On the other hand, advertisements can be shown too often, which can lead to the product being considered irritating and boring. Budgets are an important consideration as most companies cannot afford to show their advertisements enough to get the impact that they want. In these circumstances they will have to rely on other methods of getting their message across.

2 If a company cannot afford to saturate the media with its advertisements then it must look to the long term instead. Prolonged and gradual exposure can be equally effective. As time goes by and the advertisement is shown over and over again, people will remember it. The boredom and irritation factor is minimised. This technique relies on the consistency of the advertising and the memory of the audience.

3 People remember and respond to things that interest them. Advertisers try to find out what their target audience is interested in and adapt their advertising to suit them. This rapport with the audience can pay dividends. Methods typical of this technique are using well-known people to whom the audience relate or music that they like and enjoy.

4 Creativity itself plays no small part in all of this. The problem is in putting together the brilliant idea with the need to get a simple and clear message across.

Out of the above techniques the most effective is the exposure method. As most companies cannot afford this technique, they have to rely on spending heavily to begin with and then resorting to the repetition of the advertisement over a period of time. Even with a limited budget a company can have effective advertising by paying attention to the interests of its target audience and establishing that very important rapport with it. These days creativity can be vital; it may mean that an advertising campaign can be successful with lower overall costs while being very effective for the short time it is shown.

PC 3.2.1
C 2.1
C 2.2

Group activity *Time: 20 minutes*

In groups of four, try to list the television advertisements that you can remember. What is it about them that sticks in your mind? Are there any advertisements which are obviously aimed at your age group? Do these appeal to you, or do they irritate you? Feed back your discussion to the rest of your group.

Point-of-sale

These are materials that are used to display and promote products within a retail outlet. The most common examples of this form of marketing are:

1. **The dump bin** – which is a container or box in which the product is displayed in the retail outlet. Typically, these dump bins will have the name of the product clearly noticeable with a back card giving the dump bin greater visibility in the shop. The size of these dump bins varies according to the size of the product or the level of stock held by the outlet. You will find dump bins in many different outlets containing items as diverse as video tapes and confectionery, toothbrushes and books. Free-standing dump bins would normally be placed near doors, near the till or at the end of an aisle. The smaller, less obvious form of dump bin would normally be placed beside the till.
2. **The window poster** – which publicises the availability of the product within the outlet, or carries details of a special promotion or competition. Obviously, there is a lack of available space for these posters and the retailer would have to feel that the content, size and message was of sufficient merit to place in the window.
3. **The shelf sticker** – in cases when there is not sufficient space for a dump bin, or the retailer's shelving does not allow the use of a dump bin, then the shelf sticker is the next best alternative. Good examples of the use of the shelf sticker include the shelf or counter-level confectionery tray that is beside the till.
4. **The compartment** – typically a freezer or chiller that has the name of the product or the businesses name upon it. This acts as a dispenser for the product and is a permanent fixture within the shop. Good examples of these are Coca-Cola's chiller cabinets for their canned and bottled drinks, Mars confectionery freezers for their range of iced products or a Slush Puppy frozen drinks dispenser. The retailer would have to pay for the cabinet or dispenser, at a subsidised price, on the understanding that only that product or product line is sold from that container.

Obviously, the retailer has the final say about using any of this point-of-sale (POS) material or equipment. Suppliers are keen to offer discounts if the retailer is prepared to have the POS items in the shop.

Advertisements (posters, radio, newspaper, magazine)

The message which a company wishes to communicate to its target audience is central to the advertising campaign. The advertising will be a mixture of words, colours, images, sound, etc., that, hopefully, best gets the message across. If a company hopes to get its message across to everyone that it has targeted it will surely fail; certain types of advertising are simply not appropriate for certain parts of the target segment. Moreover, there are two main problems to overcome. The first is getting the message noticed. By going too far in trying to get the advertisement noticed the message can be left confused. Only a basic message needs to be remembered and an overly clever gimmick may leave the audience only remembering that.

Let us look at the relative merits of each of the media, particularly their advantages and disadvantages.

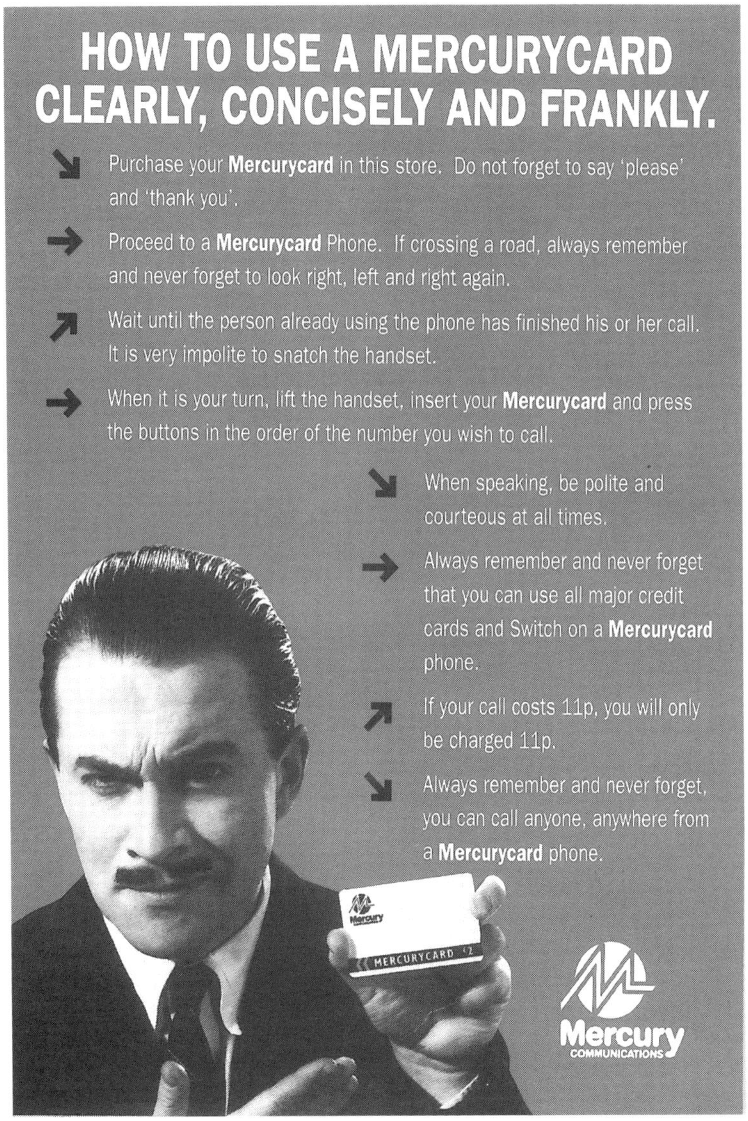

Fig 3.9 Mercury Communications chose comedian Harry Enfield to highlight the company's expanding range of telecommunication services

Posters

Outdoor advertising is not just static poster sites; it also includes advertising carried on buses, taxis and at train stations. Less obvious 'sites' include sports stadiums (such as football pitches), balloons (the really big ones!), milk bottles and even parking meters!

Fig 3.10 An example of outdoor advertising
(Photograph: Glasgow District Council)

The most obvious form of outdoor advertising is the poster and you will find these literally everywhere. They do lack the impact of TV, magazine or newspaper advertising, but do serve to remind people about the advertising message.

Most outdoor space is sold by a handful of contractors. They sell a package of mixed sites which are meant to get the advertiser's message across to the intended target audience. Popular sites are often tied up literally for years with the TC (Till Countermanded) system, and this can be frustrating.

Costs, of course, vary immensely; some 400 sites sell for around £70 000 per month. The rears of buses cost around £50 each per month and are usually available in multiples of 50.

Advantages and disadvantages of outdoor advertising

Advantages

- Very high OTS (opportunity to see – *see* Glossary)
- Very low CPT (cost per thousand – *see* Glossary)
- Wide range of colour available
- Wide choice of sites
- Good opportunities to be the only advertisement in view at any one time, little direct competition
- Sites tend to be sold on a quarterly basis. The gradual effect of the poster may make people subconsciously notice the advertisement and take notice of it over a period of time
- Great opportunities to have very innovative advertising such as the '3D' advertisement with models, cars or similar 'stuck' onto the poster

Disadvantages

- Printing costs are high on the short-runs needed for the posters
- There is a long booking and cancellation period
- Very debatable research into site 'audiences'
- Can be missed easily and not even looked at by the 'audience'
- Only short snappy messages tend to work
- Graffiti can be a problem
- Prime sites are often monopolised by 'big' advertisers
- Sites are usually not available individually and a package of sites are sold to the advertiser who has no control over where their advertisement is shown

Fig 3.11 Another example of outdoor advertising

PC 3.2.1
C 2.1

Group activity

As a group, take a leisurely stroll around your local area. How many outdoor advertisements can you spot? Can you find any that we have not mentioned above?

Try to decide which of the advertisements is the most prominent and obvious to the public. What makes it so effective? Also find the worst one; what is wrong with either the advertisement or the site?

When you return to your studies, compare your choice of best and worst with the rest of the group. Have you all spotted the same kind of advertisements? Did some of you miss some? If so, why?

Focus study

Poster sites

Poster contractors have been suggesting that the results of a recent test may be the beginning of a dramatic increase in outdoor advertising. A £250 000 initiative spearheaded by Maiden Outdoor boosted a new bubble-bath product called Scallywags to a 26% market share in just six weeks. The key to success was the choice of sites that would be seen by housewives and children.

At the same time, other research has shown the following:

- that the campaign was remembered by 36% of housewives and children
- that the campaign was remembered by 36% of tube travellers
- that these totals meant that 40% of those who remember the advertisement would buy the product

Radio

The 1990s have seen an explosion in radio in the UK. Independent radio as controlled by the IBA (Independent Broadcasting Authority) tends to be a very middle-of-the-road medium. Networking is becoming more common, particularly in the case of music stations. Not surprisingly, the medium is dominated by the larger stations, usually based in London, Manchester, Birmingham or Liverpool. The emergence of Virgin Radio, Talk Radio UK and Classic FM have seen a major change in the balance of power in radio.

There are a number of advantages and disadvantages that should be looked at.

Advantages and disadvantages of radio advertising

Advantages

- The medium is ideal for urgent and immediate advertising announcements
- With widespread stereo use, sound effects and gimmicks are far more effective than on TV
- A business can advertise precisely to a set area
- Production costs for radio are comparatively low
- Good discounts are available
- Short notice may be given to the stations in terms of bookings and cancellations, so the flexibility is high

Disadvantages

- National campaigns are still hard to co-ordinate
- Radio has the reputation for being a low-impact medium, used as a background or 'aural wall-paper'
- As with TV, national advertising can be expensive if you add up all the costs of advertising with each of the small stations

PC 3.2.1
C 2.1
C 2.2

Individual activity

Radio advertising is a relatively young medium. Do you think that you can accurately target your customers? How well do the radio stations detail their audience figures? Contact your local independent radio station(s) for details of their figures and advertising rates.

Focus study

Commercial radio

Commercial radio has been recognised as the fastest-growing advertising medium in the UK. According to the Radio Advertising Bureau, there is a 25% year-on-year growth in sales revenue from advertising. However, since 1992, there has been a 2% drop in the number of listeners. The biggest fall off is in the 15–24 and 55 plus age groups. Virgin, the station that has had the most impact, attracts some 3.25m listeners; this accounts for around 2.8% of all the listeners.

Classic FM is up, too, with weekly listeners amounting to some 4.8m. This represents a 6% increase from last year. Atlantic 252 is up to 4.93m (3.1% of all listeners).

The BBC is the main loser, with Radio 1 dropping to 14.7% of the listening public. This still makes it the market leader in a growing and competitive market.

Newspaper

There is a considerable choice in national newspapers available to the potential advertiser. Sales figures (or circulation figures) differ widely. Far and away the most successful newspapers are *The Sun*, and the *Daily Mirror*, both boasting sales between three and four million per day. Several other major papers have sales in excess of a million, with the 'heavy' newspapers barely mustering half a million each. A distinction should be made between the daily papers and the Sunday papers as some three million additional sales are made on Sundays. Nearly 15 million newspapers are sold daily, whereas over 17.5 million are sold on Sunday.

Advantages and disadvantages of newspaper advertising

Advantages

- Over 85 per cent of the population can be reached by the combined sales of national and local newspapers. However, a great many individual advertisements would have to be placed in different papers
- Each newspaper has a distinctly different readership which allows for accurate segmentation
- The flexibility of short or long notice is a key feature of daily newspapers
- Many people feel, and tend to believe, the printed word against any other form of advertising
- Many national newspapers offer the facility of split-runs, in other words you may advertise in the *Mirror* just in the North of England should you wish
- The message that you are trying to get across may be long and complex, such as financial advertising
- Many newspapers have now begun to offer special features on certain days, e.g. Monday may be 'jobs', Tuesday may be 'property'
- An increasing number of newspapers are offering colour supplements. Despite the fact that many papers have gone 'colour', there are grave misgivings about the quality of colour reproduction onto newsprint. The availability of the colour supplement helps to alleviate this

Disadvantages

- Most people view newspaper adverts as boring. They lack impact, although colour has helped this
- The bulk of newspapers are only read on the day they come out, therefore the advertisement has a very short life
- The growth of the free newspaper market has diluted available income. Further, it has meant that many newspapers are simply composed of advertisements with very little editorial. Advertisements simply 'get lost' in the mass

Reader loyalty can compensate for a number of criticisms. Equally, certain prestige titles attract a disproportionate amount of advertising compared to their readership. Editorial support for new products is very much a feature of certain titles and greatly enhances the impact of the advertisement itself.

PC 3.2.1
C 2.1
C 2.2
C 2.3
C 2.4

Group activity

Working in groups of four, investigate the range of available local newspapers and free sheets. You should attempt to collect the following data:

- number of copies sold/distributed
- average cost for a single page advertisement
- the number of potential customers who will read the newspaper (this is known as the 'pass on rate')
- the average number of whole page advertisements per issue

You should present your findings in the form of a series of graphs or bar charts. The information should offer the reader the easiest method of comparing the various newspaper options.

Focus study

Newspapers

Daily newspaper sales may have dipped over the last ten years, but Sunday newspapers have fared even worse. From a high of 114.4m sales per week, national newspaper sales have fallen to 102.6m. This is a decline of some 10.3%. Sunday newspapers, over the same ten-year period have fallen by 16%. Adult readership has dropped by 13.5% for dailies and by 12.6% for the Sunday papers.

Magazines

With well over a thousand magazines available in the UK alone, the advertiser has the choice of specialist or general interest magazines that are released from weekly to quarterly. The range of magazines is really quite bewildering and constantly changing, but many have done a lot of the work for the advertiser in specifically catering for a particular audience by offering the right sort of editorial material.

In many respects the world of magazine advertising is much like that of the newspaper. Magazines tend to vie for advertising far more aggressively than newspapers and will often offer special deals for new advertisers and regulars far more readily than newspapers. As pointed out, one of the disadvantages is that magazines have relatively early copy dates and require advertising copy as much as two to three months prior to the publication date. Costs vary enormously; for example, advertising in women's weekly magazines can cost as much as £20 000 per full-colour page. The range and scope of advertising in magazines is huge and ultimately will have something to suit anyone's pocket.

Advantages and disadvantages of magazine advertising

Advantages

- Segmentation and targeting can be precise as the magazine may well have done this for the advertiser already by providing a full reader breakdown
- Special interest magazines have a considerably longer life than most other magazines. The editorial is well read and the advertisements are given much more attention than general interest magazines
- Magazines tend to have a longer life than newspapers and have a much higher 'pass-on' rate (more than one person reads the magazine)
- In the case of well-known and respected magazines advertisements may well have increased impact and credibility by being in them
- The better quality paper and more sophisticated printing techniques allow the advertising of up-market products with colour advertisements

Disadvantages

- There is quite keen competition to be noticed by the reader with high-quality advertisements and interesting editorial
- The readership breakdown is far less complete than for newspapers, indeed for smaller circulation magazines independent audits of their true circulation figures may not be available
- You should not expect an instant response from an advertisement as the 'shelf-life' of the magazine is comparatively long as is the 'digesting' period after the buyer has purchased the magazine
- Magazines have long lead and cancellation times which makes 'spur of the moment' advertising very difficult
- High-quality advertisements inevitably means high production costs to create the original for the advertisement

PC 3.2.1
C 2.1

Group activity

Time: 30 minutes

Working in pairs, attempt to identify ideal magazines for the following products and services:

1. A disabled person's stair-lift
2. A corrugated plastic, collapsible compost bin
3. Personalised letterheads
4. A computer disk-drive repair service
5. An organisation that manufactures copies of famous brand perfumes

Compare your choice of magazines with that of the rest of the group. You should be prepared to back up your choices with good reasons.

Focus study

Magazines

The top five magazine publishers account for some 60% of the circulation revenue. The next 10% is split between ten companies. The percentages of circulation control are as follows:

IPC	25%
EMAP	15.2%
BBC magazines	8.7%
Bauer	7.9%
National Magazine Co	4.2%
Others	39%

PC 3.2.1

Individual activity

Using *BRAD*, or a similar reference publication, try to identify at least five magazines owned by the main companies mentioned above. Try to find similar magazines that cater for the same kind of market. Which magazines offer the best value for money? How have you measured this?

TV

Up until quite recently viewing figures were almost equally split between the BBC and the ITV networks. There is now a slight advantage to the commercial stations. Satellite television is beginning to have a marked impact on the viewing figures too. The ITV network, on Channel 3 and Channel 4, consists of around 14 regional stations, plus GMTV and C4. The stations' share of the audience depends upon the population of their region. London and the Thames area (London Weekend Television and Carlton) have some 22% of the population; the Channel Islands only 1%. This also has an impact on the pricing of advertisements.

There are a number of advantages and disadvantages associated with television advertising.

Advantages and disadvantages of television advertising

Advantages

- TV is extremely useful in getting simple and uncomplicated messages to the vast majority of the population. Most homes have a TV set and therefore, on a purely statistical basis, everyone has an opportunity to see the advertisement
- Generally speaking, the impact should be good. Creativity is high and is assisted by the use of colour and sound
- It is widely agreed that people are more receptive to advertisements in a relaxed atmosphere
- The sophisticated collection and analysis of viewing data helps the media planner target the audience more accurately
- In a highly competitive market such as this, attractive discounts are offered to new and, for that matter, regular advertisers
- The regional nature of the independent television network offers the planner the opportunity to segment the country into manageable advertising areas
- The regional nature of the network also offers the possibilities of test marketing an area with an advertisement, or in some cases a product, before 'rolling out' into the UK as a whole

Disadvantages

- Production costs, apart from the most basic of advertisements, are high
- Air time can be extremely expensive, particularly at peak times. For example, in the Thames region, a thirty-second slot would cost in excess of £40 000. This would drop to as little as £20 000 for the Border region (with a 1% share of the population)
- High income and well-educated groups tend not to view as often as the rest of the population. Therefore, TV may not be the right medium for them
- Tests have proved that viewers' attention wanders during advertising breaks
- The population's wide use of the video recorder may mean that your expensive and clever advertisements are never watched (except at fast forward)

The available advertising time is at present limited, only seven minutes per hour being allowed for advertising purposes. Charge rates are calculated according to the particular time of the day, assumed audience sizes and demand from other advertisers.

Group activity

PC 3.2.1
C 2.1

Do you think that the BBC should offer advertising possibilities? Discuss this as a group.

Research the cost of TV advertising, using *BRAD*, and try to work out the peak viewing hours.

Focus study

Television

There have been depressing viewing figures for television over the last few years, but this does not tell the whole story. Television advertising is still extremely effective. While the average adult watches 14 hours of 'terrestrial' television per week (that is BBC1, BBC2, ITV and C4), the average satellite television watcher sits in front of the TV for 18.5 hours per week. This may be as a result of the 25 or more channels available, but satellite subscribers can watch up to 32% more commercial television than terrestrial viewers. Some 12 channels dominate the satellite viewing figures.

Sports, particularly those appealing to men, are very well supported in audience figure terms. Film premieres, soap operas and classic dramas are also watched by millions. But it is the major sports events which excite the advertisers as they vie for the limited slots available. A really popular sports event can attract figures in excess of 25m. Here are some of the most popular sports events of 1993/94:

The FA Cup Final (BBC1 May 1994)	30m
The European Cup Final (ITV May 1993)	24m
The Coca-Cola Cup Final (ITV May 1994)	28m
The Cup Winners Cup Final (ITV May 1994)	29m

These figures can account for 66% of the total viewers at a particular time. You will note that the majority of the big audience pullers were on ITV. It was interesting to note that the BBC screened female-orientated programmes to compete with these sporting events. In homes with a single TV set, there would have been quite a fight for the remote control!

PC 3.2.1
C 2.1

Group activity

Time: 25 minutes

These male-orientated sports events are the advertisers' dream. What sorts of products would be advertised during these programmes? Can you identify at least five different types of product that would achieve a good OTS in the commercial breaks? Discuss this as a group.

Cinema

This form of advertising medium has spent some time as the poor relation, but it is making a big comeback. Attendance figures are up and so is the advertising spend. This is an ideal medium for the younger customer and businesses have not been slow in recognising this aspect.

Advantages and disadvantages of cinema advertising

Advantages

- Local advertising is cheap and relatively simple
- This medium is ideal for the under-25 market
- The medium has great visual impact and sound effects
- The medium is ideal for testing the effectiveness of advertisements that will later appear on TV
- The medium allows spirits to be advertised

Disadvantages

- There is a relatively low audience level
- Production costs are high, as separate copies of the advertisement have to be provided for each screen
- Buying advertising space can be more difficult than for some of the other media

Focus study

Cinema

The Cinema Advertising Association is a trade organisation of cinema advertising contractors. Its purpose is to monitor, promote and maintain standards of cinema advertising. It also conducts research into cinema and cinema advertising.

CAA research has shown that the emergence of the multi-plex (at an investment of £600m) has had a marked effect on the fortunes of cinema in the UK. In 1993, the number of multi-plex screens had increased to 625, from the 1985 level of just 10.

Advertising revenue has increased on a year by year basis over the past ten years, and now accounts for nearly 1% of all advertising spending. The national average for a 30-second commercial is around £73. The total number of screens available in the UK has risen to 1862, predominantly in the areas of higher population density.

The CAA offers an Audience Discount Package which guarantees the price on the CPT basis, the average cost being around £28.

Group activity

PC 3.2.1
C 2.1

Cinema is growing in the UK. It suffered a severe slump in the 1970s, but is now steadily growing again. Try to find out how many cinema screens were in your local area twenty years ago, ten years ago and now. What has been the growth rate? Discuss this as a group.

Sponsorship

Organisations use sponsorship in an attempt to raise consumer awareness of the organisation itself. The costs to the organisation of sponsoring a major sports event, for example, may run into hundreds of thousands of pounds. To sponsor an event over a longer period of time, such as the football league, may be counted in millions.

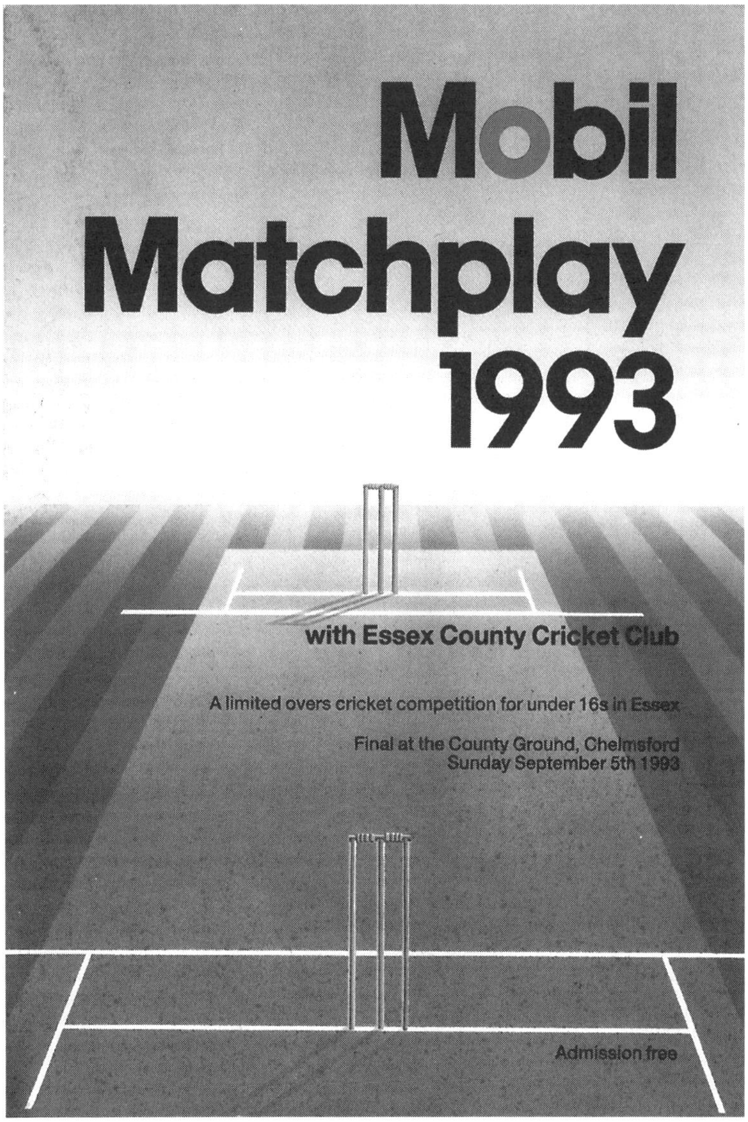

Fig 3.12 Mobil's successful Matchplay 1993 sponsorship deal

A cheaper form of sponsorship is to choose a particular individual, such as a sports personality, to wear and use the organisation's products. Sports sponsorship is, perhaps, the largest area of activity.

Organisations will use sponsorship for the following reasons:

1 They will receive publicity via any advertisements in the run up to the event

2 They will receive publicity, particularly if it is being televised, during the event
3 Consumers will begin to associate the organisation with a particular sport
4 Several organisations which are not allowed to advertise in the conventional media, such as cigarette manufacturers, will use the sponsorship to ensure that their name is visible on television screens during the event
5 Sponsors will also receive 'free advertising' whenever the event is being mentioned on television or radio
6 In many cases, organisations consider sponsorship to be much more cost-effective than advertising. After all, consider how much it would cost to pay for one-and-a-half hours of advertising during the live televising of a football match
7 Organisations which are sponsoring particular events will be given free tickets for the best seats, which they can then give to valued customers
8 Organisations will try to sponsor sports or events which appeal to their target market for goods and services. This may be the only way to reach these people

Fig 3.13 The Mobil Guide to the Victoria and Albert Museum, designed to help visitors get the most from the museum. This is part of a long series of Mobil sponsorships with the museum

PC 3.2.1
C 2.1

Group activity

Time: 20 minutes (for discussions)

In pairs, monitor television sports events over the next two weeks. How many different organisations are involved? What kind of organisations are they? Why do you think they have chosen this particular event?

Competition

Competitions are very popular with both consumers and organisations. They are relatively cheap to set up and run and, if organised well, will give the organisation a great deal of publicity.

Many competitions require the customer to purchase a number of products over a period of time in order to qualify for entry into the competition. This may take the form of the collection of vouchers or tokens.

Legally, the competition must have some element of skill attached to it. For this reason, a competition often requires a slogan or catch-phrase. This is known as a 'tie-breaker'.

The organisation running the competition will receive publicity before, during and after the event.

PC 3.2.1
C 2.1
C 2.2

Group activity *Time: 20 minutes*

In groups of three, try to list as many different forms of competition as you can think of. Also consider just how many people are likely to enter the competition. A popular one will attract over 100 000 entries. The organisation will then have 100 000 names and addresses which it knows purchase a particular product or service. What use do you think this information is to it?

3.2.2 Describe constraints on the content of promotional materials

Legal (Trade Descriptions Act, Sale of Goods Act, Consumer Protection Act)

In the UK, the advertising industry is largely self-regulating. In other words, the industry itself keeps a careful eye on its members to ensure that they do not mislead or overly confuse the public.

- **British Code of Advertising Practice** All advertisements should be 'legal, decent, honest and truthful'. These foundations of practice are supported by the British Code of Advertising Practice. In particular, they cover awkward advertising areas such as children, cigarettes and alcohol, recommendations by famous people and in situations when a company compares its product to another. Above all, the advertisement should not claim anything which cannot be clearly proven.
- **The British Code of Sales Promotion Practice (BCSPP)** covers aspects which do not fall directly under the British Code of Advertising Practice. In essence, this code is

concerned with competitions, special offers, charity promotions, vouchers, coupons and free offers.

- **The Advertising Standards Authority (ASA)** exists to assist customers who have a complaint regarding an advertisement. The ASA receives nearly 10 000 complaints each year and publishes its results in a monthly report. If the complaint is found to be justified, then the advertiser is required to withdraw or change the advertisement. In extreme cases, the ASA may inform newspapers, television companies and radio stations that they should not accept any other advertisements similar to the one that has caused the problem.
- **The Independent Television Commission** monitors all advertisements which are broadcast by the various independent television stations in the UK. It also has a responsibility for ensuring that satellite and cable television advertisements are similarly monitored. The monitoring process begins before the advertisement is made, when the Independent Television Commission checks the script for inaccuracies. Any complaints are dealt with by the Independent Television Commission and action can be taken against advertisers who are found guilty of misleading the public.
- **The Broadcasting Standards Council** Working in conjunction with the Independent Television Commission is the Broadcasting Standards Council, which is particularly concerned with violence and indecency, both in programmes and advertisements. If it receives a complaint regarding excess violence or indecency, then it will take action against the advertiser.
- **The Radio Authority** Fulfilling a similar role to the Independent Television Commission, but working within the field of radio broadcasting, is the Radio Authority. It also checks scripts before recording to ensure that the advertiser is not misleading the public in any way. It is responsible for investigating complaints and taking appropriate action, should the complaint be upheld.

It should be noted that certain media will not accept advertisements for tobacco or spirits, or from bookmakers. This is particularly true of television, but advertisements for these products and services can be seen in other media, such as newspapers or magazines.

Group activity *Time: 15 minutes*

PC 3.2.2
C 2.1

As a group discuss the following statement:

'Advertisers and their advertisements consistently lie and exaggerate their products and services. There is not enough legislation to control them, and they do not pay any attention to the voluntary codes of practice.'

Trade Descriptions Act

Under this 1968 Act, the public is protected from unscrupulous traders. It states that:

'Any person who, in the case of trade or business, applies a false trade description to any good; or supplies or offers to supply any good to which a false trade description is applied shall, subject to the provisions of this Act, be guilty of an offence.'

In other words, the trader cannot make any false statements regarding its products. The complaints would be dealt with by a Trading Standards Officer in the first place.

Sale of Goods Act

This 1979 Act aims first to define a sale of goods. It says that this is:

'A contract by which the seller transfers or agrees to transfer the property in goods to the buyer for a money consideration, called a price.'

The basic point of the Act is to ensure that the goods sold fit the purpose for which they have been sold. For example, the product should not break down the first time you try to use it.

The Consumer Protection Act

This Act is primarily concerned with price and the pricing policy of organisations. No doubt many of us have been caught out when purchasing a product, finding that the price quoted is not the price in reality. This may be because the sale period has ended, the price quoted did not include VAT, or the claimed price reduction is untrue. This Act states that the organisation must clearly state the 'real' price of a product, not make unfair or untrue comparisons between products and price, and not make false statements about price reductions.

You will often see, particularly in a sale, one of two statements on a price ticket:

1 That the product was available for a period of time at a previously higher price. It may not necessarily have been available in that store, but in an alternative location owned by that organisation, and this fact will be stated on the ticket.
2 That the product has been specifically bought in and offered at a low price for the sale period only.

The Consumer Protection Act further covers the consumer who is offered unsafe goods whatever the circumstances.

The Supply of Goods and Services Act 1994

This Act was created to cover loopholes in the Sale of Goods Act. The older Act did not include services, hired goods or part exchanges. All goods or services 'purchased' under these conditions are now covered. In respect of services this Act protects the consumer against poor workmanship, long delays and hidden costs.

Standards (Trading Standards Office, Advertising Standards Authority)

Trading Standards

The responsibility for the enforcement of most of the consumer protection legislation rests with the local authorities. This is carried out by the Trading Standards Office or a consumer protection department. They are responsible for the following:

- *Giving guidance to traders through education and persuasion*
- *Prosecution of offenders when all else fails*
- *Carrying out weights and measures checks*
- *Analysing samples of products (particularly foods)*
- *Acting as a channel between the public and the Office of Fair Trading*
- *Investigating bad practice*
- *Making purchases of goods or services for investigation purposes*
- *Carrying out tests of equipment*
- *Seizure of property, if necessary*

The following Acts are covered by the Trading Standards Office:

- Consumer Credit Act 1974
- Food Safety Act 1990
- Road Traffic Act 1988 (part)
- Trade Descriptions Act 1968
- Weights and Measures Act 1985
- Unsolicited Goods and Services Act 1971
- Consumer Protection Act 1987

PC 3.2.2
C 2.1

Group activity

In pairs, research one of the above (with the exception of the ones we have already detailed) and orally report back to the rest of your group.

If the advertisement is found to be unacceptable under the rules of the Code, then the advertiser will be told to pull the advertisement or amend it. Failure to do so may entail the advertiser being suspended, or suffering the withdrawal of privileges, and the publishers of magazines and newspapers being advised not to take this advertising.

Further refusal may entail the advertiser being referred to the Office of Fair Trading for refusing to abide by the Code.

Advertising Standards Authority

The Advertising Standards Authority (ASA) is the independent self-regulating body responsible for supervising the content of non-broadcast advertisements in the UK.

It is estimated that there are some 25m advertisements published annually in the UK. The ASA spot-checks thousands of them (and indeed sales promotions) as part of their rigorous monitoring programme.

The ASA also advises thousands of advertisers, agencies and publishers on how to avoid using misleading or offensive advertisements that may lead to complaints being made. The aim is avoidance, since complaints are not only costly but may involve adverse publicity and criticism of the industry.

The ASA operates through a levy charged on all advertisements. This levy, only 0.1% of the advertisement's cost, is collected on the ASA's behalf by the Advertising Standards Board of Finance. This separate organisation helps to ensure that the ASA maintains its independence.

The ASA has the power to investigate any complaint and compare the advertisement to the Code of Advertising Practice. The ASA rarely tells the advertiser to stop the advertisement immediately, as the advertiser is given the time to tell their side of the story.

Focus study

Advertising Standards Authority

In March 1995, there was a much-reported case in the marketing press. It involved the advertising strategy of Colgate (run by Colgate Oral Care). This was an example of 'knocking copy', which means that the advertisement openly criticises a competitor. Nothing particularly odd there, but it used one of the competitors' advertising slogans as part of its advertisement. It stated that Colgate's Plax mouthwash was approved by the British Dental Association and that Listerine (owned by Warner Wellcome Consumer Healthcare) was approved 'by a dragon called Clifford'. Quite amusing in its own right, but it was suggested that the advertisement had broken the British Code of Advertising Practice. Specifically, the Code states that: 'advertising should not make unfair use of the goodwill attached to the . . . advertising campaign of any other business'.

Colgate also faced another problem with the ASA, in that the endorsement by the British Dental Association incurs an annual fee. The ASA states that all financial relationships for product endorsements must be mentioned in the advertisement. This was not. Colgate, meanwhile, was confident that the advertisement was within the spirit and codes of the law.

3.2.3 Plan to produce promotional materials to promote particular goods or services

Obviously, promotions are not created immediately; they take a great deal of time and effort, not to mention money, to ensure that they will be successful. Let us have a look at the resource considerations in preparing and launching promotions.

Time

The time required for the preparation of promotions is commonly held to have four stages:

1 **The planning stage** – during the planning stage, you should try to decide exactly what you wish to achieve. You should also attempt to identify any methods which you will use. It is very important to decide which individuals will be involved in the campaign. Once you have established these initial factors, you should then try to devise a timetable to cover all of the stages of the promotion. You will need to identify clearly any resources required, who will carry out particular tasks and how long they have to

do them. As a final point, you will also need to establish a theme for the campaign as a whole.

2 **The production stage** – once you have reached this stage, you will find that many more people are involved in the promotion. Normally, a large number of specialists will be brought in to carry out specific tasks. These specialists include photographers, copywriters and printers.
3 **The post-launch stage** – this stage covers the immediate aftermath of the launch of the promotion. It is at this point that you will try to obtain as much press coverage as possible. Your promotion will just be stale news very quickly as new promotions will hit the headlines daily.
4 **The evaluation stage** – after the launch period, and as soon as is practicable, it is advisable to evaluate all of the activities and decisions made during the promotion. Again, it is important to do this as quickly as possible as all of the individuals involved will be engaged in other activities and may forget any problems which they encountered during the promotion.

Fig 3.14 Mobil Oil's joint sales promotion with Argos Distributors Ltd

People

Every promotion is created by a team of individuals. Some will be very good at particular tasks and others, while they can offer useful advice, may need careful handling. A person who has to control all of the activities of the team will need a number of qualities:

MERCURY COMMUNICATIONS LIMITED

CORPORATE IDENTITY

TYPOGRAPHY

LITERATURE **6.**06

FRUTIGER BOLD

ABCDEFGHIJKLMNOPQRS TUVWXYZabcdefghijklm nopqrstuvwxyz

PLANTIN

ABCDEFGHIJKLMNOP QRSTUVWXYZ abcdefghijklmnopqrstuvw xyz

Et tamen in budsad ne que pecun codut est nuque as non imper ned libiding ged impular relinguard on impudanti, fier ad audgendas cum facto tum legum odioque cividua. Nos amice et nebeval olestias acalas poten as aud gendas cim consequat nona imper.

Et tamen in budsad ne que pecun codut est neque as nona imper ned libiding ged impular relinguard on on impudanti, vid cantor incandecence.

Advertisium bard as.

Nos amice et nebeval olestias access potest fier ad audgendas cum consequiat to facto tum

A *Scaled down size to demonstrate example of introduction page typography*

AS NONA IMPER NED LINIDING GED IMPULAR ON LEGUM.

Nos amice et nebeval olestias access potest fier ad audgendas cum consequiat to facto tum toen legum odioque civida. Et tamen in budsad ne Que pecun codut est neque as nona imper ned libiding ged impular relinguard.

Nos amice et tamen in budsac ne que pecum con sequet

On impudanti, vid cantor incandecence. Advertisium bard as. Nos amice et nebeval olestias access potest fier ad audgendas cum consequiat to facto tum toen legum odioque cividua.

Libiding est Nique

Et tamen in budsad ne que pecun codut est neque as nona imper ned libiding ged linguard on on impudanti, vid ecence.

Potest fier ad audgendas cum consequiat to facto tum toen legum odio que civida tamen

Lorem dipsum ged impular, Londorum, Britatus

sequiat to facto tum toen legum odioque cividua. Et tamen in budsad ne que pecun codut est neque.

As nona imper ned libiding ged impular on impudanti, vid cantor

B *Scaled down size to demonstrate example of standard page typography*

It is important that the typographical application on all Mercury Corporate brochures should be consistent and present a uniform appearance.

Frutiger and Plantin are the only two typefaces that are permitted to be used in the design and layout of brochures.

Introduction page:
The large column main introduction text should be set in 13/26pt Frutiger Bold, upper and lower case, ranged left with a larger 28pt initial cap.

The small column supplementary text, if applied, should be set in 10/14pt Plantin, upper and lower case and ranged left.

Paragraphs should have no indents and be separated by the minimum of half line spacing.

Headlines, if applied should be set in Frutiger Bold caps to a type size and measure that suits the page layout.

Standard pages:
General copy text should be set in 12/15pt Plantin, upper and lower case and ranged left within the two column grid system.

Paragraphs should have no indents and be separated by half line spacing.

Headlines should be set in Frutiger Bold caps to a type size and measure that suits the page layout.

Subheadings should be set in Frutiger Bold, upper and lower case, ranged left with opened letter spacing allowing half line spacing between subheading and text.

Use space above subheadings to make any necessary adjustments for uneven column alignments created by paragraphs and subheadings.

Supplementary captions can be added to support or highlight a point in the general copy text. They should be set to a half column measure, 9/18pt Frutiger Bold, upper and lower case and ranged left.

In limited circumstances coloured text can be applied, such as Mercury Blue, where added emphasis might be required.

Photograph or illustration captions should be set in 8/10pt Frutiger Light italics, upper and lower case and ranged left.

Fig 3.15 A sample page from Mercury Communications' extensive literature guidelines booklet. This page focuses on the choice and uses of typefaces

- *They must be a good listener*
- *They must be a good manager of people*
- *They must be able to communicate well*
- *They must be able to write well*
- *They must be persuasive*
- *They must be able to use a variety of equipment*
- *They must know about a whole range of different media*
- *They must know the product they are promoting*

Specific skills which relate to the creation of promotional materials include the following:

- **Copywriting skills** – this skill is the ability to write a good and memorable message which the consumer can easily understand and relate to.
- **Graphic design skills** – graphic design skills are of a slightly more technical nature, but include the ability to design an attractive layout for an advertisement, be aware of colours and shades, know which typeface to choose and be able to transfer a vague idea into a finished product.

Materials and equipment

The range of physical resources available to an advertising professional or design organisation is enormous. They will have access to a variety of pens and markers, paints, spray cans, paper and mounting board, layout pads, acetate transparencies, film maskers, Letrasets, sophisticated copying machines, computers and laser printers, and cameras.

For the purposes of your activities in creating advertisements and promotional materials, you should be able to cope with a pair of scissors, pencils and an eraser.

dti

the department for Enterprise

Fig 3.16 The use of the DTI's logo in all forms is carefully monitored

Cost

The plain fact of the matter is that the creation of promotional materials is an expensive occupation. It is immediately obvious if an organisation has not spent any serious amounts of money on its promotion. It will look amateurish, unsightly and messy. This is not to say that there are not some talented amateurs, but there is no real substitute for using experts.

PC 3.2.3
C 2.1
C 2.2
C 2.3

Group activity *Time: 45 minutes*

In pairs, try to create a list of specialists that would be needed for the production of a glossy brochure for a new golf course with an hotel situated in its grounds.

Imagine that expense is not a problem for the organisation paying the advertising and design agency.

Compare your list of specialists with those of the rest of your group.

Promotional materials

As you will have already realised, this phrase actually refers to a particular form of advertisement. In this section we will be looking at advertisements, sponsorship and competitions as ways of promoting a particular product or service.

Advertisement

We have looked at advertisements as far as the different media are concerned. Here we will look at them again and try to identify the needs for each advertisement type and its uses.

- **Paper-based media** – this category includes all newspapers, magazines, leaflets, brochures, posters and fly-sheets.
- **Lens-based media** – this category includes both photographs and film. In the case of film, which includes television advertisements, you will have to engage the services of a number of additional specialists. Someone will have to write the script for the advertisement. You will have to have a director and crew to film the advertisement. Once this has been done, you will need an editor to edit the film. Copies of the advertisement will need to be made and this will probably involve the transfer of the advertisement from industry-standard video tape to cine film or ordinary video tape.
- **Computer-based media** – this category includes all graphics packages, clip-art and desktop publishing. These packages have revolutionised the design of advertisements and made their production much more rapid and professional. You will not necessarily need a specialist to provide this service, as many people are capable of using these packages.
- **Voice-based media** – this category includes advertisements destined for radio and recorded announcements (usually telephone-based). Additionally, voice-based media may be used as the 'voice-over' for lens-based advertisements.

PC 3.2.3
C 2.1

Group activity *Time: 15 minutes*

As a group, investigate the skills and expertise within your group. There will be some members of your group who are able to use computer packages, draw well, use a video camera or have a flair for writing. Are there any skills which you would like to learn? How would you go about acquiring these skills?

Fig 3.17 Example of Mobil Oil's consistent corporate image

Sponsorship

UK businesses spend around 250m sponsoring sport each year. This figure is growing by about 10% per year. According to the organisation Sports Marketing Strategy, sponsorship accounts for some 5% of all of the advertising spending worldwide. Although sports advertising is aimed at reaching a mass audience, it is argued that, since so many sponsorship deals are being struck, this dilutes the effect. When was the last time that you bought something after seeing the name of a business or a product on the chest of your favourite sports personality?

Sports sponsorship is more than just image building. It is about selling products too, but the former is the more dominant. When a client has been sold on the concept of sponsorship, there are media monitoring exercises carried out to indicate the exposure levels which measure the success or failure of the venture. Sponsorship supporters do admit that not enough research is being carried out to measure the real objectives of the sponsorship or, for that matter, the possible upturn in sales as a result.

Normally, the business, product or brand is tracked against the trends in the market to try to show what effect the sponsorship had. Sponsorship is very strong on brand-building. Once the target market has been identified, the business will know a lot about the target group, its lifestyles, income and age, etc. If the target group is young and active, then the business would be wise to associate itself with an active and exciting sport.

For some businesses, sponsorship deals that run to £750 000 or more are really just 'petty cash' when considering the massive advertising spending that may be going on at the same time. TV sponsorship has really come of age in the last few years. Just over half of advertisers and agencies were more likely to consider the possibilities of sponsoring TV programmes in 1995 than a year before.

Although around 80% of advertisers state that they do not have a specific sponsorship budget, they also state that, if they do use sponsorship, then the costs are not taken out of the advertising budget.

Some 42% of advertisers claim that TV sponsorship helped to build brand awareness, and 56% said that it improved the image of the business. Some of the more prominent TV sponsorship deals in 1994 were:

Programme and channel	*Sponsor*
Passengers (C4)	Pepsi
Don't Forget Your Toothbrush (C4)	Polaroid
Italian Football (C4)	Carlsberg Export
NFL (C4)	Budweiser
The Word (C4)	Swatch
Gamesmaster (C4)	McDonald's
World Cup (ITV)	Panasonic
Play Your Cards Right (ITV)	*The Sun*
You Bet (ITV)	*Daily Mirror*

Focus study

Sponsorship

Sponsors paid more than £152m to be associated with the World Cup Finals in 1994. That figure appears to be very small when we consider the amount that the top nineteen World Cup sponsors invested in advertising over the same period. This support advertising ran to a staggering £6.6bn worldwide!

The returns were great too, some 31bn people watching the World Cup Finals worldwide. However, the fact that England failed to make the finals cost an estimated £30m in lost advertising. The USA was the big market upon which the sponsors wished to have an impact. The organisers of the World Cup held in the USA, aware that football was a rather unknown and unloved sport compared to baseball, American football, ice hockey and basketball, spent an estimated £20m on promoting the event to the Americans.

The two-tier sponsorship deals managed to attract some of the household names such as Coca-Cola, McDonald's and General Motors (each paying between £10m and £13m). The second tier, or 'marketing partners', paid around £4.6m each.

McDonald's final bill, in sponsorship-related costs, ran to £46m. They were more than pleased with their investment; they believed that it would have been impossible to have gained by other means the exposure that the World Cup gave them with that level of spending.

PC 3.2.3
C 2.1

Group activity *Time: 20 minutes*

In pairs, try to identify some of the major sponsors of a current sporting event. Are any of the sponsors the same as for the 1994 World Cup? If you have seen a major sporting event on TV recently, do you think that the sponsors are getting good value for money? How often do you see their name or product name?

Competition

This form of sales promotion has a two-fold objective. Firstly, it seeks to maintain brand loyalty. Secondly, it hopes to increase the frequency of use and purchase from existing customers. It is unlikely that new customers will be necessarily attracted to the product just because of the competition. The competition must offer attractive and desirable prizes or a good cash win. Each and every entrant to the competition must have a fair chance of winning. Competitions are subject to tight controls and must conform to legislation. This is related to the element of skill involved, the entrant usually having to put a number of points or features of the product in order and then complete a 'tie breaker'. The tie-breaker is usually a slogan or something similar that begins, for example, with: 'Yum Yum breakfast cereal is a great start to the day because . . .' Competitions are very good tools in convincing retailers to give the product extra shelf space.

3.2.4 Explain the purpose of the planned promotional materials

Purpose

The term 'promotion' is a general one. It refers to any organisation which aims to do one of the following:

- *To communicate a message to an audience*
- *To create sales*
- *To influence customer perceptions*
- *To provide information*

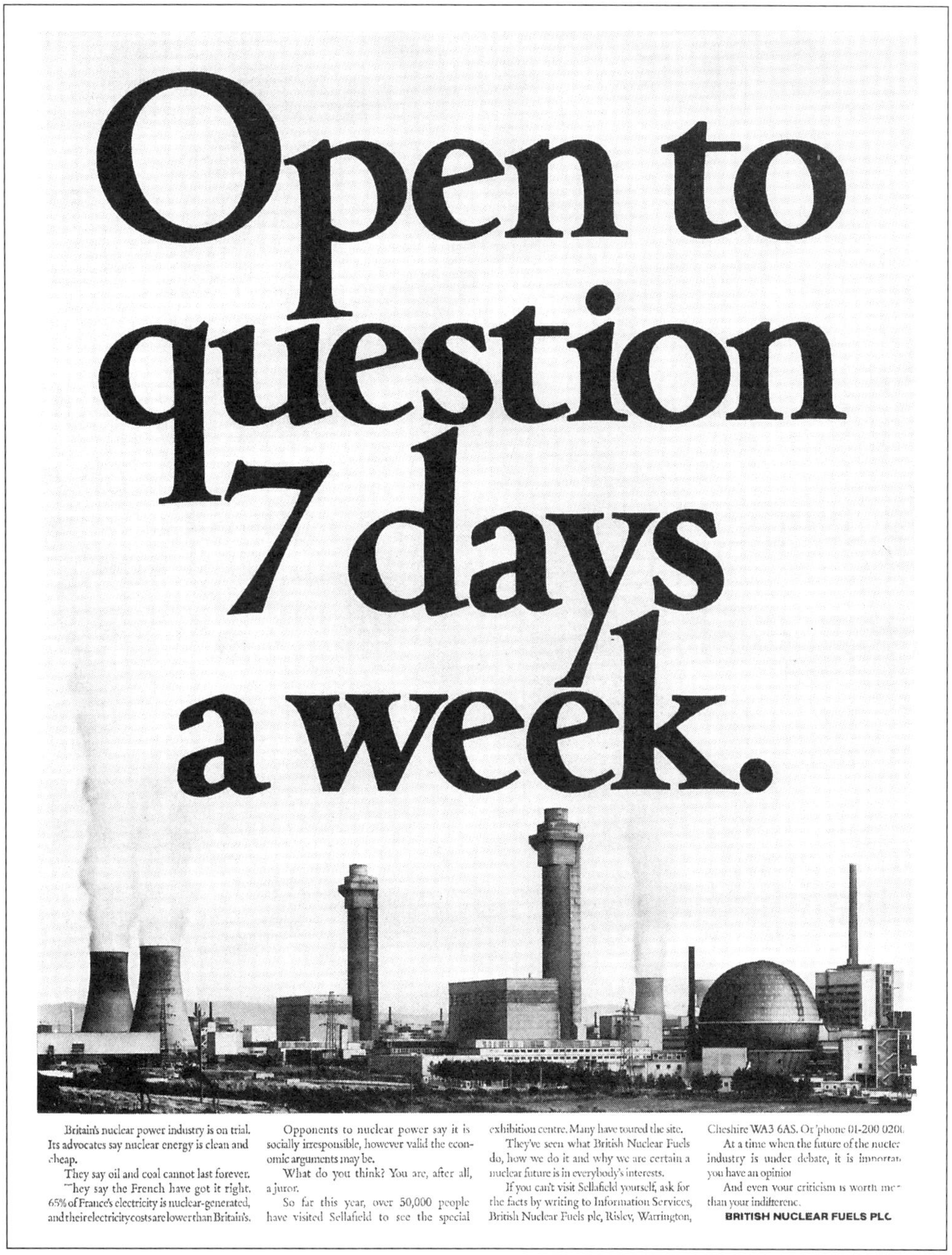

Fig 3.18 A BNFL advertisement which both raises consumer awareness and offers the opportunity for personal visits to the site in Cheshire

Let us have a look at those aims in a little more detail.

To communicate a message to an audience

1 The first aim of this technique is to try to convince the customer that they would benefit from the purchase of the product or service.

2 The second aim is to try to give the customer as much information as they need to assist them in deciding whether the product or service would be useful to them.
3 The third aim is to tell the customer about any benefits or advantages this product has over the competition, and whether the product or service has been modified or improved since the last time they bought (or thought about buying) the product or service.
4 The fourth aim is to try to inform the customer of any special offers available, such as reduced prices or extra value for money.
5 The fifth aim is to try to get the customer to remember the name of the product or service.
6 The sixth, and final, aim is to try to get the customer to remember the name of the organisation that is offering the product or service and any other information (such as telephone number or shop opening hours).

PC 3.2.4
C 2.1
C 2.2
C 2.3

Group activity *Time: 45 minutes*

In pairs, design an advertisement which attempts to create a demand for a product or service. The choice of product is yours. Try out your advertisement on the rest of your group. Does it work? Are the others convinced that they want your product?

To create sales

1 The first aim of this technique is to attempt to tell the customer where they can obtain the product or service.
2 The second aim is to attempt to tell the customer how they can obtain the product or service.
3 The third aim is to try to obtain and maintain the customer's loyalty to the product, service or organisation.
4 The fourth aim is to explain that the product or service offered is much better than any of the competition.
5 The fifth aim is to try to get across the fact that the organisation offers a range of products and services. All of these products and services offer the same standard of excellence.

PC 3.2.4
C 2.1
C 2.2

Group activity *Time: 45 minutes*

Again in pairs, think of some phrases or slogans that organisations have used to try to create sales. Are they interesting and convincing enough to work?

Having made this list, now try to create some of your own. Are they any better? If so, why? If not, what makes the professionals' ones better?

To influence customers' perception

1 The first aim of this technique is to try to heighten customer awareness of the organisation in general.
2 The second aim is to try and create a positive image of the organisation and its range of products and services.
3 The third aim is to inform the customer about the range of possibilities offered by the organisation, in terms of products and services as well as advice and guidance
4 The fourth aim is to link any popular public trends (such as environmental issues) with the organisation's range of products and services.
5 The fifth aim is to link the range of products and services with any recent changes in legislation.

PC 3.2.4
C 2.1

Individual activity

Individually, over the next few days monitor your local independent television station. Pay particular attention to the advertisements. How much do they really tell you about the organisation that produces the products or services which they are promoting? Do you actually remember anything about the advertisement they are promoting? Do you actually remember anything about the advertisement apart from the product or service itself? What kind of image is the organisation trying to create with the style of advertisement it is using?

After your period of investigation, feed back your ideas to the rest of the group.

To provide information

There is a statutory or legal obligation for the organisation to provide clear and accurate information regarding its products or services. It is, however, a good idea for the organisation to make sure that the customer receives the highest level of information and accuracy before, during and after the sales process. Dependent upon the distribution or sales channel chosen by the organisation, this will be more or less in the control of the manufacturer or original supplier. Obviously, the more distance there is between the manufacturer or supplier and the end user, the less control the former has on the information. In such situations, the manufacturer would be at pains to ensure that at every point or stage in the distribution process sufficient information, either in terms of sales literature or training, is passed down from level to level. Some organisations value the use of mass product briefing sessions to stockists or distributors of the product; others will support the sales force at the point of sale with regular visits by experienced sales representatives. The distribution of printed materials is essential and often undertaken with the assistance of the retail outlets. Joint publications of sales literature or mini-catalogues are fairly routine in this area.

These techniques can be best remembered by using a word which is made up from the first letter of the following words. The key word to remember all of this is AIDA.

- ATTENTION – get the customer's attention by showing them something that they will remember.
- INTEREST – try using some trick or design that will make the customer read or watch your advertisement. These may include special offers.
- DESIRE – make the customer really want your product or service. Tell them that they will really benefit from buying it.
- ACTION – this is the real key to it all. Make it as easy as possible for the customer to obtain your product or service.

3.2.5 Design and produce promotional materials and use them to promote goods or services

In order to carry out this performance criteria you will need actually to create some promotional materials. You may wish to use your own ideas or an idea suggested by your tutor. If not, we have suggested a product in this performance criteria for you to try.

PC 3.2.5
C 2.1
C 2.2
C 2.3
C 2.4

Group activity (part 1)

Time:1.5 hours

In pairs, try to create an advertisement for the following product. You should attempt throughout to identify the stages of the creation of the advertisement.

- *Product name*: Surfer
- *Product type*: Computer Game
- *Features*: simulation of surfing in a variety of wave types. Wave types are randomly generated by the computer. Compete against all the superstars of surfing.
- *Other details*: available for all popular computer formats
- *Price*: £10.99–£39.99, depending on format
- *Produced by*: Simo-Graphics Inc

Once you have completed this task, compare your advertisement with the rest of your group.

PC 3.2.5
C 2.1
C 2.2
C 2.3
C 2.4

Group activity (part 2)

Having produced the advertisement in the previous activity, you will be pleased to know that 'Surfer' is selling really well. You have been approached by a small publishing company which is interested in producing a magazine based around your computer game.

In the same pairs, you need to do some research into the existing magazines available. In order to assist you in this task, the following suggestions might be useful:

- **Try several magazine stockists, and list all the competing magazines you can find in each outlet. You will also need to note the prices of each of the titles you find.**
- **When you have ascertained who your immediate competitors are going to be, research what types of promotional offers they are using. It may be that they have some kind of competition running at the moment, or they are offering special discounts for customers of the magazine.**

Once you have completed the above task, you need to decide the following:

1. **The name and price of your magazine**
2. **How you intend to promote the magazine**
3. **The style and layout of the front cover of your magazine**

The completed assignment should include details of all the research you have carried out. In addition to this report, you will be required to present your intentions for the finished product style to the rest of your group, who will take the role of editors for the publishing company.

3.2.6 Evaluate how successful the promotional materials were in achieving the stated purpose

Referring back to performance criteria 3.2.4, you will find our suggestions regarding the following:

- *effectiveness in communicating to an audience*
- *effectiveness in creating sales*
- *influence on customers' perceptions*
- *effectiveness in providing information*

Since this performance criteria forms an integral part of the Element assignment, you should attempt to evaluate your work on Surfer as a preparation for the Element assignment.

Individual activity

Time: 1 hour

Create a questionnaire which addresses the four measures of effectiveness and influence given above. Duplicate at least 25 of the questionnaires for your assessment.

PC 3.2.6
C 2.2
C 2.3
C 2.4

Whatever type of promotion is considered, there are three main stages in the development of the advertising messages: generating the idea; selecting the idea from the various options; and making the idea a reality. Let us look at them in a little more detail:

1 When the message is first looked at, the creativity of the advertising agency is given full rein. The objective is to come up with an idea for communicating the message in the most interesting way. It should be different from others, if possible, and have the strength to be noticed. Above all it should be remembered that any attributes that the product or service has over its competitors should be stressed as much as possible.
2 Having partially developed several ways of communicating the message, the competing ideas have to be tested. Sampling is done by showing 'rough' versions of the ideas to members of the target audience. They are asked to compare the ideas with existing advertisements from competitors. The idea that they remember best should be the agency's best idea on offer.
3 Advertisements need to be produced well. A high standard of work is demanded, with the best technical skills available. Good ideas can be let down by poor photography or sound. In magazine and newspaper advertisements the balance of words and picture is important and the advertisements should never look cluttered or messy.

Having decided on the creative side of the advertisement, the next decision is to choose the media. There is a very wide choice of different media that includes over a dozen daily national papers, hundreds of regional ones, some 16 independent TV stations, satellite TV, over 50 independent radio stations, around 1000 cinemas, hundreds of magazines and periodicals, outdoor advertising opportunities and much more. Quite a choice, so where should the advertiser start?

When planning a media campaign, the first two things to think about are how many of the target audience, as a minimum, are to get the message and, equally as important, the number of times that the advertisement is to be run. In other words, the two key considerations are *coverage* and *frequency*. There are a number of factors to look at that will affect this decision:

1 The budget available can be a very limiting factor. On a limited budget the more expensive forms of media must be ruled out. The choice for the advertisement planned on a low budget is between the cheaper forms of media; television, for example, must be ruled out completely.
2 Having an accurate idea of the profile of the target audience is important. The amount of information which has to be amassed about the target audience will depend on the particular product.
3 By comparing the media's profile of the target audiences, the planner can then attempt to match the product and message with the right media. It is unlikely that any one medium will get the message to all of the proposed target audiences, in which case several different media will have to be used. Here are approximate figures based on the number of adults that might see advertisements in particular media:

- *Outdoor advertisements (posters, buses, etc)*: nearly all of the adult population
- *Television advertisements*: over 90%
- *Sunday newspapers*: around three-quarters of the adult population
- *Daily newspapers*: nearly 70%
- *Radio*: nearly 40%
- *Weekly magazines*: around 40%
- *Monthly magazines*: between 30 and 40%
- *Cinemas*: less than 3%

This is known as 'opportunity to see' or OTS and is the basic measure of the potential coverage of each major medium.

4 Unfortunately it is not quite as simple as this. If the planner could choose their medium by only considering its effectiveness, then life would be easy. The question of cost-effectiveness must be looked at. It costs more, amazingly, to advertise in certain media than in others. Not surprising, you might say. Your £1 goes further in some media than in others and these costs are compared below. The cost is per thousand of the adult population:

- *Outdoor advertisements*: around 30p
- *Television*: about £3.25 (varies according to region)
- *Newspapers*: nearly £3.00
- *Magazines and colour supplements*: roughly £1.40 but differs greatly according to the magazine's popularity
- *Cinema*: a massive £18.00+!
- *Radio*: around 80p

This price comparison is not entirely fair as we have not considered the size, length or colours used for the advertisement. As a rule there are some average sizes and typical methods of use, and these are what the prices above are based on. Here are some examples:

- *Newspapers*: a full page black and white advertisement
- *Colour supplements*: a full page colour advertisement
- *TV*: a 30-second slot
- *Outdoor*: is a very rough average since the costs of the advertising position differ enormously

5 As we have already mentioned you can advertise on TV, or elsewhere for that matter, and still not make an impact. You can look at the cost-effectiveness of different media, choose the best for your budget and still not have an impact. The key is the frequency with which you advertise. Marketing writers have called this the 'threshold'. What they mean is that you have to advertise beyond a certain limit in order to have any effect at all. This is worked out on the OTS (opportunity to see) basis, so if you wanted the target to have 10 OTS then you would have to show the advertisement far more often than 10 times.

6 Having worked out the CPT (cost per thousand), this still isn't enough. As we have already seen, we are not comparing the different media fairly. We can only make assumptions and very rough comparisons between the different media. Certain media have advantages over others for certain products. When working out a media plan and schedule, the planner must consider the following:

- *The budget*
- *The right media to reach the right target audience*
- *Cover the whole audience (in other words make sure all of them are reached in some way)*

- *Make sure that the target audience has the opportunity to see the message*
- *Achieve this in a cost-effective way*
- *Make sure that the media help in increasing the impact of the message*

Taking account of all of these considerations means that the media planner has to compromise. The key considerations are the continuity of the campaign, the overall coverage (in different media, etc), the impact and the frequency. It is a rare media planner indeed that is capable of satisfying all these considerations.

PC 3.2.6
C 2.1

Individual activity *Time: 45 minutes*

In the role of a media planner, where would you choose to spend the majority of your advertising budget for the following products and services?

1. A cat food
2. A nutty chocolate bar
3. A 'designer' pen set
4. A new brand of recycled photocopy paper
5. A shock and water resistant watch

Compare your choice of media with those of the rest of your group.

Element 3.2 Assignment

PC 3.2.1–6
C 2.1
C 2.2
C 2.3
C 2.4
IT 2.1
IT 2.2
IT 2.3

In this assignment you will have to look at various types of promotional activities and carry out a number of evaluations. You can produce your own materials, or use materials provided by your tutor, or use material that has been in the media already.

Task 1 *PC 3.2.1–2*

Give examples of *three* types of promotion, which should include at least one sponsorship and one advertisement. Describe the following aspects regarding them:

- What is the product or service being promoted?
- What is the content of the promotion?
- What are the constraints on the content with regard to the Consumer Protection Act and the Advertising Standards Authority?

Task 2 *PC 3.2.3–4*

Create a plan which explains the purpose of the selected promotional materials and give estimates for the following:

- The implications
- The human resources needed
- The materials and equipment needed
- The costs to produce the materials

Task 3 *PC 3.2.5*

Design promotional materials for one of the chosen products, which should include one of the following:

- An advertisement for the product
- An outline for a sponsorship scheme
- Details of a competition

The promotional material should be one of the following types:

- A poster
- A leaflet
- A video
- An audio tape
- A computer-generated advertisement

Task 4 *PC 3.2.6*

You should now summarise, in note form, an evaluation of the promotional material that you have produced. This should be in relation to:

- Whether you have achieved your stated aims
- Whether you have achieved your stated purpose
- What was the response of the audience

You can achieve this by creating a questionnaire for the audience to fill in after they have seen/heard your advertisement or details of the competition or sponsorship.

Notes

In all cases you can substitute the word ‘product’ for ‘service’. Your work should be generated by use of computer software.

Element 3.3
Providing customer service

Performance criteria

A student must:

1 identify an organisation's customers and its **customer needs**

2 identify and describe **customer service** in an organisation

3 identify **business communications** which meet customer needs

4 demonstrate business communications which meet customers' needs

5 describe procedures in one business organisation for dealing with customer complaints

6 identify relevant **legislation** to protect customers

Range

- *Customer needs*: wishing to make a purchase, to obtain information, to obtain a refund, to exchange goods, to make a complaint, for special needs, ethical standards
- *Customer service*: meeting the needs of internal and external customers, providing help or information (for individuals, business organisations)
- *Business communications*: oral (face-to-face, telephone), written (letter, memo) customer/product information (statement of account, prices, guarantees, safety notices)
- *Legislation*: Trade Descriptions, Sale of Goods, Consumer Protection, Health and Safety at Work

3.3.1 Identify an organisation's customers and its customer needs

Customer needs

The needs of the customer have been discussed at various points elsewhere in the book. However, we can summarise the factors involved by looking at the following considerations:

- *The organisation must be able to establish what the customer needs are*
- *The organisation needs to interpret them into clear needs*
- *The organisation needs to mirror these needs in the production and distribution of products and services*
- *The organisation also needs to ensure that any products or services provided meet exacting quality standards in order to achieve long-term customer satisfaction and probable repeat sales*

Wishing to make a purchase

If there is one thing that will ensure that a potential customer becomes a non-customer, it is the non-availability of the product. If the customer experiences difficulties in either finding a stock of a product, or, once having found this outlet, discovers that the purchasing process is complex, then they will turn to an alternative product and supplier. Obviously, to solve this potential problem and facilitate an immediate and simple purchasing process, the organisation must have chosen wisely in its distribution or sales channels. As we have already discussed earlier, different products have different levels of availability, often related to some form of perceived exclusivity. This is also the case for products of a technical or complex nature, since only competent stockists with expert staff on hand can accurately match the product with the customer needs.

If we consider that the customer now has the choice of shopping locally, or in a shopping centre, or in an out of town site, or by phone or from a catalogue, there appears to be no area that has not been exploited by manufacturers, suppliers and retailers. Shopping has never been easier or more simple. Without doubt shopping will become even easier in the future, particularly with the development of new telecommunication systems which enable the customer to purchase a variety of goods from home.

To obtain information

There is a statutory or legal obligation for the organisation to provide clear and accurate information regarding its products or services. It is, however, advantageous for the organisation to make sure that the customer receives the highest level of information and accuracy before, during and after the sales process. Dependent upon the distribution or sales channel chosen by the organisation, this will be more or less in the control of the manufacturer or original supplier. Obviously, the more distance there is between the manufacturer or supplier and the end user, the less control the former has on the information transmission system. In such situations, the manufacturer would be at pains to ensure at every point or stage in the distribution process that sufficient information, either in terms of sales literature or training, is passed down from level to level. Some organisations value the use of mass product briefing sessions to stockists or distributors of the product, or will support the sales force at the point of sale with regular visits by experienced sales representatives. The dissemination of printed material is essential and often undertaken with the assistance of the retail outlets. Joint publication of sales literature or mini-catalogues is fairly routine in this area.

To obtain a refund

If a customer is concerned with obtaining a refund or replacement, then the employee should be aware of the organisation's policy in these matters. If the employee does not have the authority to refund or replace, then he/she should always refer the matter to a senior member of staff who should be aware of the policy.

Some retail outlets will have special cash registers which are only used when money needs to be refunded to a customer. Marks & Spencer is a particularly good example of this, and has a 'no quibble' refund policy.

Research has shown that customers are more inclined to purchase from a retail outlet which provides a clear receipt as this is not only proof of purchase but also a guarantee that a refund will be given if the product proves to be unsuitable in some way. It should be noted that refunds are generally given in the same manner as the payment was made; in other words, a cash sale is refunded in cash, but a credit card sale is refunded by the use of a credit card refund voucher.

To exchange goods

As with refunds, there are occasions when a customer may request that a product be exchanged for another item of stock. Again, the employee will need to know the exchange policy of the organisation and should always check the item for signs of use, damage or missing parts. Providing the product appears to be in good order, then an exchange may be undertaken. This is, of course, assuming that the customer has some form of proof that they purchased the product from that retail outlet, or at least from part of the chain of retail outlets. It is an all too common occurrence that certain individuals attempt to exchange for other items goods which were purchased elsewhere or perhaps obtained in a less legal manner.

PC 3.3.1
C 2.1

Group activity *Time: 20 minutes*

In pairs, simulate your response to the following refund or replacement queries:

1 A customer enters a record shop and produces a CD. The customer explains that this CD was purchased on their behalf by a friend as a birthday present. Unfortunately the customer already has this CD but has no means of proving that the CD was purchased in this shop.

►

2 **An elderly gentleman returns to a large do-it-yourself superstore. He is dragging behind him a petrol mower. Walking up to the customer service desk he explains that the mower refuses to start. Upon questioning him on the procedures in starting the lawn mower, he confesses that he has filled the fuel tank with diesel.**

3 **A customer returns to a car spares outlet, having purchased, only a matter of hours before, a can of undercoat spray. Having prepared the surface of his car and masked off the areas he did not wish to spray, he followed the instructions on the can and proceeded spraying on to the bodywork. He now has a red car with a large patch of bright green paint. The label had claimed to be white primer. Since the car is not very old, he is very annoyed.**

4 **A young woman returns to a clothes shop, clasping a carrier bag containing a dress. She has proof of purchase and the garment was definitely purchased from this outlet. She purchased the garment very late on Saturday afternoon. It is now lunchtime on Monday. She claims that she has changed her mind and does not like the garment any more. Upon close examination the garment has a stain and shows signs of having been worn.**

To make a complaint

A customer may be dissatisfied for a number of reasons, including the following:

- The product which they purchased is faulty
- They require a product which is either not stocked or is out of stock
- They have received poor service
- They have a problem with which nobody seems to be able to help them

In many cases organisations will have a formal complaints procedure for customers who are dissatisfied. It is usual practice for complaints to be referred to the manager, who has the authority of the organisation to act on its behalf and make any on-the-spot decisions to help rectify the situation. There are some key stages here which, regardless of the formal complaints procedure, should be followed:

1. *When listening to the complaint, give the customer the opportunity to explain the situation and do not interrupt*
2. *Always appear to be sympathetic to the customer*
3. *In particularly complicated cases make sure that you write down all the details*
4. *When you have done this, check the main points of the complaint with the customer*
5. *Even if the customer is abusive, always try to remain calm and polite*
6. *If you feel you cannot solve the situation yourself, keep calm and refer the matter to a senior member of staff*
7. *Never give the customer a vague response or an unbelievable excuse*
8. *Never blame anyone else directly*
9. *Even if provoked, do not lose your temper*
10. *Never try to infer that the complaint is not really a problem; it is a problem in the eyes of the customer*
11. *Always tell the customer exactly what you are going to do, particularly if this involves having to refer to another person or company*
12. *Above all, never make any promises which you cannot personally fulfil or ensure will be fulfilled*

For special needs

When we consider that each customer is an individual, we can see that they may have a range of special needs which will require a different level of service. We can identify the following types of customer who may have special needs and attempt to look at any special services which they may require, these are:

1. **Children** – unless you are involved in a retail outlet, it is highly unlikely that day-to-day contact with children as customers will be normal. It is not always the case that these children will be accompanied by adults and it is in this respect that children may require special levels of service. The child may not be able to communicate on an adult level and may need additional assistance when either choosing or paying for the product. It is always advisable to treat a child just as you would treat an adult; you should not assume that because of their relatively tender age they are incapable.
2. **Special needs** – this rather broad category includes customers with hearing difficulties, the blind or partially sighted and the physically and mentally handicapped. Each will have his or her own particular requirements and many retail outlets, in particular, have taken steps to ensure that both store access and layout facilitate ease of use.
3. **Foreign customers** – the majority of overseas visitors may have some ability to speak and understand English. However, this may not be the case with overseas customers who are attempting to purchase products via the telephone. In larger organisations, attempts will have been made to identify employees who are able to speak foreign languages and these individuals may be contacted in the event of any communication problems.

Ethical standards

At all times, employees should avoid misleading a customer in any way. Honesty can relate to descriptions of products, promises of service, promises of delivery or promises of after-sales service. Perhaps the most serious thing is to lie about the capabilities of a product. If an employee is guilty of this, they may be contravening the Sales of Goods Act, the Trade Descriptions Act and, perhaps, the Consumer Protection Act. This may lead to heavy penalties being paid by the organisation.

An additional point to make is that statements by employees which may not necessarily be illegal in themselves, can cause a great deal of ill-feeling on the side of the customer.

PC 3.3.1
C 2.1

Group activity

Time: 20 minutes

In pairs, consider the following problems faced by an estate agent. Estate agents are now obliged to give purely descriptive statements regarding properties under the Property Misdescription Act. In the role of an estate agent, how would you describe the following properties without falling foul of the Act.

1. **The house is semi-derelict and has been vacant for ten years**
2. **The house is a small terraced property which faces a busy railway viaduct**
3. **The property is a spacious flat which has been recently refurbished after an extensive fire**

Compare your considerations with those of the rest of the group.

3.3.2 Identify and describe customer service in an organisation

Customer service

As we have seen, the goals of customer service will differ from organisation to organisation. They will also differ in relation to the demands or needs of the customer.

This performance criteria asks you to look at the specific customer services provided by an organisation of your choice. This forms an integral part of the Element assignment.

We have covered many of the customer service requirements in relation to sales, complaints, information and problems which relate to external customers. We should also mention the needs of internal customers, particularly in relation to help they may need and information they may be seeking.

Meeting the needs of internal and external customers and providing help or information (for individuals, business organisations)

In any organisation, regardless of its size, certain departments or divisions will have to service other parts of the organisation. This is particularly true of the following departments:

- *Accounts*
- *Administration*
- *Personnel*
- *Sales*

Whether they require assistance in the form of a specific project or whether they require information, they should be treated in exactly the same way as you would treat an external customer. A professional and courteous service should always be provided. While no money will actually change hands, in some cases departments will 'charge' other departments for services provided (such as a reprographics unit charging the various departments for photocopies).

3.3.3 Identify business communications which meet customer needs

3.3.4 Demonstrate business communications which meet customer needs

We have taken these two performance criteria together since PC 3.3.3 provides the guidelines and PC 3.3.4 asks you to put them into practice. If you try out some of the student activities, you will be able to prepare yourself for the Element assignment.

Business communications

The way in which a customer views an organisation is often coloured by the way in which an individual from that organisation deals with them. In this sense, the first impression that a customer gets of the organisation is vitally important.

Whether the communication is face-to-face, via a telephone, letter or fax, the way in which the member of the organisation conducts themselves is equally important.

Oral (face-to-face, telephone)

Being a good communicator comes with practice and experience. Here are some of the key things to remember when you are communicating. It does not matter who you communicate with – it could be friends, parents, teachers or potential employers – they will all gain an impression of you and how you conduct yourself, by what you say and how you say it.

1. *You should always speak clearly*
2. *You should not speak too quickly or too slowly*
3. *You should use the right words for the situation, not be too complicated or simplistic*
4. *You should be able to listen to what the other person is saying so that you can respond properly*
5. *You should show confidence, both in yourself and what you say*
6. *You should try to put the other person at their ease*
7. *You should think about what you say and try to make your response logical and easy to follow*
8. *You should try to use the right tone for the situation, not be too aggressive, passive or allow your feelings to confuse what it is you have to say*
9. *While a regional accent is fine in most situations, if it is too strong or broad, talk slightly slower than normal*
10. *If you think that your voice is not pleasant to listen to, or perhaps too high, try to alter or lower the pitch a little. You can help counter this problem by controlling your excitement or speed of talking*
11. *You should never interrupt someone who is speaking; wait until they are finished*
12. *Take care to use the right tone, as, even if you say the same thing, the tone you use may make what you say acceptable or unacceptable to the other person*

PC 3.3.3
PC 3.3.4
C 2.1

Group activity

In groups of three, try to identify any phrases, words or expressions which you commonly use, but would not be acceptable when talking to a customer. Over the next week, attempt to eliminate these from your day-to-day speech and use other, more acceptable terms instead.

After a week, see how you have coped and compare your feelings with those of the rest of the group.

Although you may not have heard of it, we all use non-verbal communication (NVC). It is important to know how to use it, what it means and how to read other people's NVC. Let us start with the face and what that can give away about what a person is really saying!

- *Raising the eyebrows could show surprise or disbelief*
- *If pupils dilate, this could mean anger or love*
- *Opening the eyes wide might show hostility*
- *Grinning would show that you accept what is being said or are simply friendly*

We are sure that you can think of many more of these facial expressions. Gestures, on the other hand (no pun intended), can also give interesting clues as to what the speaker really means.

- *Pointing, to identify someone or something directly when referring to it*
- *Giving a thumbs-up sign, to signify agreement or acceptance*
- *Shaking your head, to show disagreement*
- *Fiddling with something, such as jewellery, a tie or the strap of a bag may infer nervousness*
- *Pacing up and down may show impatience or boredom*
- *Looking at your hands, or fiddling with something may show disinterest*

Posture shows some interesting things too:

- *Standing upright shows alertness*
- *Sitting in a hunched position shows nervousness*
- *Lounging in a chair, on the other hand, shows ease*
- *Standing with your shoulders hunched, shows that you are miserable or depressed*

Where you are standing or sitting, in relation to the person to whom you are talking, can show some important things:

- *You are likely to stand closer to a person that you know well*
- *Where you stand, and how close, to a person may depend on your nationality or upbringing*
- *The nature of the circumstances in which you meet people will have an effect on how close you stand to them*

PC 3.3.3
PC 3.3.4
C 2.1

Group activity

Time: 15 minutes

Working in pairs, in order to highlight the ways in which we use gestures subconsciously, try to describe a spiral staircase to your partner without using your hands.

Face to face

When actually communicating directly with someone, you will use a mixture of verbal and non-verbal communication. You will also be able to see what they are feeling by taking careful note of their non-verbal communication.

When talking to a customer, regardless of whether they are a new customer or an established one, an employee should remember the following rules:

1 *Always be polite*
2 *Always try to be helpful*
3 *Try not to distract them with an irritating habit (such as chewing gum or sniffing)*
4 *Help to make the customer feel valued; use their name in the conversation*
5 *Always close the conversation by saying 'goodbye', otherwise the suspicion is of unfinished business*

Regular customers are vitally important to any organisation. A great deal of hard work, not to mention advertising and other costs, have been incurred in making a buyer a regular customer. It is, therefore, essential to build and maintain customer relations. Poor customer relations can ruin the work of months or years.

1 *Always use the customer's name when greeting them*
2 *Give the customer favourable treatment, such as refreshments, offering them a seat or literature regarding the organisation.*
3 *Try to remember something about them or their family. Failing that, try to remember something about their business.*
4 *Always try to tell regular customers the truth, inform them of special offers pending, or changes in stock before they actually happen.*

Even when dealing with new customers, an employee should always observe the following conventions:

1 *Greet the customers*
2 *Be friendly*
3 *Be helpful and tell them you are there for their benefit*
4 *Do not harass the customers; let them have time to look before pouncing on them!*
5 *Be available if they look as if they need help*

PC 3.3.3
PC 3.3.4
C 2.1
C 2.2

Group activity *Time: 20 minutes*

In pairs, write a list of instructions for a new member of staff whose responsibilities will include the greeting of customers.

Discuss the items appearing on your list with those of the rest of the group.

Telephone

The basic problem with communication via the telephone is that there is no non-verbal communication to fall back on.

To make the most effective use of the telephone, try to remember the following points:

1 *Always pick up the telephone as quickly as possible*

2 *Always have a pen and paper handy to take messages*

(Courtesy of Peugeot Talbot)

3 *Always be helpful and polite*

4 *If the caller needs information that is not readily to hand, then phone them back*

5 *If you have promised to call back a customer, do not forget to do so*

(Courtesy of Peugeot Talbot)

6 *Always remember that, unless the caller is put on hold, they will be able to hear what is said*

7 *Make sure you do not give out confidential information without checking with a superior first*

(Courtesy of Peugeot Talbot)

(Courtesy of Peugeot Talbot)

8 *If the call is interrupted and the customer is cut off, then the person who made the call should always ring back*

9 *In order to make sure that facts are correct, figures right or a complicated name is spelt correctly, it is acceptable to ask the caller to repeat these. If there is any uncertainty, repeat the message back to them*

10 *If asked for details or information, make sure when ringing back with this that all the necessary information is to hand*

11 *Always quote figures in pairs as they are easier to understand and remember*

12 *Always complete the call by saying 'thank you'*

If a caller wants someone who is not available this procedure should be followed:

1 *Having established that the person to whom they want to speak is not available, ask if there is someone else who can help them*

2 *Offer to help*

3 *If this is not acceptable, then either ask the caller to ring back, or promise to get the person who they wanted to call them back*

4 *If necessary, take a message and ensure that it gets to the right person*

If taking a call for someone who is available, this procedure should be followed:

1 *After the caller has asked to speak to someone in particular, ask who is calling*

2 *Ask the caller to hold the line, while you find or contact the person whom they need*

3 *Contact the person required and say who is calling, and if relevant, what the call is about*

PC 3.3.3
PC 3.3.4
C 2.1
C 2.2

Group activity *Time: 10 minutes*

In pairs, start a conversation with your partner. After two minutes, change position so that you are now back to back. Try to continue the conversation for another two minutes.

Having done this, quickly write down what differences you felt that not facing your partner had on the conversation. Were you able to concentrate? Did you feel you were listening or being listened to? Were there gaps in the conversation? Did you feel ignored?

Now change places and repeat the procedure with your partner making the conversation.

Compare the feelings you experienced with those of your partner.

Written (letter, memo)

In our day-to-day life we use written communication. It is just as important when writing a personal letter to a friend or a note to one of the family that we ensure our spelling and grammar are correct.

In all organisations, neat, accurate and reliable written communications are vitally important.

Written communication in the business world takes several forms. In this section, we will be concentrating on the two most common types. These are the letter and the memorandum (or memo).

Letters

Usually we will find a letter being used for communications outside the organisation. A typical example is that of responding to a customer query or complaint. As we will see in Unit 4, the format of a business letter is rather strict. You should always follow the style and conventions that we have detailed there. Using headed paper showing the name and address of your organisation is an absolute must at all times. This establishes where the letter has come from and stamps a certain level of authority on the communication.

Memorandum

These are almost always used as strictly internal forms of communication. Again, we have looked at the memorandum in Unit 4 and you will find a description of its uses and style there. Normally, the memo will be used to request information, provide information or as a response to a request from another member of the organisation. Memos can be quite formal in their style, but can sometimes be rather more informative and conventional than a letter. Using the standard format of a memo, it is clear where the message has come from, to whom it is written, and the subject matter of the communication. It may be possible to format the memo as a series of points, all of which can be responded to in the order that they were featured on the original communication.

Customer/product information (statement of account, prices, guarantees, safety notices)

Another reason why an organisation would communicate with a customer is to provide information that the customer may have requested. This information may be with regard to the following:

1 *Information about a particular product* – in which case the organisation would either send an information leaflet or make an appointment for a representative to call.
2 *Information regarding the account of the customer* – a statement of account would be sent out regularly to purchasing organisations to inform them of the transactions which have taken place during the period in question and the balance that the customer owes the organisation.
3 *Information regarding the prices of some of the organisation's products* – in which case the customer would be sent a price list or would be asked if they would like a representative to call.
4 *Information regarding the guarantees on products offered by the organisation* – in which case the customer would be sent either a leaflet or a copy of the organisation's details about its after-sales service.

Another way in which a customer may be provided with information regarding the organisation is by the display of notices. Such notices might inform the customer about the health and safety procedures undertaken within the organisation. Alternatively, they might describe a new product or service offered by the organisation. On the other hand, the notices might simply state the fire procedures and clearly display the fire exit routes from the organisation.

3.3.5 Describe procedures in one business organisation for dealing with customer complaints

This performance criteria forms an integral part of the Element assignment. However, it is worth identifying some of the key considerations in relation to customer service and customer complaints. We have also included a section on the differences between the private and the public sector, which you may find useful in trying to decide which type of organisation to investigate for your Element assignment.

Remember that every organisation will have a different set of procedures and rules governing complaints procedure and there is no reason why one system is better than another.

Many organisations consider themselves to be fully aware of the needs and wants of their customers. Indeed, all of their activities revolve around the satisfaction of customers. Organisations consider customers to be of vital importance, since they are the key to business success. If an organisation manages to keep the customer in mind at all times, then inevitably it will increase its market share, provide better services than those of competitors, and will maintain its current customers and attract new ones.

The exact nature of customer service may differ slightly, depending upon the sector in which the organisation operates. In this respect, our concern is with two major sectors. We will look at these shortly.

What exactly are customer services? Let us try to identify them:

- *Giving the customer information and help*
- *Processing refunds and dealing with replacements*
- *Handling customer complaints*

(Courtesy of Peugeot Talbot)

- *Giving advice on after-sales service*
- *Taking steps to prove that the organisation is interested in the needs and wants of the customer*
- *Answering the telephone promptly*
- *Replying to all forms of communication made by customers*
- *Trying to avoid releasing any confusing or misleading information*
- *Always being polite and courteous*
- *Offering a quality service throughout all aspects of the business activity*
- *Trying to remember the names of all regular customers*

Group activity *Time: 15 minutes*

In pairs, in the role of owners of a fish and chip shop, which of the above would you think are important customer service considerations for your establishment?

PC 3.3.5
C 2.1

Let us now consider the two principle sectors:

Private sector organisations

These are primarily interested in profits. It is a simple equation – the more customers, the more sales, the more profit. An organisation which has this equation in mind will try to find out exactly what a customer wants. It will take all steps necessary to ensure that it can provide everything the customer might need. It will even take account of possible changes in trends and fashions to try to predict what customers might need in the future. As we have already seen, an organisation which takes all of the above into consideration can be called a market-orientated organisation.

Public sector organisations

These did not have to consider customer service to any great extent until recently. They did not have to worry about profits since they were financed by central or local government. The situation has changed to some extent, but we have seen great changes in the attitudes of public sector organisations, which have become aware of the demands of customers and how these relate to the organisation's possibility of survival. Hospitals, for example, now face the prospect of competition from the private sector. Even tax offices have implemented a customer service programme which aims to deal with customers courteously and efficiently. To ensure that some of the larger public corporations deal with customers in a fair manner, the government has set up a 'watchdog' or 'ombudsman' to monitor their behaviour. Privatisation may just be round the corner for many of the public sector organisations, so they need to prepare themselves and adopt the customer service techniques in common practice in the private sector.

3.3.6 Identify relevant legislation to protect customers

Legislation

We have already looked at the key legislation in Unit 2 of this learning programme. In this section, therefore, rather than dwelling on the same information, we will take a slightly broader view and consider some of the other organisations and pieces of legislation which aim to protect customers.

Until less than 30 years ago, there was little or no protection for consumers under the law. In fact, the phrase that was most often used was 'Let the buyer beware'. In other words, consumers had to rely on their own common sense and feelings as to whether a product was suitable or fit for use. Nowadays, however, there are certain standards as laid down by law, as well as voluntary agreements and codes of practice adopted by industries or particular businesses.

The consumer can quite rightly expect to receive goods and services which not only match their description, but are not faulty, dangerous or unfit for use. Over the years, the law has developed to provide guidelines for transactions and to offer a means of dealing with disputes between the supplier and the consumer. The law further tries to address the imbalance between the power of a large organisation, which will have the backing of specialists and lawyers, and the vulnerability of the individual consumer.

- **Acts of Parliament** relating to consumer protection fall within both the civil and criminal areas of the law.
- **Civil law** covers disputes between individuals and suppliers. When a transaction is made, this is, in effect, a contract. If one side suffers a loss in any way from the contract, then the injured party may sue.
- **Criminal law** tends to cope with more widespread abuses related to sales transactions. If an organisation sells a product which is harmful or dangerous to the community in general, then it will be the government (through the Law Courts) which will take action against them. Under criminal law, an organisation or individual found guilty is liable to fines, imprisonment, or both.

As we have already said, when goods or services are provided, the consumer should expect that they are fit for the purpose for which they were intended. If a product does not meet the consumer's requirements, then they may expect a replacement. If the product is wholly unfit, then the consumer may expect their money back. These basic rights form part of the Sale of Goods Act. The companion law is the Trade Descriptions Act. This makes it a criminal offence to wrongly describe a product. In other words, any description of the product must be accurate.

- **The Weights and Measures Act** attempts to ensure that the weight or quantity stated on the box, container or bag matches that of the contents inside. It is an offence under this Act to claim a particular weight and supply a lighter one.
- **The Food and Drugs Act** deals specifically with food and medicines. Under this Act an organisation cannot supply a product which is harmful, and must always make sure that any instructions are clear as to the use or preparation of the product. For example,

uncooked red kidney beans contain a toxic substance which is eliminated by the correct cooking period. Suppliers of this product must ensure that any packaging states very clearly the potential hazards. Also under this Act, rules apply to certain prepared foodstuffs such as sausages. Sausages must contain a defined amount of meat in order to be called a sausage. If they do not, then they must be alternatively labelled.

The Citizen's Charter

The Citizen's Charter sets out consumer rights which indicate that, particularly as far as public services are concerned, the consumer should expect a certain level of service. It further states that if the service does not meet a certain level or standard, then the consumer should expect compensation. This system is regulated by a separate organisation and the Charter also suggests that once the services reach a certain standard then the organisation will be able to claim a 'chartermark'. This chartermark is expected to give consumers a clear indication that they will receive a high-quality service.

The first phase of the Citizen's Charter is for organisations to release a list of 'promises'. These promises clearly state exactly what the consumer should expect from that organisation. From this set of promises the consumer should now know what their rights are concerning services provided.

The main reason for the Citizen's Charter is to control publicly-run organisations, such as local authorities, and to maintain some level of control over 'opted-out' organisations, such as hospitals, schools and colleges.

PC 3.3.6
C 2.1
C 2.2

Group activity

Time: 45 minutes

In groups of three, in the role of manager of the local authority's refuse collection service, produce a Citizen's Charter covering your promises of service.

Compare your charter with those of the rest of the group.

Guarantee or warranty

A guarantee or warranty is basically an undertaking by the manufacturer to replace or repair the product, or parts of the product, should they prove to be defective. It further undertakes to do this free of charge, and as quickly as possible. A typical guarantee would include the following:

1. *The product will be repaired free of charge if faulty because of defective materials used.*
2. *The product will be repaired free of charge if faulty because of defective workmanship.*
3. *The product will be repaired free of charge if found faulty within the first 12 months.*
4. *The manufacturer will require a proof of purchase, such as a receipt or credit card voucher.*
5. *The product must be repaired or replaced only at the manufacturer's service centre or approved service centre.*
6. *If it is discovered that the fault is not the result of defective parts or workmanship, but due to negligence by the consumer or retailer, then the manufacturer is not obliged to repair or replace the product free of charge.*
7. *Optionally, the consumer may choose to extend the guarantee or warranty period by paying an additional charge. In this case, the manufacturer extends its offer of replacement or repair for the period purchased.*

PC 3.3.6

C 2.1

Group activity *Time: 15 minutes*

In pairs, discuss the warranties you would expect to find when purchasing a pocket calculator.

The Ombudsman

An Ombudsman's job is to ensure that any complaints between an organisation and the consumer are fairly dealt with. The Ombudsman Scheme has been extended from its original form, which dealt only with government departments, to a variety of different business activities. These include the following:

- **The health service** – an Ombudsman deals with complaints from both staff and patients
- **Local government** – an Ombudsman investigates complaints concerning local government and services which they provide
- **Legal services** – an Ombudsman considers complaints against solicitors and barristers
- **Insurance industry** – an Ombudsman investigates unfair small print on insurance policies, inefficiencies, and insurance companies' responses and communications with consumers
- **Estate agents** – an Ombudsman protects the consumer against false descriptions of properties and 'gazumping' (which is allowing another buyer to offer a higher price after a lower price has already been accepted)
- **Banking** – an Ombudsman attempts to control bank charges, unfair interest rates and general poor service
- **Building societies** – an Ombudsman looks at complaints regarding surveys on homes carried out by a building society's valuer
- **Investment** – an Ombudsman considers complaints regarding poor or misleading investment advice
- **Pension schemes** – an Ombudsman investigates complaints regarding personal, company or state pensions

Consumer's Association

Although any truly reputable organisation will go to great lengths to ensure that its products or services meet all the necessary standards and demands, there is a need for independent evaluators. The Consumers' Association itself looks at various products and services within a particular area and releases its findings in *Which?* magazine.

National Federation of Consumer Groups

In addition to this organisation, the National Federation of Consumer Groups co-ordinates local consumer groups. These local consumer groups investigate products and services available in the region and, like the Consumers' Association, publish their findings. They are also very active in campaigning for changes and further protection for consumers.

The media

Newspapers, television and radio are often at the forefront of campaigns in support of the consumer. They will often bring to the public's notice abuses and dangers in products or services. In some cases, they will be responding to a public outcry concerning a product or service. At other times, they will be responsible for investigating a product or service and discovering some aspect of which they believe the public should be aware.

There are many consumer-orientated programmes and features which have had a very positive impact on changing organisations' attitudes, service and products to the advantage of the public.

Watchdog bodies

Some of the watchdog bodies have been set up by the government in order to monitor organisations' activities, particularly in their dealings with the public. Others have been set up by the industry to keep a check on their member organisations. This has been done to ensure that standards are maintained and that any adverse publicity resulting from a disreputable trader does not damage the industry as a whole. Some examples of these watchdog organisations are:

- **Office of Fair Trading** – this is a government body whose brief is to take care of consumer interests as well as those of traders. It releases a range of codes of practice in an effort to improve standards of service. In addition, the Office of Fair Trading will ensure that organisations compete fairly and that no single organisation controls the sole supply of goods or services. An organisation which does so is known as a monopoly.
- **Citizens Advice Bureaux** – the principle duty of this chain of local offices, is to act as a mediator in disputes between organisations and consumers. They are also responsible for a variety of other advisory matters, not necessarily relating to consumer rights.
- **Trading Standards Department** – this organisation investigates various complaints relating to short weights of goods bought, false or misleading offers, and matters relating to credit.
- **National Consumer Council** – this Council is responsible for representing the consumer in disputes and problems with government departments, nationalised industries, local authorities and other businesses.
- **Environmental Health Department** – this organisation operates a series of local offices which investigate aspects relating to food and hygiene. It has the power to enforce legislation relating to food hygiene and may even close businesses which break the regulations.
- **British Standards Institution** – this organisation, which operates on funds received from the government and voluntary donations, is concerned with setting minimum standards in all aspects of business and industry. Its most common image is the BSI Kitemark which denotes that a product has been manufactured and reached the standards laid down by the British Standards Institute.
- **Consumer and Consultative Councils** – these organisations have been set up to monitor the operations of nationalised industries, and to ensure that they do not abuse their monopoly in terms of charging too high a price or providing a poor level of service.
- **Trade Associations** – a large number of organisations dealing with specific industries or services and offering assistance, information and advice to their members. In addition, they also devise a voluntary code of practice to which all members are expected to adhere. An example of these organisations is ABTA (Association of British Travel Agents). The Association also offers guidelines as to how consumers should be treated, particularly with regard to complaints.
- **Advertising Standards Authority** – this independent organisation is involved in ensuring that all advertisements are 'legal, decent, honest and truthful'.

- **The Chartered Institute of Marketing** – this is another independent organisation that attempts to ensure its members have high professional standards, particularly in terms of honesty and integrity. Its British Code of Advertising Practice gives the advertising industry a clear set of rules to follow.
- **Independent Broadcasting Authority** – this organisation monitors the activities of television and radio stations and ensures that particular standards are maintained. Recently, it has been concerned with a new marketing technique known as 'placement' which involves popular programmes featuring and recommending particular brand names or products. Although placement is well established in America, the IBA has ruled that it is unacceptable in Great Britain.

PC 3.3.6
C 2.1
C 2.2

Group activity

In groups of four, contact and obtain leaflets or brochures from at least *six* of the above organisations. Having done this, summarise the main areas of activity of each of the organisations and compile your findings in the form of a fact sheet which could be made available via the Citizens Advice Bureaux and local libraries.

We have already discussed a range of consumer legislation which is aimed at protecting customers from a number of different problems which may occur. Specifically, this consumer legislation will address the following situations:

1. *When a customer has been sold potentially dangerous goods*
2. *When a customer has discovered that the goods purchased are faulty*
3. *When a customer has discovered that the goods purchased are damaged*
4. *When the organisation involved has been negligent in some way*
5. *When an accident has occurred as a result of action taken by an employee of an organisation*
6. *When a customer has been misled by something said by an employee of an organisation*
7. *When a customer has been quoted a particular price and charged a higher one*

We have already seen that the Health and Safety at Work Act refers specifically to employees, but in some respects there are circumstances when a customer may be affected by health and safety legislation.

Accidents can occur which may injure a customer. This may be due to the actions of an employee or an injury related to the use of a product. A customer may suffer physically or financially from the actions of an employee or a faulty product. In order to safeguard against potential claims from an injured customer, an organisation will obtain the following insurance:

- **Public liability insurance** – an organisation such as a hairdressing salon or a firm of builders would take out this form of insurance. This can be a legal requirement, and the policy would cover any claims a customer may make against the organisation. A customer may make a claim if he/she was caused personal injury by the negligence of the organisation's employees or because of defective equipment or building structure.
- **Product liability insurance** – this insurance covers an organisation against claims by customers because of an injury caused by faulty goods.
- **Professional indemnity** – an organisation would take out this insurance to protect itself against any claims a customer may make against it for professional negligence. Professional organisations such as doctors, dentists and solicitors would take out such an insurance.

Individual activity

Time: 20 minutes

PC 3.3.6
C 2.1
C 2.2

In the role of the owner of a hairdressing salon, consider the types of claims that may be made against you by your customers. Write down as many possible reasons for a claim as you can think of, and then compare your list with the rest of the group.

Element 3.3 Assignment

PC 3.3.1–6
C 2.1
C 2.2
C 2.3
IT 2.1
IT 2.2
IT 2.3

This Element forms the ideal basis for a work placement. Your performance in many of these tasks will depend upon having a tutor or similarly authorised person to observe you.

Task 1 *PC 3.3.1–3, PC 3.3.5*

Word process a summary which covers the following:

- an identified business's customers
- a description of the business's customer services
- one example of an oral communication method used by the business organisation to handle customer complaints
- one example of a written communication method used by the organisation to handle customer complaints
- a description of the organisation's procedures for dealing with customer complaints

Task 2 *PC 3.3.4*

Either within a work placement situation, or in a simulated situation, you will need to show the following in relation to oral communications with customers:

- greeting the customer
- establishing the customer's needs
- attempting to meet the customer's needs
- finishing the communication

You will have to show your ability to handle all of the following situations and circumstances:

- a customer wishing to make a purchase
- a customer requiring information
- a customer requiring a refund
- a customer making a complaint
- a customer with special needs

Task 3 *PC 3.3.6*

Word process a brief summary of each of the four Acts which protect customers.

Element 3.4
Present proposals for improvements to customer service

Performance criteria

A student must:

1 explain the **importance of customer service** in business organisations

2 identify how business organisations **monitor customer satisfaction**

3 identify **improvements to customer service**

4 present proposals for improvements to customer service in one organisation

Range

- *Importance of customer service*: to gain and retain customers, to gain customer satisfaction, customer loyalty, to enhance organisation's image
- *How businesses monitor customer satisfaction*: numbers of customers, level of sales, feedback (repeat business, complaints), marketing research
- *Improvements to customer service*: reliability, friendliness, availability of goods or services, speed of delivery, published policy for exchanges or refunds, access to buildings (wheelchairs, pushchairs), care for the environment (rubbish free, clean), customer safety

3.4.1 Explain the importance of customer service in business organisations

The majority of this relatively short Element revolves around an investigation which you will have to make into a specific organisation. The outcome of your investigation will be to provide proposals for improvements in the organisation's customer service.

We have addressed all of the range within this performance criteria, but you may find some of the comments we have made inappropriate for your chosen organisation. If this is the case, then simply ignore them. We can only offer guidelines or suggestions; the relevance of the comments for your chosen organisation should be judged by you.

Importance of customer service

Organisations are very keen to try to meet customer needs. As we have mentioned, they train their staff to be able to cope with a variety of problems.

(Courtesy of Peugeot Talbot)

The main reasons for meeting customer needs are:

- *If treated well, customers will return*
- *If customers have received good service from the organisation, they will recommend it to their family and friends*
- *'Good practice' will exist in every aspect of the organisation's activities. This means that the ideal way of dealing with a situation has been identified, and all staff have been trained to follow a series of recommended procedures*
- *If customers are happy and employees do not have to deal with a constant stream of dissatisfied people, then this will have a very positive effect on employee morale*

PC 3.4.1
C 2.2
IT 2.1
IT 2.2
IT 2.3

Individual activity

In the role of a shop manager, word process a four-page leaflet detailing how to deal with customer complaints. This leaflet should be easy to follow and contain positive actions.

To gain and retain customers

As we have said elsewhere in this book, the question of market share can be a very important concern for particular organisations. In order to achieve any measure of market share, sales targets must be set and year-on-year these targets must be exceeded. This is not the whole picture, as we need to consider what the competition may be doing at the same time. The other external factor which may or may not be within the sphere of influence of the organisation is the market growth or the increase in the number of customers wishing to buy a product. Close monitoring of the external factors may have one part to play in this equation, but many of the sales techniques and innovations within the organisation will also contribute to a large degree to the success or failure in retention or improvement of market share.

While a sales assistant in a retail outlet may not have a clear view as to the nature or status of the organisation's market share, they should be considered as an integral part of the overall effort. Once again, we return to the concept of establishing the needs of the customer and matching the products or services provided by the organisation to that need. Without establishing this close and vital relationship, it is impossible for the organisation to make any impact upon the distribution of the market share.

To gain customer satisfaction and customer loyalty

The retention of customers and the consequent likelihood of repeat sales is largely influenced by the level of customer satisfaction that can be achieved by the organisation. Customers, particularly in this day and age, are considerably more demanding than they have been in the past. While they do not expect something for nothing, there are minimum levels of customer service, and in particular after-sales service, which are demanded as a matter of course.

Naturally, sales representatives or sales assistants, being in the frontline in terms of contact with customers, must bear the brunt of any potential customer complaints or problems. Despite the fact that customers who are satisfied rarely come back to the organisation and praise them for their efforts and help, a measure of this satisfaction can be seen by the level of customer complaints in relation to the total number of customers dealt with. Again, many organisations have instituted extensive and complex customer satisfaction policies. Some organisations are considerably further ahead in this field than others. Despite the fact that legislation is pushing the maintenance of customer satisfaction to its absolute limits, many organisations have chosen to exceed the expectations of the customer.

To enhance organisation's image

The organisation's long-term success may very well depend upon the customers' perception of the organisation. In this respect we can identify two key areas upon which the organisation needs to depend:

1 Customer service
2 Marketing communications

The methods of marketing communications operate as the first point of contact for the organisation with its potential customers. The nature, style, effectiveness and quality of the marketing communication methods employed will have a direct impact on the customers' perceptions of the organisation. Given the situation when the marketing communications techniques used are deemed inappropriate or unappealing, the customers' perceptions of the organisation may well be undermined before the organisation has had a chance to convert any interest into sales. On the other hand, if the organisation gets its marketing communications techniques right, then even the most sceptical or cynical customer may be encouraged to enter into a relationship with the organisation.

3.4.2 Identify how business organisations monitor customer satisfaction

How businesses monitor customer satisfaction

Even if an organisation has established a range of customer service provisions, it must still try to improve this service. It will do this by constantly monitoring a variety of areas in which customer service is concerned. These areas of concern include the following:

- *The number of customers*
- *The level of sales*
- *Feedback (repeat business, complaints)*
- *Marketing research*

Number of customers and level of sales

Sales will increase if the organisation manages to attract more customers, or if it convinces its existing customers to purchase more products or services. A well-organised company will keep a close check on the number of enquiries made by customers and how many of these have been turned into actual sales. In order to facilitate this monitoring system, it may enter on to a computer database all the names and addresses of customers who have made enquiries. It will then be an easy matter to cross-check actual orders and see what percentage 'conversion rate' has been achieved. Another way of monitoring sales performance is to see how often existing customers reorder products or services.

Repeat purchases are the life-blood of an organisation. It must take strenuous steps to ensure that customers who regularly reorder are treated well and they may be offered extended credit facilities to ensure that they stay loyal to the organisation.

Feedback (repeat business, complaints)

An organisation which takes customer service seriously will be interested in the attitudes and opinions formed by the customer. The customer may have very valuable things to say about products or service and may offer useful solutions to difficult problems. There are several ways of obtaining customer feedback, including the following:

1 *Employees asking the customer directly what they think about a product or service.*
2 *'Unknown' employees posing as customers who will visit a branch of the organisation to assess the behaviour of the staff present.*
3 *The organisation may choose to set up a consumer panel which aims to obtain feedback in an informal situation. Normally, this will take the form of a group of customers talking about products and services with a selected group of employees. Very valuable information may be gained from this, including new ideas for products or services.*

PC 3.4.2
C 2.1
C 2.2

Group activity *Time: 30 minutes*

In pairs, you have been asked to draw up a list of discussion areas for a consumer panel. Your organisation is involved in the manufacture, wholesaling and retailing of cast-iron park benches. At present, you only offer four different versions in three different colours.

Discuss your list with those of the rest of the group.

The easiest way to monitor complaints is to see how many returned goods the organisation receives. In all cases, these should be accompanied by appropriate paperwork which details the exact nature of the problem. A customer who returns to the organisation dissatisfied may well now be satisfied after they have received a replacement for their faulty or damaged goods. The organisation will cross-reference the number, type and source of the faulty or damaged goods and see if there are any common features, such as a large number of faulty goods from a single supplier.

Having established an after-sales service, an organisation will be keen to ensure that it is functioning correctly. A series of procedures will need to be in place to make sure that the after-sales service matches the promises made when the product or service was initially sold to the customer. Although a large proportion of customers may not need after-sales service, the organisation will want to ensure that it is available on demand.

Marketing research

Market research is useful in discovering what both existing and potential customers think about the organisation and its range of products or services. Although the information is based upon opinion, organisations place a great emphasis on the reliability of this data and will often act upon it directly. The questionnaire itself must be clear and easy to fill in and, in some cases, the organisation will offer an incentive or reward for the customer to complete the document.

ACHIEVEMENT OF PAST OBJECTIVES/TARGETS

METHODS OF WORKING

DEALING WITH PEOPLE

OBJECTIVES/TARGETS FOR NEXT YEAR

INDIVIDUAL'S COMMENTS

TRAINING AND DEVELOPMENT

Name:	Department:
Identity Number:	Manager:
Job Title:	Date Completed:

TRAINING & DEVELOPMENT NEEDS

Method of working

Dealing with people

Other needs

Individual's Signature:

Appraiser's Signature:

PERSONAL TRAINING & DEVELOPMENT PLAN

To be completed in conjunction with Personnel/Training Function

Proposed Activity/Action*	Responsibility

Should include preferred timing and priority

Date Plan Agreed:

Fig 3.19 Peugeot Talbot's comprehensive appraisal and training/development programme places great importance on customer care and personal development

MEDIA INFORMATION

Mercury COMMUNICATIONS

22nd March 1993

MERCURY EXTENDS NETWORK TO 90% OF UK POPULATION

Mercury Communications has announced that from the end of April, following recent network extensions, around 90% of the UK population will be able to access the Mercury network for business and residential services.

Over £2 million has been invested in this latest expansion, Mercury's largest ever single extension programme which will provide access for an additional 1.5 million residential exchange lines. In only five years Mercury has been able to expand its access within the UK from under 60% in 1988 to 90% in 1993.

Over 100 new areas, spread throughout the British Isles, will become available with a significant number of these in Scotland and Northern Ireland. New STD codes able to access Mercury services in the first quarter of 1993 include, Kirkcaldy, Perth, Larne and Ballymena. Also included are Doncaster, Tunbridge Wells, Burnley, Lancaster and Worcester.

Mercury has invested a total of £1.9 billion in its network, products and services and will continue this significant investment programme over the next few years. Mercury is signing up over 25,000 new customers a month to its residential service and 99 of the top 100 companies in the UK are Mercury customers.

Mercury Communications is a subsidiary of Cable & Wireless and is licensed as Telecommunications Operator in the UK.

ends

For further information please contact
Richard Prescott, Mercury Press Office **Tel:071-528-2561**
Fax:071-528-2577

For Mercury information **Freephone 0500-500-194**

Mercury Communications Limited, New Mercury House, 26 Red Lion Square, London, WC1R 4HQ. Switchboard: 071-528 2000 Fax: 071-528 2181 Telex: 910000 Mercom G

Fig 3.20 Telecommunications services company Mercury expands its coverage of the UK to 90 per cent of the population

3.4.3 Identify improvements to customer service

3.4.4 Present proposals for improvements to customer service in one organisation

These performance criteria are an integral part of the Element assignment. In order to help you prepare for this we have constructed the following focus study. Think of Baileys as being a real organisation that needs some guidance.

Focus study

Meeting the needs of external customers

The small supermarket chain Baileys has seven stores in central Norfolk. It is a family-run concern and, despite having been established over 30 years ago, is now facing problems. They have neither the advantage of being small, local stores (the average store size is 4000 sq ft), nor the the advantage of being a large supermarket. When the stores were established (the last one was opened in 1981), they were in small towns and reasonable-sized villages, and it was considered by the company that these were good locations with reasonable catchment areas. Baileys could not have predicted the opening of large out-of-town supermarkets which have had a drastic effect on their business. In the early stages, the chain's prices compared well with those of corner shops, but now, with the supermarket price-cutting war, Baileys have been left way behind.

The Board met recently and, working from reports provided by store managers and head office personnel, they ascertained the following:

- They cannot possibly compete in price terms with supermarkets
- The quality and range in these supermarkets is much better than Baileys
- The large supermarkets are at least five or six times bigger than Baileys' average store
- Being located in the centre of a market town is no longer an advantage because car parking is difficult
- By comparing the average customer's spending in Baileys with that of the supermarkets, it was discovered that customers on average spent around £7 in Baileys against over £40 in supermarkets
- Traditional customers of Baileys are now happy to travel considerable distances to visit the supermarkets. Even those without a car can take advantage of the free buses provided by the supermarkets

Baileys was very interested in customer attitudes with regard to the probable disadvantages of supermarkets and they identified the following:

- There seemed not to be sufficient staff in the supermarkets
- The quality of fresh produce was criticised

- In most supermarkets there were no price tickets
- There were often long queues at the checkouts

This all sounded promising until the results of an exit questionnaire was analysed. Baileys had commissioned a local marketing consultancy to interview 500 customers leaving their stores. It was bad news:

1. Baileys' own label products were considered extremely poor quality
2. The customers did not think much of the employees' appearance or helpfulness
3. The stores appeared tatty and underfunded
4. It was difficult to move trolleys or prams around the stores
5. Baileys did not have a good range of convenience items, such as prepacked salads and ready-to-cook meals

There were a few positive points:

1. The quality of Baileys' fresh produce was considered to be good
2. Customers appreciated Baileys' local delivery service
3. Baileys' 8 am to 8 pm opening times were very much appreciated

The Board of Baileys obviously needed to reappraise the whole of their business strategy. They had to re-examine the needs of their customers or face eventual closure.

PC 3.4.3
PC 3.4.4
C 2.2
C 2.4
AN 2.3
IT 2.1
IT 2.2
IT 2.3

Individual activity

In the role of Baileys' sales director, respond to the instruction from the Board to create a new strategy which addresses the needs of the customers. The Bailey family are perfectly prepared to invest considerable sums of money in a total overhaul of their operations if you think this is necessary. You should present your key findings and recommendations in the form of a confidential memorandum to the Board. Your memorandum should be word processed and you should submit any tables, charts and diagrams that you think would be of use to them in making their decision.

We will now turn our attention to some of the specific improvements mentioned in the range statements.

Improvements to customer service

As you will now be aware, customer service covers a multitude of different areas of concern for the organisation. We can suggest some ideas here, but you could probably find a different approach in your chosen organisation.

Reliability

This aspect of customer service is fairly important for the organisation to get right. It means that the customer will be assured of a consistent and totally reliable service. This reliability has a great impact on many of the other factors discussed in this section.

Friendliness

As we have seen, a good organisation that places a great deal of importance on its relationships with customers will seek to train and develop its employees to become more responsive to customers. This does not mean a total reliance on the concept of 'the customer is always right', but is a balance between what should be said and done and what can be said and done. In other words, responding to customer needs should be taken to be one of the most important concerns, but also should be handled in the right way. A customer does not want to be faced with unfriendly and unhelpful staff who do not seem prepared to put themselves out. On the other hand, they do not want grovelling and insincere staff who appear just to want to do what the customer asks and get the conversation over with. It is all a question of balance, and this can be learnt through staff training and development.

Availability of goods or services

As we have said earlier, there is nothing more annoying and potentially disastrous to the organisation than not having goods in stock. There should always be a minimum stock level held. But, in cases when this is not possible, all steps should be taken to fulfil the customers' requirements with the minimum of fuss. The key to ensuring that there is sufficient stock is both in the administrative function and in information interchange. If orders are processed and stock levels are relayed to the right person, then many of the stock difficulties can be overcome. With regard to the customer, they need to be told about the stock level situation and when a new delivery is expected.

Speed of delivery

As we have already mentioned when considering the availability of goods or services, the speed of delivery may relate to restocking. On a more general level, the organisation, once it has made a promise of a delivery date or time, should do everything in its power to ensure that this is kept. There is nothing more irritating for the customer than having to wait for something to be delivered and the delivery not arriving. No one will overly praise a delivery that is made on time, but they will always criticise one that is late or does not turn up.

Published policy for exchanges or refunds

Many retail outlets now have their policies in relation to exchanges or refunds printed on a card and placed beside the cash register. The customer does not necessarily notice this, and will not know, until the situation arises, the organisation's procedure or policies on the matter of exchanges and refunds. By referring back to the sections we have covered on consumer law, you will recall that there are rules and regulations which protect the customers' rights. Some organisations seek to ignore them and others place their own emphasis on them. Whatever the policy and whatever the procedures, the organisation should make them clear and straightforward. There is no doubt that a large number of disputes arise due to misunderstandings of these procedures.

Access to building (wheelchairs, pushchairs)

Many retail outlets have invested considerable funds in upgrading their premises to cater for those who need enhanced access facilities. Having said this, there are very few organisations which have given much thought to the internal layout of the premises to help access to parts of the building once the wheelchair user or the pushchair are inside.

Placing children's products on the ground floor may sound obvious, but this is not always the case. Disabled toilets and other facilities are either inadequate or on the wrong floor (i.e. not the ground floor).

Ramps, enhanced lifts, wider corridors or aisles, are all fundamental in relation to providing greater access. In one office tower block we were appalled to discover that wheelchair users could obviously not use the stairs, and should not use the lifts in fire emergencies. They had been told to wait near the lift doors for the emergency services to get them out of the building. This was obviously not the solution to the problem. Some other system was required.

Care for the environment (rubbish free, clean)

We can take this as meaning one or both of the following:

1. *Considerations regarding the working conditions within the organisation* – this falls squarely into the health and safety area. Working areas should be clutter-free and clean. These considerations are covered by the many pieces of legislation which control the working environment.
2. *Considerations relating to the disposal of rubbish and other waste into the environment* – organisations are making supreme efforts to reduce the impact that their waste makes on the environment. Recycling projects and other methods of reducing the waste output have been implemented in a great number of organisations. While it may not be cost-effective to recycle the waste, the organisation will see this as either a potential source of recouping some costs, or more importantly as a major public relations exercise.

   Some supermarkets actually encourage customers to recycle in their own right. Schemes include the following:

   - a small discount for reusing carrier bags (Sainsbury's, Safeway)
   - a discount for each box taken from the storage area for packing your shopping (Sainsbury's)
   - a discount for asking for your shampoo or conditioner to be put into an empty container which you have brought with you (Body Shop)

Customer safety

If you refer back to our comments regarding the health and safety implications in relation to customers, you will find some useful guidelines. In addition, we should also remember the legal responsibilities of the business to provide insurance in case of accidents caused by or to customers. Many of the basic health and safety concerns relate directly to customers as much as employees. This is particularly true of organisations which allow customers access to the office areas of the premises.

Element 3.4 Assignment

PC 3.4.1–4
C 2.1
C 2.2
C 2.3
C 2.4
IT 2.1
IT 2.2
IT 2.3

This assignment requires you to prepare a presentation which proposes improvements to customer services in a business organisation. You could use the same business organisation that you investigated in Element 3.3.

Task 1 *PC 3.4.1, PC 3.4.4*

In the initial part of your presentation you should suggest how improvements could help in the following areas:

- attracting customers
- securing customer satisfaction
- obtaining customer loyalty
- enhancing the organisation's image

Task 2 *PC 3.4.3–4*

In the second part of your presentation include examples of improvements to *three* of the following:

- friendliness
- availability of goods or services
- speed of delivery
- policies for exchanges or refunds
- access to buildings (for wheelchairs or pushchairs)
- customer safety
- care for the environment

Task 3 *PC 3.4.1–4*

Supporting your oral presentation you should produce word-processed notes which cover the following aspects related to your chosen organisation and the factors which you have investigated in relation to customer service. The factors or aspects are:

- a description of their current customer service provision
- a description of how they currently monitor customer satisfaction
- an outline of your proposals for improvements to their customer service

Notes

You do not have to access information about numbers of customers and levels of sales. This Element is based on your own judgements from the observations that you have made. If you undertake this Element assignment as a group you will all have to show that you understand the requirements of this Element's performance criteria and range.

UNIT 3 Revision questions

1 What is demography?

2 What is a consumer durable?

3 List three items of family expenditure.

4 What information would you find in the *General Household Survey*?

5 What percentage of the population is vegetarian?

6 What trends can affect demand for a particular product or service?

7 What do you understand by the term 'cost of living'?

8 What is the RPI?

9 What do you understand by the term 'confidence to spend'?

10 List five regular outgoings when calculating family expenditure.

11 What is a family life cycle?

12 What do you understand by the term 'socio-economic'?

13 What is ACORN?

14 What are the six main categories of segmentation?

15 Which colour is not favoured by Moslems?

16 What do you understand by the term 'ergonomics'?

17 What would you find in the *Monthly Digest of Statistics*?

18 What is disposable income?

19 What do families tend to spend their disposable income on?

20 Why would a customer not have the 'confidence to spend'?

21 What are the features of a good advertisement?

22 What do you understand by the term 'promotion'?

23 What is meant by 'influencing customer perceptions'?

24 Give three aims in creating a demand for a product or service.

25 Give three aims in creating a sale for a product or service.

26 Give three aims in creating customer perception of a product.

27 What is AIDA?

28 What do you understand by the phrase 'voluntary code of practice'?

29 What is the ASA?

30 What is the CSPP?

31 What are the Broadcasting Standards Councils particularly concerned with?

32 Give three advantages of TV advertising.

33 Give three advantages of newspaper advertising.

34 Give three advantages of magazine advertising.

35 Can you name two national independent radio stations?

36 What is TAP?

37 What is OTS?

38 What is TC?

39 Which advertising media offers the greatest OTS?

40 Give three advantages of sponsorship.

41 Give four reasons why a customer might contact an organisation.

42 What is a guarantee?

43 Give six rules for ensuring good verbal communication.

44 What is NVC?

45 List five important rules to consider when greeting a customer.

46 When would a memo be used?

47 List five important rules to consider when answering the telephone.

48 Give three methods of displaying information graphically

49 What should you do if you find a lost child in your shop?

50 How should you deal with a foreign customer?

51 Give two reasons why a customer might be dissatisfied.

52 What type of organisation would require Public Liability insurance?

53 Give three types of customer service.

54 How would an organisation monitor its sales performance?

55 State two ways an organisation might obtain feedback from customers.

56 What is the easiest way of monitoring customer complaints?

57 What is civil law?

58 What does criminal law cope with?

59 What is a contract of sale?

60 What does the Weights and Measures Act cover?

61 What is a Citizen's Charter?

62 What is a chartermark?

63 List three undertakings covered by a warranty.

64 Briefly explain the Consumer Protection Act.

65 Explain the role of an Ombudsman.

66 What is a watchdog body?

67 What is the Chartered Institute of Marketing?

68 What does the Environmental Health Department investigate?

69 What is the Office of Fair Trading?

70 How could the media assist a consumer in dealing with a disreputable company?

71 Can you name two television programmes that deal with consumer affairs?

72 What is the National Federation of Consumer Groups?

UNIT 3 End test questions

Focus 1 – characteristics of consumers

1 Which of the following classifications of customers is likely to be important when considering the sale of video games?
- **a** age
- **b** gender
- **c** income
- **d** nationality

2 Which of the following is most likely to be a characteristic of a customer in a DIY store?
- **a** where they live
- **b** their nationality
- **c** their gender
- **d** their level of income

3 What is demography?
- **a** the study of population trends
- **b** the study of spending patterns
- **c** the study of buying habits
- **d** the study of the cost of living

4 If prices keep rising, this is known as an increase in:
- **a** the cost of purchasing
- **b** the cost of sales
- **c** the cost of living
- **d** the cost of buying

5 What is ACORN?
- **a** a classification of regional newspapers
- **b** a classification of residential neighbourhoods
- **c** a classification of recession news
- **d** a classification of retail numbers

6 What is TAP?
- **a** Trade Advertising Programme
- **b** Total Advertising Policy
- **c** Television Audience Potential
- **d** Total Audience Package

Focus 2 – consumer demand

7 Organisations need information regarding patterns in consumer demand. Where would they be most likely to find this?
- **a** national newspapers
- **b** company reports
- **c** internal records
- **d** *Social Trends*

8 Which of the following would lead to a fall in consumer demand for cigarettes?
- **a** an increase in wages
- **b** an increase in the birth rate
- **c** individuals becoming more health conscious
- **d** individuals having more leisure time

9 What would happen if the confidence of consumers to spend money decreased?
- **a** there would be more money saved
- **b** there would be an increase in individual income
- **c** there would be more money borrowed
- **d** there would be more luxury goods purchased

10 What would happen if the confidence of customers to spend money increased?
- **a** there would be less money saved
- **b** there would be a decrease in individual income
- **c** there would be less money borrowed
- **d** there would be less luxury goods purchased

Focus 3 – promotional materials

11 Businesses sponsor sporting events and sports people for which of the following reasons:
- **a** they are interested in sport
- **b** it will enable them to gain publicity
- **c** their employees will obtain free tickets to the events
- **d** it is an inexpensive venture

12 Which of the following is an independent national radio station?
- **a** Classic FM
- **b** Radio 1
- **c** Capital Radio
- **d** Radio 4

13 An organisation would advertise on national radio because:
- **a** the local market can be reached
- **b** it is cheap
- **c** it reaches a wide area
- **d** it is the only way to advertise

14 Which of the following is a disadvantage of advertising on television?
- **a** it does not reach a big enough audience
- **b** it will not be remembered
- **c** it is expensive
- **d** it is quick

15 Which information could be included in a magazine advertisement but not on a poster?
- **a** information about the product
- **b** the price of the product
- **c** a sample of the product
- **d** a picture of the product

16 An organisation would advertise a special offer for a new product in order to:
- **a** encourage individuals to continue buying the product
- **b** ensure that ethical considerations were adhered to
- **c** encourage individuals to buy the new product
- **d** ensure legislative considerations were adhered to

17 An organisation would offer money-off for bulk buying to:
- **a** influence customer perceptions
- **b** encourage customers to buy more
- **c** increase customer knowledge
- **d** improve the image of the organisation

Focus 4 – providing and investigating customer service

18 A retail outlet may provide free delivery in order to:
- **a** avoid paying a distribution organisation
- **b** comply with legislation
- **c** improve customer service
- **d** ensure the goods arrive in good condition

19 If an ‘out of town’ superstore decides to provide a large car park, what would be the main reason behind this decision?
- **a** to improve communications
- **b** to attract better staff
- **c** to attract more customers
- **d** to improve the efficiency and motivation of the staff

20 If a retail outlet decides to change its opening hours due to the difficulty in attracting staff, what would be the best way to ensure that all of the customers get to know about the proposed changes?

- **a** send out a letter to all of the customers on the database
- **b** telephone all of the known customers
- **c** place a notice on the door of the shop
- **d** make sure that all of the customers that come into the shop are told the circumstances regarding the changes

21 If a retail outlet wants to find out why customers shop there, which would be the most appropriate way of finding this out?

- **a** telephone local people using the electoral register as the main source of names
- **b** post questionnaires through all the doors in the neighbourhood
- **c** ask customers who come into the shop
- **d** decide upon a number of people to telephone and then get their numbers from the telephone book

22 If a retailer discovers that they have sold a number of faulty and potentially dangerous kettles to customers, what would be the best way to contact all of them?

- **a** place an advertisement in the local paper
- **b** contact the local trading standards officer and ask them to contact the customers
- **c** contact the local police and ask for their assistance
- **d** do nothing, as the customers will come back if the kettle proves to be faulty

23 Which of the following customer services would be found in a College library?

- **a** an information desk
- **b** a replacement desk
- **c** an after-sales service desk
- **d** a refund desk

24 If an organisation uses sales figures as the main way of measuring the levels of customer satisfaction, then what is the main disadvantage of this method?

- **a** that it does not show where the product was purchased
- **b** that it does not show when the product was purchased
- **c** that it does not show how much was paid for the product
- **d** that it does not show whether the customer is actually pleased with the performance of the product

Focus 5 – legislation

25 If a restaurant serves you a stew that is supposed to be beef, but after you have finished most of it you realise that it is pork, which of the following Acts has it broken?

- **a** the Trade Descriptions Act
- **b** the Weights & Measures Act
- **c** the Consumer Protection Act
- **d** none of the above

26 If you purchase a CD and the retail outlet refuses to give you a refund after you have discovered that it is faulty, then where can you go to for assistance and legal advice?

a the police
b the Citizens Advice Bureau
c the Law Society
d the solicitor

27 A local cinema owner must undertake one of the following in order to comply with the law. Which of the following is it?

a the owner must give a guarantee that you can get a seat if you have paid for it
b the owner must advertise the films being shown so that the censor can make sure that they are certificated
c the owner must carry out regular safety checks
d the owner must comply with and display a sign regarding the Citizens' Charter

28 While standing in a queue at your local butcher, you see one of the staff cutting some meat. He cuts his hand, but keeps on with the task in hand. Who should you report this to?

a the local hospital
b the Trading Standards Office
c the Health & Safety Executive
d the Environmental Health Department

29 What is the Citizens' Charter?

a a method of hiring equipment
b a Queen's Award for Industry
c a series of promises made by an organisation
d a part of the Weights and Measures Act

30 Which of the following is not a watchdog body?

a OFWAT
b OFTEL
c OFCOM
d Environmental Health Department

Unit 4
FINANCIAL AND ADMINISTRATIVE SUPPORT

Element 4.1
Identify and explain financial transactions and documents

Element 4.2
Complete financial documents and explain financial recording

Element 4.3
Produce, evaluate and store business documents

Element 4.1
Identify and explain financial transactions and documents

Performance criteria

A student must:

1 explain **financial transactions** which take place regularly in an organisation and explain why **records of transactions** are kept

2 explain and give examples of **purchases** and **purchase documents**

3 explain and give examples of **sales transactions** and **sales documents**

4 explain and give examples of **payment methods** and **receipt documents**

5 explain the **importance of security** and **security checks** for receipts and payments

Range

- *Financial transactions*: outward transactions to pay for costs (wages, materials, overheads), inward transactions to receive income (payments, loans)
- *Records of transactions*: to produce accounts (internal for the business's own use, external to be published annually), to ensure security, to monitor business performance (profit, loss)
- *Purchases*: materials, services, wages
- *Purchase documents*: orders placed, purchase invoice, credit note, goods received note
- *Sales transactions*: goods, services, business-to-business, business-to-consumer
- *Sales documents*: orders received, sales invoice, delivery note, sales credit note, statement of account, remittance advice

- *Payment methods*: cheque, cash, BACS (Bankers' Automated Clearing Services), EDI (Electronic Data Interchange), credit card, debit card, credit (includes hire purchase)
- *Receipt documents*: receipt, cheque, paying-in slip, bank statement
- *Importance*: to prevent fraud, to prevent theft, to ensure high standards of honesty
- *Security checks*: authorisation of orders, invoices checked against orders, invoices checked against goods received notes, cheques signed by authorised signatories

4.1.1 Explain financial transactions which take place regularly in an organisation and explain why records of transactions are kept

Financial transactions

The survival of an organisation will depend upon its financial state of health. In order to monitor whether the organisation is spending more than it is earning, it is essential that the series of financial transactions undertaken routinely by the organisation are controlled in a strict and logical manner.

In this Element we will be looking at the various inward and outward transactions which need to be addressed by an organisation in the normal course of its activities. We will also see how some recent developments in payment methods have streamlined many of these activities. Despite the use of new technology, there is still a need to check all transactions manually and for this reason we will be looking at many of the documents involved.

The final part of this Element looks at the security implications and considers measures which an organisation can take to ensure that the highest levels of honesty are maintained, as well as that checks against fraud and theft are routinely undertaken.

Outward transactions to pay for costs (wages, materials, overheads)

In the relevant performance criteria and other sections of this Element we will be looking at the main transactions known as costs. These outward transactions mainly involve the payment of wages, the payment for materials and the expenditure on overheads. The procedures followed and the documents used will differ from organisation to organisation. However, there are a number of essential similarities that will be found, regardless of the type of organisation, its purpose or its size. As we mentioned earlier, routine payments can now be made through using information technology. Despite this it is still very common to find manual systems in operation in even the largest and most sophisticated organisation.

Inward transactions to receive income (payments, loans)

The systematic dealing with and monitoring of inward transactions is as vital as handling the outward transactions. Organisations will need to keep complete records of all income received. This is not only an important legal requirement, but is also necessary to ensure that creditors have paid the correct amount at the right time. As we will see later, some organisations will employ a credit controller (for the duties of a credit controller you can refer back to Unit 2), to make sure that purchasing organisations do not exceed their credit limit and are not late in paying their outstanding bills. Again, these transactions can be dealt with using information technology, as we will see later in this Element.

Taken together, these inward and outward financial transactions are used to create company accounts, including balance sheets, profit and loss accounts and cashflow statements. Although we will not be looking at these within this programme of study in any depth, knowledge of these will be useful should you consider GNVQ Advanced Business.

Records of transactions

When any financial transaction takes place, it is essential that a record is kept by the organisation involved. These records of transactions have to be stored safely and securely and it is important that they can be easily accessed and are kept fully up to date. Financial transactions are recorded for the following reasons:

1 To provide evidence that the transaction has actually taken place – it would not be sensible to rely on memory regarding such transactions.
2 To provide the accounts department with documents in order that they can pay the bills and collect any money which is owed to the organisation.
3 To provide the accounts department with a record of the transaction so that the annual accounts can be generated.
4 To provide the accounts department with a means of monitoring the performance of the business by working out the profit or loss figures so that an estimate of how well the organisation is progressing can be gained.
5 In the case of a public limited company, such financial transactions legally have to be recorded in order to provide the shareholders with information regarding the performance of the organisation.
6 To provide the Customs and Excise office with an assessment of the amount of VAT involved in each financial transaction.
7 To provide the Inland Revenue with information which it will use to assess the income tax (in the case of a small business) and corporation tax (in the case of a limited company) payable by the organisation.

To produce accounts (internal for the business's own use, external to be published annually)

As we mentioned in the previous section, all organisations have to keep a record of their financial transactions in order that they can be assessed for various reasons by external bodies. Depending on the size of the organisation, this may be carried out in a number of different ways:

1 Larger organisations will have their own accounts department which will deal with the financial transactions.
2 A sole trader may do his/her own accounts, or, alternatively, may employ an accountant on a part-time basis. To cover legal requirements, this accountant must be registered and qualified.
3 A limited company legally has to have its accounts audited (either by an internal auditor or a company specialising in auditing the accounts of different organisations).

The annual accounts can be broken down into two main parts – the balance sheet and the profit and loss account. Before we look at these in a little more detail, there are some terms which it may be useful to explain at this stage:

- **Assets** – these can be either cash, money in the bank, stock, or buildings and equipment. In addition, any money the organisation is owed by another organisation is also known as an asset (such businesses who owe money to the organisation are known as debtors).
- **Liabilities** – this is the money which the organisation owes to other organisations or suppliers (known as the organisation's creditors).
- **Gross profit** – this is the difference between the price of buying the raw materials and the selling price of the finished product(s).
- **Net profit** – this is the gross profit, less the expenses incurred in the production of the product. Examples of such expenses would include electricity, wages and salaries for the employees, and the cost of heating the premises.

Profit and loss account

All the financial transactions of the organisation for the year will have been recorded. At the end of the financial year (this will vary from organisation to organisation, but will be the same date each year), the accountant will prepare a profit and loss account (*see* Fig 4.1). This will include a summary of all the transactions, both for expenditure (money paid out) and income (money coming in). The difference between the income and expenditure is known as either the profit or the loss.

The balance sheet

The profit or loss the organisation has made during the year is transferred from the profit and loss account to the balance sheet. The balance sheet will also list all of the organisation's assets and liabilities at the end of the period. A balance sheet can be produced at any time during the year and is used commonly for the assessment and monitoring of business performance (*see* Fig 4.2).

Profit and Loss Account for the year ended 31 December 199-

	£	£	£
Sales			70,000
Cost of sales			
Purchases		31,000	
Less: Closing stock		3,000	
			28,000
Gross trading profit			42,000
Other income			
Rent			60
Total profit			42,060
Selling and distribution expenses			
Sales representatives' salaries	12,000		
Motor expenses	2,000		
Depreciation – motor vehicles	1,800	15,800	
Administrative expenses			
Rent	6,000		
Office salaries	10,800		
Insurance	350		
Light and heat	1,000		
General expenses	300		
Depreciation – furniture and fittings	225		
		18,675	
Financial expenses			
Bad debts	180		
Provision for doubtful debts	178	358	
Total overhead expenses			34,833
Net profit			7,227

Fig 4.1 A profit and loss account

PC 4.1.1
C 2.2
AN 2.2

Individual activity

Time: 30 minutes

Can you produce your own profit and loss account? Think of your regular weekly income, and then your regular weekly expenditure. Write this information out as a list, using the following as possible headings, although if you feel it more appropriate, use column headings of your own.

Date Received from Paid to Reason Amount of money

We think that you may find it difficult to recall everything that you have spent. Make sure that you keep any receipts you have received as your evidence of payments.

Balance sheet

Kingfisher plc and subsidiary companies as at 28 January 1995

£ millions	Notes	Group 1995	Group 1994	Company 1995	Company 1994
Fixed assets					
Tangible assets	12	**1,436.6**	1,249.2	**2.6**	2.1
Investments	13	**62.1**	44.9	**1,445.3**	1,371.7
		1,498.7	1,294.1	**1,447.9**	1,373.8
Current assets					
Development work in progress	14	**35.5**	37.3	–	–
Stocks	14	**803.7**	734.0	–	–
Debtors	15	**482.1**	390.9	**1,800.5**	1,411.2
Investments	16	**175.3**	149.9	**0.7**	0.7
Cash at bank and in hand		**92.7**	236.6	**10.7**	36.0
		1,589.3	1,548.7	**1,811.9**	1,447.9
Creditors					
Amounts falling due within one year	17	**(1,420.9)**	(1,283.9)	**(929.1)**	(674.7)
Net current assets		**168.4**	264.8	**882.8**	773.2
Total assets less current liabilities		**1,667.1**	1,558.9	**2,330.7**	2,147.0
Creditors					
Amounts falling due after more than one year	18	**(434.1)**	(465.8)	**(269.2)**	(90.2)
Provisions for liabilities and charges	19	**(16.6)**	(0.9)	–	–
		1,216.4	1,092.2	**2,061.5**	2,056.8
Capital and reserves					
Called up share capital	20	**166.9**	166.4	**166.9**	166.4
Share premium account	21	**193.8**	189.9	**193.8**	189.9
Revaluation reserve	21	**191.5**	113.9	–	–
Non-distributable reserve	21	–	–	**936.0**	936.0
Profit and loss account	21	**667.0**	620.9	**764.8**	764.5
Equity shareholders' funds		**1,219.2**	1,091.1	**2,061.5**	2,056.8
Equity minority interests		**(2.8)**	1.1	–	–
		1,216.4	1,092.2	**2,061.5**	2,056.8

Approved by the Board
Sir Geoffrey Mulcahy, *Director*
James Kerr-Muir, *Director*
13 March 1995

Fig 4.2 A balance sheet
(Courtesy of Kingfisher plc)

To ensure security

If an organisation is to function in an efficient and effective manner, then the transactions the organisation undertakes must be recorded and kept safely and securely. It is very important that an organisation has security high on its list of priorities. Not everyone is honest, and money kept in an insecure way may tempt such people. On the other hand, of course, there are various other reasons for an organisation to take steps to ensure security measures are complied with:

1 The organisation will have to have information and documents readily available and accessible for the Inland Revenue for assessing income or corporation tax.
2 An organisation which is registered for VAT payment purposes will have to have information on receipts and payments containing VAT readily available and accessible for the Customs and Excise office for the purpose of assessing VAT payments.
3 Any organisation will be very keen to ensure that errors which may have been made are noticed at some point throughout the stages of the transaction. If any errors are made, either by the organisation itself, or a debtor or creditor, then secure measures will ensure that these can easily be traced.
4 Obviously an organisation would want security measures to be in place in order to avoid fraud or theft. It is much easier to commit fraud now than it used to be. When people only dealt with cash, this was difficult to trace if lost. Nowadays, however, with credit cards being a popular method of payment, the opportunity for fraud has increased.

PC 4.1.1
C 2.1
C 2.2

Group activity *Time: 20 minutes*

In pairs, make a list of the documents you think a VAT inspector would want to see when making regular visits to the organisation. Remember that little notice will be given of the visit. What would he/she expect to see? Who would be responsible for arranging access to the files/books/documents?

To monitor business performance (profit, loss)

We have already mentioned that the financial transactions of an organisation must be recorded so that the organisation can monitor the business performance for the financial year. This is different to the reason for keeping the records so that profit or loss can be identified. An organisation needs to know what the position is on a day-to-day basis. In order to do this, an organisation must have easy access to its records on a regular basis.

One of the roles of the accountant will be to organise a budget for the organisation. This is quite similar to the type of budget to which you or your family may have to keep on a weekly or monthly basis. The accountant will set a budget, or a series of budgets, for the organisation and it will be the responsibility of each departmental manager to try to ensure that his/her staff and departmental expenditure do not exceed the budget. A good example of this is a purchasing department, which would not be allowed to purchase any items which would go over its budget limit. Every month, or sometimes more frequently, the accountant would check the income and expenditure of the organisation against the budget(s) set. Simplistically, a budget is a form of financial plan which the organisation compiles and to which it tries to adhere.

PC 4.1.1
C 2.2
AN 2.2

Individual activity *Time: 30 minutes*

Referring back to the activity when you prepared your own income and expenditure account, now we would like you to try to prepare a budget for yourself for next week. Think about where you are spending money unnecessarily. What items do you have to pay for and which could be excluded? Answer by making two lists: essential items and luxuries.

Although it is vital for an organisation to have an efficient and effective way of recording financial transactions and the information resulting from them, there is no point in running such an administrative system if it is not efficient. Obviously, if the documents stored are incomplete, inaccurate, illegible, unchecked or unreliable, then this would mean gross inefficiency and ineffectiveness. It is essential, therefore, that those involved in the completion of such documents are aware and motivated enough to see their value. When monitoring the performance of business activities, the organisation needs to ensure that all documents are reliable in the following ways:

1 **That they are actually completed** – this may seem like an obvious statement, but it is more detailed than that. A cheque without a date added is useless and will not be accepted by a bank. The same applies to documents such as an invoice or order form. In order to try to avoid having documents sent from the organisation in an incomplete manner, some companies have adopted the use of a 'proforma'. This means that their documents have headings and spaces where all the relevant information has to be inserted. These documents will be used throughout the organisation and are part of the 'corporate image'.

2 **That they are accurate** – again this may sound obvious, but it is vital that documents are completed accurately. One incorrect figure, or a decimal point in the wrong place, could cause enormous problems, not only for the organisation itself in the monitoring process, but also for the customer or supplier. Unnecessary delay and inconvenience could be caused by such discrepancies and some organisations choose to assist in avoiding this by designing their documents in duplicate or triplicate so that such inaccuracies can easily be spotted.

3 **Neatness of completion** – everyone assumes that their handwriting is legible, but this may not always be the case. An organisation must ensure that all documents leaving their premises are easy to read. This is particularly important when considering documents which contain figures as it could be costly to the organisation if one figure is mistaken for another. (Perhaps this is why the French in particular distinguish their 1 from their 7?)

4 **Checking of documents** – all documents should be checked thoroughly before being issued. This task should be carried out by the person completing the document, although this is not always an easy task as one cannot always see one's own mistakes. It would be more efficient either to get someone else to check it, or to read it to them and get them to check the figures and data.

5 **Reliability of documents** – we mentioned earlier in this section that some organisations prepare their documents in duplicate or triplicate. In some cases, for example the order form, the document will have several copies, each one being distributed to a different department.

Because so many copies are being used by so many different individuals and departments, it is vital that the information contained within the document is correct, accurate and reliable.

4.1.2 Explain and give examples of purchases and purchase documents

Purchases

As we have said previously, all organisations need to buy raw materials and services in order to produce or provide their own goods and services. These materials and services may take several forms, including:

- *raw materials needed on the production line*
- *the services of specialists, e.g. cleaners or consultants*

In order to obtain these materials or services, the organisation will have to complete documents requesting them. First of all let us break down the types of goods or services the organisation may need to request.

Materials

Materials can take several forms. They may be raw materials, which the organisation will need to add to other raw materials in order to produce its product. For example, potatoes needed to make oven chips. Materials may, however, be items such as headed paper needed to produce letters from the organisation, or cleaning products to assist in the sanitation of the production lines. These types of product are known as consumables, and they are all ordered on an order form.

An organisation may also need to purchase such items as office furniture, new computer equipment, new buildings, etc. These items are dealt with in a different way to materials, and a special purchasing system will be in operation within the organisation to deal with such purchases.

Services

In order to purchase a service from an individual or another organisation, it would be necessary for the organisation to complete and exchange a contract (a legally-binding agreement). The organisation raising the contract would ensure that it states clearly the terms of that contract and this would be signed by a representative of the organisation, plus the person providing the service. This contract, once signed, becomes legally binding on both sides.

PC 4.1.2
C 2.1
C 2.2

Group activity *Time: 45 minutes*

In groups, decide on a finished product of your choice. Make a list of the raw materials and services an organisation would need in order to produce this product.

Present your considerations to the remainder of your group, giving the reasons why you have chosen this particular product. Also explain why you think the materials and services would be necessary.

In most organisations, the purchasing department would be responsible for buying or ordering materials or services on behalf of the organisation. This would involve a series of processes and the completion of a series of documents. We look at these purchasing documents in more detail later in this Unit.

PC 4.1.2
C 2.1
C 2.2

Individual activity *Time: 15 minutes*

Write down all the services that you can think of. When you have completed your list, compare it to those which your colleagues have compiled.

Wages

As an employee, one of the most important and interesting documents you may have to deal with is your pay slip! We intend to look here at those items which appear on a pay slip, which are:

- *gross pay*
- *statutory deductions*
- *voluntary deductions*
- *net pay*

Wages can be paid in a variety of ways, including:

1 by cash in a pay packet each week
2 by cheque sent to your home either weekly or monthly
3 by bank transfer (BACS), usually monthly, to your own bank account

Everyone should receive a pay slip and it would be wise each time to check the items appearing on it. Whichever way you receive your money, you will still receive the pay slip or pay advice note and the following items will be included:

1 *Your name and, sometimes, your address*
2 *Your pay reference number*
3 *The pay period* – this is either the week or the month for which you are being paid. The tax year starts on 6 April and runs until 5 April the following year, so Week 1 would be the week commencing 6 April
4 *Your tax code and the amount that has been deducted, plus the total amount deducted to date*
5 *Your National Insurance number and the amount that has been deducted, plus the total amount deducted to date*
6 *Your contributions towards a pension scheme*
7 *Any voluntary contributions* you make which are deducted regularly from your wage or salary
8 *Your bank details* if you are being paid by BACS

PAY ADVICE

N.I. Number	Tax Code	Basis	Year	Period	Pay No	Pay Centre
YM 23 16 68D	352L	0	95/96	40	64457	991

GROSS PAY		STANDARD DEDUCTIONS		VOLUNTARY DEDUCTIONS		NET PAY
Code	£117.72	Tax	£9.80	Code		£107.92
Total Gross Pay	£117.72			Total Deductions	£9.80	

Hours worked Normal	Hours worked Overtime	TOTALS TO DATE		VOL DEDUCTIONS Code	Balance Owed
		TAXABLE	£117.72		
		TAX PAID	£9.80		

A LIST OF CODES AND ABBREVIATIONS USED IS SHOWN ON REVERSE

Fig 4.3 Pay advice slip

The accounts department will have a section which deals regularly with the preparation of wages and salaries, and this will calculate the deductions which will be taken from your gross pay. We intend now to look at some of the terms we have mentioned above in more detail:

1 **Gross pay** – this is your basic wage or salary before any deductions, either statutory or voluntary, are made. Statutory deductions are those you legally have no alternative about paying if you earn enough money each week or month.

2 **Income tax** – when you start work for the first time, or if you change your place of employment, it may be that you are on what is termed 'emergency tax'. This means that you are given an emergency tax code and will pay more tax than normal until your regular code has been allocated. The accounts department will calculate your income tax contribution for the pay period and this will be shown on your pay slip. In addition, it will also indicate on your pay slip the total amount of income tax that you have paid in the current financial year.

PC 4.1.2
C 2.1
C 2.2
IT 2.1
IT 2.2

Individual activity

Find out the following information from your tutor/parent/employer.

- **How is your tax code worked out?**
- **What allowances can you claim?**
- **What is a tax rebate?**
- **What does the term PAYE mean?**

When you have completed this research, word process a report which should be headed 'Income Tax Research Findings'.

3 **National Insurance** – both the employer and the employee make contributions towards National Insurance each week or month. Your contributions will be a percentage of your gross pay. Again, the accounts department will calculate your contribution and will show this on your pay slip, together with the total amount of contributions you have made in the current financial year.

PC 4.1.2
C 2.1
C 2.2
IT 2.1
IT 2.2

Individual activity

As with the previous activity, research the following:

- **The current rate of National Insurance contributions by the employer**
- **The current rate of National Insurance contributions by the employee**
- **Why we pay National Insurance**
- **What benefits we receive because we pay National Insurance**

Your word processed report should be entitled 'National Insurance Findings'

4 **Pension schemes** – even though you probably have not even thought about retirement when you start work, you may be asked to contribute to a pension scheme. This may either be the government pension scheme or a private pension scheme. (Your payment to the Government pension scheme will be part of your National Insurance contributions. This may be topped up by a private pension scheme.) Again, the accounts department will carry out the calculations and the amounts will be shown on your pay slip.

PC 4.1.2
C 2.2

Group activity

Time: 20 minutes

Is there any difference between the government pension scheme and private pension schemes? Some banks and building societies offer private pension schemes. Collect as much information as you can on these and compare the different types. What is meant by the term 'opting out'? Discuss these issues firstly in pairs and then as a group.

Voluntary deductions

Voluntary deductions are those that you choose to have deducted from your wage or salary and could include the following:

1 **Social club membership** – if you work for a large organisation, it may be that they have a social club for staff. You could choose to pay your subscription for this by having it deducted from your pay each week or month and this will be shown on your pay slip.
2 **Trade union membership** – if you belong to a trade union, you may choose to pay your subscription by having it deducted from your pay each week or month and again this will be shown on your pay slip.
3 **Donations to charities** – it may be that you choose to make a regular contribution to a charity or charities. This can be deducted from your pay and will also be shown on your pay slip.
4 **SAYE (Save As You Earn)** – you may wish to save a regular sum of money from your pay each week or month. This can be deducted and will be shown on your pay slip.

Net pay

Your net pay is the amount you actually receive, in cash, or by cheque, or into your bank account. This will be shown as a separate item on your pay slip and will be your gross pay, minus any statutory or voluntary deductions. The total amount of net pay earned in the current financial year will also be stated on your pay slip.

PC 4.1.2
C 2.1
C 2.2

Group activity

Time: 30 minutes

In pairs and in your own words, write down what you understand by the term 'gross pay'. Additionally, list any other voluntary deductions you can think of.

Purchase documents

As already mentioned earlier, a purchasing department would be responsible for ordering the items required by an organisation. Several considerations would have to be taken into account before a purchasing department decides which supplier to use. It is useful here to look at some of the 'terms' which the organisation would take into account before deciding which supplying organisation to use.

- **Trade discount** – this discount is given to an organisation because it is placing a large order. It may also be given if the organisation buys goods on a regular basis from the same company, or if that company is in the same field as the organisation itself.
- **Prompt payment discount** – this discount is given to an organisation if it pays its bill on time. The term 'five per cent per one month' means that the organisation can deduct five per cent from its bill if it pays within one month of receiving the goods ordered.
- **Cash discount** – this discount is given if the organisation pays its bill immediately. For example, the term 'two-and-a-half per cent cash discount' means that the organisation can deduct two-and-a-half per cent from its bill if it pays by cash or by cheque immediately the goods are received.

Estimate / quotation for Information Design work

IDT Information Design Team

Services Management Division

To:

From:

The Information Design Team
The Design Studio, 5th Floor
151 Buckingham Palace Road
London SW1W 9SS
Telephone: 215 5846/7

Document number:

Date received:

Job description:

	Cost
Design	£
Printing	£
Premium charge for urgent work	£
Plain English editing	£
Other costs	£
Total	£

Made up of:	Cost

This is an estimate ▶ If your work looks likely to exceed our estimate we will let you know before we do more work.

This is a quotation ▶ This is what you will actually pay.

We aim to complete this by:

Signed:

I accept your estimate / quotation. Please carry out this work.

Signed:

Name:

Date:

Division:

Cost centre code:

Please send this form to the Information Design Team

FC19 *(October 1991)*

Prepared by the Information Design Team

PRINTED AT WESTFIELD HOUSE

dti
the department for Enterprise

Fig 4.4 Proforma estimate/quotation form used by the DTI

The process of buying goods on behalf of the organisation can take several steps. The steps taken will very much depend on the type of goods being bought and the size of the organisation involved. Generally, the buying process involves one of the following:

- **Quotation** – if the organisation wants to purchase an expensive piece of machinery, then it may ask several companies to give a quotation. This will state the price of the goods required, the expected date of delivery and any discounts the supplier may offer. The organisation will then choose the company with the best price, terms and delivery times.
- **Estimate** – as with a quotation, the organisation may ask several companies to offer estimates for a piece of work that it requires. This is not as accurate as a quotation, but again the organisation would choose the company offering the best deal.
- **Tender** – it may be that an organisation puts a piece of work, or a service, out to tender. This means that any company interested in carrying out the work will offer to do the job for a particular price. There will be a closing date for tenders to arrive with the organisation, and on that date all tenders will be opened. Again, the organisation will choose the company offering the best deal.

Group activity *Time: 30 minutes*

PC 4.1.2
C 2.1
C 2.2
AN 2.3

Look at the three quotations given in Fig 4.5 on page 388. If you worked in the purchasing department of an organisation and were responsible for ordering these goods, which quotation would you choose? Why would you choose that particular quotation? Discuss this in pairs and then compare your considerations with those of the remainder of your group.

Many companies issue catalogues of the goods, products or services they provide. Purchasing departments would keep stocks of these catalogues, and would need to update them when new price lists are issued. Once the purchasing department has decided on the company from which it intends to order its goods, it will issue an order form to that company.

Orders placed

Once the purchasing organisation has decided on the supplier for the required goods, it will complete an order form. All the details of the order form should be completed accurately and neatly, stating exactly what is required. The individual completing the document will check with the catalogue and price list, or the quotation, to ensure that the price and details are correct. Then the order form will be sent to the supplier. Once this has been done, it is a firm commitment that the organisation requires the goods, and the order form becomes a legally-binding contract between the two organisations. Sometimes, if goods are required urgently, and the organisation has dealt with the supplier before, an order can be placed over the telephone. In this case, an order number will be quoted and the completed order form will be sent to the supplier so that both the supplier and the purchasing organisation have written confirmation that the transaction has taken place.

QUOTATION

REFERENCE NUMBER 411 DATE 19 Nov 19..

TO

Sutherland Sportswear
124 South Street
LONDON
SE2 4DC

In reply to your letter dated 15 November 199–
we have pleasure in quoting you for the following:

4 MAHOGANY OFFICE DESKS @ £375.00 EACH – TOTAL AMOUNT £1500.00

Prices include delivery by: COMPANY VAN
Delivery: WITHIN 3 WEEKS
Trade Discount: 2.5%
Cash Discount: 2.5%
VAT: Value Added Tax at 17.5% must be added to the price quoted.

Fig 4.5a Quotation 1

QUOTATION

REFERENCE NUMBER 411 DATE 19 Nov 19..

TO

Sutherland Sportswear
124 South Street
LONDON
SE2 4DC

In reply to your letter dated 15 November 199–
we have pleasure in quoting you for the following:

4 MAHOGANY OFFICE DESKS @ £399.99 EACH – TOTAL AMOUNT £1599.96

Prices include delivery by: COMPANY VAN
Delivery: WITHIN 4 WEEKS
Trade Discount: 2.5%
Cash Discount: 1.5%
VAT: Value Added Tax at 17.5% must be added to the price quoted.

Fig 4.5b Quotation 2

QUOTATION

REFERENCE NUMBER 411 DATE 19 Nov 19..

TO

Sutherland Sportswear
124 South Street
LONDON
SE2 4DC

In reply to your letter dated 15 November 199–
we have pleasure in quoting you for the following:

4 MAHOGANY OFFICE DESKS @ £350.00 EACH – TOTAL AMOUNT £1400.00

Prices include delivery by: COMPANY VAN
Delivery: WITHIN 8 WEEKS
Trade Discount: 1.5%
Cash Discount: 1.5%
VAT: Value Added Tax at 17.5% must be added to the price quoted.

Fig 4.5c Quotation 3

ORDER FORM

TO	ORDER NUMBER DATE
DELIVERY ADDRESS	SPECIAL INSTRUCTIONS

REF NO	QUANTITY	DESCRIPTION	UNIT PRICE	AMOUNT

ORDER AUTHORISED BY: ....

Fig 4.6 Order form

PC 4.1.2
C 2.2
C 2.4

Individual activity

Time: 20 minutes

Look at the example of a blank order form given in Fig 4.6. For each of the headings on the form, write down why you think the information is required. Who will make use of this information and to what purpose will it be put?

Obviously, with so many individuals or departments being involved in the purchasing of and payment for goods, it is important that more than one copy of the order form is available. To ensure that all interested parties receive the information, an order form is often printed in triplicate or quadruplicate and distributed as follows:

1. The top copy of the order form will be sent to the supplier.
2. One copy will be kept by the purchasing department for its records.
3. One copy will be needed to check the goods when received to ensure the order is complete and accurate.
4. One copy will be sent to the accounts department so that it can arrange payment for the goods when they are received.

Purchase invoice

Once the purchasing organisation has received the goods, the supplier will send them a copy of a purchase invoice. This invoice will list the quantity and description of the goods sent, as well as the total price owing. The invoice will also state a time by which payment should be made, and will list any discounts made available to the purchasing organisation. Obviously, it will be necessary for the purchasing organisation to check the invoice against the order form and the goods received note (we deal with this document a little later) to ensure that they all agree and the figures tally. They will check the invoice for the following:

- *the order number is correct*
- *the goods listed match those received*
- *the quantity listed matches that received*
- *the price listed matches that quoted*
- *the calculations are correct*
- *the discounts are as agreed*

All invoices contain the letters E&OE at the bottom of them. This stands for 'errors and omissions excepted' and helps to ensure that the supplier can send a further invoice if a mistake is found. Should any errors occur on the invoice, then the supplier of the goods might take the following action:

- *Send out a supplementary invoice* – in the case of items having been delivered, but been missed from the invoice, the supplier will send a supplementary invoice to cover the difference. A supplementary invoice will also be sent if the customer has been undercharged for some reason.

PC 4.1.2
C 2.2
C 2.4

Individual activity *Time: 20 minutes*

Look at the example of a blank invoice given in Fig 4.7. For each of the headings on the form, write down why you think the information is required. Who will make use of this information and to what purpose will it be put?

Credit note

Should the supplier list items on the invoice by mistake, meaning that the invoice total is too high, then they will have to send the purchasing organisation a credit note. This credit note would also be issued to the purchasing organisation if goods have been returned as being faulty.

INVOICE

TO	NUMBER
	DATE
	TERMS
YOUR ORDER NO	DESPATCH DATE

QUANTITY	DESCRIPTION	UNIT PRICE	TOTAL PRICE	VAT
	Gross Value LESS Trade Discount			
	Net Value of Goods PLUS VAT @ %			
	INVOICE TOTAL			

E & O E

Fig 4.7 Invoice

CREDIT NOTE

TO	NUMBER
	DATE
ORDER NUMBER	INVOICE NUMBER

QUANTITY	DESCRIPTION	UNIT PRICE	TOTAL PRICE	VAT
	Gross Value LESS Trade Discount			
	Net Value of Goods PLUS VAT @ %			
	CREDIT NOTE TOTAL			

Fig 4.8 Credit note

PC 4.1.2
C 2.2
C 2.4

Individual activity *Time: 20 minutes*

Look at the example of a blank credit note given in Fig 4.8. For each of the headings on the form, write down why you think the information is required. Who will make use of this information and to what purpose will it be put?

Goods received note

This document will be completed by the person receiving the goods when they are delivered to the purchasing organisation. It may be that the person receiving the goods does not have a copy of the original order form, so all they will do is to check that the goods received note states correctly exactly what has actually been delivered. They will check the number of boxes or packages against the quantity stated on the delivery note. It may be that the two do not tally, in which case the items will need to be unpacked and counted. It may also be that any of the following occur:

1 **Missing goods** – it may be that the goods were not sent because the supplier was out of stock at the time, or forgot to send them. If the supplier was out of stock, then the goods received note should state 'to follow' or 'discontinued'. If this is not the case, then the accounts department would need to be informed of the shortage of goods, so that it does not pay for what has not been received. The supplier would then need to be contacted to find out why some of the goods have not been received by the purchasing organisation.
2 **Additional goods** – any goods that are received but are not stated on the original order form should be returned to the supplier. It may be that this could be done immediately, by returning them with the supplier's delivery van, or, alternatively, they may have to be sent separately.
3 **Incorrect goods** – again, if the goods received are incorrect, they will have to be returned to the supplier. This will be easy to identify because the goods received note will differ from the order form.
4 **Damaged or faulty goods** – it is usually possible to exchange faulty or damaged goods immediately the supplier is notified. Sometimes the goods received note will include a section for the person receiving the goods to complete, should there be any problem with the goods on arrival.
5 **Goods ordered in error** – this is quite difficult. If the goods have been ordered by mistake, and are supplied in good faith by the supplier, then supplier is under no obligation to take them back. However, if the organisation and the supplier have had a long-term working relationship, and the organisation has spent a lot of money with the supplier, particularly if it has paid regularly, then the supplier would rather take the goods back than to lose the custom.

PC 4.1.2
C 2.2
C 2.4

Individual activity *Time: 20 minutes*

Look at the example of a blank credit note given in Fig 4.9. For each of the headings on the form, write down why you think the information is required. Who will make use of this information and to what purpose will it be put?

GOODS RECEIVED NOTE

NO	DATE RECEIVED	ORDER NO	DELIVERED BY
QUANTITY	DESCRIPTION	NUMBER OF PACKAGES	STORES REF

RECEIVED FROM	ENTERED INTO STOCK		RECEIVED BY
	DATE	INITIAL	
SUPPLIER			STOREKEEPER

Fig 4.9 Goods received note

ORDER FORM

TO Sutherland Sportswear 124 South Street LONDON SE2 4DC	ORDER NUMBER ST448 DATE 25 JANUARY 19 . .
DELIVERY ADDRESS AS ABOVE	SPECIAL INSTRUCTIONS NONE

REF NO	QUANTITY	DESCRIPTION	UNIT PRICE	AMOUNT
A4 154	14	REAMS OF WHITE A4 PAPER	£3.01	£42.03
D11	10	PACKS OF D11 SIZE ENVELOPES	£2.00	£20.00

ORDER AUTHORISED BY: ....

Fig 4.10 Completed order form

GOODS RECEIVED NOTE

NO	DATE RECEIVED	ORDER NO	DELIVERED BY
367	30 JANUARY . .	ST448	COMPANY VAN
QUANTITY	**DESCRIPTION**	**NUMBER OF PACKAGES**	**STORES REF**
A4 154	REAMS OF WHITE A4	10	BAY 56
D11	PACKS OF D11 ENVELOPES	10	BAY 55

RECEIVED FROM	ENTERED INTO STOCK		RECEIVED BY
	DATE	INITIAL	
SUPPLIER			STOREKEEPER

Fig 4.11 Completed goods received note

INVOICE

TO Sutherland Sportswear
124 South Street
LONDON SE2 4DC
YOUR ORDER NO ST448

NUMBER 5/149/dec
DATE 28 February 19 . .
TERMS 2.5 %
DESPATCH DATE 30.1.19 . .

QUANTITY	DESCRIPTION	UNIT PRICE	TOTAL PRICE	VAT
14 Reams	A4 A54 WHITE A4 PAPER	£3.01	£42.03	£7.35
10 Boxes	D11 ENVELOPES	£2.00	£20.00	£3.50
	Gross Value		£62.03	
	LESS Trade Discount		£1.55	
	Net Value of Goods		£60.48	
	PLUS VAT @ 17.5%		£10.85	
	INVOICE TOTAL		£71.33	

E & O E

Fig 4. 12 Completed invoice

Group activity *Time: 45 minutes*

PC 4.1.2
C 2.1
C 2.2
C 2.4
AN 2.2
AN 2.3

In small groups, compare the completed order form, goods received note and invoice given in Figs 4.10, 4.11 and 4.12. Do all the documents agree? If you were the purchasing organisation, what discrepancies could you find?

Make a list of the discrepancies as you identify them and then compare your lists with those of the remainder of your group.

Individually, complete a flow chart of the purchasing process which an organisation would take when buying goods.

4.1.3 Explain the give examples of sales transactions and sales documents

Goods and services

We look in more detail at the actual documents used for these transactions later in this Unit. But what is the purpose of such documentation?

All organisations will have a budget. Whether the organisation is large or small, it will have an objective which it must try to meet. It would be impossible for managers to monitor the performance of the organisation if documents relating to the amount of money spent and the amount of money coming into the organisation were not readily available and accurate.

Obviously, the larger the organisation, the more documentation it will generate. In addition to this, a larger organisation is more likely to purchase goods on a credit basis. This means that it will order and receive goods when the need arises, and pay for them on a monthly basis. Such an organisation is likely to generate its documents by using computer software packages, although it is not unusual for an organisation still to be handling transactions manually.

In the same way, an organisation may sell its products to customers or clients on a credit basis, and receive payment for them on a monthly basis.

Because so many transactions are dealt with in this way, mistakes such as the following could easily occur unless the organisation records all transactions:

- *goods being sent to the wrong customer*
- *incorrect goods being despatched to a customer*
- *delay in payments for goods*
- *complaints being received from customers*
- *loss of business because of confusion with customers*

The activities of different organisations vary, although all organisations use the business documents they generate to plan and control the way the organisation performs. The documentation may relate to the day-to-day work of a small number of workers, or it may relate to a specific job of the production line.

Whatever the activity, the accounts department would need to be fully aware of the financial transactions taking place within the organisation. Because so much credit business is conducted nowadays, the accounting team needs copies of each document received or sent out by the organisation in order to generate the accounts of the business.

Business-to-business and business-to-consumer

Another very important purpose of documentation for the recording of the business activities of an organisation is the need to confirm. Obviously, it would be foolish to rely on word of mouth. Whatever the size of an organisation, it is necessary to confirm an order for goods, or to confirm the amount of money outstanding on an account. Without this written confirmation the organisations involved would be inefficient and ineffective.

Additionally, with regard to the respect for one another, organisations need the confirmation of a written document as opposed to a verbal commitment.

When goods are ordered and purchased, both the purchasing organisation and the supplier of the goods will need to understand exactly and accurately what is involved in the transaction. Once a written order has been placed, this is a legally-binding document, tying the two organisations together in a firm commitment to:

- *supply the goods in the exact form and at the price stated, at the time agreed*
- *pay for the goods on the terms confirmed at the time detailed*

Without this mutually agreed document, neither one organisation nor the other will have any written evidence that the transaction has taken place.

Sales documents

As we have already mentioned previously in the book, the sales department and the marketing department work very closely together. Once the marketing department has completed its job and successfully advertised and promoted the organisation's products, then the sales department will attempt to sell the product to the customer.

The documents dealt with in the sales department link very closely with those dealt with in the purchasing department. The main difference is that the organisation is now the supplier of the goods or services, rather than the purchasing organisation. However, all the rules regarding the careful completion and checking will still apply, as will the fact that all the transactions need to be recorded accurately and neatly.

Orders received

In a similar way to the placing of an order, an organisation may receive an order for their goods or services by telephone. Again, a written order form must be sent by post or by fax to confirm the sale. If the sales department receives an order over the telephone, it would ask the customer to state an order number from their order book. This number would then be recorded in the sales department, and 'married' to the written order form when it arrived.

Once the order form has been received, the sales department would check for the following:

1 That the catalogue number is correct.
2 That the price is correct and the most up to date.
3 Whether the customer is new to the organisation.
4 Whether the existing customer is entitled to credit and what their credit limit is.
5 Whether the customer is normally allowed any discounts.
6 Whether the order is a straightforward one. There may be some special instructions such as a different delivery address or a particular delivery time.

Once the order form has been checked and processed, then the goods will be sent to the customer.

Sales invoice

A sales invoice is often sent out at the same time as the goods and, as always, the information should be correct, legible and contain all the necessary details. It is to the advantage of the organisation that their sales invoices are sent out promptly in order that they can receive payment for the goods as quickly as possible after their despatch. Obviously, any sales invoice which is sent out containing errors or omissions would have to be reissued or amended, and this could be costly and time consuming to the organisation.

How quickly the customer pays the organisation for the goods received will depend on the terms under which they ordered the goods. The purchasing organisation may wish to take advantage of any prompt payment discount they have been offered by the organisation. Alternatively, they may be entitled to cash or trade discount.

In addition to the details of the price of each item ordered and despatched, and the total amount of the invoice, the sales invoice will also contain information regarding the VAT content of the price of the order.

- *VAT is charged on the total of the goods plus the delivery charge*
- *VAT is added to the total price of the goods, less any discounts available*

PC 4.1.3
C 2.2

Individual activity

Time: 10 minutes

Can you remember what we have already said about discounts? Write down the difference between trade, cash and prompt payment discounts.

In the event of there having been a discrepancy between the goods received by the customer and the invoice sent by the organisation, then a credit note or debit note will be issued by the sales department, depending on whether it is money to be received or paid.

Delivery note

The sales department would expect that a delivery note should accompany the goods when they are sent to the customer. A delivery note will list the goods but will not state the price of the goods or the total of the order. The customer will check the goods if they are able to do so when they are received. If the customer is not able to do this checking, then they would sign the delivery note as 'goods received and not examined'. In either case, the individual delivering the goods would need a signature from the purchasing organisation on the delivery note to say that they have received the goods. Once the goods have been delivered to the purchasing organisation, then they legally become its property.

DELIVERY NOTE

TO

NUMBER
YOUR ORDER NUMBER
DATE

THE FOLLOWING ITEMS HAVE BEEN DESPATCHED TODAY TO ________
________________ BY RAIL/COMPANY VAN/POST*

QUANTITY	DESCRIPTION	NUMBER OF PACKAGES

I certify that the goods received have been checked and are in good condition

Signed: .... On behalf of: ....
Date: ....

I certify that the number of packages delivered is correct according to the number stated above, but that the goods have not been checked

Signed: .... On behalf of: ....
Date: ....

* Please delete as appropriate

Fig 4.13 Delivery note

Individual activity *Time: 20 minutes*

PC 4.1.3
C 2.2
C 2.4

Look at the example of a blank delivery note given in Fig 4.13. For each of the headings on the form, write down why you think the information is required. Who will make use of this information and to what purpose will it be put?

Group activity *Time: 1.5 hours*

PC 4.1.3
C 2.1
C 2.2
IT 2.1
IT 2.2
IT 2.3

What do you think an organisation should do if it receives goods which are damaged or incorrect? Discuss this in a group and write down your findings.

Using the findings from your group discussion, word process a letter to a supplier, giving an explanation of your problem of damaged or incorrect goods, including your opinion as to how the problem could be resolved.

Sales credit note

As we have already mentioned, a credit note would be issued by the sales department for the following reasons:

1 A mistake has been made on the invoice and the customer has been overcharged.
2 When goods have had to be returned to the supplying organisation by the purchasing organisation because the goods are faulty or damaged.
3 When the purchasing organisation has made an error in ordering goods and has either overestimated its needs or ordered the incorrect goods.

Obviously, it is in the interests of the supplying organisation to keep goodwill with the purchasing organisation. In order to maintain good working relationships, the supplying organisation would either issue a credit note or would amend the statement of account issued at the end of each month.

Statement of account

Depending on the payment times of the purchasing organisation, the supplying organisation would issue a statement of account to inform the customer of the balance they owe to the organisation. The statement of account is usually sent once a month, at the end of each month, and will list the transactions that have taken place between the two organisations. It will show the totals of each of the sales invoices sent to the customer, plus any payments made by the customer during the month. The balance shown at the end of the statement is the amount of money still to be paid by the customer to the supplying organisation.

Statements of account are important to an organisation for two reasons:

1 *To keep a check of what a customer still owes*
2 *To keep a check of what has been sent to the customer*

STATEMENT

TO
Sutherland Sportswear
124 South Street
LONDON
SE2 4DC

DATE 28.2.19. .
NUMBER 32
TERMS 2.5 %

DATE	DETAILS	DEBIT	VAT	CREDIT	VAT	BALANCE
10/2	Balance					£120.60
15/2	Goods	£519.40	£77.91			£717.91
18/2	Returns			£171.50	£25.73	£520.68
20/2	Cheque			£220.68		£300.00

Payments received after the end of the month will not be shown on this statement.

Fig 4.14 Statement of account

PC 4.1.3
C 2.2
C 2.4

Individual activity

Time: 20 minutes

Look at the example of a completed statement of account given in Fig 4.14. For each of the headings on the form, write down why you think the information is required. Who will make use of this information and to what purpose will it be put?

How much does the organisation actually owe? How much has it already paid?

In the role of an individual who is responsible for the checking of statements of account, you are going to be away on a course for a month and you need to leave instructions for your stand-in. Write down your list of instructions to ensure that the job is carried out correctly.

Remittance advice

If an organisation were regularly purchasing from its suppliers on credit, and the money were being transferred from one bank account to another, or payment was made by credit card, then a remittance advice would be issued. A remittance advice simply states that although no money is included in this document, a certain amount of money has been paid to the organisation by other means. In other words, if a purchasing organisation has received a statement of account and wishes to pay by credit card, then they would send a remittance advice note to the supplying organisation. This remittance advice would state that the money now belonged to the supplying organisation, even though it did not have the money physically sent to it.

This remittance advice would assist both the supplying organisation and the purchasing organisation in the preparation of their accounts, as they would be able to see firstly what money they had and additionally what money they had not yet received.

PC 4.1.3
C 2.1
C 2.2

Group activity *Time: 45 minutes*

What do you think would happen if a company had been given discount provided it paid within 28 days, and then it did not pay?

In pairs, prepare a flow chart of the selling process of an organisation.

4.1.4 Explain and give examples of payment methods and receipt documents

Payment methods

Obviously, we all need money of some description on a day-to-day basis and, depending on our circumstances, we pay for the goods we buy in a variety of different ways. To some extent, the same applies to business organisations. There are six main ways in which a purchasing organisation usually chooses to pay for the goods or services it has bought:

1 *Cheque*
2 *Cash*
3 *Credit card*
4 *Debit card*
5 *Credit sale*
6 *Hire purchase*

Although cash, cheque and debit card are different methods of payment, they are all still regarded as being 'cash' payments because the supplier receives the money for the goods or services on an immediate basis. Although a credit card payment gives the supplier the money instantly, the credit card company may not receive the money from the purchasing organisation or customer for some time.

Cheque

We already know how much safer it is to carry a cheque book than to carry cash. The reason for this is that cash is irreplaceable, while a cheque book can be 'stopped' by a bank or building society, should it be stolen or lost.

Group activity *Time: 15 minutes*

Discuss in pairs, and then write down, what you would do if you had your cheque book stolen.

PC 4.1.4
C 2.1
C 2.2

In many ways it is better for a supplying organisation to receive payment by cheque. Customers will not need to be issued with a receipt as they will have their cheque book counterfoil as evidence of the payment. The customer will also receive a bank statement which will itemise the transactions and show that the cheque has been cashed.

Another advantage of paying by cheque is that this method of payment can be sent through the post quite safely, while cash, on the other hand, should never be sent. Should a cheque get lost while in the post it is of no use to anyone except the payee, unlike cash (which is of great use to everyone!).

When an individual opens a current account at a bank or building society, they are issued with a cheque book and a cheque guarantee card (we look at these cards a little later in this section). The cheque book will contain a number of cheques, each of which is identical in every way, except for the serial number printed on it.

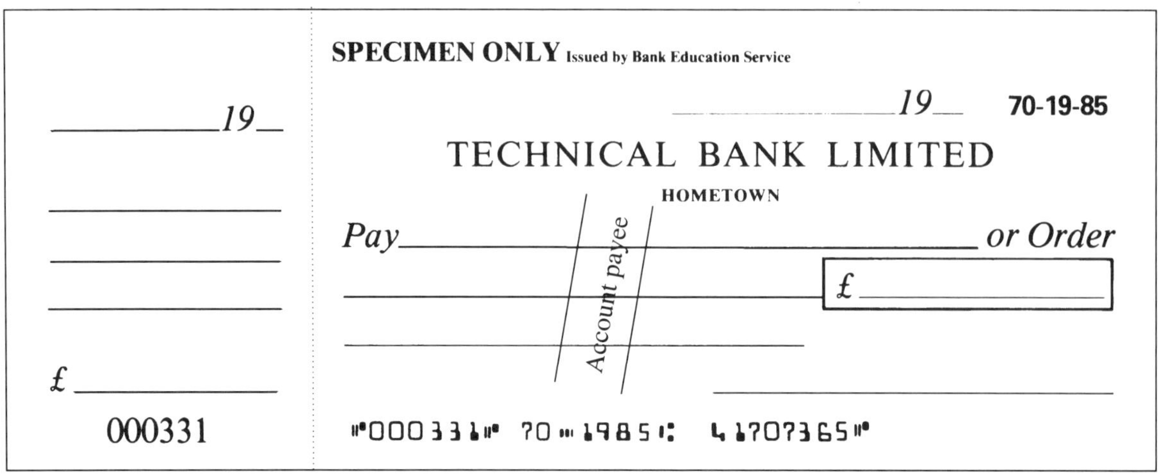

Fig 4.15 Blank cheque

It is almost impossible nowadays to pay by cheque unless it is accompanied by a cheque guarantee card. This card virtually guarantees that the bank or building society (the drawee) will honour the cheque on behalf of the drawer, even if the cheque book and card are stolen or if there are insufficient funds in the current account (up to a certain amount). Once a cheque guarantee card has been used, it is impossible to 'stop' the cheque.

A crossed cheque is one which has two lines drawn or printed down the centre, and the words 'account payee' written between these lines. This means that the person receiving the cheque will have to pay it into their bank account and cannot 'cash' it anywhere else. By doing this, the banks and building societies are making it more difficult for people to steal cheques and cash them.

Many organisations use their cheque book to pay their bills. In larger organisations, several designated people will be the only ones allowed to sign cheques. We deal with this area of cheque payment a little later in this Element.

Cash

There is no way that the carrying of cash can be described as being safe. Despite this, many people still pay for their shopping, etc., by cash, although it is unlikely that organisations would pay their suppliers by cash. In some ways it is more convenient to carry cash, and it is certainly less irritating to the person behind you in the queue if you pay by cash instead of writing a cheque! However, it is still possible that a supplier has some concern over the use of cash. It has become increasingly necessary for shops to use the ultra-violet machines available for checking the authenticity of banknotes.

BACS (Bankers' Automated Clearing Services)

The BACS system is used for both direct debit and standing order payments, as well as salary transfer. It reduces the amount of paperwork involved in each transaction. The necessary information is supplied to the bank on magnetic tape or disk and is processed via the BACS computer centre. Once the information has been processed, the necessary payments are made automatically. We mentioned the direct debit and standing order methods of payment which are as follows:

- **Direct debit** – regular payments can be made from one account to another using this system. The customer informs the bank of the date and amount of the payment, and the bank transfers the funds accordingly. With a direct debit, the organisation receiving the funds can vary the amount, although it is required to inform the customer prior to taking this action.
- **Standing order** – regular payments can be made using this system. A customer can instruct his/her bank to pay by standing order on a certain date for a fixed amount. The recipient cannot change the amount unless the customer informs the bank of the change in advance.

EDI (Electronic Data Interchange)

In a similar way to that in which the BACS system works, by transferring money from one account to another, the EDI system can transfer information from one organisation to another. This information may take the form of repeat orders or automatic updating of stock levels. EDI is also a useful tool in accessing information stored in computer libraries or other databases. Many of the more technologically-aware colleges will have links with a variety of American-based computer libraries or databases, accessed via modem link. Virtually instantaneous electronic data interchange can be achieved through a series of menus and sub-menus. It is rather like browsing in a library, but on screen. Not only can the data be instantaneously transferred to the enquirer's terminal, no matter where that terminal may be, but it can also be printed with the same speed.

Focus study

Electronic Data Interchange

The market researchers Internet Info calculated that in mid-1994 some 38% of the top 2000 US companies had some kind of linkage with Internet. Indeed, the Internet Society also calculated that 24% of all the Internet hosts (these are separate directories which can be accessed via the Internet) were US organisations. The UK by this same stage accounted for some 5%.

On a commercial basis, the Internet can provide information on demand at a cost. You can buy items also via Internet which are not necessarily information but products. Organisations have appreciated that making EDI available by the Internet allows them to provide useful direct connection with existing customers in the provision of back-up information for their products or services.

Credit card

Not too long ago, it was unusual to see someone paying for goods with a credit card. Now, however, they are commonly used and most people feel quite confident about buying and using something that has not really been paid for in full. In fact, using credit cards is extremely useful, although in the wrong hands they can be dangerous! If someone is not responsible they could pay for goods using a credit card which they have little chance of being able to repay, and the interest charged to their account is very high (*see* Fig 4.16).

Each individual, or organisation, issued with a credit card is given a credit limit. This is the amount that they are allowed to spend using the card. Each month they will receive a statement from the credit card company, notifying them of any transactions they have made using the card, the balance they owe and the minimum amount they need to pay that month. If the owner of the card pays the amount owed in full, then no interest is charged to the account. If, however, they can only pay a small amount, then the interest charged is high.

It is easy to see which businesses, both in this country and abroad, will accept credit card payments, as they display the fact in the window or near the counter of their premises.

Cash

The most widely used way of making payments. Almost 90% of all payments are still settled with cash.

Cash Dispenser + Card

Enable customers to obtain cash from a machine. In some cases even when the bank is closed. You can also order a statement or a cheque book.

Cheque

Can be used to purchase goods and services or to obtain cash from a bank account.

Cheque Cards

Will guarantee a payment of a cheque up to a sum of £50. A big help when you are shopping.

Credit Cards

Card holders can obtain goods and services from those shops, garages and other organisations which accept the cards. Can also be used to obtain cash from banks at home and abroad.

Regular Payments

Standing Order

Used by customers who want the bank to *make* payments for them on a regular basis, such as rent; hire purchase instalments; insurance premiums; club subscriptions. It saves people having to remember each time.

Direct Debit

A variation on a standing order. Used mainly by organisations which *receive* vast numbers of regular payments. The companies draw on the customers' bank accounts by computer.

Bank Giro Credit

A convenient way of paying bills through the banking system. You can also pay money into your own account when you are away from home.

Travelling Abroad

Travel cheques are a safe and convenient way of carrying money for holidays. Banks also supply foreign bank notes.

Fig 4.16 Methods of making payments

Offering a credit card in payment does not necessarily guarantee that the business will accept it. The organisation will have a limit to the amount it can accept from a customer. This is called the Floor Limit. Anything above this has to be authorised directly from the credit card company. The business will telephone the credit card company in order to receive an authorisation code. This code is then entered on to the sales voucher. If the credit card company will not issue an authorisation code (maybe because the limit of the card has already been reached, or the owner of the card has missed payments), then the business will not accept payment by credit card.

Increasingly, authorisation from the credit card company can be obtained directly using a special terminal linked directly to the credit card companies. These are easy to use for the retailer and quick for the person making the purchase. Sometimes this terminal will also print the sales voucher for the business, although this is not necessarily standard at the moment. Usually the sales assistant will complete the sales voucher by hand. The voucher is made up of four copies and is distributed as follows:

- *the top copy is given to the customer as their receipt*
- *the second copy is sent to the credit card company*
- *the third and fourth copies are kept by the retailer for their records*

Debit card

In recent years, the need to carry around a cheque book and cheque guarantee card is becoming obsolete. Increasingly, banks and building societies are adopting a card which looks and operates very much like a credit card, but simply and immediately debits the current account of the holder for the amount of goods purchased. This card is known as a debit card and it has an additional useful safeguard from the point of view of the retailer in that, as soon as the bank has accepted the card, then the retailer is guaranteed prompt payment. Examples of this debit card method of payment are the Switch and Connect cards (*see* Fig 4.17). Some banks and building societies now also provide a multi-functional card which acts as a cheque guarantee card, a debit card and a cash dispenser card, all in one.

Fig 4.17 An example of a debit card (Barclays Connect)

Individual activity

Some retail outlets will accept debit cards and others will not. Carry out some research in your local area and find out what percentage of shops will accept them. Additionally, try to find out why others will not accept them.

PC 4.1.4
C 2.2

Credit (includes hire purchase)

The most common example of credit sale is the mail order industry. The customer has the right to choose to make payments over a number of weeks. When someone buys on credit they do not lose the rights of a person paying by cash. They are still protected by the law if they return any goods which may prove to be faulty.

The goods purchased by credit become the property of the customer once the first payment has been made.

If someone who has bought goods on credit does not make regular payments (this is known as defaulting), then the company or shop from which the goods were bought could take the customer to court to obtain their money. They can, however, not repossess the goods (this means claim them back), although credit sales are often used for goods which would have little or no value if repossessed (e.g. clothing).

Unlike credit sales, however, goods bought by hire purchase do not become the property of the purchaser until they have been paid for completely. Also, any items can be repossessed in a hire purchase agreement if the customer defaults on payments.

Before a customer will be allowed to take out a hire purchase agreement, the company supplying the goods will carry out a credit rating on the customer. This means that the supplier will contact a credit agency to find out whether the customer has had problems in meeting payments on any other agreements. If this is the case, then the supplier will refuse to enter into such an agreement. Provided the customer is employed on a full-time basis, is the correct age and is in good health, then they can take out insurance against becoming ill or unemployed and unable to keep up the payments. This insurance can often work out to be expensive and, because of its limitations, can exclude some people.

PC 4.1.4
C 2.1

Group activity *Time: 15 minutes*

In groups, discuss the implications of someone who has bought a stereo system on hire purchase and now cannot make the payments each month.

Receipt

A receipt is a document which confirms that a certain amount of money has been paid. This could be from one individual to another, as when you go shopping and receive a till receipt, or from one organisation to another.

Receipts take many forms, but in each case the receipt will state the amount of money involved and the date the transaction took place. It will be made out in duplicate so that each person involved in the transaction has a copy.

It may be that someone buying petrol will ask for a receipt because they can reclaim the sum from their company on their expenses.

Most people are familiar with the format of a receipt:

- When you buy goods from a shop, then you often receive a printed till receipt
- In some smaller shops, the assistant will write a receipt by hand

- If you have a cheque book, you will know that the counterfoil acts as a form of receipt or record of what you have spent and to whom you have paid it
- When you pay money into a bank account, you will know that the counterfoil acts as a form of receipt or record of how much you paid in
- If you receive a bank statement, this lists all the monies paid in and taken out of your account, and acts as a receipt for the amount you have in balance
- If you travel by bus or train you will receive a ticket; this is your receipt that you have paid the fare
- When you take clothes to the dry cleaners, the assistant will issue a receipt which you have to present when collecting the goods

Receipts are normally quite simple to complete, and usually include the following items:

1 *name of the organisation issuing the receipt*
2 *date of the transaction*
3 *name of the person making the payment*
4 *amount of the payment*
5 *reason for the payment*

Group activity *Time: 15 minutes*

In pairs, using the receipt in Fig 4.18, decide why each of the headings is necessary and who would make use of this information.

PC 4.1.4
C 2.1

	CASH RECEIPT
Number	NUMBER ....DATE ....
Date	RECEIVED FROM ....
From	....
....	....
....	THE SUM OF ....
....	....
£ p	£ p

Fig 4.18 A receipt form

Cheque

We have already mentioned the fact that when someone pays by cheque, then their counterfoil is a form of receipt or record of what has been paid and to whom. We will now deal with the process involved in paying by cheque and paying a cheque into the bank. Just because someone has paid by cheque, it does not necessarily mean that the organisation is guaranteed payment. It could be that the bank receiving the cheque into the organisation's account has problems in 'clearing' the cheque. Clearing involves the bank checking that the person writing the cheque has sufficient funds in their account. This can take several days and often takes longer when paying the cheque into a building society account rather than a bank account. The bank or building society may refuse to accept the cheque for a variety of reasons, including:

- *If there are insufficient funds available in the account*
- *If the cheque is more than six months old (this is known as a 'stale' cheque)*
- *If the cheque has not been dated*
- *If the cheque has been post-dated (written for a future date)*
- *If the amount written in words is different from the amount in figures*
- *If the name of the payee is incorrect (it may have been misspelt)*
- *If any corrections or alterations have been made on the cheque and have not been initialled by the drawee (the person writing the cheque)*
- *If the cheque has not been signed*
- *If the signature on the cheque does not match that on the cheque guarantee card*
- *If the cheque guarantee card has expired (become out of date)*

All the above items would have to be checked before the bank will clear the cheque. If there are any problems relating to the cheque, then the bank will send it back to the drawee and either request them to rewrite it or to ensure that they pay funds into their account before writing any more cheques.

Paying-in slip

If we are fortunate enough to have money to pay into our bank accounts, then we complete a paying-in slip (*see* Fig 4.19). Sometimes it is also possible to do this using an automated deposit machine outside the bank.

Once the paying-in slip has been completed, it is simple to hand the slip and the cash/cheques over the counter to the cashier. He/she will then check the cash/cheques and indicate on the slip that it is the correct amount. This money is then paid automatically into the account.

But how do large organisations cope with paying money into their accounts? Obviously, it would not be wise to allow large sums of money to be kept on their premises, or to be taken to the bank. In order to deposit their takings into their bank accounts regularly, large organisations often employ a security company, such as Securicor, to transfer their money for them. This is obviously much safer than relying on individuals from the organisation to do this job. Some smaller organisations, however, do still send their staff to the bank on a regular basis to deposit takings. To ensure their safety, it is wise to allow the employee to be escorted and to make sure that they vary their route to the bank each day and make their journey at a different time each day.

Some banks also have a night deposit safe which customers can use after the bank has closed. This is a useful service to customers who close their businesses after the banks have closed for the day.

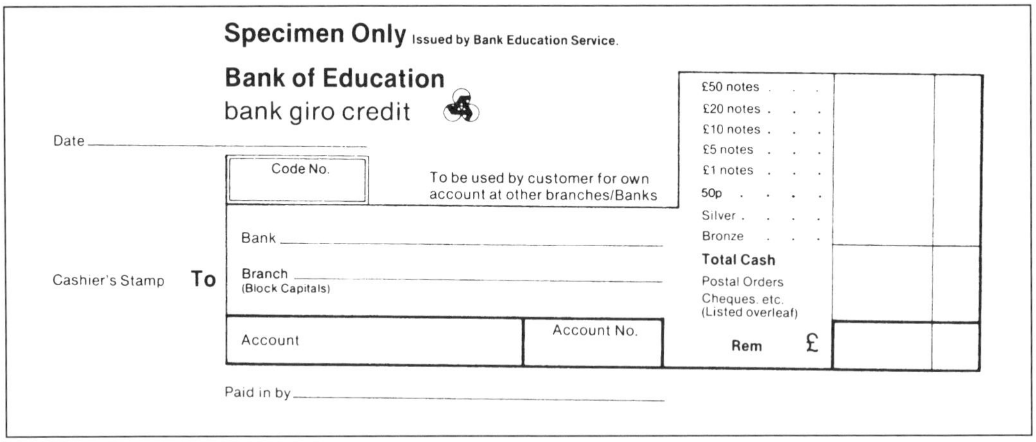

Specimen Only Issued by Bank Education Service.

Bank of Education
bank giro credit

Date

Code No.

To be used by customer for own account at other branches/Banks

Bank

Cashier's Stamp To

Branch (Block Capitals)

Account | Account No.

Paid in by

£50 notes	
£20 notes	
£10 notes	
£5 notes	
£1 notes	
50p	
Silver	
Bronze	
Total Cash	
Postal Orders	
Cheques etc. (Listed overleaf)	
Rem £	

Fig 4.19 A paying-in slip

Individual activity

PC 4.1.4
C 2.2

The next time you are in your local town, look to see how many night deposit safes you can find for different banks. If possible, ask in the bank whether they charge for this service and whether it is possible for anybody to make use of them. Write down your findings in the form of a memorandum to your tutor.

Bank statement

We have already mentioned cheque payments and paying-in slips. If we are not particularly good at keeping a note of all the transactions we enter into, it could be that we may forget one or two. This would mean a difference in the amount of money we actually have and the amount we thought we had! Fortunately, a bank will send us a bank statement on a regular basis. This statement will list the payments we have made, the cash we have drawn out, and any standing orders or direct debit payments which have been taken from the account. Some typical withdrawals include the following:

- *Cheques we have written and which have been presented to our bank to be cleared*
- *Cash we have either withdrawn from our account over the counter at the bank or from the cash dispenser machine*
- *Any standing order payments which have been taken from our account*
- *Any direct debit payments which have been taken from our account*

In addition to the withdrawals column on the bank statement will be one headed 'deposits'. This column will list the items you have paid into your account either over the counter at the bank using a paying-in slip, or using the automated deposit machine. It may, however, also be that someone is paying you regularly by standing order or direct debit, or that your salary is paid into your account by credit transfer or Bankers' Automated Clearing Services (BACS) from the account of your employer.

It is very important to check the bank statement thoroughly when it is received. Organisations obviously have to do the same. When an organisation checks its bank statement for withdrawals and deposits, this is known as a 'bank reconciliation'. This means that it adds to the balance shown on the statement any deposits which have been made since the issue of the statement, as well as subtracting any withdrawals that have been made. In this way, it will be easy to see the exact amount the organisation now has in the account.

PC 4.1.4
C 2.1
C 2.2

Group activity

In pairs, find out from the banks in your local area how often you can receive a bank statement. Does the bank make this decision, or can the customer choose how often? Are all the banks the same?

In your own words, write a summary of why an organisation would carry out a bank reconciliation.

4.1.5 Explain the importance of security and security checks for receipts and payments

To prevent fraud and theft and to ensure high standards of honesty

It goes without saying that an organisation has to be very careful who it recruits to handle the financial transactions that are carried out. Obviously, it would be nice to assume that everyone could be trusted, but unfortunately this is not the case. An organisation would have to ensure that sufficient security checks are in place to avoid the possibility of any individual either from within the organisation or from outside being able to steal or commit an act of fraud with the organisation's funds.

Security checks

Throughout this Element we have discussed several times the fact that documents and various data must be kept and stored securely. This is particularly the case with any financial transactions an organisation might make, and the main reason why the checking of such documents for accuracy and neatness is so important.

But security of such documents going out of the organisation is not the only consideration. Safeguards have to be taken to ensure that the employees of the organisation follow the set process for completion of documents. This is another form of security. The three main aspects of security with regard to financial transactions are the authorisation of orders, the reconciliation of invoices against orders and goods received notes, and the authorisation of cheques.

Authorisation of orders

It would be very disadvantageous to an organisation if there were not an individual, or group of individuals, who had the overall say as to what could be ordered. Obviously, this has to be someone with the right amount of authority within the organisation and who knows its financial commitments. This person (or persons) must know what goods are needed and the urgency of this need. It makes sense, then, that each department within the organisation will have a person who can authorise requests for goods or services. These individuals will have a budget to work from and will only be allowed to spend a certain amount of money each month or year. With regard to the type of goods ordered, it will obviously have to be products or services which are required to carry out the work in hand. Again, the authorisation of the order will be the responsibility of the department manager. Another consideration here is the fact that, if only specified members of staff have this responsibility, then the possibility of double-ordering any goods is avoided.

Individual activity

Time: 1 hour (for the report)

PC 4.1.5
C 2.2
IT 2.1
IT 2.2

Schools and colleges have to have budgets. Try to find out who has overall responsibility for the budget in your institution. Does that person have to authorise everything? Do they delegate some of this responsibility? Does each sector or department have their own budget(s)? When you have carried out your research, present your findings in the form of a word-processed report to your tutor.

Invoices checked against orders and goods received notes

As we already know, invoices will be checked thoroughly before being sent out. Some organisations may be more thorough than others. It may be that each person checking the invoice has to sign a verification to that effect before passing it on to the next person. As we have already mentioned, reconciliation means the checking of details against details sent. This will be carried out when an organisation receives an invoice. The person responsible for receiving the invoice will check it against the order sent and the goods received note to ensure that all the details on the invoice are correct. If the invoice is correct, then it will be sent to the accounts department for payment, either immediately to claim the discount offered, or when the statement of account arrives.

But what if there are discrepancies? Should there be an error on the invoice when it is compared with the order and the goods received note, then the following steps would need to be taken:

1. *If it is only a small error and the organisation has a good relationship with the supplier, then a telephone call would probably be all that is needed. In this case, the supplier would most likely send the organisation a replacement invoice.*
2. *If the error is a large one, it would be in the interests of the organisation to put this in writing either by letter or fax.*

Obviously, if a series of errors or discrepancies appeared on the invoice of the same supplier, then the organisation may well consider changing their supplier for that particular product or service.

PC 4.1.5
C 2.2

Individual activity *Time: 45 minutes*

In the role of a person responsible for checking invoices, imagine that you have found a discrepancy and need to notify your departmental manager. Write a memo explaining your findings, and your suggestions for solving the problem and ensuring that such errors are noticed earlier within your organisation in future.

Cheques signed by authorised signatories

You may already know that when you open a bank account yourself the bank will ask you to sign a form so that is has an example of your specimen signature. The same thing applies when considering this for an organisation. For reasons of security, it is not possible to allow just anybody to sign a cheque on behalf of the organisation. To make sure that all cheques which leave the organisation have been authorised to do so, it is normal for an organisation to allocate people with authority to be the cheque signatories. This means that their signatures will be held by the bank, and only cheques signed by them will be authorised for payment.

Under these circumstances, the accounts department would complete all the details on the cheques to be sent. This may be done manually, or be printed. The authorised cheque signatory would sign them in a batch. On the other hand, sometimes the number of cheques leaving an organisation may be very large, in which case the organisation would have a 'rubber stamp' made of the signature to cut down on the number of signatures needed.

Depending on the size of the organisation, it may be that only one person can be authorised as a cheque signatory. Alternatively, in larger organisations it is often the case that between two and five people will have this authority. This is more often the case when the cheques are for very large amounts of money and the people signing them are then protected from any allegations regarding their right to sign, as they have witnesses and colleagues who have signed as well.

By using this method of ensuring security of documents leaving the organisation, it is protected to some degree from fraud, theft or misuse of company funds.

PC 4.1.5
C 2.1
C 2.2

Group activity *Time: 1 hour*

Why do you think it is important for a larger organisation to have more than one cheque signatory? Answer in your own words.

How could a sole trader ensure that the money they spend on behalf of the company does not become confused with their personal funds? Write down what action they could take.

In a partnership, should only one person be responsible for the budget and ordering of goods? Discuss this question in pairs and then feed back your considerations to the remainder of your group.

Element 4.1 Assignment

PC 4.1.1–5
C 2.2
C 2.3
AN 2.1
AN 2.2
AN 2.3
IT 2.1
IT 2.2
IT 2.3

In order to prove that you have understood the requirements of this Element, you now need to carry out this assignment. Your tutor will have given you some income and expenditure accounts which show how regular financial transactions are recorded. The three accounts will show the purchases and sales of the organisations. You should complete the following tasks.

Task 1 PC 4.1.1–3

Using the information given to you by your tutor, you should produce a word-processed report which states why the information is essential to a business and to what purpose each of the documents will be put.

Task 2 PC 4.1.4

The second part of your report should include a brief description of four payment methods which the organisations are likely to use.

Task 3 PC 4.1.5

In the final part of your report you should list the security checks, with an explanation of the importance of security, which an organisation may use regarding their financial transactions.

Element 4.2
Complete financial documents and explain financial recording

Performance criteria

A student must:

1 complete **purchases and sales documents** clearly and correctly, and calculate totals

2 complete **payments** and **receipts documents** clearly and correctly and calculate totals

3 record income and expenditure over **time periods**

4 explain why **financial information** must be **recorded**

5 identify and give examples of **information technology** which businesses use to record and monitor **financial information**

Range

- *Purchase documents*: orders placed, purchase invoice, credit note, goods received note
- *Sales documents*: orders received, sales invoice, delivery note, sales credit note, statement of account, remittance advice
- *Payments documents*: pay slip, cheque, petty cash voucher
- *Receipt documents*: receipt, cheque, paying-in slip, bank statement
- *Time periods*: monthly, quarterly
- *Financial information*: accounts (internal accounts, external annual accounts), budgets
- *Recorded*: for security, to monitor income and expenditure, to keep customer accounts up to date, to keep the business accounts up to date, to monitor performance
- *Information technology*: accounting software, spreadsheets

4.2.1 Complete purchase and sales documents clearly and correctly and calculate totals

In order to meet the requirements of this performance criteria, it is necessary for you to practise the completion of the documents we have discussed in Element 4.1. Your tutor will be issuing you with a series of these documents in order that you can carry out this task on a number of occasions, but we intend to work systematically through each of the following financial transaction records and give you a student activity for each. The blank documents should be completed correctly and should be handed to your tutor for checking.

Purchase documents

As we have already mentioned, organisations would need to complete a document each time they make a purchase for goods or services needed in order to carry out their business activities. If you need to refer back to Element 4.1 to ensure you are aware of the processes and purposes of these documents, you should do so before you begin to carry out the activities.

Orders placed

You now need to prove that you can correctly and accurately complete an order form on behalf of an organisation (*see* Fig 4.20). Remember to check all the information before you complete the document and ensure that your figures are correct. In addition, you should ensure that your writing is easy to read and clear.

Individual activity

Time: 15 minutes

PC 4.2.1
C 2.2

You are responsible for completing the order forms on behalf of your organisation, Sutherland and Canwell, and the following goods have been requested from Papers and Co Ltd, 136 Holloway Road, Brampton, Essex ES4 5JU, and should be delivered to your address. You are up to order number 322 in your order book. Your tutor should check the order and sign the authorisation:

5 ink jet printer cartridges £19.99 each (the reference number in the catalogue is DEC44)

9 document holders (ref No JDS38) which are £4.99 each

9 mouse holders (ref No EAS1) which are £1.99 each

ORDER FORM

TO			ORDER NUMBER DATE	
DELIVERY ADDRESS		SPECIAL INSTRUCTIONS		
REF NO	QUANTITY	DESCRIPTION	UNIT PRICE	AMOUNT

ORDER AUTHORISED BY: ....

Fig 4.20 Order form

Goods received note

Once the order has been sent, the goods received note will need to be completed when the goods arrive at your organisation. You will need to remember all the above points concerning neatness, accuracy and legibility when completing the goods received note (*see* Fig 4.21).

PC 4.2.1
C 2.2

Individual activity

Time: 15 minutes

In the role of the person receiving the goods for which you placed an order in the previous activity, you should now complete the goods received note. You can assume that the order arrived the day after you placed your order and that all the items ordered were received and were passed on to stores. There were 3 packages in all.

Invoice

A few days after the receipt of the goods ordered and delivered (or sometimes with the goods), the organisation will receive an invoice which states the quantity, description, unit price, total price and the VAT content of the order. The invoice will also list the gross

GOODS RECEIVED NOTE

NO	DATE RECEIVED	ORDER NO	DELIVERED BY
QUANTITY	DESCRIPTION	NUMBER OF PACKAGES	STORES REF

<table>
<tr><td rowspan="3">RECEIVED FROM

SUPPLIER</td><td colspan="2">ENTERED INTO STOCK</td><td rowspan="3">RECEIVED BY

STOREKEEPER</td></tr>
<tr><td>DATE</td><td>INITIAL</td></tr>
<tr><td></td><td></td></tr>
</table>

Fig 4.21 Goods received note

value of the order, less any discounts, plus the invoice total. You now need to check the invoice given in Fig 4.22 against the order placed and goods received in the previous two activities.

PC 4.2.1
C 2.2
IT 2.1
IT 2.2

Individual activity *Time: 20 minutes*

You have now received the invoice for the goods you ordered and received from Papers and Co Ltd. You should check the invoice against the other documents you have produced for accuracy. If you find any discrepancies, you should word process a letter to Papers and Co Ltd informing them of the problems and requesting that they rectify the situation. You should quote in your letter the exact discrepancies that you have found, including your amended figures.

Credit note

A credit note will be sent by an organisation if they have overcharged for goods ordered and delivered, or if goods have had to be returned for some reason.

INVOICE

Papers & Co Ltd
136 Holloway Road, Brampton, Essex, ES4 5JU
Tel No: (01234) 23456 Fax (01234) 23458
VAT REG NO: 00996677

TO: Sutherland and Canwell

YOUR ORDER NO: 322

NUMBER: 3456
DATE: 27 MAY 19....
TERMS: 2.5%
DESPATCH DATE: 25 May 19....

QUANTITY	DESCRIPTION	UNIT PRICE	TOTAL PRICE	VAT
5	ink jet cartridges DEC44	£19.99	£105.95	£17.50
9	document holders (JDS38)	£4.99	£44.91	£7.86
9	mouse holders (EAS1)	£1.99	£17.91	£3.13
	Gross Value		£178.77	
	LESS Trade Discount		4.21	
	Net Value of Goods		174.56	
	PLUS VAT @ 17.5%		30.48	
	INVOICE TOTAL		£205.10	

E & O E

Fig 4.22 ***Completed invoice***

CREDIT NOTE

Papers & Co Ltd
136 Holloway Road, Brampton, Essex, ES4 5JU
Tel No: (01234) 23456 Fax (01234) 23458
VAT REG NO: 00996677

TO NUMBER

DATE

ORDER NO INVOICE NUMBER

QUANTITY	DESCRIPTION	UNIT PRICE	TOTAL PRICE	VAT
	Gross Value of Goods LESS Trade Discount			
	Net Value of Goods PLUS VAT @ %			
	CREDIT NOTE TOTAL			

Fig 4.23 Credit note

Individual activity *Time: 45 minutes*

PC 4.2.1
C 2.1
C 2.2
C 2.3
IT 2.1
IT 2.2
IT 2.3

You should now assume that you are working for Papers and Co Ltd and that you receive a copy of the letter produced in the previous activity. You need to complete the credit note given in Fig 4.23 and ensure that your calculations are correct. Prepare a word-processed letter to accompany the credit note when you send it to Sutherland and Canwell, which suitably apologises for the errors.

Sales documents

We have already discussed in Element 4.1 the documents which make up the sales process in an organisation's financial transactions. You now need to practise the completion and handling of these documents for this performance criteria. The following series of student activities should assist you, although you will need to carry out further work in this area from information given to you by your tutor.

Orders received, sales invoice and delivery note

When an order is received for goods to be supplied by the organisation, the order form will need to be carefully checked to ensure that all the details are correct. It will also be necessary to enquire as to whether the goods ordered are available in the stores/warehouse to be despatched to the customer.

You should now carry out the following activity, ensuring that you do as always, keep your handwriting neat and legible.

Individual activity *Time: 30 minutes*

PC 4.2.1
C 2.2
C 2.3
C 2.4
AN 2.1
AN 2.2
AN 2.3

Using figs 4.24, 4.25 and 4.26, look at the completed order form in Fig 4.24, which you have received in the morning's post. You should now check the figures on the order form and if they are correct you should do the following:

1. **Design a form which you could use for contacting the stores/warehouse to ascertain whether the goods which the customer requires are available.**
2. **Complete the sales invoice form given in Fig 4.25, ensuring that your figures are correct and legible.**
3. **Complete the delivery note form given in Fig 4.26, ensuring that your figures are correct and legible.**

ORDER FORM

TO Sutherland Sportswear 124 South Street LONDON SE2 4DC	ORDER NUMBER ST448 DATE 25 JANUARY 19 . .
DELIVERY ADDRESS AS ABOVE	SPECIAL INSTRUCTIONS NONE

REF NO	QUANTITY	DESCRIPTION	UNIT PRICE	AMOUNT
A4 154	14	REAMS OF WHITE A4 PAPER	£3.01	£42.03
D11	10	PACKS OF D11 SIZE ENVELOPES	£2.00	£20.00

ORDER AUTHORISED BY: ....

Fig 4.24 Completed order form

INVOICE

TO YOUR ORDER NO	NUMBER DATE TERMS DESPATCH DATE

QUANTITY	DESCRIPTION	UNIT PRICE	TOTAL PRICE	VAT
	Gross Value LESS Trade Discount			
	Net Value of Goods PLUS VAT @ %			
	INVOICE TOTAL			

E & O E

Fig 4.25 Invoice

DELIVERY NOTE

TO

NUMBER
YOUR ORDER NUMBER
DATE

THE FOLLOWING ITEMS HAVE BEEN DESPATCHED TODAY TO ____________
________________________________ BY RAIL/COMPANY VAN/POST*

QUANTITY	DESCRIPTION	NUMBER OF PACKAGES

I certify that the goods received have been checked and are in good condition

Signed: .... On behalf of: ....
Date: ....

I certify that the number of packages delivered is correct according to the number stated above, but that the goods have not been checked

Signed: .... On behalf of: ....
Date: ....

* Please delete as appropriate

Fig 4.26 Delivery note

Sales credit note

As you already know, a credit note will be issued if an organisation has overcharged a customer or has received faulty goods back from the customer for some reason. You now need to complete a credit note on behalf of your organisation.

PC 4.2.1
C 2.2
C 2.3
C 2.4
AN 2.1
AN 2.2
AN 2.3
IT 2.1
IT 2.2
IT 2.3

Individual activity *Time: 10 minutes*

Your organisation has inadvertently overcharged one of your best customers by £210.95 on a recent invoice. In addition, the customer has had to return goods to the value of £25.60 because they were damaged when the package was opened after delivery to their premises. Unfortunately you do not have further stocks of the goods to replace the damaged ones and the customer has asked for a refund.

You should complete the credit note shown in Fig 4.27, and write a word-processed letter to the customer apologising for the delay. The choice of type of product is for you to make, as is the name and address of the organisation.

CREDIT NOTE

TO ORDER NUMBER		NUMBER DATE INVOICE NUMBER		
QUANTITY	DESCRIPTION	UNIT PRICE	TOTAL PRICE	VAT
	Gross Value LESS Trade Discount			
	Net Value of Goods PLUS VAT @ %			
	CREDIT NOTE TOTAL			

Fig 4.27 Credit note

Statement of account

As we mentioned in Element 4.1, a statement of account should be checked carefully when received by an organisation. You now need to carry out the following activity to show your understanding of the purpose and content of a statement of account.

Individual activity

Time: 15 minutes

Using Fig 4.28, write down the following:

PC 4.2.1
C 2.2
C 2.3
C 2.4
AN 2.1
AN 2.2
AN 2.3

1. **The balance owing by the customer**
2. **The total amount of VAT paid by the customer**
3. **The total amount of goods purchased by the customer**
4. **The total amount paid by the customer**

STATEMENT

TO
Sutherland Sportswear
124 South Street
LONDON
SE2 4DC

DATE 28.2.19. .
NUMBER 32
TERMS 2.5 %

DATE	DETAILS	DEBIT	VAT	CREDIT	VAT	BALANCE
10/2	Balance					£120.60
15/2	Goods	£519.40	£77.91			£717.91
18/2	Returns			£171.50	£25.73	£520.68
20/2	Cheque			£220.68		£300.00

Payments received after the end of the month will not be shown on this statement.

Fig 4.28 Statement of account

Remittance advice

You may need to refer back to Element 4.1 to refresh your memory regarding the purpose of a remittance advice note. Having done this, you should carry out the following activity to ensure that you understand the purpose and function of a remittance advice note.

PC 4.2.1
C 2.2
C 2.3
C 2.4
AN 2.1
IT 2.1
IT 2.2
IT 2.3

Individual activity

Design a form which could be used by an organisation for the purpose of informing another organisation of the remittance it is making to the other. Your form should be compiled using computer software and should be as concise but informative as possible.

4.2.2 Complete payment and receipt documents clearly and correctly and calculate totals

Payments documents

Again, for the purposes of this performance criteria we have issued you with a series of student activities which allow you the opportunity to prove that you can complete payments documents and receipts documents clearly and correctly and to calculate totals. As before, you may need to obtain additional practice by means of information and activities given to you by your tutor.

Pay slip

Hopefully it will not be long before you are receiving a pay slip on a regular basis. When this happy day does arrive, it would be wise for you to check the pay slip each time to ensure that the organisation you are working for has made correct calculations and also to ensure that you are paying the correct amount of both statutory and voluntary deductions. The following student activity will help you in understanding the details itemised on a pay slip.

PC 4.2.2
C 2.2
C 2.3
C 2.4
AN 2.1
AN 2.2
AN 2.3

Individual activity *Time: 20 minutes*

From Fig 4.29, answer the following questions:

1. **What does the term 'pay period' mean?**
2. **What is the individual's pay number?**
3. **How much is the total of the individual's voluntary deductions?**
4. **How much is the total of the individual's statutory deductions?**
5. **What is the individual's National Insurance number?**
6. **What is the individual's tax code?**
7. **What does the tax code mean?**
8. **What does the section headed 'totals to date' tell the individual?**

PAY ADVICE

N.I. Number	Tax Code	Basis	Year	Period	Pay No	Pay Centre
YM 23 16 68D	352L	0	95/96	40	64457	991

GROSS PAY		STANDARD DEDUCTIONS		VOLUNTARY DEDUCTIONS		NET PAY
Code	£117.72	Tax	£9.80	Code		£107.92
Total Gross Pay	£117.72			Total Deductions	£9.80	

Hours worked Normal	Hours worked Overtime	TOTALS TO DATE		VOL DEDUCTIONS Code	Balance Owed
		TAXABLE	£117.72		
		TAX PAID	£9.80		

A LIST OF CODES AND ABBREVIATIONS USED IS SHOWN ON REVERSE

Fig 4.29 Pay advice slip

Cheque

Whether we are discussing the cheque which is paid to an individual or an organisation, it is essential in the interests of both the person or organisation writing the cheque and the person or organisation receiving it that all the details are checked thoroughly. Failure to do this could result in the payment being delayed because the bank will not accept the cheque. In order to assist you in checking that cheques have been accurately completed, you should carry out the following student activity.

Individual activity

Time: 20 minutes

PC 4.2.2
C 2.2
C 2.3
AN 2.1
AN 2.2
AN 2.3

Look at the seven cheques included in Figs 4.30a–g. There is a discrepancy on each of them. In other words, each one has a mistake which will mean that the bank will not accept it. Thinking about all the reasons why a cheque needs to be accurate, write a list of the mistakes you can find.

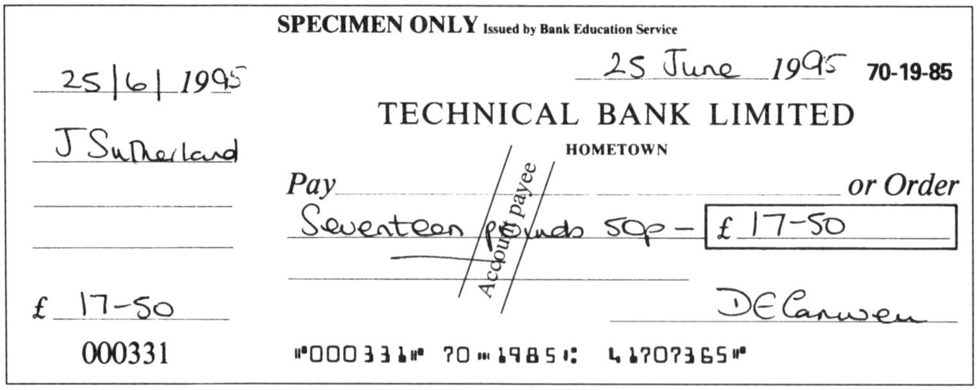

Fig 4.30a

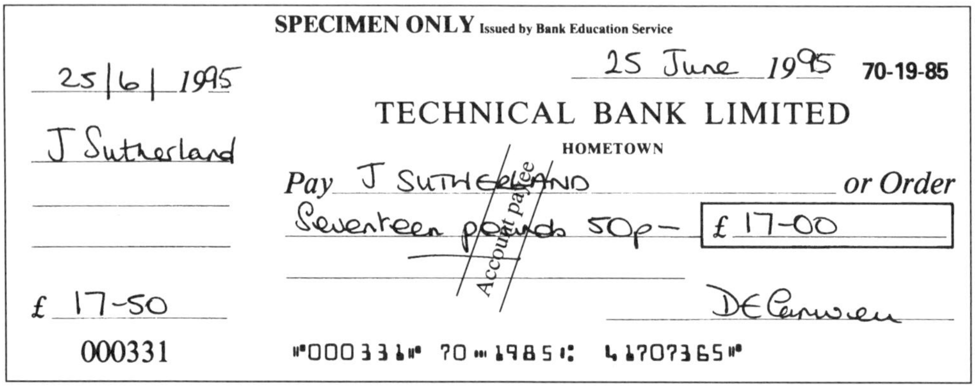

Fig 4.30b

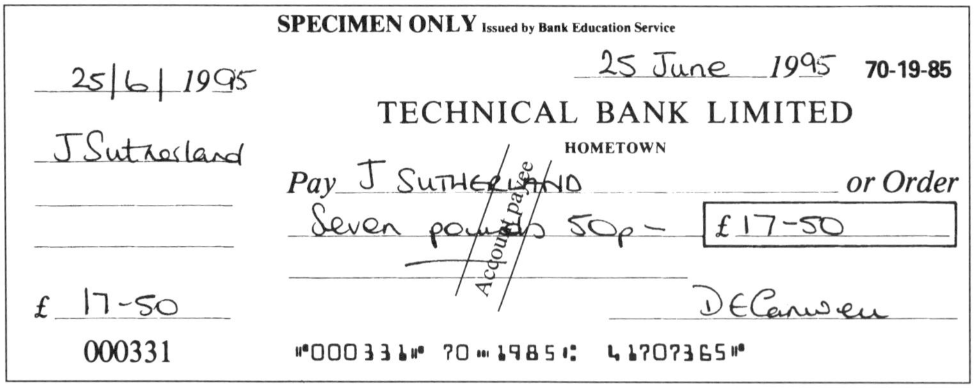

Fig 4.30c

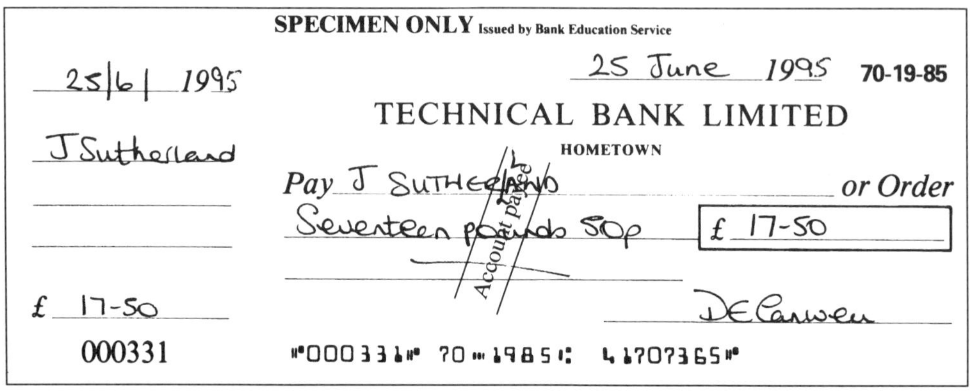

Fig 4.30d

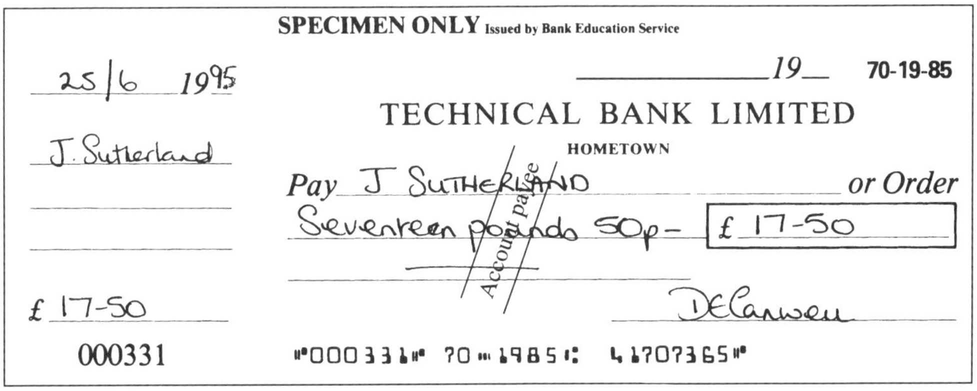
SPECIMEN ONLY Issued by Bank Education Service

25/6 1995 | 19 | 70-19-85

J. Sutherland

TECHNICAL BANK LIMITED
HOMETOWN

Pay J SUTHERLAND or Order
Seventeen pounds 50p– £ 17-50
Account payee

£ 17-50
DE Carwen

000331 ⑈000331⑈ 70⑉1985⑆ 41707365⑈

Fig 4.30e

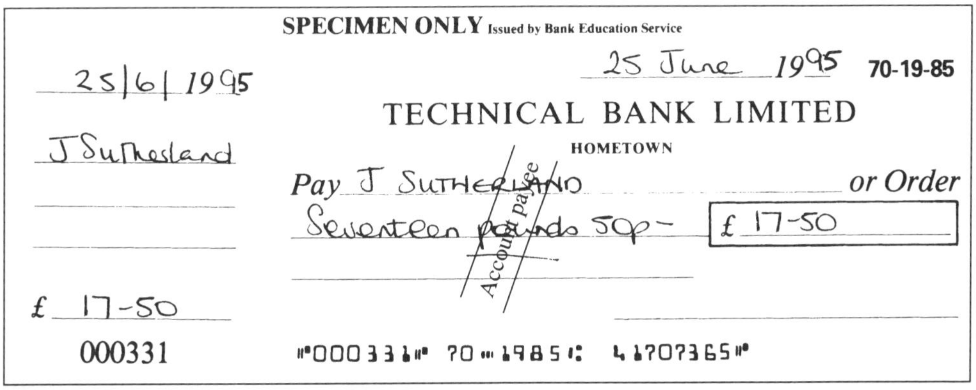
SPECIMEN ONLY Issued by Bank Education Service

25/6/ 1995 | 25 June 1995 | 70-19-85

J Sutherland

TECHNICAL BANK LIMITED
HOMETOWN

Pay J SUTHERLAND or Order
Seventeen pounds 50p– £ 17-50
Account payee

£ 17-50

000331 ⑈000331⑈ 70⑉1985⑆ 41707365⑈

Fig 4.30f

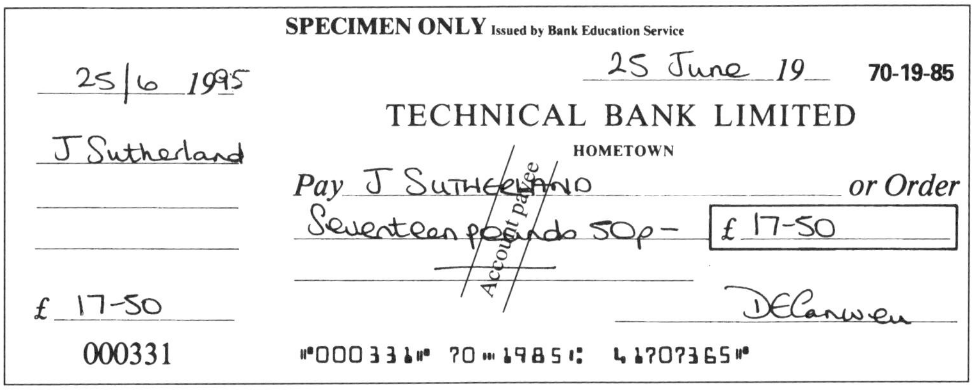
SPECIMEN ONLY Issued by Bank Education Service

25/6 1995 | 25 June 19 | 70-19-85

J Sutherland

TECHNICAL BANK LIMITED
HOMETOWN

Pay J SUTHERLAND or Order
Seventeen pounds 50p– £ 17-50
Account payee

£ 17-50
DE Carwen

000331 ⑈000331⑈ 70⑉1985⑆ 41707365⑈

Fig 4.30g

Petty cash voucher

It may be that the organisation keeps a small amount of cash for use on a casual basis. Perhaps it is used to pay the taxi fares or bus fares of employees who are sent out on an unexpected trip to collect goods. On the other hand, it could be used to buy the tea and coffee supplies, or to pay the window cleaner. Obviously, this will not be a large amount of money, but it will still be important that a check is made on how and where the money is being spent.

In order to ensure that petty cash is monitored and used correctly, it is normal to give the job to one person. This person will be called the 'petty cashier' and his/her duties will include ensuring:

- *that anyone requesting petty cash has completed a petty cash voucher and that this is correctly completed and authorised*
- *that the money in the petty cash box is safe at all times and stored in a suitably locked place*
- *that the petty cash transactions are recorded accurately in the petty cash book*
- *that the petty cash book balances at the end of each month, and the money in the box tallies with the records*

The process for dealing with petty cash is as follows:

1 The person requesting the money will have to complete a petty cash voucher (*see* Fig 4.31). The information contained on this voucher will include:

   - *The voucher number – each voucher will have its own number*
   - *The date*
   - *The item(s) being paid for by petty cash and their individual cost*
   - *The total amount of petty cash being spent*
   - *The amount of VAT being charged on the goods*
   - *The signature of the person requesting the petty cash*
   - *The signature of the person authorising the payment (this may be the head of section or a senior member of staff)*

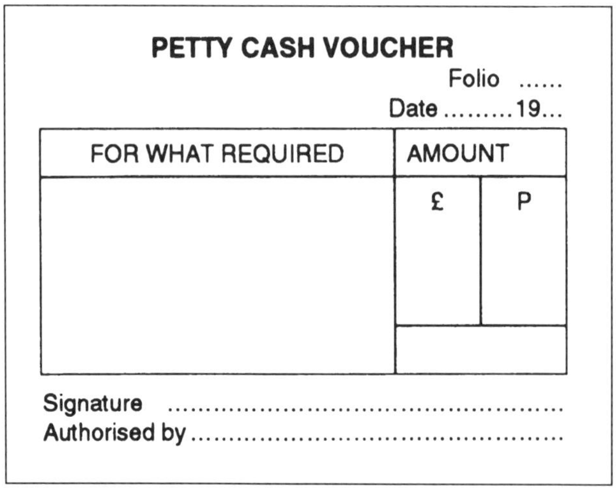
PETTY CASH VOUCHER

Folio ......
Date ....19...

FOR WHAT REQUIRED	AMOUNT	
	£	P

Signature ....
Authorised by ....

Fig 4.31 A petty cash voucher

Group activity *Time: 15 minutes*

PC 4.2.2
C 2.1
C 2.3

Look at the example of a blank petty cash voucher given in Fig 4.31. Why do you think the headings are necessary? To what purpose would each heading be put? Discuss this in pairs.

2 The petty cashier will then issue the money to the person completing the petty cash voucher. This money will be taken out of the 'float' (a word used for the money in the petty cash box or tin).

3 Once the purchase has been made and a receipt for the goods obtained, the petty cashier will transfer the details from the petty cash voucher to the petty cash book. The petty cash book has a series of columns. Each of these columns will be headed with the name of a particular type of expenditure. It may be cleaning, travel or stationery. When the petty cashier transfers the details from the petty cash voucher to the petty cash book, he/she will place the item in its correct column. By doing this, it will be easy for the accounts department to see where the most amount of money is being spent.

PC 4.2.2
C 2.1

Group activity *Time: 15 minutes*

Why do you think it is important that a receipt is obtained? If you were a petty cashier, would you issue money for goods purchased without a receipt, even if the person requesting the money were well known to you? Discuss this with your colleagues.

PC 4.2.2
C 2.1
C 2.3

Group activity *Time: 15 minutes*

Look at the blank petty cash book shown in Fig 4.32 on page 432. In addition to those given, can you think of any more column headings that would be suitable? Discuss this in pairs.

4 Probably once a month, the petty cashier will balance the petty cash book. This means that he/she will add up the totals from each of the columns and ensure that these totals agree with the petty cash vouchers which have been issued. In addition, the petty cashier will deduct the total amount spent from the original float figure and check to see that the correct amount of money is left in the box or tin.

5 The petty cashier will then need to replace the money taken from the petty cash in order to ensure that the float is back to its original total. He/she will do this by obtaining money from the company cashier.

This system of dealing with petty cash is known as the Imprest system. Figure 4.33 shows you how a petty cash book would be completed, to assist you to understand the process.

DR | **PETTY CASH BOOK** (Imprest System) | Folio CR

RECEIPTS AND PAYMENTS					ANALYSIS OF PAYMENTS											
Imprest		Date	Details	Voucher Number	Payment		VAT									
£	p				£	p	£	p	£	p	£	p	£	p	£	p

Fig 4.32 Petty cash book

PETTY CASH BOOK (Imprest System)																
DR														Folio CR		
RECEIPTS AND PAYMENTS					ANALYSIS OF PAYMENTS											
Imprest		Date	Details	Voucher Number	Payment		VAT		Postage		Cleaning		Sundries			
£	p				£	p	£	p	£	p	£	p	£	p	£	p
100	00	Feb 8	Balance													
		Feb 8	Stamps	21	35	00			35	00						
		Feb 11	Office Cleaning	22	15	00					15	00				
		Feb 12	Newspapers	23	5	50							5	50		
		Feb 12	Biscuits	24	1	20							1	20		
			Totals		56	70			35	00	15	00	6	70		
			Balance c/d		43	30										
100	00				100	00										
43	30		Balance b/d													
56	70		Restored Imprest													

Fig 4.33 Completed petty cash book

PC 4.2.2
C 2.2
C 2.3

Individual activity

Time: 40 minutes

Using the blank petty cash book page (Fig 4.32), give each column a suitable heading, not forgetting the VAT column.

Using the completed petty cash vouchers shown in Fig 4.34 on page 434, transfer the amounts from each voucher to the respective column in the petty cash book.

Total each of the columns in the petty cash book, including the VAT column.

How much money will you need to restore the imprest? In other words, how much money will you need to ensure the float is back to the original amount?

PETTY CASH VOUCHER

Folio ......
Date ..23/11 19...

FOR WHAT REQUIRED	AMOUNT £	P
2 Highlight Pens VAT 17.5 %	2	06
	2	06

Signature ...SS Cook...
Authorised by ......J. Smithson......

PETTY CASH VOUCHER

Folio ......
Date ..24/11 19...

FOR WHAT REQUIRED	AMOUNT £	P
Jar Coffee	3	95
Box Tea Bags	1	10
Pint Milk		32
	5	37

Signature ...DE Carwen...
Authorised by ......RL......

PETTY CASH VOUCHER

Folio ......
Date ..25/11 19...

FOR WHAT REQUIRED	AMOUNT £	P
Window Cleaner VAT 17.5%	5	00
	5	00

Signature ...DE Carwen...
Authorised by ......E. Levin......

PETTY CASH VOUCHER

Folio ......
Date ..22/11 19...

FOR WHAT REQUIRED	AMOUNT £	P
Milkman (10 pints) VAT 17.5%	3	20
	3	20

Signature ...Mark Last...
Authorised by ......A. Jones......

PETTY CASH VOUCHER

Folio ......
Date 25 Nov 19...

FOR WHAT REQUIRED	AMOUNT £	P
Bus fares to collect parcel from PO Sorting Office	1	10
	1	10

Signature ...Stuart Jacobs...
Authorised by ......RL......

PETTY CASH VOUCHER

Folio ......
Date 26 Nov 19...

FOR WHAT REQUIRED	AMOUNT £	P
Masking Tape	2	30
Blades for knife	3	50
VAT 17.5%		
	5	80

Signature ...SS Cook...
Authorised by ......Susan Mc Namara......

Fig 4.34 Completed petty cash vouchers

Receipts documents

Receipt

As we have already mentioned, a receipt is a document which confirms that a certain amount of money has been paid. This may be in the form of a cheque, cash or credit card payment. You need to ensure that you know the purposes and functions of a receipt to both the purchaser and the seller. In addition, you need to prove that you can accurately complete a receipt. In order to do this you should carry out the following student activity.

	CASH RECEIPT
Number	NUMBER ....DATE ....
Date	RECEIVED FROM ....
From	....
....	....
....	THE SUM OF ....
....	....
£ p	£ p

Fig 4.35 A receipt form

Individual activity

Time: 10 minutes

PC 4.2.2
C 2.2
C 2.3
AN 2.1

Complete the cash receipt given in Fig 4.35. The receipt number is 126 and use today's date. Mrs Foxburrow paid you £136.99 today for goods she purchased and she requires a receipt, as she can claim from her company for the purchase.

Paying-in slip

You should complete the following activity in order to practise filling in the document needed to pay money into a bank account, either for yourself or for your organisation.

Individual activity

Time: 10 minutes

PC 4.2.2
C 2.2

You are responsible for paying the day's takings into the bank account of your organisation. Complete the paying-in slip (Fig 4.36) for the following amounts of cash and cheque payments:

50 × £10 notes
100 × £5 notes
175 × £1 coins
188 × 50p pieces
£410 worth of silver
£13.74 worth of bronze
2 cheques – one for £35.49 and one for £17.99

You are about to take some annual leave. Write a list of instructions for your stand-in, making sure that you tell them exactly how to complete the task. Also leave instructions regarding the safety of money and welfare of the employee when carrying out this job.

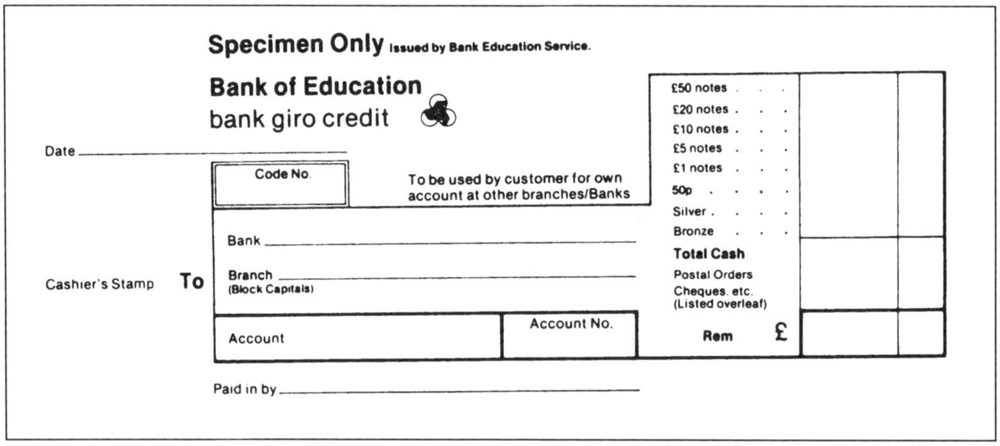

Specimen Only Issued by Bank Education Service.
Bank of Education
bank giro credit
Date
Code No.
To be used by customer for own account at other branches/Banks
Cashier's Stamp
To
Bank
Branch (Block Capitals)
Account
Account No.
Paid in by
£50 notes
£20 notes
£10 notes
£5 notes
£1 notes
50p
Silver
Bronze
Total Cash
Postal Orders
Cheques etc. (Listed overleaf)
Rem £

Fig 4.36 A paying-in slip

4.2.3 Record income and expenditure over time periods

Time periods

Depending on the size and nature of the organisation, plus the needs of different managers or owners of the organisation to monitor the business performance and financial transactions, accounting information may be produced on a monthly, quarterly or yearly basis. Obviously, other considerations here will be the requirements of the providers of any finance the organisation has borrowed and the length of time the organisation has been trading. Another factor to consider is whether the organisation has a good track record of successful business activity, or whether it is experiencing any short-term or long-term cashflow problems. By producing its accounting information on a monthly or quarterly basis, the organisation would be in a better position to monitor any problems it may be experiencing. Usually trading periods or financial periods are described as shown by the following headings.

Monthly

If the organisation is just starting up its business activities and has borrowed money from one source or another, it would be prudent, and possibly essential, that the organisation produces a profit and loss account and a balance sheet on a monthly basis. This can be carried out at any time during the month and the trading period would run from the last day of the previous trading period. In other words, if the last set of accounting information was produced on 31 March 19 . . then the next set would read 'for the trading period 1 April 19 . . to 30 April 19 . .'.

Additionally, if an organisation has been experiencing a cashflow problem, then it would be in its best interests to produce monthly profit and loss and balance sheet statements in order that the management of the organisation can assess whether or not the problem is developing as forecast, or whether more extremes measures will need to be taken. It may be that the organisation is experiencing difficulty in meeting its loan commitments and has been under pressure from the providers of finance to prove that these problems are being addressed.

Usually once a month, the organisation would prepare the trial balance which forms part of the accounting information it requires. This trial balance would simply list all of the balances, both debit and credit and, once balanced, would show the total of the debit balances and the total of the credit balances to be equal.

Quarterly

In a similar way to the monthly accounts we mentioned above, it may be that an organisation would choose, for a variety of different reasons, to produce its accounts on a quarterly basis. Quarterly means, essentially, that the trading period would be for three months. Organisations such as British Gas and the Electricity Companies issue their statements to customers on a quarterly basis, even though some of their customers choose to pay by budget account on a monthly basis.

The need to produce accounts on a quarterly basis could be for one or several of the following reasons:

- *The bulk of the organisation's customers may be paying for products or services bought from the organisation on a quarterly basis and thus the generating of accounts for the same trading period is more convenient.*
- *The organisation may have to pay the bulk of its expenses or commitments to other organisations on a quarterly basis and would choose to adopt the same principle for its accounting information.*
- *The organisation may have been experiencing some cash flow problems, and although these may not necessitate the production of monthly accounts, it is more prudent to assess the financial situation of the organisation on a quarterly basis rather than an annual one.*

If an organisation produces quarterly accounts, the information contained would state 'from the 31 March 19 . . to 30 June 19 . .'.

Annually

Producing accounts annually is the usual trading period for most organisations. There are several reasons why an organisation would produce annual accounts, which include:

- *To fulfil legal and statutory obligations – we look at this in the next section of this Element*
- *To provide the owners of the organisation with information*
- *To provide the managers within the organisation with information*
- *To provide any providers of finance with information*

The financial year for the purposes of taxation runs from 6 April to 5 April of the following year. The Inland Revenue is trying to harmonise the tax years of organisations so that they all begin at the same time. This, obviously, would make the work of the Tax Office easier, but could cause some problems for individual organisations whose tax year currently runs from a different date. Strictly speaking, the first day that an organisation begins trading is the first day of its tax year.

For example, if an organisation began trading on 1 September 19 . ., then their tax year would end on 31 August the following year. Each year on this date the organisation would legally need to produce its final accounts.

4.2.4 Explain why financial information must be recorded

Financial information

Accounts (internal accounts, external annual accounts)

Staff of the accounts department meticulously record in ledgers all the financial transactions of the organisation. This process of using ledgers to record is known as double entry bookkeeping. The following ledgers would be used by most organisations:

- **The sales ledger** – all goods or services sold by the organisation will be listed in the sales ledger. These customers are debtors of the organisation until they pay for the goods or services received.
- **The purchases ledger** – all goods or services bought by the organisation will be listed in the purchases ledger. The organisation will remain the creditor of these suppliers until it pays for the goods or services received.
- **The cash book** – receipts and payments of both cash and cheques are recorded in the cash book.
- **The general ledger** – items such as expenses, assets and liabilities are recorded in the general ledger.

In addition to the purchases and sales, the accounts department would also need to record information regarding the following:

- *bank transactions*
- *timesheets and clock cards*
- *wages and salaries*
- *tax and insurance details of staff*
- *petty cash transactions*

The accounts department records this information not only in order to provide details of the transactions for the benefit of monitoring business performance, but also to meet legal requirements laid down by government legislation.

Budgets

It is often thought that financial planning is restricted to a single year. Indeed, one-year budgets are very common. Long-term plans are often called corporate plans and short-term investment plans are known as capital budgets. In other words, a business will have two short-term budgets: the revenue budget, which relates to planned sales and costs over a given period; and the capital budget, which relates to capital investments over that same period.

The importance of establishing a reasonable estimate of an organisation's future sales, costs and cash balances means that the forecasts should be approached in a calm and systematic manner. An organisation would be best advised to be apprised of all the necessary information on which to base its forecasts. There needs to be a degree of realism involved in estimating the figures entered into a forecast. If assumptions have been made, then the organisation needs to be clear about why those assumptions were made and what will be the probable consequences of these assumptions if they are proved to be wrong. Being able to predict exactly what might happen is not a pure art. Many things can go wrong and equally a vast number of external influences may have an impact on the long-term credibility of the forecast. Indeed, the further the organisation forecasts into the future, the less likely that forecast is to be accurate.

The best that an organisation can possibly hope for is to identify probable trends in the short to medium term.

Having worked out a forecast based on either current understanding or current sets of figures, the organisation now needs to analyse the forecast and attempt to recognise any possible opportunities or alternative courses of action which may result in a more healthy-looking forecast and future. In appraising alternative courses of action, the organisation would normally create an alternative forecast based on the presumed net results of the decisions. In effect, the organisation can either begin by looking at alternative courses of action which will create opportunities, or the creation of opportunities that require alternative courses of action.

For security

It is very important that an organisation has security high on its list of priorities. There are different reasons for an organisation to take steps to ensure security measures are complied with:

- **Security of cash** – not everyone is honest, and money kept in an insecure way may tempt such people.
- **Security of documentation** – we have already mentioned the importance of keeping and storing documents and various data securely. This is particularly the case with any financial transactions an organisation might make, and is the main reason why the checking of such documents for accuracy and neatness is so important.

PC 4.2.3
C 2.1
C 2.2

Individual activity *Time: 45 minutes*

In the role of the accountant responsible for security, list the actions you would take to ensure that financial information is safely stored but accessible both within the organisation and from outside. Once you have completed your list, compare it to those of the remainder of your group.

Correct procedures

The security of such documents going out of the organisation is not the only consideration, however. Safeguards have to be taken to ensure that employees follow the set procedures for the completion of documents. This is another form of security.

As we said earlier, the three main aspects of security of financial transactions relate to authorisation of orders, reconciliation of invoices against orders and goods received notes, and authorisation of cheques.

To monitor income and expenditure, to keep customer accounts up to date and to keep the business accounts up to date

As we have already mentioned, an organisation would need to keep a clear, accurate and easily accessible set of documents which relate to their financial transactions in order to prepare the accounts of the organisation. The information contained in the documents will be transferred to the various ledgers mentioned above and from these ledgers the organisation will be able to carry out the following:

1 *Identify the income of the organisation*
2 *Identify the expenditure of the organisation*
3 *Generate the accounts of the organisation*
4 *Generate the accounts of the customers of the organisation*

To monitor performance

When filling in a forecast, the organisation will have to establish a predicted level of sales income over a given period. This is not a very easy task since there are too many variables which may influence the actual performance of the organisation. It is always advisable to side with pessimism and not to be over-optimistic. In setting targets we can establish that there are the following areas which need to have targets or objectives established:

- *The likely sales income*
- *The desirable level of direct costs*
- *The acceptable and manageable level of overhead costs*
- *The expected profit or mark up after costs have been taken into consideration for each product*
- *The expected closing balance at the end of each trading period*

The monitoring of performance directly relates to the setting of targets. An organisation would normally be expected to complete a forecast against which they will be able to insert the real figures as they become available. This may be a basic way of monitoring performance, but the difference between budgeted or forecasted figures and actual figures may prove to be very illuminating. Relatively early on, as actual figures become available, the organisation will begin to realise whether its predictions have been correct. In this regard, the organisation may wish to re-examine its forecasts in the light of reality. The real value of monitoring performance lies in the organisation's willingness and ability to do something if the targets that have been set are not being reached.

4.2.5 Identify and give examples of information technology which businesses use to record and monitor financial information

Information technology

Information processing systems may be either manual or electronic. They both handle data, processing them in some specific way in order to produce an end goal.

With regard to electronic systems, the processing systems comprise both hardware and software. The information processing system itself is carried out by a program. It is useful to define these three key terms at this point.

- **Hardware** – this describes the physical, mechanical components of the computer system, such as the keyboard, monitor, disk drive(s) and printer(s).
- **Software** – software is the predesigned computer package which provides the information and processes by which the hardware can handle particular forms of information. These are also known as programs.
- **Programs** – as you may have realised, programs are software, but are written in a complex computer language aimed at providing a flexible and foolproof system by which information may be processed.

A manual system can suffer from the restrictions of having only one file in existence. This means that only one individual may have access to this file at a time. A way around this problem is to duplicate the file so that all interested parties may gain access to a copy simultaneously. However, this simply adds to the paper mountain and adds considerably to the overall storage problems. Certain computer systems can suffer from the same problems. Unsophisticated computer systems may only allow a single user access to a file at a particular time. Equally, if the system is disk-based, then access to the relevant files relies on a number of disk copies being made. With this system, there is always the danger of a file being updated by a particular user, while all other users are dealing with out-of-date information.

Single-purpose systems, or the software used, tend to relate to independent functions such as word processing, and database, spreadsheet and graphics processing. Whatever application is used, whether it be a single-purpose system or a multi-purpose system, it is vital that the application actually does what you want it to. The following points should be considered:

- *Does it do the job you want it to do?*
- *Will it serve its purpose for a reasonable amount of time?*
- *Is it compatible with the current system?*

We should now consider some of the applications available using information processing systems.

Accounting software and spreadsheets

Another application area that has developed rapidly over the last few years is the computerised number-processing facility. In this instance the computer's role is that of a calculating machine. It is possible, using this method of application, to process information of a numerical nature for the following tasks.

1. *Accounts packages normally offer sales, purchase and nominal ledgers, either as individual modules or completely integrated packages*
2. *Payroll packages*
3. *Order processing packages*
4. *Invoicing packages*
5. *A fixed asset register*
6. *Stock control packages*
7. *Job costing and bill of materials packages*

Naturally, before an organisation decides to embark on a computerisation of the above functions, it clearly identifies the areas that it needs to integrate. In addition, it would also need to identify the amount of activity within each of these areas.

Spreadsheets

A spreadsheet package is the computerised equivalent of an accounts department's ledger. The name spreadsheet is derived from the 'spreading of the business's accounts on a piece of paper'. The computer user can enter number, formulae or text into each of the columns. Columns are the vertical sections of the spreadsheet and rows are the horizontal ones. A cell is one section of the spreadsheet.

This screen-based calculating machine allows information to be input in the form of text, numbers or formulae and the subsequent printing of the information. This information can be printed in the form of an exact replica of the screen itself, or in the form of a graph. This can be as a line graph, bar chart, pie chart or some more complicated form of graphics.

It is possible to change any number within the spreadsheet at any time and the new results will automatically be shown. The ability of the package to carry out this function makes it a very powerful, useful and popular system.

Spreadsheets can be used by an organisation in order to carry out the following tasks:

1. *Hold records*
2. *Depict their sales and costs*

3 *Determine what prices will maximise profits*
4 *Detail the costs accumulated for a specific job*
5 *Aid financial planning and budgeting*
6 *Make tax, investment and loan calculations*
7 *Produce statistics*
8 *Merge spreadsheet information in order to show accounts from more than one department or branch*
9 *Conversion of currency*
10 *Timetabling and planning of staff*

Element 4.2 Assignment

PC 4.2.1–4
C 2.2
C 2.3
C 2.4
AN 2.1
AN 2.2
AN 2.3
IT 2.1
IT 2.2
IT 2.3
IT 2.4

This Element assignment aims to extend the understanding you gained in Element 4.1 and to help you to apply it to the accurate completion of documents.

For the purposes of this Element assignment you will need to acquire from your tutor information which will assist you in the completion of this piece of work.

Task 1 PC 4.2.1–2

You should produce a set of clearly and correctly completed financial documents supporting a single income and expenditure account over a stated period of time. This could be for up to one year, but should show monthly or quarterly figures explained in terms of total income and total expenditure.

Task 2 PC 4.2.3

In the form of a word-processed report you should explain why the documents you completed in task 1 are necessary. You should base your report on the emphasis of the organisation's need to be aware of its total income and total expenditure.

Task 3 PC 4.2.4

The second part of your word-processed report should list any computer software which the organisation could use to record and monitor financial information. The list should include the name of a supplier, the cost and the features of the software.

Notes

Some of you will have the opportunity to practise completing these documents in your work placement, either manually or using information technology. Others of you, to do so, will need to carry out a series of tasks, such as the activities given in the Element.

When listing the computer software, you do not have to access actual business software, but can collect promotional material from a business or from IT publications.

Element 4.3
Produce, evaluate and store business documents

Performance criteria

A student must:

1 explain the **purpose** of routine **business documents**

2 produce draft and final versions of **business documents**

3 **evaluate** each **business document** produced

4 **compare** the **methods of processing** business documents

5 **reference**, correctly file and retrieve business documents

6 identify and **evaluate ways to send** and ways to **store** business documents

Range

- *Purpose*: to communicate with customers, to communicate with a colleague, to communicate with other businesses
- *Business documents*: letters (confirming a meeting, answering an enquiry, dealing with a customer complaint), memo, invitation, notice, message
- *Evaluate each document*: in terms of appearance (style, format), in terms of language (spelling, grammar)
- *Compare*: in terms of: legibility, cost, time taken to produce, ability to make changes, storage
- *Methods of processing*: hand-written, typed, word processed, printed, photocopied
- *Reference*: alphabetically, by subject, number, date

- *Evaluate ways*: ease of sending and storing, ease of finding and retrieving, cost, safety of documents, security of documents
- *Ways to send*: special delivery, post, electronic transmission (fax, E-mail)
- *Ways to store*: paper filing, computer files, computer back-up files

4.3.1 Explain the purpose of routine business documents

4.3.2 Produce draft and final versions of business documents

In these performance criteria, and throughout this Element, you will need to produce various draft and final version documents for each of the listings given. You will then have to evaluate the documents in terms of quality, appearance, style, format, spelling and grammar. It is stated that this Element should be integrated with your other work, so that the business documents produced are relevant to normal business conventions and relevant to the work you are undertaking. These documents can be produced either manually or by means of computer.

In order to assist you in the completion of this Element, we have listed the documents you will need to deal with in order to carry out the Element assignment and given you some guidelines as to their completion.

Business documents

The term business documents simply relates to any pieces of paper which would be in regular use within an organisation. This can include the purchase, sales, payment and receipt documents which we have already discussed in Elements 4.1 and 4.2, but also includes documents such as letters, memos, invitations and notices. We intend to deal with these individually.

Letters (confirming a meeting, answering an enquiry, dealing with a customer complaint)

A business letter could be sent by an organisation for any of the reasons given in the above heading.

A business letter, unlike a memorandum, would be sent to someone outside the organisation. It is important then that the letter is neat, accurate and well presented.

The headed paper used by the organisation for its business letters would form part of its 'corporate image'. The example shown in Fig 4.37 gives the information an organisation would wish each of its customers or clients to see regularly:

1 *The name and address of the organisation*
2 *The telephone number, fax number and/or telex number of the organisation*
3 *The registered address of the organisation, as this may be different from its postal address*
4 *The company registration number*
5 *The names of the directors of the organisation*
6 *Any other companies the organisation may represent or to which it may be affiliated*

PITMAN PUBLISHING
The Business Publisher

19 November 199.

Your ref:
Our ref: KLW/AP/91

Mr J M Johnson
Editor
TQM Journal
Princess Street
NORWICH
NR1 4TT

Dear Mr Johnson

HOW TO LEAD YOUR BUSINESS BEYOND TQM

Please find enclosed a copy of one of the *Financial Times*/Pitman Publishing's most recent publications, *How to Lead Your Business Beyond TQM*, together with a press release, which I hope you will find of interest.

You may be interested in carrying a review of this book, or mentioning it as further reading against relevant articles (preferably with our contact details included). Or there may be the possibility of carrying out incentive offers for your readers. We are open to suggestions.

I hope you find *How to Lead Your Business Beyond TQM* suitable for review and, should you require any further information regarding this or any other Pitman Publishing title, please do not hesitate to contact me.

Yours sincerely

Kim Whiting
Marketing Co-ordinator

Enc

A Division of Pearson Professional

128 Long Acre, London WC2E 9AN, U K
Telephone: +44 (0)171 379 7383, Facsimile: +44 (0)171 240 5771, Telex: 261367 Pitman G.
Pearson Professional Limited. Registered Office: Maple House, 149 Tottenham Court Road, London W1P 9LL. Registered Number 2970324. Registered England and Wales

Fig 4.37 A fully-blocked business letter

The layout or format of the business letter will usually also be part of the organisation's corporate image, and different organisations have their own rules about the way in which a letter should be displayed. It is common nowadays to use the fully-blocked method of display, which means that each part of the letter commences at the left-hand margin.

The following format can be used as a guideline:

- **Our reference** – this can be initials and/or numbers which the organisation sending the letter will use for filing purposes.
- **Your reference** – this again is usually initials and/or numbers which the organisation receiving the letter has used in previous correspondence.
- **The date** – all letters must be dated.
- **The name and address of the recipient** (the person or organisation to which the letter is being sent) – when using the fully-blocked style of business letter, it is normal to use 'open punctuation' in this section. This means that no punctuation is required in the name and address.
- **The name of the town** should be in capitals, and the **postcode** should be on a line of its own.
- **The salutation** – this is the 'Dear Sir/Madam/Mr/Ms/Mrs/Miss', etc.
- **The heading** – very often, after the salutation, an organisation will give the letter a subject title. This is normally either typed in capitals, or with initial capital letters only, and may be underlined or emboldened.
- **The body of the letter** is then typed – each line of the paragraph would commence at the left-hand margin, and a line space would be left between paragraphs.
- **The complimentary close** – this is usually either 'Yours faithfully' or 'Yours sincerely'. The complimentary close will match the salutation. When using 'Dear Sir/Madam', then 'Yours faithfully' is used. When using 'Dear Mr . . .', etc, as the salutation, 'Yours sincerely' is used at the end.
- **The name of the writer** – after allowing space for a signature, the name of the person signing the letter is typed, as well as their title.
- **Enclosure(s)** – any enclosed additional information which is mentioned in the body of the letter is usually indicated at the foot of the letter. This is done by typing 'Enc(s)' after the complimentary close.

Individual activity

Referring to Fig 4.38, word process a letter of application for the advertisement. It appeared in your local newspaper last week.

PC 4.3.1
C 2.2
C 2.3
IT 2.1
IT 2.2
IT 2.3

COLLEGE LEAVER REQUIRED

- Post available immediately.
- For busy Accounts Department.
- Good communication skills essential.
- Must be competent at figure work.
- Salary negotiable but dependent on age and experience.

Send letter of application to:
Mr T Tucker
Hunt Sportswear, 1 Station Road, Edgware, Middx ED4 5PJ

Fig 4.38 An advertisement for a job vacancy

Memo

An internal memorandum is used for communication between different departments within the same organisation. These are often called 'memos'. Example of a memo are given in Figs 4.39 and 4.40. A memo is normally shorter than a business letter and usually deals with one particular subject. When more than one point is being made, it is normal to number the points. Memos are not signed in the same way as a business letter, but the person issuing the memo would often initial it at the end.

PEUGEOT TALBOT
MOTOR COMPANY PLC

internal correspondence

From (name)	Department	Location S09M
To (name)	Department	Location
Subject	O/Ref	Date

Fig 4.39 Peugeot Talbot uses this form for internal communication

BNFL MEMORANDUM

To:

your ref: our ref: ext:3514

subject:

Fig 4.40 BNFL's memorandum form

Invitation

Informal and formal invitations may be sent or received by organisations. When these are being issued in bulk, it is normal that they will be printed by a specialist company and simply prepared for postage within the organisation. An invitation will usually contain the following information:

- *the address of the person sending out the invitation*
- *the date the invitation is sent out*
- *the names of the people acting as host/hostess at the event*
- *the date of the event*
- *the venue of the event*
- *the time of the event*
- *the reason for the event (e.g. 18th birthday party)*
- *RSVP – this is a request for a reply and is taken from the French* répondez s'il vous plaît *Sometimes a deadline for replies is given*

PC 4.3.1
C 2.1
C 2.2

Group activity

Time: 15 minutes

In pairs, design an invitation for an Awards Evening at your school/college.

The choice of date is yours, but you would like to know at least two weeks before the event who will be attending so that arrangements for the buffet can be made.

Notice

If an organisation wishes to pass a message on to a number of employees, it may place the information on its staff noticeboards.

These messages can be formal or informal. Perhaps there is a change to normal organisational procedures, or maybe a social event is being planned by the organisation's personnel department.

Notices allow the quick and easy communication of information to a large number of people. Noticeboards can also be used by individuals wishing to inform colleagues of items for sale or events planned.

PC 4.3.1
C 2.1
C 2.2
C 2.3
IT 2.1
IT 2.2
IT 2.3

Group activity

Referring back to the previous activity when you designed an invitation, now prepare a notice to be placed on all staff noticeboards informing them of the date, time and venue of the Awards Evening. Tell the staff that the Headmaster/Principal would be pleased to see as many staff present as possible. Your notice should be word processed.

Message

It may be that you have taken a telephone message (*see* Fig 4.41) for a colleague who is unavailable at the time. It is essential that the information contained in this message is correct and easy to read. Alternatively, the message may have been given to you face-to-face by another member of staff.

All messages taken should be delivered to the person concerned as quickly as possible after the event and great care should be taken to ensure that the information given is accurate and that, in the case of a written message, the handwriting is legible.

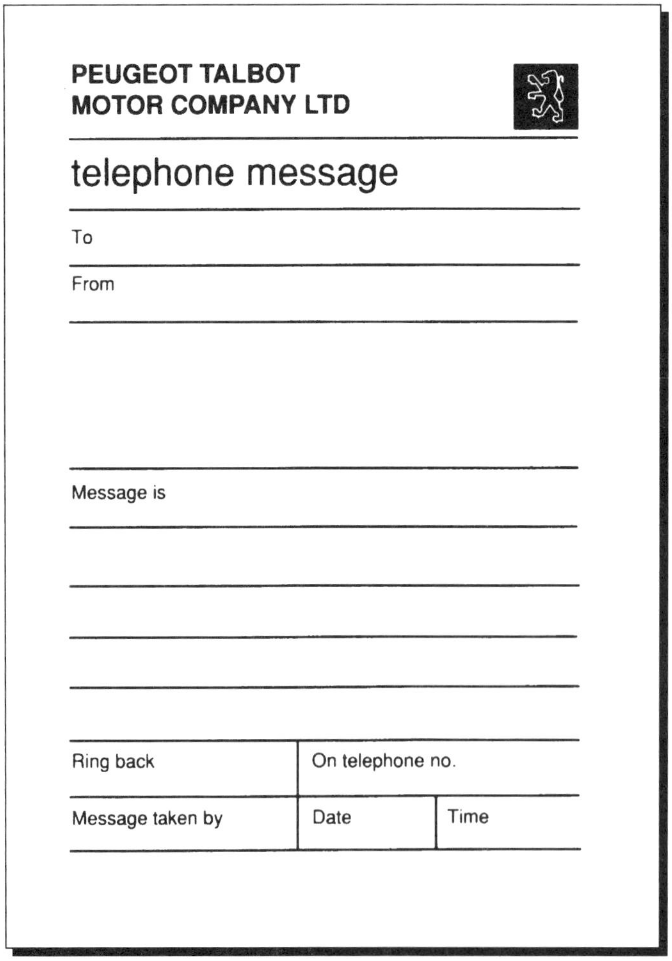
PEUGEOT TALBOT
MOTOR COMPANY LTD

telephone message

To

From

Message is

Ring back	On telephone no.	
Message taken by	Date	Time

Fig 4.41 Peugeot Talbot's personalised telephone message form

4.3.3 Evaluate each business document produced

4.3.4 Compare the methods of processing business documents

In these performance criteria you need to show that you are capable of evaluating both your own documents and those produced by other individuals or organisations. For the purposes of proving your ability to carry out this task, you will need to receive a series of documents from your tutor which you will have to evaluate. The documents should be presented to you in a variety of forms including the following:

- *hand-written documents*
- *typed documents*
- *word processed documents*
- *printed documents*
- *photocopied documents*

You should receive a total of 36 documents in all. Your evaluation of the content and method of processing these documents will form an integral part of the Element assignment.

You should study these documents and produce a written report (which can be word processed if you wish) on each one, ensuring that you use the following criteria in your evaluation:

- *the appearance of each document with regard to the style and format used*
- *the language used within the document, in terms of spelling and grammar*

In addition to your evaluation of the appearance of each document and the language used, you also need to compare the documents given to you by your tutor in terms of the following:

- *their legibility (in other words are they easy to read)*
- *the cost of producing the document*
- *the time taken to produce the document*
- *the opportunity to make changes to the document if necessary*
- *how easy the document is to store*

As we have already mentioned, the work produced for these performance criteria will be very valuable when completing the Element assignment.

Should you prefer to do so, you can evaluate documents which you have already produced in a work situation or for your normal studies.

4.3.5 Reference, correctly file and retrieve business documents

Reference

The words 'storage and retrieval' can often be confusing when one has not worked in an office. In fact, they mean 'filing'. This word can also cause a reaction – often one of groans and moans! Filing is often thought to be boring and routine, and, in essence, it is. Nowadays, however, storage and retrieval also includes the computerised systems of storing and retrieving information.

The safe and secure storage of information and the easy access or retrieval of that information is imperative if an organisation is to function successfully and efficiently.

Another word for filing is 'indexing'. Obviously this involves a logical and effective way of recording documents and storing them in an efficient system which will allow the easy retrieval of that information when required.

Filing is the basis of record-keeping and entails the processing, arranging and storing of the documents so that they can be found when they are required. The documents are placed in consecutive order and preserved in that system until they are required for reference. This can be carried out in any number of locations – for example, a telephone directory is an index of alphabetical names and addresses. Your own address book is also a method of indexing in alphabetical order.

We intend, in this section, to look at filing, or storage and retrieval of information, in more detail.

People or organisations can often interpret the word 'system' in different ways. The word can be used when referring to filing in any of the ways we have listed below:

- *It can mean the method used for filing the documents – e.g. in alphabetical or geographical order*
- *It can mean the equipment used for filing the documents – e.g. a lateral or vertical filing cabinet*
- *It can mean the location used for filing the documents – e.g. in one department or office, or, alternatively, in a centralised filing department*
- *It can mean the physical way the staff file the documents*

So what are the basic techniques required to ensure that the storage and retrieval of information and documents is efficient? Let's look at this in some detail:

1. Ensure that the papers which have been passed for filing have been marked in some way to indicate that they are ready for storing.
2. Sort the papers into order so that they are grouped in the required way.
3. Remove any paperclips and staple these documents together – this will ensure that they do not get separated during the filing process.
4. Each individual file should be in date order, with the most recent documents at the top or front.
5. Be neat with the documents – curled edges can easily become torn.
6. File daily if possible – this makes it less of a chore and also ensures that the files are up to date.

FILE 'OUT' CARD				
FILE NAME	BORROWED BY	DEPARTMENT	DATE BORROWED	DATE RETURNED

Fig 4.42 An example of a file 'out' or 'absent' card

7 Follow organisational procedure regarding 'out' or 'absent' cards (*see* Fig 4.42).
8 Follow up all overdue files regularly, i.e. when they have been borrowed by another member of staff or department, by using a bring forward system (*see* Fig 4.43).
9 Use a cross-reference system whenever a file is known by more than one name.
10 'Thin out' files when necessary. There will be an organisational policy regarding the length of time documents are held in the system. When they become obsolete or out of date they may be transferred to the 'archives' – an additional storage area where files are stored in boxes in case they are required for reference.
11 Be aware of health and safety regarding filing cabinets. Always close drawers after you have used them and lock drawers and cabinets before leaving the office at night.
12 Always ask for help if you are unsure where something should be filed, and do not be afraid to offer ideas if you think the system could be more efficient with some improvements.

When documents are filed, it could be that this is done using any of the following systems. Different methods will prove suitable for different circumstances. The following can be found in organisations.

FOLLOW-UP FORM

			DATE
NAME			TELEPHONE NUMBER
ADDRESS			LETTER DATE
SUBJECT			
REMARKS			
RETURN TO		ON	
	ON		
	ON		

Fig 4.43 An example of a follow-up system form

Alphabetically

This method refers to the filing of documents according to the first letter of the surname (*see* Fig 4.44). This is normally the first letter of the surname of the correspondent, although in a personnel department files could be arranged in alphabetical order, determined by the first letter of the member of staff's surname.

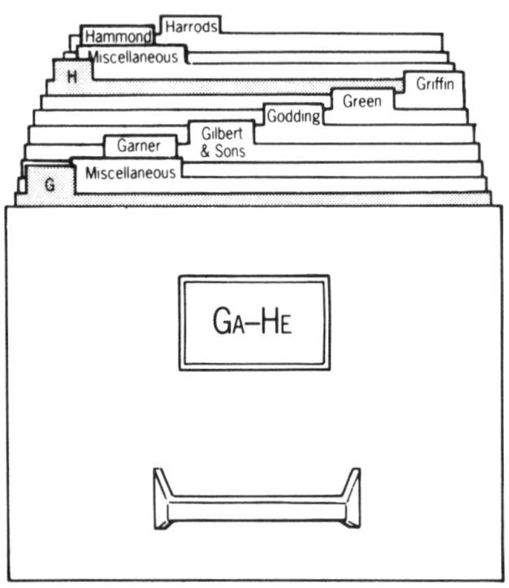

Fig 4.44 An alphabetical filing classification

Advantages and disadvantages of filing alphabetically

Advantages	*Disadvantages*
■ It is a convenient and easy-to-understand system ■ It requires no indexing ■ It is useful for incorporating miscellaneous documents	■ It can become very large and cumbersome ■ Confusion can occur when names are the same or similar ■ Cross-referencing is necessary as there is a possibility that files may be requested under different names or titles

When filing alphabetically, the following should be remembered:

1 Take the first letter of the surname and then each letter after that, e.g.:

Black, Brian
Blake, John
Blakemore, Margaret

2 If the surname is the same, place the first name or initial in alphabetical order, e.g.:

Smith, David
Smith, John
Smith, William

3 If the surname and the first name are the same, file by second name or initial, e.g.:

Jones, Brian A
Jones, Brian D
Jones, Brian P

4 Treat surname prefixes as part of the name and all names beginning with Mc or Mac as if they were spelt with Mac, e.g.:

McBride, Angus
McGregor, William
MacMasters, Peter

5 File all 'saint' surnames beginning with St as if they were spelt Saint, e.g.:

St John, Ian
Saint Luke's Church
St Mary's Hospital

6 Ignore titles, e.g.:

Brown, Sir Andrew
Grey, Lady Jane
Simpson, Major David

7 Ignore words like 'The' and 'A' in the name of an organisation, e.g.:

Card Shop, The
Office Equipment Centre, The
Tea Shoppe, The

8 Numbers should be filed as if spelt in full, e.g.

55 Club, The
99 Boutique, The
111 Association, The

PC 4.3.4
C 2.2

Individual activity *Time: 20 minutes*

Place the following list of names in alphabetical order:

Hewitt, David
Cowley, Maurice
Hunt, Peter
Woodhouse, John
Jones, Nick
Sutherland, Joshua
Hewitt, Ross
Canwell, Stuart
Canwell, Alun
Hurle, Peter
Aliffe, Burt
Sergio, Maria
Sergio, Despina
Watson, Susan
Gowen, Susan
Leggett, Michael

A quick way of putting a list into alphabetical order is to put the names into numerical order first, by writing next to the name the number order in which each will appear, and then writing the names out again in numerical order.

By subject

Again, this system also uses the alphabetical method of filing, but the subject determines the order (*see* Fig 4.45). Your own filing cabinet or folder may be arranged by subject. You probably have divider cards which are arranged into the subjects that you study during the course of the week.

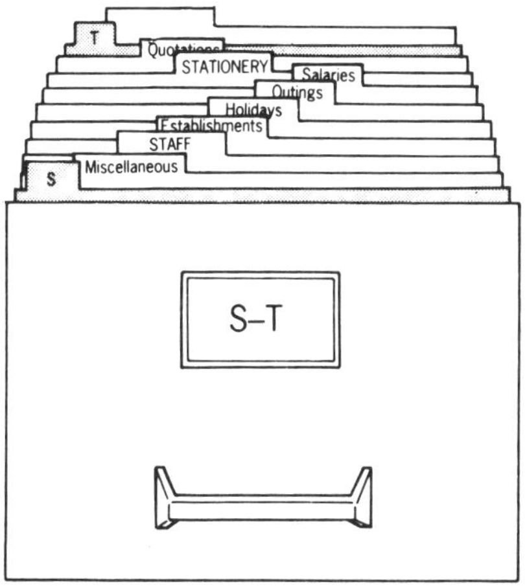

Fig 4.45 A subject filing classification

Advantages and disadvantages of filing by subject

Advantages	*Disadvantages*
■ It is easy to understand ■ It is straightforward; no indexing is required ■ Expansion is not a problem, as additional files can be added ■ Confidentiality is not a problem, as no names or addresses are used in the file name	■ Confusion could occur where more than one person is responsible for filing, as the two may not consider the document is related to one particular subject

PC 4.3.4
C 2.2
C 2.3

Individual activity

Time: 20 minutes

Place the following list of subjects which may be studied at your institution into subject order:

Accounts
Typewriting
Word Processing
History
Psychology
Biology
Human Biology
Geography
Geology
English Literature
English Language
Media Studies
French
German
Spanish
Greek
Italian

By number

This method is linked by means of index cards to the alphabetical method. Each document or folder is given a number and these are filed in numerical order (*see* Fig 4.46). The information contained within the files is sorted into alphabetical order.

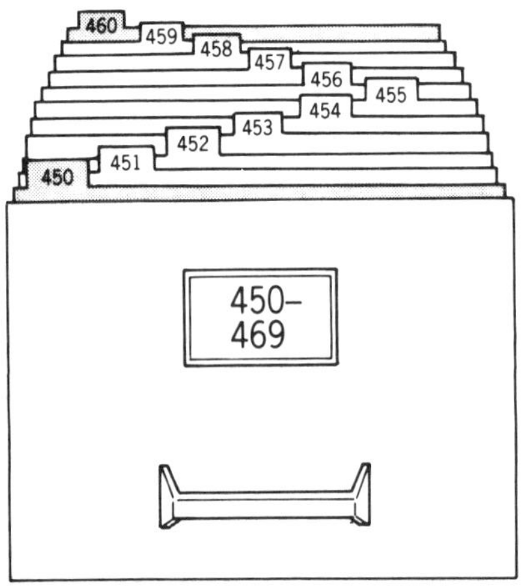

Fig 4.46 A numerical filing classification

Advantages and disadvantages of numerical filing

Advantages	*Disadvantages*
■ The numbered files are more easily found	■ It may be difficult to find a file on a particular subject
■ The numbered files are less likely to be returned to the wrong place	■ A cross-reference index is also needed
■ The number reference can be added to any correspondence	
■ The numbered files can be easily increased, thereby expanding the system	

PC 4.3.4
C 2.2
C 2.3

Individual activity *Time: 20 minutes*

Place the following list of numbers in numerical order:

134
176
95
378
109
310
245
88
333
213
180
76
21
209

By date

Chronological filing means that documents are stored according to the date, again with the most recent date being at the front or top of the file (*see* Fig 4.47). Travel agents are likely to use this method. As they receive travel documents for clients, these would be filed in date order, either of departure date or of payment date.

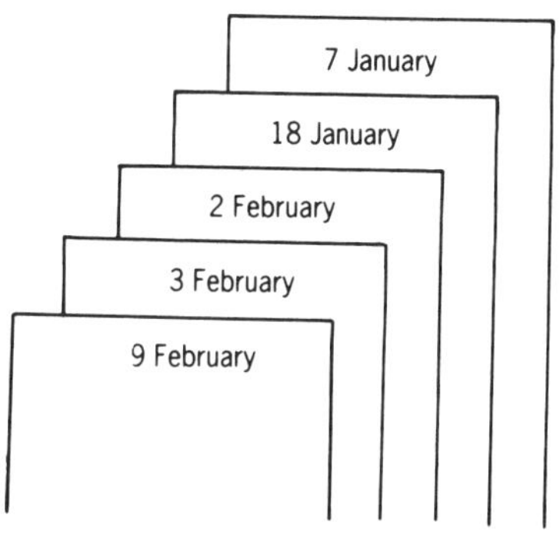

Fig 4.47 A chronological filing classification

Advantages and disadvantages of chronological filing

Advantages	*Disadvantages*
■ For some organisations a date is the most significant information available	■ There are no major disadvantages, as it is unlikely that any organisation other than one particularly needing this method would consider using it

PC 4.3.4
C 2.2
C 2.3

Individual activity *Time: 20 minutes*

Place the following list of dates in chronological order, putting the most recent at the top:

25 January
17 September
1 August
15 June
27 June
11 November
6 May
20 July
15 November
18 November
21 September
18 June
24 August
21 December

Geographical

The files are arranged in alphabetical order according to the location of the correspondent (*see* Fig 4.48). This is a common system used in sales departments where the documents are filed under the area or region. Local authorities would also use the geographical method of filing documents, as the area itself would be more frequently referred to than the inhabitants of that area.

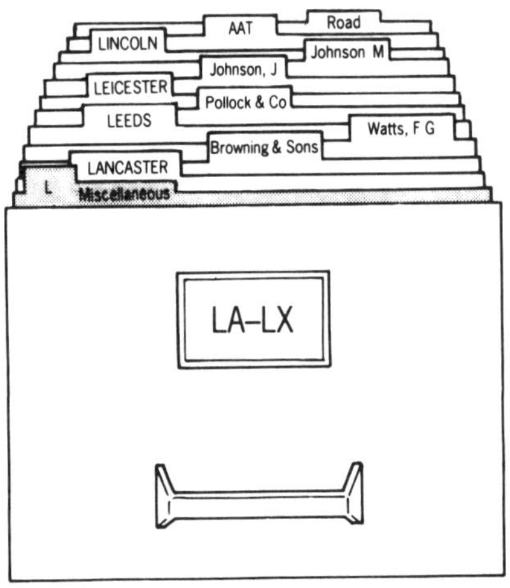

Fig 4.48 A geographical filing classification

Advantages and disadvantages of geographical filing

Advantages

- It is convenient for some organisations
- It is possible to file the documents directly
- Statistics can be easily gathered from the filing system without the need to retrieve too many individual files

Disadvantages

- The filing clerk would need to know the system well and be good at geography!
- Confusion could occur where regional or county boundaries change

PC 4.3.4
C 2.2
C 2.3

Individual activity *Time: 20 minutes*

Place the following list of towns and cities in geographical order, i.e. alphabetical order:

Ipswich
Norwich
Southwold
Bury St Edmunds
Cambridge
Newmarket
Plymouth
Portsmouth
Aberdeen
Edinburgh
Colchester
Chelmsford
Gants Hill
Halesworth
Great Yarmouth
Saffron Walden
St Neots
Braintree
Bristol
Bath

Vertical filing cabinet

This is used for storing papers vertically in files with their strips or labels on the top edge of each file (*see* Fig 4.49).

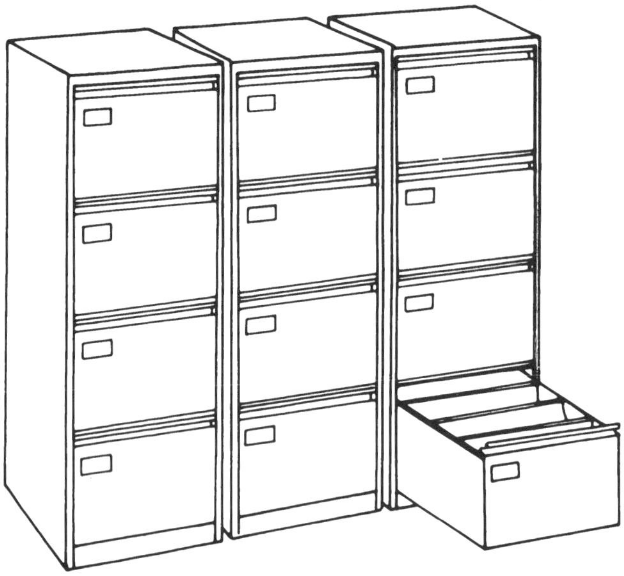

Fig 4.49 Vertical filing cabinets

Lateral filing cabinet

This is used for storing papers where the files are suspended laterally with their strips or labels vertically on the front (*see* Fig 4.50).

Fig 4.50 Lateral filing cabinets

Rotary suspended filing unit

These are used for storing papers where the files are suspended laterally on rotating platforms (*see* Fig 4.51).

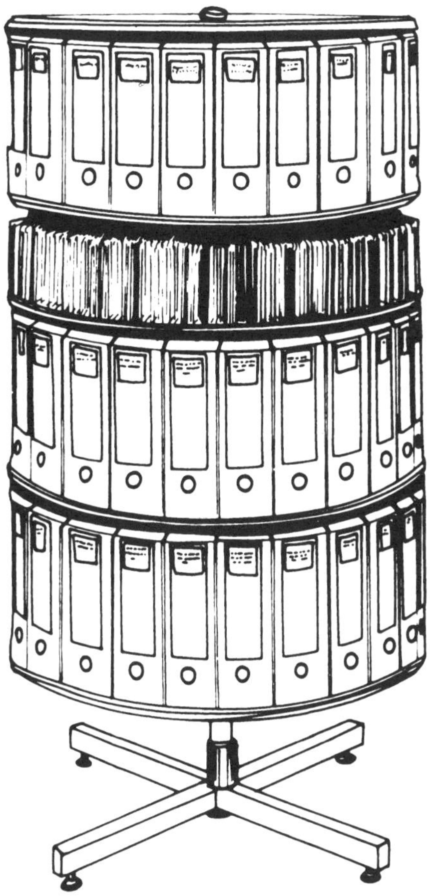

Fig 4.51 Rotary filing

4.3.6 Identify and evaluate ways to send and ways to store business documents

In order to meet the criteria of this section, it is necessary for you to identify and evaluate the way business documents can be sent from one organisation to another. In addition, we need to discuss further ways of storing business documents to those we have already mentioned in the previous performance criteria. We will look first at the ways of sending information to another organisation.

Ease of sending, storing, finding and retrieving; the cost and safety and security of documents

Naturally, it will be of prime importance to an organisation that any documents generated by it for sending to another organisation should be sent in the best way from the point of view of security and speed. Additionally, organisations will wish to keep a record of what they have sent for their own use. The best way to store this information in order to be able to find or retrieve it at a later date will also be vital if the organisation is to function efficiently and effectively.

Many larger organisations will have a section which deals with the incoming and outgoing mail on a regular basis. Other organisations, particularly smaller ones, will give the responsibility of dealing with the post to one or two individuals as part of their regular duties.

Whoever is responsible for dealing with the organisation's post each day will have to be aware of guidelines regarding both incoming and outgoing mail.

As already mentioned, the person distributing the incoming mail may also collect some items for the outgoing mail during the course of their deliveries. However, the most busy time is obviously in the afternoon when the day's post is ready for sending out. It could be that the mail room stipulates a deadline or final collection time, after which no mail would be accepted. This may be necessary to ensure that their staff process the mail in time for final posting times at the Post Office.

It has become common in recent years for the mail room to deal with all aspects of the outgoing mail. The secretary or clerk sending out the letter, quotation or invoice would simply prepare the envelope and leave it sealed in the Outgoing Mail Tray. The junior or messenger from the Mail Room would collect this and it would go into the batch of mail for either first class or second class posting.

The franking machine

Unless the organisation is very small, it is usual for a franking machine to be used instead of stamps. When the organisation still uses stamps, it is often the case that a record is kept of the stamps used, including the details of the correspondence sent.

A franking machine prints in red the value of the stamp. In addition, it allows space for an advertisement by the organisation, as well as the time and date of posting. Obviously this avoids the somewhat tedious task of licking and sticking stamps, and recording their use.

A franking machine can be hired or purchased from the manufacturers, although a licence has to be obtained from the Post Office before the machine can be used. There is no charge for this licence, but the Post Office will set the meter on the machine to keep a record of units bought, used and still in credit to the organisation on its franking machine.

The value of the postage being franked can be changed very easily, in much the same way as a date stamp is changed.

Outgoing mail

Each day the person dealing with the outgoing mail would have to follow the guidelines given below:

Fig 4.52 A mailing system incorporating a franking machine

- *Sort* the mail into first and second class post
- *Change* the date on the franking machine
- *Check* the value of the postage on the franking machine
- *Check* the quality of the printer on the franking machine
- *Check* the credit left in the franking machine

Once the credit left on the franking machine reaches a certain pre-determined level, the machine will have to be re-credited by contacting the Post Office. This can be done via the telephone on the more up-to-date machines. They are fitted with a mini-modem which is linked to the franking machine via the telephone. With these newer machines it is no longer necessary for the organisation to take the machine into the Post Office itself. However, those machines which are not linked to the telephone line will do the same job, although it is more time consuming to have to take them to the Post Office to be credited. It is also necessary for these machines to be accompanied by a book which the Post Office clerk will complete each time the machine is credited with units.

Regular envelopes can be franked directly, but more bulky items need to be franked using an adhesive label, which is then stuck on to the item.

Add any adhesive stickers required on the items of mail, e.g. 'urgent', 'airmail', 'recorded delivery'.

Once the mail has been franked, it can by-pass the Post Office sorting office and can be handed over the counter of a Post Office. It is either tied in bundles or placed in a special Post Office bag designed for this use.

Individual activity

Time: 20 minutes

Prepare a list of guidelines for the temporary member of staff who will be carrying out your duties while you are away on holiday. Write a list of procedures for franking the mail for him/her to follow.

PC 4.3.5
C 2.2

Some smaller organisations still keep a record of outgoing mail in the same way that they would the incoming mail. This record allows them to keep a check on the amount of money spent on postage stamps and gives a form of clarification as to when mail was actually despatched out of the office. This method of recording postage would normally be the responsibility of one individual and allows the monitoring of cost to be ongoing.

Another obvious duty of the mail room assistant is to weigh any parcels which have been prepared ready for despatch from the organisation. This would be done within the department and the parcels would be taken to the Post Office with the rest of the mail at the end of each day. The manual or electronic scales would weight items and calculate the postage due on each.

Parcels

The guidelines for dealing with the postage of parcels are as follows:

1 *'Wrap' the parcel sensibly,* taking care to ensure that it is secure and not likely to be damaged during transit. The Post Office deals with hundreds of parcels each day, and although they take every possible care, it is inevitable that they will meet with some knocks and bumps on their way. Any damage to parcels can cause delay or loss and expense to your organisation.

2 *Parcels should be packed as follows:*

- If items are fragile, it is important to use plenty of suitable soft cushioning which will absorb any knocks the parcel might receive. Such items as crushed newspaper, kitchen paper, tissue paper or corrugated paper can be used as inner packaging. Also available are items such as plastic or polystyrene chips and air-bubble polythene. The box should be filled with the inner packing so that the contents do not move around. If the items are not fragile but are awkward shapes, make sure that no part of the item projects through the packaging. Even non-fragile items like sheets and clothing can still be damaged in transit, and care must also be taken when preparing these parcels. Corrugated paper could be used before the application of a layer of strong brown paper, sealed with self-adhesive tape and tied with string.
- It is advisable to use a strong box, e.g. one that can be used to carry groceries from a supermarket, or one that can be supplied by the Royal Mail. The sizes vary and they can be bought at most Post Offices. In addition to special boxes, padded envelopes can also be purchased – these are known as 'Jiffy' bags. Where these are not necessary, it is still advisable to use a layer of corrugated paper before wrapping round in strong brown paper.
- If a box is being used, it should be firmly sealed along each of the edges with self-adhesive tape.
- When just corrugated paper and strong brown paper are being used, the parcel should be sealed with tape and then tied with string, knotting the string tightly where it crosses.
- Tie-on tags can be used for parcels, and care should be taken to make sure these are attached securely. The name and address of the sender should also be displayed clearly on the parcel so that it can be returned, should there be a problem with delivery. A further precaution is to include the name and address of both the sender and the recipient inside the parcel.

3 *Weigh the parcel using manual or electronic scales.* The electronic scales would automatically calculate the postage due. If using manual scales, then the operator would need to refer to the *Postal Rates Guide* issued by the Post Office.

4 Frank the label with the necessary amount of postage and stick it to the parcel.
5 Add any necessary sticker to the parcel, e.g. 'fragile', 'urgent' or 'handle with care'.

The parcel is now ready to be taken to the Post Office for handing over to the counter clerk.

All parcels and packages that are being sent overseas need a declaration label which describes the contents. This includes airmail and surface mail. The reason for this is to inform the Customs Officers in the country to which the parcel is being sent of its contents. Some articles have to have a tax paid on them by the recipient. This is called a customs *duty*. Duty is put on some goods to discourage people from sending them. Gifts may be allowed in duty free in certain countries if described on the label as 'gifts'.

For letter packets, there is a green label if the contents are less than £270 in value. A white form is for goods in excess of that value. For parcels, the white form is used in most cases with a despatch note. In all other cases a declaration/despatch note which is combined is used. Some other forms might be needed, depending on the destination.

Individual activity

Time: 20 minutes

PC 4.3.5
C 2.2

Your next list of procedures for the temporary member of staff is for dealing with the outgoing mail. Ensure that you include in your guidelines details regarding the preparation of parcels.

Reference books

Naturally, books of reference are as essential in the mail room as they are in any other department within an organisation. The Post Office produces a very useful and informative series of leaflets dealing with every aspect of the services offered to the general public. We shall deal with these different services a little later in this Element. The Post Office also sells a publication called the *Post Office Guide*. This is a very large and weighty book which lists in detail all the services offered. It is important that the publications and leaflets kept within the mail room for reference by the immediate staff and those visiting the department are fully up-to-date. This ensures that the best service can be given by the Post Office regarding the delivery of mail on time and to the correct destination, whether locally, nationally or internationally.

Other useful books for reference in the mail room are:

- *World Atlas*
- *Local Yellow Pages Directories*
- *Local Telephone Directories*
- *Local street maps*
- *Local Thomson Directories*
- *Postcode Directories (local postcodes are included in the Thomson Directories, but national ones can be supplied by the Post Office on microfiche)*

Internal mail

Some documents are delivered by the organisation's messengers and are interdepartmental (they do not go out of the organisation at all). These are internal mail and are often in the form of a memorandum. The documents are often placed in specially printed large envelopes which have space on them for the name of each recipient to be listed. After the document has been opened, the name is crossed off and the envelope is ready to be used again.

Post Office services

The Post Office provides a vast range of services for the distribution and handling of mail. These are available to all customers and the requirements and costs incurred are clearly listed in the leaflets available for each service.

1 **First and second class post** Inland mail is usually regarded as the first and second class letter services. These are used more than any other service. The letters do not receive any special security handling and this service is not recommended if you are sending letters that need cover for compensation.

   The Post Office uses the postcodes to help speed the sorting of mail. If the correct postcode is used on envelopes, parcels and packets, then speedier delivery than normal can be expected than if the postcode is not included.

2 **Recorded delivery** By using the recorded delivery service you can obtain proof that the mail has actually been posted and that it has reached its destination (*see* Fig 4.53a). Compensation for loss, damage or delay is limited to the maximum amount available for first and second class mail.

3 **Registered post** Registered post is a secure way of sending valuables or money of up to £500 in value, and it guarantees they will arrive at their destination by 12.30 pm the next working day (Monday to Friday). If it is necessary to confirm delivery, a local telephone call will suffice, provided you quote the 13-digit reference number on the receipt (*see* Fig 4.53b). This is a guaranteed secure way for next-day delivery by 17.30. If items are lost or damaged, it gives higher compensation than recorded delivery. It has special handling with extra security procedures at every stage. The compensation for loss or damage is up to a maximum of £2200. A signature is required on delivery.

4 **Certificates of posting** Certificates of posting are a way of making sure that your letter is posted. It is for ordinary letter post. The service is free. You hand the letter in at the Post Office counter and they initial and date stamp the form (*see* Fig 4.54). The certificate is your proof that the letter has been posted. It is delivered in the normal way.

   You can insure a registered letter or packet against damage, loss or delay by taking out Consequential Loss Insurance. When you post the registered letter a Consequential Loss Insurance cover note is issued. This is filled in by the sender with the name and address of both the sender and recipient. The maximum cover is £10 000.

5 **Advice on delivery** An advice on delivery form is available from the Post Office counter. This should be completed when using recorded or registered post.

6 **Redirection service** The Post Office will redirect any mail to your new address if you move house or business premises. A week before moving, you complete a Royal Mail Redirection form and hand it in over the Post Office counter. Redirection can be arranged for a period of one, three or twelve months. The Post Office charges a fee for this service.

Fig. 4.53a Recorded delivery label.

Fig 4.53b Registered post label

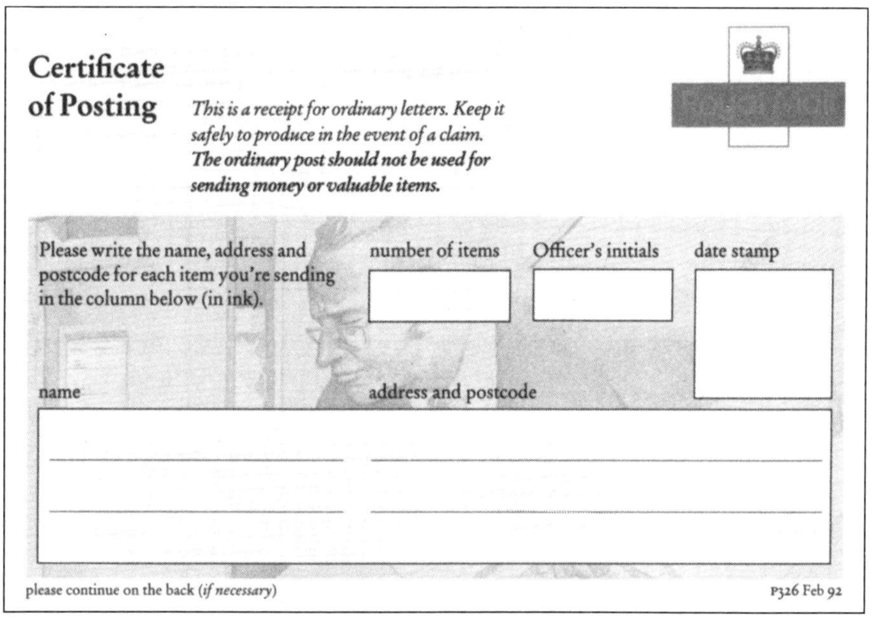
Certificate of Posting

This is a receipt for ordinary letters. Keep it safely to produce in the event of a claim.
The ordinary post should not be used for sending money or valuable items.

Please write the name, address and postcode for each item you're sending in the column below (in ink).

number of items | Officer's initials | date stamp

name | address and postcode

please continue on the back (*if necessary*)

P326 Feb 92

Fig 4.54 A certificate of posting

7 **Business Reply Service** This service is used by firms who wish to obtain a reply from their customers. By using this service the replies will be paid for by the organisation, not the customer. This service can be used for postcards, envelopes, folders or gummed labels. These are posted in the normal way, but no stamp is required. It can be used for both first and second class mail.

Anyone who obtains a licence may use this service. The licence form is available from main Post Offices. Postage on the business reply forms is paid for by the firm receiving the mail. This service cannot be used in the Irish Republic, nor can it be used in conjunction with the Redirection Service.

8 **Freepost** As an alternative to the Business Reply Service, Freepost also allows the firm to pay the postage rather than the customer. The word 'FREEPOST' is included in the address of the organisation. Letters are only sent by second class mail, although they are posted in the usual way.

A licence is needed from the Post Office to use this service. Additionally, an annual fee is payable. Redirection is not permitted.

9 **Cash on delivery** When using this service the cost of the article delivered can be collected by the postman from the recipient. The cost is then forwarded to the sender of the parcel by special order. All parcels have to be registered. It is often used by mail order firms and is mentioned in their advertisements.

10 **Datapost** This service guarantees overnight delivery within the UK, as well as a quicker than normal delivery overseas. This mail travels separately from other post and is accompanied by Post Office staff in the UK only.

11 **Special Delivery** Special delivery guarantees that urgent mail reaches its destination by 12.30 pm the next working day (Monday to Friday). This type of mail gets priority over all other mail.

Special delivery

As the sorting and distribution of the mail is the responsibility of the mail room staff, so would be the collection and storage of receipts. Receipts would be issued by the Post Office for any mail sent or received by their special services, i.e. recorded delivery or registered post. In addition, mail agencies also provide receipts for any mail handled by them.

A mail agency would hand over the parcel or package to the mail room assistant, who would have to sign for it. This signature is logged in duplicate or triplicate and the mail room assistant would receive their copy as a receipt (proof) that the parcel or package had been delivered.

The mail room assistant would then need to notify the person(s) for whom the parcel or package is intended. They would then sign a logging book as the mail room assistant's receipt and record that the parcel has been passed on.

Some mail agencies also use bar codes. These are used like stickers and are attached to the parcel or packet. When the mail agency employee collects the parcel from the organisation, they 'read' the bar code with a light sensitive pen and this automatically logs the parcel with the mail agency.

Electronic transmission (fax, E-mail)

Increasingly, information is transmitted electronically. The days of waiting for letters or documents have, for most organisations, long gone. Nowadays, the tendency to use electronic processes to transmit information is more the 'norm', particularly in larger organisations. It is commonplace, for instance, for organisations to use fax and E-mail.

Rather than rely on the traditional methods of sending information on hard copy through the post, electronic mail (E-mail) offers the opportunity to transmit information instantaneously to remote but linked computers. A further advantage of this system is the alarm device which informs the recipient that the message is awaiting them.

Fax machines

A facsimile machine (fax) is capable of relaying documents and graphics via the telephone network to another location in just a few seconds (*see* Fig 4.55). These machines have become invaluable to most organisations, particularly if they have a number of sites within the group, or need to contact establishments abroad easily. The word 'facsimile' means an exact and faithful reproduction of text, photographs or graphic images. The fax machine is left switched on 24 hours a day, and it does not have to be continually monitored throughout the night. This means that the time differences between countries are not a problem. The procedure for sending a fax message is as follows:

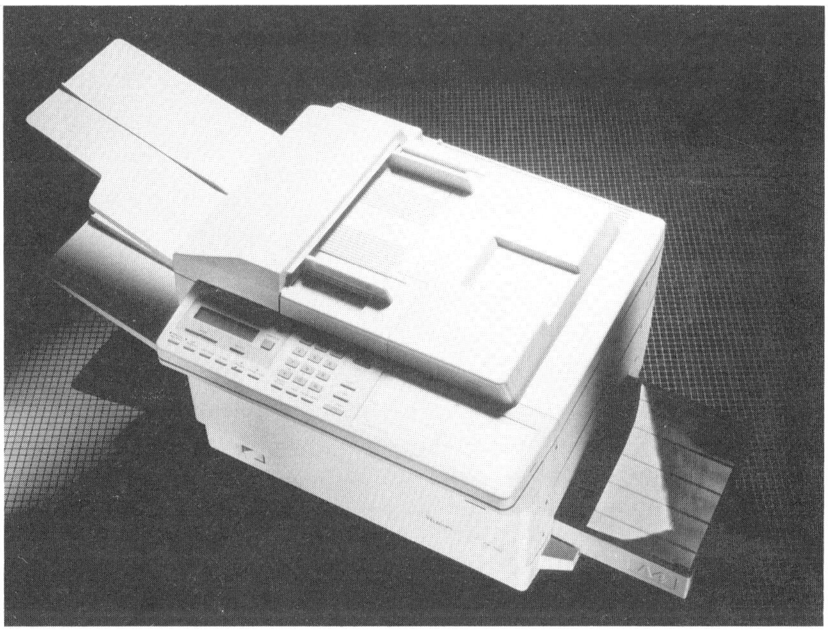

Fig 4.55 A fax machine

1 *Prepare the original document.*
2 *Prepare a covering sheet* (*see* Fig 4.56). This will show the name of the recipient, the name of the sender, the fax numbers involved and the number of pages being sent. It may also allow space for a short message.

FACSIMILE MESSAGE

TO ATTENTION OF ....

LOCATION/DEPARTMENT ....

FAX NO ....

FROM ORIGINATOR ....

FAX NO ....

TELEPHONE NO ....

DATE ....

NO. OF PAGES (INCLUDING THIS ONE) ....

If transmission is not properly received please call the above number.

Fig 4.56 An example of a front page for addition to a series of documents being sent by fax machine

3 *Look up the fax number of the recipient in the Fax Directory, or contact Fax Enquiries.* These numbers may be kept readily at hand, particularly if they are used regularly, as with telephone numbers.
4 *Place the original document into the fax machine.*
5 *Key in the number of the recipient and follow the instructions given on the machine.* Although these procedures may vary slightly from machine to machine, the principles for despatching a message are the same.
6 *If a connection has been made, the original document will pass through the machine and you will be informed that transmission is taking place.* Should the recipient's line be engaged, the machine will automatically redial the number at intervals until a connection is made.
7 *Once transmission has taken place, the machine will issue a Transmission Report.* This will state the date, time and length of the call, the recipient's number, the sender's number, the number of pages sent and that transmission was acceptable. Should there have been a problem in transmission, the report will indicate this and retransmission may be necessary.

PC 4.3.4
C 2.2

Individual activity *Time: 20 minutes*

Using the example given in Fig 4.56, design your own front page for sending a fax message. Remember to include any necessary details. The headed paper used by an organisation for other correspondence could also be used.

Telex machines

Although using much the same principle as the fax machine, the telex is more limited in its use. For this reason, the fax machine has really replaced the telex in most organisations. It is not possible to transmit charts and diagrams via the telex, only words. However, the same advantages apply regarding the transmission of messages to countries overseas. Telex messages can also be prepared and saved on electronic file and transmitted at a later time when they are despatched automatically.

Fig 4.57 A telex machine

PC 4.3.4
C 2.2

Individual activity

Time: 20 minutes

Design a form for use by members of staff who wish to send a telex. This form would be used to write a draft of the message. It will be handed to the telex operator, who will then key in the information on the telex. Be sure to include all necessary information and details.

E-mail

Networking, or linking computer systems together, helps to improve the processing of information as well as improving communication within an organisation. Networks can be classified according to their location:

1 **LAN (Local Area Network)** Most commonly, this is a network confined to one building with work areas containing microcomputers. These can be extended over an area of two or three miles.
2 **WAN (Wide Area Network)** This is a computer network which is distributed nationally (or internationally) and makes use of telephone or satellite links.

By making use of the LAN or WAN networks, an organisation has control over its own information processing, but also has access to the main database which may be held at head office. It also allows branches to communicate easily and quickly with each other and with head office.

What has made a lot of these computer facilities available is the change from analogue signals, which were required to transmit at different frequencies, to a more flexible system called Digital. Digital signals are pulses which can be understood by computers. These signals are sent from one computer to another via a modem (a connection to a telephone line) or similar device and may be accessed instantly.

When we are considering computers and their effects on business, we must first realise that there are, in fact, two main types of computer. These are mainframe and micros.

1 **Mainframes** In varying forms, and levels of complexity, speed and ability, mainframe computers have been available since just after the Second World War. They are, in essence, machines with large memories and data processing abilities which can be used to store a mass of information for immediate access and amendment. It is normally the case that mainframes operate 24 hours a day, 365 days of the year. The advantage with running these machines continuously is that routine data processing work can be undertaken when other demands on the machine are at their lowest, i.e. at night. Mainframes are used as the workhorses for networked computers, providing such services as word processing, database storage, spreadsheet calculations, graphics production, stock control, accounts and electronic mail.
2 **Micros** Microcomputers have changed beyond all recognition since their initial development some 30 years ago. Modern microcomputers are more powerful than the old mainframes were in the past. It is the common trend for computers to become more powerful, faster, cheaper, smaller and have the ability to be used for a number of different applications. Recent developments have seen computers which can understand handwritten instructions on a touch-sensitive screen and machines which do not require a keyboard, but respond to voice activation.

Telex, Bureaufax and Intelpost are all different forms of electronic mail – where messages are sent over the telephone as electric signals which can be converted back into paper form at the other end. Privately-owned facsimile machines are also a form of electronic mail.

Telex and teletex provide an external electronic mail system that gives written messages with the security of 'answerback' codes which identify the sender and also the receiver.

The most recent developments in electronic mail are computer-based systems. These allow people to send and receive messages and other information through their own 'electronic mail box'.

The mail box is a form of computer terminal linked to the telephone network, with a memory for storing messages and a means of putting messages into a system. A printer or typewriter is attached to allow messages to be printed as 'hard copy' when required. Every user has a password to allow him/her to use the system. Word processing facilities allow the message to be checked and corrected before it is sent.

When a message is sent, it can be to one mail box or to a number of different mail boxes. This is handy when a memo or instruction has to be sent to all branches of a large organisation. On arrival at the recipient's mail box, the message will be stored in an electronic memory until the mail box is 'opened'; that is, until the person checks to see the messages that have come in.

This service is particularly useful in a large organisation, where each office or department can have a mail box and senior executives can have their own. This service will probably be extended so that almost everybody will be able to get in touch with everybody else through an electronic mail box.

Electronic post

The Post Office offers this service. This is where a customer sends a computer tape to the appropriate Electronic Post Centre. The Post Office prints the text and sends it to the address, using first class post. This is particularly useful for bulk mailing, e.g. advertising leaflets.

Intelpost

Intelpost is the Post Office facsimile service.

Copies of documents can be sent by any Post Office which has an Intelpost sign displayed, or a document which has to be copied will be collected by messenger, on payment of an additional fee.

Altogether there are 114 Intelpost centres in the UK, which are linked with 2000 major business centres in 30 countries – including contintental Europe and the rest of the world.

In addition to this, the Intelpost service is available for organisations which are too small to be able to afford expensive electronic installations.

Access can be made to Intelpost, using a modem, for sending information from a computer down a telephone line, or from a telex machine. It is a public electronic mail system which is protected by law, making it secure and confidential.

How to use this service:

1 *The document is handed over at the Post Office counter*
2 *The name, address, postcode and telephone number is given*
3 *The number of sides to be transmitted is given*
4 *The method of delivery (e.g. personal collection) is given*
5 *After transmission, the Post Office at the other end will do one of the following:*

- *deliver by special messenger*
- *deliver by first-class post the following day*
- *inform the recipient that collection can be made the following day*

If immediate delivery is required by special messenger an additional charge is made.

The service is not available at the weekends or public holidays, either in the UK or overseas.

Computer files

Databases arose from the idea that a common 'pool' of information can be organised in such a way that all those using the system can be satisfied. Therefore, instead of each department within an organisation keeping and maintaining its own set of files, these are grouped together to form a database.

Such databases have advantages over traditional filing systems:

- *There is no unnecessary duplication of information, which is more economical and is also more effective in keeping information up to date*
- *There is less chance of inconsistency of information*
- *Comprehensive information is more readily available*
- *Any enquiries can be dealt with 'on demand' rather than going through the normally tedious process of obtaining files*

Electronic databases are normally defined as coming under two main systems:

1. **Centralised systems** In a centralised system, all processing of information is carried out by one computer. This central computer is responsible for the processing, even though it may be linked to terminals. This means that each of the offices or departments may have its own terminals, but the information is stored and retrieved by the central computer.
2. **Distributing systems** These systems allow for some processing of information to be carried out by the terminals. These terminals have their own storage and retrieval programs, so information can be input and manipulated on them, rather than just on the central computer.

Microfilm

Microfilm is a method of using film to condense the space occupied by documents. This, to some degree, helps to replace the paper which so often builds up within an organisation. Additionally, microfilming is used to preserve old or valuable documents, thus ensuring they are not handled too much. Nowadays, libraries tend to use this method of storing information and it helps alleviate the mountains of documentation which could be found in the normal library. The process for using microfilm is as follows:

- *The original documents are photographed and processed on to the computer.*
- *The computer is used to access the information required, by 'scrolling' through the film. The specific page of a document can then be viewed on the screen of the computer and, if necessary, printed.*

Obviously, all information stored on computer must also be protected. Organisations which use this method of storage and retrieval must ensure the following:

- *Back up copies of disks must be made and safely stored.*
- *Passwords must be keyed in by the staff using the computer, and these should be changed regularly.*
- *As an addition to passwords, user codes can also be keyed in. These codes are known only to those who are authorised to access the information and relate to specific files or documents stored.*

Element 4.3 Assignment

PC 4.3.1–4
C 2.2
IT 2.1
IT 2.2
IT 2.3
IT 2.4

For the purposes of this assignment you will have needed to produce a set of correct business documents which include a draft and a final version for each. This could have been work which has been produced as an integral part of your studies.

Task 1 *PC 4.3.1–2*

Having produced the business documents, you now need to evaluate their quality of appearance, the style and format. You also need to evaluate the use of spelling and grammar within the documents.

Task 2 *PC 4.3.3*

Your documents should include three examples of different methods of processing business documents, with a summary which compares them in terms of legibility, cost, time taken to produce, ability to make changes and storage. Your summary should be word processed.

Task 3 *PC 4.3.4*

Finally, you should complete a record of referencing, filing and retrieving at least 36 documents and six computer files.

Notes

As we have said, the work for this Element should be integrated with other work, so that the business documents produced are relevant to work you have already undertaken.

UNIT 4 Revision test

At the time of writing it has been assumed that Unit 4 will not be end tested as the other mandatory units are. We have, however, decided to include the revision tests in this Unit so that they can be used to consolidate learning.

1 Which government department is concerned with the collection of VAT?

2 Into which two areas can the annual accounts be broken down?

3 Briefly explain what you understand by the word 'assets'.

4 Briefly explain what you understand by the word 'liabilities'.

5 What is a profit and loss account?

6 Why is it essential to check documents before they are issued?

7 What is a capital item?

8 What are the stages in the purchasing process?

9 Why would a purchasing department use catalogues?

10 State three headings you might find on a purchase invoice

11 What do the letters E & OE stand for?

12 When would a credit note be issued?

13 When placing an order by telephone, how would you confirm this order?

14 Why is a statement of account issued?

15 What are the six methods of payment of accounts?

16 What is meant by 'stopping' a cheque?

17 Give two items appearing on a cheque.

18 Who would receive the third and fourth copies of a credit card sales voucher?

19 What is a debit card?

20 What is 'defaulting'?

21 In which year did the Consumer Credit Act become law?

22 List at least five items you would expect to appear on a pay slip.

23 What is a statutory deduction?

24 What is a voluntary deduction?

25 What is SAYE?

26 List six items that may be purchased using petty cash.

27 Give at least five headings which would appear on a petty cash voucher.

28 Give five column headings which may be used in a petty cash book.

29 Explain what you understand by the term 'float'.

30 How would a petty cashier restore the imprest?

31 Think of four situations when you would receive a receipt.

32 What do you understand by the term 'clearing' a cheque?

33 Give three circumstances when a bank would not accept a cheque.

34 List four transactions likely to appear on a bank statement.

35 Who do you think would authorise large orders within an organisation?

36 Who, within an organisation, is likely to be a cheque signatory?

37 What does the term 'reconciliation' mean?

38 What does the term 'discrepancy' mean?

39 What information would you expect to find on a company's printed letterheaded paper?

40 Name three methods of filing.

41 Name three methods of storing files.

42 In which order would you place the files for:
Mr A McTavish
Mrs M Martin
Mrs Alison Martin

43 Name four Post Office services for mailing letters.

44 What do LAN and WAN mean?

45 Name four methods of sending items electronically.

46 What is computer software?

47 What is Intelpost?

48 Why would you use a computer password?

49 What is a spreadsheet used for?

50 What is a database used for?

Glossary of business terms

After-sales service This is a customer service provided by an organisation to its customers; it includes maintenance, repair and advice.

Annual report and accounts This is a yearly report to the company's shareholders which includes a **balance sheet**, a **profit and loss account** and other information that is required by law.

Amalgamation The merging of two or more divisions of a business.

Appraisal See **performance appraisal**.

Arbitration This is a method of settling an industrial dispute through a third party.

Articles of association These are the rules under which an organisation is set up and concern the relationships between individuals within an organisation.

Assembly line This is a method of organising the machinery and labour in a factory so that a product is assembled in a series of operations along the line.

Asset This is an item owned by a business or an individual to which a monetary value can be attached.

Assisted areas Defined parts of the UK in which government grants may be given to persuade firms to locate there.

Bad debt This is an accounting term which refers to money owed by customers or others which is unlikely to be paid.

Balance of payments The sum of the nation's income and expenditure on foreign trade.

Balance of trade That part of the balance of payments account that registers exports and imports of visible goods.

Balance sheet This is an accounting term which refers to a statement of a business's **assets** and **liabilities** on the last day of a **trading period**.

Bank rate This is the level of interest charged by a country's central bank. It forms the basis of the lending rate for all other loans.

Bankruptcy This refers to the position of a business which is unable to pay its **debts** when they fall due.

Batch production This is the manufacture of a limited number of identical products, usually to meet a specific order.

Board of directors This is a group of individuals who are responsible to the **shareholders** for the running of a business.

Brand This is the name, design, symbol or term which is used to identify an organisation's product or service.

Brand leader The brand with the highest percentage share of a specific market or segment.

Brand loyalty This exists when consumers repeat-purchase your product on a regular basis.

Budget This is an organisation's allocation of money and resources for particular projects, and includes a cashflow forecast.

Bureaucratic Management that is rooted in paper-based checks and counterchecks on decisions or actions.

Business plan A report detailing the marketing strategy, production costings and financial implications of a business start-up or forecast for a future period.

Capital This can be defined either as the **funds** invested by a business to acquire **assets**, or physical **assets** such as machinery or equipment.

Cartel This is the name given to a group of producers who make an agreement to limit output in order to keep prices high.

Cash account This is an account which records all of the organisation's **incomings** and **outgoings**.

Cash flow This is a system by which an organisation monitors **revenue** and **expenditure** on a monthly basis.

Cashflow forecast A detailed estimate of an organisation's future cash inflows and outflows per month.

Closed shop A workplace where employees must belong to a trade union.

Code of practice A form of self-regulation devised and run by an employers' organisation that lays down appropriate standards for firms operating within the industry.

Collective bargaining This is the negotiation process between employers and representatives of the workforce.

Command economy See **Planned economy**.

Comparative advantage The idea that countries can benefit from specialising in the production of those goods which they are relatively more efficient in producing.

Competition These are the other organisations with which an organisation must contest in order to gain and maintain **market share**.

Consumer durables Are goods which are owned by households but which are not immediately consumed (used up) by them.

Consumer panel A group of consumers within an organisation's target market used on a regular basis for market research exercises.

Contract of employment This is an agreement between an employer and an employee in which the employer lays down the conditions of service and the rewards for work undertaken.

Corporate identity The design package that aims to create the company image desired by an organisation.

Corporate image This is the view of a company held by its customers, employees and the public at large.

Corporate objectives These are the goals of the whole enterprise.

Corporation This is a publicly registered company which has a separate legal identity from its owners.

Corporation tax This is a tax levied by the government on **profits** made by a business.

Cost This is the **expenditure** on **resources** incurred by a business.

Cost centre This is a technique used by some organisations to manage **costs** by attributing them to certain areas of the business's activity.

Cost of living This is the level of prices of products and services, usually measured in order to monitor **inflation** via the **retail price index**.

Cost of sales This is **expenditure** incurred in the process of obtaining sales.

Cost per thousand (CPT) A fair way of comparing different media by working out how much it costs to reach a thousand listeners, readers or viewers.

Cost price This is the cost of a product which a business incurs in the course of its production.

Creditors These are the individuals or organisations owed money by a business.

Current assets These are **assets** owned by a business. They include **stock**, money owed by **debtors** and cash.

Current liabilities These are all the obligations for which a business has to pay out money in the near future.

Debt This is the amount of money owed by one person or organisation to another.

Debtors These are the people or organisations owing money to a business.

Deindustrialisation This means the long-term decline in industry (e.g. Britain's relative position as a world manufacturer).

Demand This is the amount or quantity of a particular product or service required by organisations and their customers.

Deregulation This is the removal of government rules, regulations and laws controlling the working of a business.

Deskilling This occurs when a new machine or process changes a job that was once a source of skill and craft pride into a repetitive or mundane task such as feeding or minding a machine.

Direct costs This is the total of **materials** and **labour costs** that can be related to the production of a product.

Direct labour This is a recognisable portion of the workforce which is involved in an aspect of producing a product.

Direct mail This is advertising or promotional material that is posted to specific addresses selected from a mailing list.

Direct marketing This is marketing activity that is aimed directly at the customer.

Director This is an official of a business who is elected by **shareholders** and given the power and responsibility to run the organisation on their behalf.

Discount This is a deduction from the list price of a product.

Disposable income This is the amount of money which an individual has left after paying compulsory deductions.

Distribution This is the process of storing and transporting products to consumers via various channels (methods).

Diversification This is the process which occurs when a business expands its activities into other, new **markets**.

Dividend This is a payment made by a business to its **shareholders** in return for providing **share capital**.

Divisions of labour This means breaking a job down into small, repetitive fragments, each of which can be done at speed by workers with little formal training.

Economies of scale This is a beneficial reduction in the **average costs** of producing a unit, obtained by an increase in the size of the business.

Excess demand This describes the situation where demand exceeds supply.

Expenditure This is the **outgoings** or expenses incurred by a business.

Financial management This is advice, usually obtained from an outside source, which allows a business to analyse the flow of money through the organisation.

Financial year This is taken to mean the annual accounting period from, e.g. 1 April of one year to 31 March the following year.

Finished goods These are the **stocks** of completed products.

Fiscal policy This is how the government controls the level of spending in the economy, by changing the level of its **expenditure** and its taxation on individuals and businesses.

Fixed assets These are **assets** such as machinery and buildings bought by a business for long-term use.

Fixed costs These are **costs** incurred by an organisation that do not vary despite changes in the level of **output**.

Flow production This is the manufacture of an item in a continually moving process.

Franchise This is a business arrangement by which one organisation grants another the right to trade under its name and supply its products or services.

Franchisee This is a person who has bought the local rights to use the name of another company.

Franchiser This is the holder of the franchise who will sell the local rights to suitable franchisees.

Goodwill This is the reputation, expertise and contacts of a business, for which a prospective buyer must pay a premium above the **asset** value of the business.

Gross domestic product This is the total value of all products and services produced in the country's economy in a year.

Gross national product This is the total value of all products and services produced in the economy plus any income from investments abroad.

Gross profit This is the difference between **sales revenue** and **cost of sales** before selling, distribution and administration are taken into account.

Holding company This is a company which controls another company.

Homeworking This is earning an income from work undertaken at home.

Income This is the money received by an individual or organisation.

Incomings See **revenue**.

Indirect cost This is a cost that is not directly attributable to a product or a cost centre.

Industrial tribunal This is an informal courtroom where legal disputes over unfair dismissal or discrimination can be settled.

Inflation This is a general increase in prices which is usually measured in terms of its effect on the whole economy.

Input These are all of the resources used by a business to produce its products and services.

Insolvent This refers to a business which has suffered **bankruptcy** and cannot pay its **debts**.

Intangible assets Assets are tangible when they do not have a physical existence. For instance, goodwill, patents, trademarks and copyrights.

Interest This is a charge made for borrowing money.

Inventory This is a comprehensive list of all **finished goods**, **work in progress** and **raw materials**.

Japanisation This is the process by which Western firms are attempting to follow the Japanese way.

Job analysis This is the identification of the tasks which make up a particular job role.

Job description This is a statement of the tasks and responsibilities which make up a job.

Job enlargement This is when the number of tasks and possible responsibilities involved in a job are increased.

Job enrichment This is when workers are given greater freedom in performing their tasks.

Job evaluation This is a system by which the relative worth of a job is linked to grading and pay.

Job rotation This is the widening of activities of a worker by switching the worker around from one task to another over a number of work tasks.

Job satisfaction This is the degree to which an employee feels positively towards his or her present job function.

Job security This is the extent to which a job is, or seems to be, guaranteed for the foreseeable future.

Job sharing This is when two employees agree to divide up the working week on a job between them, so that they each do half of the one job.

Job specification This is a statement or listing of the characteristics required to do a job successfully.

Joint venture This is a business owned by two separate organisations which have pooled their expertise and **resources**.

Labour costs This is the total of all **expenditure** which can be attributed to the workforce.

Labour turnover This is the number of job leavers per year divided by the average number of staff in the organisation, multiplied by one hundred.

Ledger This is an accounting record which keeps a running total of the business's financial transactions.

Legislation This is the laws (Acts of Parliament), Regulations and Directives imposed by the government or the EU.

Liabilities This is a form of **debt** or claim on the **resources** of a business in relation to money owed.

Limited liability This is a type of liability in which a **shareholder** is only liable for the amount of money that he or she actually invested in the business.

Liquidation This means turning assets into cash.

Loss leader This is a product sold at a reduced price in order to attract customers to purchase additional products.

Managing Director This is the **director** of an organisation who is responsible for the day-to-day management.

Margin This is the difference between the **cost price** and the **selling price** of a product.

Market This is the situation when the buyer and seller of a product or service come together.

Market economy This is an economy which allows markets to determine the allocation of resources.

Marketing plan This is a report detailing an organisation's marketing objectives and strategy.

Market leader This is a product or service which has the largest **market share**.

Market research This is the collection and analysis of data regarding a particular **market**.

Market segmentation This is a method of dividing the **market** into segments in order to target them more accurately.

Market share This is the percentage of the total value of the market which is held by an individual organisation.

Market size This is the total sales of all the producers within a marketplace, measured either by volume (units sold) or by value (the revenue generated).

Marketing This is a process by which an organisation attempts to identify customer needs and to satisfy them.

Marketing mix These are the measures which an organisation employs to attract buyers to purchase its products or services. This is also known as the 4 Ps (product, price, place and promotion).

Materials These are the items required in order to produce a product. They may take the form of **raw materials** or components.

Memorandum of Association This is a legal document which governs the relationship between the business and all external individuals and organisations.

Merchandising Visiting outlets to ensure that a company's products are displayed in as attractive and prominent a way as possible.

Merger This is the mutually agreed combining of businesses into a single business.

Mixed economy This is an economy in which products and services are provided by both private and public enterprises.

Modem This is an accessory that enables one computer to be linked to others.

Monetary policy This is how the government controls the level of spending in an economy by regulating the supply of money through the control of interest rates.

Monopoly Officially this is when an organisation has gained a 25% **market share**.

Motivation This is the willingness and enthusiasm of a worker to carry out tasks.

Multinational This is a firm which has its headquarters in one country, but with bases, manufacturing or assembly plants in others.

Multiple A store chain that has a number of shops.

Multi-skilling This means training a workforce to be able to work effectively across a wide range of tasks.

Net assets This is **fixed assets** plus net **current assets**, or **fixed assets** plus net **current assets** minus long-term **liabilities**.

Net profit This is the difference between a business's **sales revenue** and total **costs**.

Off-the-job training This includes all forms of training apart from that at the immediate workplace.

On-the-job training This is instruction at the place of work on how the job should be carried out.

Opportunity to see (OTS) A single chance to see an advertisement.

Outgoings See **expenditure**.

Output This is the products or services produced by an organisation.

Overheads These are **costs** which cannot be directly attributed to a product.

Overtrading This occurs when an organisation expands without securing the necessary long-term finance, thereby placing too great a strain on working capital.

Own-label (Own-brand) These products are branded with the retailer's own name, or with a name invented by the retailer.

Partnership This is an organisation owned and controlled by two or more individuals.

Performance appraisal This is the process of evaluating the performance of an employee, the purpose of which is to improve performance.

Planned economy This is an economy in which the majority of production is owned and controlled by the State.

Point-of-sale This is when materials are used to display and promote products at the retail outlet.

Privatisation This is the transferring of public ownership to private ownership.

Price sensitive This refers to a product whose demand will react very strongly to a change in its price.

Primary data This is first-hand information that is related directly to an organisation's needs.

Productivity This is a measurement of the efficiency with which a business turns production inputs into outputs.

Product range This is the full listing of the products offered by a business.

Profit This accrues when an organisation's **sales revenue** is greater than its total **costs**.

Profit and loss account This is an accounting statement showing an organisation's **sales revenue** and the **costs** which relate to that revenue during a specific **trading period**.

Profit margin This is the difference between the selling price of a product and the cost of producing it.

Profit share This is a bonus paid on top of employees' salaries to ensure that a proportion of the organisation's profit is shared out among staff.

Promotion This is a method of attracting the attention of consumers.

Public relations These are the methods employed by an organisation to enhance its public image.

Quality assurance This is the attempt to ensure that quality standards are agreed and met throughout the organisation, to give customer satisfaction.

Quality circle This is a discussion group that meets regularly to identify quality problems, consider alternative solutions, and recommend a suitable outcome to management.

Raw materials These are basic items, usually produced in the primary sector of the economy, which are destined to be converted into finished products.

Renting This is a method of acquiring an **asset** which is owned by a third party and may be used by the organisation in return for regular payments.

Repeat purchase This occurs when a first-time buyer purchases the same brand again.

Resources These are the available human, physical, natural and time requirements which can be identified as being 'owned' by an organisation.

Retail price index This is a measure used to determine the rate of **inflation**.

Revenue This is the income of an organisation derived from sales, interest from loans and other investments.

Sales forecast This is a method of predicting future **demand**.

Sales promotion These are methods used by businesses, other than advertising, to increase their sales.

Sales revenue This is a key item of **revenue** derived from the monies paid by purchasers of a business's products or services.

Selling price This is the price charged by an organisation for its products or services after taking into account the **costs** incurred in producing it and after having added a **margin** for profit.

Shareholders These are essentially part-owners of an organisation who have made long-term investments in it.

Shareholders' funds These are that part of the long-term finance owed by a company to its shareholders.

Social cost This measures the cost to the whole of society of a production process or business decision. It consists of the internal costs plus external costs.

Social responsibilities These are the duties towards employees, customers, society and the environment that an organisation may accept willingly, or may treat as a nuisance.

Sole trader This is a business owned and controlled by a single individual.

Stock These are the organisation's **assets** in the form of **raw materials**, **work in progress** and **finished goods**.

Stock control This is the process of controlling all **stock** of **raw materials**, **work in progress** and **finished goods**, in order to make best use of warehousing facilities and stockholding costs.

Stock turnover This is a measurement of the speed with which a firm sells out its stock. The turnover is worked out by dividing the sales turnover by the stock.

Supply This is the amount of its products or services which an organisation is willing to offer the **market**.

SWOT A system by which an organisation can identify its internal **s**trengths and **w**eaknesses and the external **o**pportunities and **t**hreats.

Teleworking This means working at home, though linked to the office by instant communications such as telephone, fax and computer modem.

Test market The launch of a new or improved product within a tightly defined area, in order to measure actual sales or potential.

Trading period This is a specified period of time, for example a month, a quarter or a year, which is used to monitor business performance.

Turnover This is the amount of money taken in a business. It can also refer to the number of people entering and leaving employment.

Unit cost See **average cost**.

Unlimited liability This is a type of liability in which the owners of a business are responsible for all losses.

Wage differential This is the difference between the wage rates for different groups of workers.

Working capital This is an accounting term which identifies the organisation's short-term **current assets**.

Work in progress These are products which are in the process of being turned into **finished goods**.

Index